ZEW Economic Studies
Volume 48

Publication Series of the Centre for
European Economic Research (ZEW),
Mannheim, Germany

More information about this series at
http://www.springer.com/series/4041

Kai Hüschelrath • Heike Schweitzer
Editors

Public and Private Enforcement of Competition Law in Europe

Legal and Economic Perspectives

Springer

ZEW
Zentrum für Europäische
Wirtschaftsforschung GmbH
Centre for European
Economic Research

Series Editor
Prof. Dr. Clemens Fuest

Editors
Kai Hüschelrath
Centre for European Economic Research (ZEW)
Mannheim, Germany

WHU Otto Beisheim School of Management
Vallendar, Germany

Heike Schweitzer
University of Mannheim
Mannheim, Germany

ISSN 1615-6781 ISSN 1867-2027 (electronic)
ISBN 978-3-662-51414-6 ISBN 978-3-662-43975-3 (eBook)
DOI 10.1007/978-3-662-43975-3
Springer Heidelberg New York Dordrecht London

Printed on acid-free paper

Springer is part of Springer Science+Business Media (www.springer.com)

Table of Contents

Public and Private Enforcement of Competition Law in Europe – Introduction and Overview

Kai Hüschelrath and Heike Schweitzer[1]

1 Introduction

Most competition law enforcement systems are based on two enforcement pillars: public and private enforcement. Public enforcement refers to state authorities that enforce antitrust rules; such authorities are vested with special powers and use special procedures to investigate and punish infringements. Private enforcement, in contrast, is litigation initiated by individual plaintiffs before a court to remedy an infringement of competition law. Remedies include damages, restitution, injunction, nullity or interim relief. They can be asserted in stand-alone actions or they can follow an infringement decision by a competition authority. Unlike public enforcement agencies, private parties have no special powers in civil law disputes.

Although both enforcement pillars have played a significant role in most jurisdictions over the past decades, it is fair to say that their relative importance has differed substantially across countries. While private enforcement has been the driving force of US antitrust enforcement since the middle of the 20th century, it has been somewhat less important in Europe, where public enforcement has dominated. In particular private damages actions that follow competition law infringements have long been a rare phenomenon. In order to create more incentives to seek compensation before European courts, the European Commission published a Green Paper in 2005 and a White Paper in 2008 to incentivize private damages actions and remove obstacles for victims of anticompetitive conduct. The same goal is assumedly at the heart of the Draft Directive on Private Damages Actions for Infringements of Competition Law Rules[2] that has recently been published by the EU Commission. De facto, however, the focus has shifted to dealing with potential conflicts between public and private enforcement. A growing number of pro-

---

1 We are indebted to Max Göhring and Paul Hentz (University of Mannheim) for their support at the editorial stage of the project.

2 EU Commission, Proposal for a Directive on certain rules governing actions for damages under national law for infringements of competition law provisions of the Member States and of the European Union, 11 June 2013, COM(2013)404 fin.

ceedings against competition authorities for access to leniency files has raised awareness that an appropriate framework is needed, both for private enforcement actions as such, and to handle the complex interaction of public and private enforcement.

The goal of this volume is to contribute to this important discussion. The twelve chapters in this book address key questions concerning public and private enforcement.

On the public enforcement side, the following questions are discussed:

- What are the key tools that competition authorities can use to enforce anticartel laws, and how do firms react to the implementation of new tools such as leniency programmes?
- Is the recent substantial increase in fines imposed by the EU on firm legal ground? Should fine levels be based on turnover, should prior compliance efforts be valued, and to what extent should the parent company be liable for infringements of its subsidiaries?

On the private enforcement side, key issues addressed include the following:

- How should the harm created by infringements of competition law be quantified? How can we assess what would have happened in the absence of infringement? Which methods are legally acceptable, which methods are feasible?
- How should the disclosure of evidence within private enforcement of competition law be organised?
- What can we learn from the calculation of administrative fines in Germany for cartel damage claims?
- How should passing-on defence be treated in private enforcement suits?

Concerning the interaction of public and private enforcement, key issues include:

- What does the calculation of fines in public enforcement have in common with the calculation of damages in private enforcement, and, more generally, how do these calculations affect each other?
- Is it still justified to calculate the fines according to the same principles that were applicable when private enforcement was still dormant? Does the accumulation of high fines and damages create disproportionate pressure on the companies affected?
- How do best practices for expert economic testimony issued by competition authorities differ, and how relevant are they for an effective and efficient public and private enforcement of competition law?

An overarching question investigated in this volume is:

- What lessons can we learn from a fully-fledged assessment of public and private enforcement activities in certain jurisdictions?

The following section briefly introduces the individual chapters of this volume and provides first hints as to possible answers.

2 The Contributions to this Volume

The first contribution is a theoretical and empirical perspective on the public enforcement of anti-cartel laws by *Kai Hüschelrath*. Following a general discussion of ex ante and ex post tools applied by competition authorities to fight hard core-cartels, a particular focus lies on the implementation of optimal fines for detected infringements. In a simple model framework, the minimum fine that deters cartelization is found to be increasing with the cartel-induced price increase and decreasing with the competitive mark-up, the probability of detection and market demand elasticity. Within the discussion of empirical evidence on EC cartel enforcement activities, a dataset of 73 EU cartel cases – decided between 2000 and 2011 – is used to present and interpret selected enforcement characteristics over time, e.g. the number of decided cases, the sum of fines, and the number of leniency cases. Recent policy changes are clearly reflected in the data, showing, e.g., an increase in the average fine per firm and in the number of leniency applications per case.

In his contribution, *Ulrich Schwalbe* presents an economic perspective on one particular public enforcement tool that has substantially gained importance over the last two decades: leniency programmes. Within a relatively short period of time, leniency programmes have become the major 'cartel case generator' for competition authorities. Not only did leniency programmes increase the number of cartel detections, it also seems likely that they had a positive impact on both the detection rate and the deterrence effect with respect to the formation of new cartels. Schwalbe is specifically interested in the possible response of a cartel to the existence of a competition authority in general and a leniency programme in particular. He argues that it would be unreasonable to assume that a cartel would simply ignore a competition authority that aims at detecting and punishing cartels, or that it passively accepts the existence of a leniency programme. More likely, the cartel will adapt its behaviour as well as its internal structure to existing institutions and instruments. The number of contacts, the specification of contacts, and the connections between cartel members may change in the presence of a leniency programme. Applying concepts from the theory of organised crime, Schwalbe concludes that a probable reaction to leniency programmes is the increased formation of what is known as 'hub-spoke cartels'. This finding may serve as a further justification of the increased attention national cartel authorities have lately paid to vertical restrictions. As a consequence, the extension of leniency programmes to vertical relations should be taken into consideration (which has, for example, already been done in the UK).

Wolfgang Bosch presents a sharp legal critique of the EU Commission's current fining practice, questioning whether it still is on firm legal ground. Due to delays in the publication of this volume, his contribution does not consider the ECJ's most recent case law. Bosch's critique is based on fundamental legal arguments that are nonetheless still relevant. A new and legally sound approach to fines, he firstly argues, would require a more reliable legal basis in Reg. 1/2003. Secondly, turnover as a basis for the calculation of fines does not seem to be the right approach, considering that the earnings from the cartel should be given back to those who have suffered from the cartel. Thirdly, compliance efforts of companies need to be considered in setting the fine. Lastly, the current concept of parent company liability demands a detailed review as well.

A number of contributions address the interaction of public and private enforcement. The articles by Ackermann, Mäger and Paul, as well as Dannecker and Kern provide different perspectives of the interplay of the two enforcement pillars. As the intense debate on access to leniency files by private damage claimants has shown, public and private enforcement can no longer be conceived of as completely separate. Strengthening private enforcement will affect public enforcement, and these effects must be reflected in the legal regime. The contributions in this section provide important and innovative input for this big challenge ahead.

Thomas Ackermann's contribution focuses on the question how private damage payments should affect the calculation of fines. In order to answer this question, he sets out to analyse the commonalities and differences between the calculation of fines and the calculation of damages. Interestingly, Ackermann finds that despite different aims, both optimal damages and optimal fines require knowledge of counterfactuals (but-for prices and but-for quantities). Since establishing but-for prices and but-for quantities beyond reasonable doubt would be exceedingly difficult, ways must be found to overcome the problem of under-enforcement that follows from this obstacle. As the example of the German legal system shows, the law of damages and the law of fines differ with regard to the instruments they apply to cope with the risk of under-enforcement resulting from uncertainty about counterfactuals: While the assessment of fines relies on substitute criteria, the assessment of damages relies on facilitating devices. The instruments used so far in the sphere of damages, namely the application of a relatively low standard of proof, may not yet be sufficient to make private damages claims a sizeable contribution to the enforcement of antitrust law. However, the more effective private enforcement by means of damages becomes, the more significant becomes the need to take account of this in the calculation of fines.

Thorsten Mäger and *Thomas B. Paul* start from a similar intention. Given that a new private litigation culture is evolving with a view to cartel damage claims in Germany and in the EU, is it still justified to calculate the fines according to the same principles that were applicable when civil enforcement was still dormant? In order to answer this question, Mäger and Paul provide an overview of the recent discussion on the interaction between liability in fines and liability in damages, both from an economic and a legal point of view. They find that while the economic theory of optimal deterrence is not yet able to provide more than rough and imperfect clues about the socially optimal level of deterrence, economic logic nonetheless suggests that reconciliation between public and private enforcement is important, as both contribute to the aggregate deterrent effect of competition law. Assuming that over-deterrence is as much a concern as under-deterrence, rational policy-making would imply that a substantial increase in private enforcement should be reflected in a reduction of the level of fines unless new evidence suggests that previous aggregate levels of deterrence were insufficient. Measured against these standards, Mäger and Paul conclude that the current legal status at the European level and in Germany seems unsatisfactory, both with regard to leniency cases, where possible solutions have not progressed beyond the stage of policy discussions, and with regard to the general reconciliation of the level of fines and damages, where the existing legal mechanisms are rudimentary at best.

Gerhard Dannecker and *Ursula Kern* argue that the accumulation of high fines and more intense private enforcement would lead to disproportionately high sanctions that are no longer in accordance with the requirements of Art. 49 (3) of the Charter of Fundamental Rights of the European Union. In order to solve this problem, they analyse and rethink the relationship between fines, disgorgement of profits and private enforcement. Regarding the relationship between a disgorgement of profits and private damages, they find that damages payment must be deducted from the profits to be disgorged. If private damages proceedings succeed public proceedings, which is usually the case, a procedure must be introduced that allows for repaying the company. Fines, however, typically involve some element of disgorgement of illegal profits and additional deterrence. In the EU, the illegal profits to be disgorged are not clearly identified. According to the fining guidelines, actual gains have no impact on the calculation of the basic amount of the fine. The relationship between private and public enforcement is hence not adequately addressed: There is no procedure to adjust the fine retrospectively in the case of damage payments to take into account a disgorgement element. In Germany, the law allows for a separate disgorgement of illegal gains in addition to the imposition of deterrent fines. In principle, it should therefore be easier to take into account subsequent damage payments. According to Dannecker/Kern, this would also be mandated by constitutional law. In such a regime, public and private enforcement could be reconciliated.

A final set of contributions addresses the evolution of private enforcement as such. The papers by Niels and Noble, Heinemann, Burrichter and Paul, as well as Siragusa discuss important aspects of private enforcement, e.g. the quantification of damages, best practices for expert economic opinions, access to evidence, and the role of the passing-on defence.

Gunnar Niels and *Robin Noble* start out with the observation that difficulties regarding the quantification of damages remain one of the key obstacles of private antitrust enforcement in Europe. A report by Oxera published in December 2009 entitled 'Quantifying antitrust damages: towards guidance for courts' was a first attempt at providing guidance in this respect. In this report, a team of legal and academic experts tried to provide answers to crucial questions such as how to determine an acceptable and practically feasible "but for"-scenario. Niels and Noble discuss selected parts of this report. They delineate the main stages of damages estimations and describe the different types of harm caused by hard-core cartels. They develop a detailed classification of methods and models for the quantification of damages in which they differentiate between three main approaches: comparator-based, financial-based, and market-structure based. Finally, they provide guidance on how to select the methods and models to use. They conclude with a reminder not to neglect the final stage of damage calculation, i.e. calculating interests on damages, which can have a substantial effect on the final damages value. At the same time, it remains far from simple, both legally and economically.

Arndt Christiansen and *Christian Ewald* discuss the relevance and importance of 'best practices for expert economic opinions' in light of the publication of the first formal notice on binding quality standards by the Bundeskartellamt in October 2010. 'Best practices' are intended to ensure that the interaction between the parties' economic experts, the competition authorities, and the courts contributes effectively to sound decision quality. They provide important insights of "forensic economics" – a subbranch of the economic discipline that strives to apply economic theories and methods within a given legal framework. Expert economic opinions constitute one specific channel to feed forensic economics into competition law proceedings. However, in order to contribute effectively to decision-making on the basis of expert assessments, submissions have to meet minimum quality standards. A comparative analysis of the "Best Practices for expert economic opinions" issued by the Bundeskartellamt in October 2010 and similar guidance documents issued by other competition authorities reveal the following core evaluation criteria for the quality of expert economic submissions: relevance, reliability; robustness, replicability; transparency, accessibility; comprehensibility. The guidance documents do express a preference for established and tested theories and methods, but abstain from detailed prescriptions with respect to the substantive content or the methodology used in economic expert submissions. A look at the US indicates that court-based adversarial enforcement regimes apply almost identical principles to govern the admissibility of expert testimony. Apparently, there is a growing consensus concerning the minimum quality standards that should be adopted to guide forensic economics in competition law enforcement in general.

Andreas Heinemann's contribution addresses the controversial debate on the EU Commission's proposals regarding the disclosure of evidence first formulated in its 'White Paper on Damages Actions'. Critical observers have pointed to the risks associated with introducing a US style litigation culture in Europe. Some continental legal orders with restrictive disclosure obligations have opted for another way to create an effective regime of evidence: They make use of presumptions. Disclosure rules and presumptions should be looked at together when assessing the legal regime on evidence, as presumptions can compensate for weak disclosure rules. According to Heinemann, a combination of carefully shaped disclosure rules and presumptions might be the preferred solution in the European setting. With the 'more economic approach' to competition law, the need for an appropriate mix of disclosure and presumptions has increased. An effects-based analysis is particularly costly and will often require the production of economic expertise. Administrative costs as well as social costs may be reduced if the burden of proof is shifted to the respondent when it comes to the facts that respondents are better placed to produce.

Jochen Burrichter and *Thomas B. Paul* take a look at recent experiences with economic evidence in German courts. The study is motivated by the rather recent phenomenon of high stakes cartel damage claims. The former practice of determining illicit cartel profits that was relevant for the calculation of public fines until the entry into force of the 7th GWB Reform Act in July 2005 provides for some relevant prior experience that can be of use in the evolving regime of private enforcement. Hence, Burrichter and Paul discuss an important decision by the Higher Regional Court of Düsseldorf in the Cement cartel case that may well be regarded as a blueprint for the treatment of complex econometric evidence in German courts. Burrichter and Paul conclude that the initial experience with economic evidence in German courts, especially their comparatively swift and knowledgeable hearing of economic expert testimony in the Cement cartel case, may be considered rather encouraging. Yet the authors identify several significant stumbling blocks concerning, inter alia, access to the necessary data to perform economic analyses, the protection of confidentiality of raw data used in such analyses, and, perhaps most importantly, the significant technical pitfalls that lurk in almost any economic method of damage quantification and may give rise to prolonged battles over what can be considered a reliable estimate.

Mario Siragusa's contribution addresses a much-discussed and important aspect of private enforcement, the passing-on defence ('POD'). It stands for the argument of a defendant that the claimant has passed on the cartel surcharge to his own customers. At the same time, an indirect purchaser may bring an action for damages against a member of the cartel based on a claim that the cartel surcharge has been passed through to him. Siragusa first describes the Commission's position regarding the POD and discusses its consequences. He then examines various national approaches, starting with Italy and moving on to recent developments in France, Germany and the United Kingdom. The practical problems national courts will be confronted with in dealing with a POD are highlighted. Finally, Siragusa discusses how recent initiatives on collective redress will impact on the POD.

The book concludes with an overview of recent enforcement activities in England and Wales – a jurisdiction that has traditionally been somewhat hesitant in the field of public enforcement and had initially been expected to become a leader in private enforcement actions. With the entry into force of the Competition Act 1998 in 2000 and the Enterprise Act 2002 in 2004, competition law enforcement in England and Wales underwent significant changes. *Sebastian Peyer* adresses the question how public and private antitrust enforcement have developed since then. His account remains skeptical. With a view to public enforcement, Peyer argues that the OFT may have been unfortunate with some of the cases it selected for enforcement actions, and some cases that it brought may not have sent the strong signals to the markets that are required from a public enforcer. He doubts whether the imminent merger of the OFT and the Competition Commission will help to quickly improve the track record of the new competition watchdog. While the concentration of expertise is likely to bolster the central role of the future Competition and Market Authority (CMA), running a new agency needs time to establish precedents and procedure, and to learn from judicial defeats. Likewise, private enforcement of competition law is in need of more court decisions to settle important legal issues, e.g. indirect purchaser standing. One of the major challenges of private litigation in the UK is the cost of bringing a case. Private parties have to make considerable investments to successfully bring an action. The UK Government is currently rethinking the framework for private actions and has released its proposals for reform.

3 Outlook

In June 2013, the Commission published a proposal for a directive on rules governing private damages actions for competition law infringements.[3] This proposal could largely not be reflected in this volume. However, the various contributions to this volume are of great importance for the discussion of the proposal that has ensued. The tension between public and private competition law enforcement that has arisen from the intensification of private enforcement has yet not been solved on the public enforcement side, and the solutions that the proposed directive offers on the private enforcement side are unsatisfactory. Rules on disclosure, their interaction with legal presumptions and the exact rules of a 'passing-on defence' all remain subject to debate. So does the question whether harmonization is really needed, or whether the diversity of evolving national approaches provides better prospects for experiments and mutual learning. The contributions collected in this volume offer a principled and profound reflection on these issues. They promise to remain relevant in the debate for a long time.

3 EU Commission, Proposal for a Directive on certain rules governing actions for damages under national law for infringements of competition law provisions of the Member States and of the European Union, 11 June 2013, COM(2013)404 fin.

Public Enforcement of Anti-Cartel Laws – Theory and Empirical Evidence

Kai Hüschelrath

1 Introduction

The fight against hard-core cartels[1] is ranked high on the agenda of many competition authorities around the world these days. The efforts of the European Commission (EC) and other institutions are reflected in policy reforms such as new fining guidelines or leniency programmes and also in improved cartel enforcement. While the European Commission decided only ten cartel cases in the 1995–1999 period, the number increased to 30 in the period from 2000–2004 and to 33 in the 2005–2009 period.[2]

From an economic perspective, the fight against hard-core cartels is justified by the negative welfare implications of such particular 'agreements among competitors'. In addition to allocative and productive inefficiencies, hard-core cartels typically cause dynamic inefficiencies, substantially harming customers and consumers in several ways. The harm caused by hard-core cartels – together with the absence of any structural benefit of such agreements – supports their classification as a 'per-se violation' in most antitrust laws around the world.[3]

Although the moral commitment to obey existing laws and regulations is an important cornerstone of legal system function, it is usually viewed as insufficient when it comes to compliance. As a consequence, policy makers are obliged to design and implement enforcement mechanisms. For the case of anti-cartel laws, such a public enforcement system can be subdivided into two parts: *detection* of illegal conduct and *intervention* against the infringer, in the form of pecuniary

---

1 In the modern industrial organisation literature, a hard-core cartel is typically defined as '... a group of firms who have agreed explicitly among themselves to coordinate their activities in order to raise market price – that is, they have entered into some form of price fixing agreement' (L. Pepall, D. Richards and G. Norman, *Industrial Organization: Contemporary Theory and Practice* (Boston 1999), p. 345).

2 Data source: European Commission, Cartel Statistics (as of 19 May 2010), available at http://ec.europa.eu/competition/cartels/statistics/statistics.pdf.

3 See, for instance, Art. 101 of the Treaty on the Functioning of the European Union (TFEU) or Art. 1 of the German Act Against Restraints of Competition (GWB).

fines or incarceration, say. Through the implementation of such a public enforcement system, policy makers aim at deterring illegal behaviour so that potential infringers realise ex ante that the expected punishment is larger than the expected gain and therefore rationally decide to refrain from illegal conduct.

With this background in mind, I provide a theoretical and an empirical perspective on the public enforcement of anti-cartel laws. Section 2 discusses important theoretical implications of anti-cartel law enforcement. Using the broad differentiation in detection and intervention, I discuss key enforcement instruments like ex ante and ex post detection tools, the imposition of deterrence-optimal fines or the role of leniency programmes. Section 3 complements the theoretical perspective with empirical evidence from EC cartel enforcement. In addition to a description of a dataset consisting of 73 cartels detected and prosecuted by the EC between 2000 and 2011, selected enforcement characteristics like the number of decided cases, the role of leniency programmes and the duration of cartel investigations are examined. Based on this empirical evidence, together with some theoretical insights on the imposition of optimal fines, section 3.3 tries to give an answer to the question if current EU fine levels can be viewed as deterrence-optimal. Section 4 concludes the article with a review of the key findings and offers some comments on the interplay between public and private enforcement of competition law.

2 Theoretical Foundations of Anti-Cartel Law Enforcement[4]

In general, the antitrust enforcement process within a system of public enforcement consists of three steps: the respective conduct has to be detected, prosecuted and 'penalised'. Although there may be important practical differences between 'detection' and 'prosecution' (bearing in mind the fundamental difference between 'having knowledge of a certain conduct' and 'proving a certain conduct'), we combine both actions into one for the following economic analysis and distinguish between a 'detection' stage and a complementary 'intervention' stage.

As already mentioned in the introductory section, hard-core cartels are a prime candidate for *per se* prohibition. This does not necessarily preclude that hard-core cartels might occasionally raise overall welfare; but such occurrences are considered so rare that a per se ban remains the appropriate antitrust reaction. Assuming that a per se ban of hard-core cartels is codified in law, the key challenges facing competition authorities with respect to enforcement are twofold. On the one hand, they work on ways to reduce the incentives to form cartels. On the other they must address the question of how to detect and intervene against existing cartels. As shown in Figure 1, the competition authority can make use of both ex ante and ex post tools in fulfilling these objectives.

4 This section draws partly on K. Hüschelrath and J. Weigand, Fighting Hard-core Cartels, in M. Neumann and J. Weigand (eds.), *International Handbook of Competition* (Edward Elgar, 2013).

Fig. 1. Cartel enforcement options

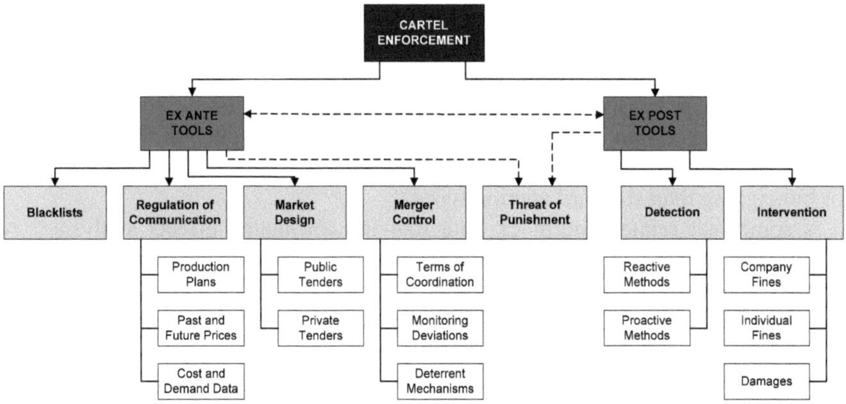

Source: Hüschelrath (2010)[5]

As shown in Figure 1, ex ante tools aim to reduce the incentives to form cartels. They include blacklisting, regulation of communication, market design and merger control. The available ex post tools can be subdivided into detection activities and intervention activities. Both categories will be characterised further below.

Ex ante enforcement tools

There are several ways competition authorities can reduce the formation of cartels ex ante. One prominent example is the development and publication of blacklists specifying the types of conduct classifiable as 'hard core'. But the potential of blacklists to reduce cartelisation is limited to cases in which firms are uncertain (or ignorant) about the illegality of their planned conduct and only decide to refrain from applying it after studying the respective blacklist. Given the informative character of blacklists, they are of exceptional importance in countries where competition policy has been recently introduced (and hence where firms might simply be unaware of the exact content and meaning of antitrust rules) and for companies that operate in foreign countries and have to comply with the interpretation of antitrust law abroad.

A second way to prevent cartel formation is the identification of communication types between competitors that indicate the intention to form a cartel (or tacitly collude). For instance, Kühn[6] proposes the prohibition of certain types of communication between firms likely to facilitate collusion but unlikely to improve social welfare (i.e. by enabling a pro-competition information exchange). The

5 K. Hüschelrath, 'How Are Cartels Detected? The Increasing Use of Proactive Methods to Establish Antitrust Infringements', 1 *Journal of European Competition Law and Practice* (2010), 522–8, p. 524.

6 K.-U. Kühn, 'Fighting Collusion - Regulation of Communication Between Firms', 32 *Economic Policy* (2001), 169–204, p. 195.

communication types Kühn identifies are private discussion of future output prices or production plans, information exchanges about past prices and quantities, and the exchange of individualised cost and demand data (in most cases). According to Kühn,[7] banning these forms of communication could 'significantly improve competition policy towards collusive practices'.

A third type of ex ante instrument for preventing cartel formation is the adjustment of market design.[8] The application of contemporary auction theory, for example, can help in designing auction mechanisms which offer fewer possibilities for bid-rigging than standard auction types.[9]

A somewhat related fourth ex ante tool is coordinated effects analysis.[10] A compulsory part of the horizontal merger control, this technique investigates whether a proposed merger is likely to create a post-merger environment in which collusion is more likely than in the pre-merger environment. For instance, suppose an aggressive firm (what is known as a maverick firm) manages to enter a mature industry with high entry barriers and several episodes of cartelisation in the past. If one of the three incumbent firms tries to get rid of this 'troublemaker' by acquiring it, merger control is likely to block its attempt with the argument that the post-merger environment would ease coordination among the incumbents. Generally, however, the history of European competition policy has shown that coordinated effects analysis is typically difficult to execute; to stand a chance of acceptance by local courts, factors such as terms of coordination, monitoring deviations or deterrent mechanisms need to be carefully considered.

Ex post enforcement tools

Although ex ante instruments are certainly useful in reducing the number of cartels in an economy, it is unlikely that these instruments alone will optimally deter cartelisation.[11] From an ex post perspective, the competition authority's fundamental challenge is to detect hard-core cartels. As cartel members are typically aware of the illegality of their agreements, they have a strong incentive to keep them secret. As a consequence, a key action for a competition authority lies in the identification of such illegal agreements (detection in a narrower sense) and the collection of sufficient evidence to prevail in court (detection in a broader sense). In general, the competition authority can use a selection of reactive and proactive detection tools to increase the probability of cartel detection. Both options will be discussed in greater detail in section 2.1.

Interventions against hard-core cartels are motivated by the belief that fines discourage attempts by firms to form hard-core cartels. Consequently, the funda-

---

7 Kühn, *supra* note 6, p. 196.

8 M. Motta, *Competition Policy* (Cambridge University Press 2004), p. 191.

9 P. Klemperer, *Auctions: Theory and Practice* (Princeton University Press, 2004).

10 Motta, *supra* note 8, p. 192.

11 In general, the theory of law and economics shows that it is typically inexpedient to deter unlawful behaviour completely; the better solution is to find the optimal degree of enforcement based on assessments of costs and benefits. See R. Cooter and T. Ulen, *Law and Economics* (Addison Wesley, 5th ed. 2008), p. 427.

mental purpose of company fines is to create and maintain a deterrence effect by signalling to the companies that substantial fines will have to be paid if their conspiracy is detected ('threat of punishment'). As shown in Figure 1 above, however, intervention does not necessarily have to stop at the imposition of corporate fines; it can also be complemented by individual penalty (monetary fines or even prison sentences). Although such penalties can certainly be effective as additional intervention tools, the detailed discussion in section 2.2 concentrates on identifying optimal fines and on the role of leniency programmes.

2.1 Detection

It has long been recognised that competition authorities can make use of various methods to detect cartels. Generally, these methods can be separated into reactive methods and proactive methods. According to the International Competition Network,[12] reactive methods rely on some external event before the competition authority becomes aware of an issue; proactive methods are initiated from within the authority and do not rely on an external event. An overview of the different methods is provided in Figure 2.

Fig. 2. Methods of cartel detection

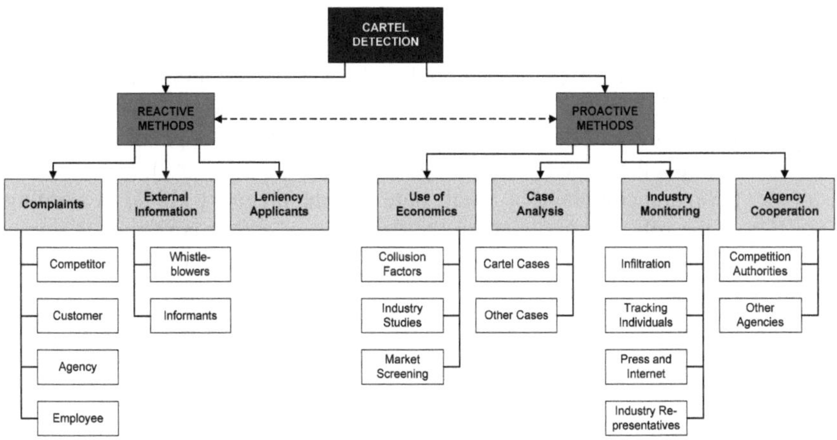

Source: Hüschelrath,[13] adapted from ICN[14]

---

12 ICN, Anti-Cartel Enforcement Manual – Cartel Working Group – Subgroup 2: Enforcement Techniques (Istanbul 2010).

13 Hüschelrath, *supra* note 5, p. 525.

14 ICN, *supra* note 12.

As shown in Figure 2, reactive methods to detect cartels include complaints, other external information and leniency applicants. Following the detailed characterisation in ICN,[15] complaints about an alleged cartel agreement can be filed by competitors, customers, other agencies or current or former employees of the respective companies. A whistleblower is typically a current or former employee who is aware that his employer is involved in a cartel but was not personally involved. An informant is typically an outsider who receives access to information from within the cartel. A leniency applicant is a cartel member who reports the respective cartel to the authority to reduce or even eliminate the penalty that would otherwise be applicable.

Proactive methods offer a variety of tools to actively detect cartels. The explicit use of economics, for instance, can play a role in how to investigate collusion factors across industries, in the conduct of market or industry studies or inquiries, and in the implementation of a market screening approach. Competition authorities can supplement these approaches by analysing past cartel cases or other competition cases. Furthermore, constant monitoring of industries through infiltration of informants, career tracking of industry managers, press and internet monitoring as well as regular contact with industry representatives promise to increase the probability of detecting cartels. Last but not least, cooperation between agencies – competition authorities, other national or international agencies – can promote cartel detection.

There is little evidence about the relative importance of reactive and proactive methods in detecting cartels. In their seminal paper, Hay and Kelley[16] identified 12 different methods of both categories applied by US competition authorities between 1963 and 1972, and which identified a total of 49 cartels. In 70% of the cases, however, one of the following four methods was actually applied: Grand Jury investigation in another case (24%), complaint by competitor (20%), complaint by customer (14%) and complaint by local, state or federal agency (12%). According to the ICN,[17] the role of complaints in the detection of cartels continues to dominate today. Leniency applications are catching up in importance, however. Although detailed statistics are not available, proactive methods seem to play a small role relative to reactive methods. Increasingly, there are signs that a collection of complementary proactive methods is being applied to raise the probability of cartel detection.[18]

---

15 ICN, *supra* note 12, p. 7.

16 G. Hay and D. Kelley, 'An Empirical Study of Price Fixing Conspiracies', 17 *Journal of Law and Economics* (1974), 13–38.

17 ICN, *supra* note 12, p. 10.

18 Hüschelrath, *supra* note 5.

2.2 Intervention

Interventions against hard-core cartels are motivated by the belief that fines discourage attempts at cartel formation. Accordingly, the fundamental purpose of corporate fines is to create and maintain a deterrence effect by signalling to potential conspirators that substantial fines will have to be paid if they are caught. This belief requires an examination of how to derive deterrence-optimal fines.

2.2.1 Derivation of Deterrence-Optimal Corporate Fines

In this section, we discuss the derivation of deterrence-optimal corporate fines. We start with a discussion of several basic mechanics followed by an analysis of the key drivers of a minimum fine with a deterrence effect in an extended model framework. This model permits the use of several simulation exercises that help us understand the determinants of optimal fines for infringements against anti-cartel laws.

Deterrence-optimal fines – Basic mechanics

In general, an ex ante deterrence effect is determined by two factors: the severity of the sanction and the probability of detection.[19] A certain behaviour will be deterred if the fine equals the offender's gain from the illegal conduct divided by the probability of detection. For example, if the excess profit of a cartel agreement is given by g=200 and the probability of detection p=0.2, the corresponding fine F to deter such behaviour can be calculated to be F=(200/0.2)=1,000.[20]

Although focusing on the offender's gain seems to be straightforward, research in law and economics offers an alternative – the 'net harm to others' caused by the offender. Let the net harm to others be given by h and the probability of detection continue to be p. Polinsky and Shavell[21] show that the optimal harm-based fine F is given by $F=h/p$, as long as individuals are risk neutral.[22] This reasoning is in line with the policy conclusion that, to deter harmful conduct optimally, the expected fine must equal the net harm the offender causes to others.

---

19 See M. Gal, 'Harmful Remedies: Optimal Reformation of Anticompetitive Contracts', 22 *Cardozo Law Review* (2000), 91–132, for a detailed assessment.

20 The basic model was developed by Gary S. Becker in his seminal paper 'Crime and Punishment: An Economic Approach', 76 *Journal of Political Economy* (1968), 169–217. He examined a utility maximisation problem for an individual who faces the introduction of a law enforcement regime. Translated into the cartel world, the expected profits of the cartel agreement are given by E(Gc)=p(Gc-c-F)+(1-p)Gc=0. It immediately follows that the deterrence-optimal fine is given by F=(Gc/p)-c, where c is used as a measure of costs incurred by the detection process (which is set to 0 for the time being).

21 M. Polinsky and S. Shavell, 'The Economic Theory of Public Enforcement of Law', 38 *Journal of Economic Literature* (2000), 45–76, p. 50.

22 An individual is risk-neutral if he or she is indifferent about an expected cost or value and its certain equivalent.

Although there is still scholarly debate whether 'gain' or 'harm' is the appropriate basis for antitrust fines, recent commentators have favoured the harm-based approach.[23] This trend is based on a seminal paper by Landes[24], in which he showed under fairly general conditions that '[t]he optimal penalty should equal the net harm to persons other than the offender, adjusted upward if the probability of apprehension and conviction is less than one. This sanction encourages efficient behaviour'.[25] One fundamental advantage of the harm-based fine over the gain-based fine is that the former would not deter those types of efficient conduct that cause more gain to the offender than harm to society and should therefore not be deterred (but punished) from a welfare perspective. As Wils writes, 'The optimal fine thus set makes the offender internalise all the costs and benefits of the violation, thus leading the offender to commit the 'efficient violations' whose total benefits exceed the total costs while deterring 'inefficient violations' whose total costs exceed the total benefits.' [26]

With respect to cartel enforcement, Souam[27] investigates two different regimes of pecuniary punishment: a fine based on revenues of the respective industry and a fine which relates to the damage caused to customers. Given the fact that investigations are costly and have a declining social benefit, he finds that it is welfare-optimal in both systems to tolerate some degree of collusion. As long as the damage is less than the ex ante costs of deterrence, it is welfare-optimal not to intervene. Souam's results imply that both approaches are similar insofar as they both reach similar deterrence levels. However, in industries in which the likelihood of collusion is small, a revenue-based fine has certain advantages over a damages-based fine, while in industries with a high likelihood of collusion, a damage-based fine achieves slightly better performance.

Assuming that harm is chosen as the appropriate basis for antitrust fines generally, the harm caused by a cartel is determined by market size, duration of the infringement and size of the price rise compared with the competitive level (i.e., the overcharge).[28] If such a fine were a credible threat to market participants – and the probability of detection were 100% – cartel agreements would be completely deterred. But ensuring a 100% detection rate would be an extremely expensive undertaking. For example, a study by Bryant and Eckard[29] estimated that the probability of detecting cartel agreements in the US over a 12-month period is about

---

23 See W. Wils, 'Optimal Antitrust Fines: Theory and Practice', 29 *World Competition* (2006), 183–208, p. 12 for a discussion.

24 W. Landes, 'Optimal Sanctions for Antitrust Violations', 50 *University of Chicago Law Review* (1983), 652–78.

25 Landes, *supra* note 24, p. 678.

26 Wils, *supra* note 23, p. 13.

27 S. Souam, 'Optimal Antitrust Policy under Different Regimes of Fines', 19 *International Journal of Industrial Organization* (2001), 1–26.

28 These three parameters also determine the damage caused by the cartel needing to be calculated in private damage claims.

29 P. Bryant and E. Eckard, 'Price Fixing: The Probability of Getting Caught', 73 *Review of Economics and Statistics* (1991), 531–6.

15% on average.[30] More recently, Combe *et al.*[31] developed a general stochastic detection model and used it to estimate the annual probability of detection for a sample consisting of all cartels convicted by the Commission from 1969 to 2007. The authors found an annual probability of detection of between 12.9% and 13.3%. Despite the relatively low probability of detection, it would still be theoretically possible to reach a full deterrence effect, as the size of the fine could be adjusted upward to compensate for the reduction in the probability of detection. However, studies have also shown that such a proposal is hardly practicable for general economic reasons (the social and economic costs of high fines, say) and for practical reasons (inability of firms to pay such fines, say).[32] In other words, it is neither possible nor economically desirable to completely deter cartelisation.

However, even if antitrust fines and the probability of detection are not high enough to deter cartelisation completely, they still benefit consumers. The economic rationale behind this claim was formalised by Block *et al.*[33], who studied the relationship between antitrust enforcement and optimal collusion in a simple theoretical framework. The authors assume that the cartel objective is to maximise joint profits. Hence, in a world without a competition authority all firms in the industry collude and charge the monopoly price. If a competition authority is introduced, and it decides to investigate (and impose fines) if the mark-up exceeds a threshold level, the price-cost mark-up now significantly affects the probability of detection – that is, the higher the price-cost mark-up, the greater the likelihood of an investigation by the competition authority. In such a model setup, a profit-maximising cartel will not set the monopoly price but still charge a price above the competitive level. The price level is determined by the size of the expected fine *and* the probability of detection (i.e., the enforcement efforts of the competition authority). In other words, Block *et al.*'s model shows that an increase in either the size of the fine[34] or the probability of detection leads to a reduction in the price-

30 In a recent study, Connor collects views on the probability of cartel detection and found that most evidence seems to suggest a 10–20% chance of detection. See J. Connor, 'Optimal Deterrence and Private International Cartels', *Working Paper* (Purdue University 2006), p. 9.

31 E. Combe, C. Monnier and R. Legal, 'Cartels: The Probability of Getting Caught in the European Union', *Working Paper PRISM-Sorbonne* (Paris 2008).

32 Wils, *supra* note 23, p. 18. This poses the more general question why it is not optimal to introduce capital punishment for price fixers. Although such a step might come near to full deterrence, it would very likely avoid any kind of procompetitive cooperation that could be interpreted as a cartel. Additionally, managers threatened by capital punishment would have a huge incentive to invest in compliance systems or in ways of hiding their criminal acts. Both types of investment are costly to society.

33 M. Block, F. Nold and J. Sidak, 'The Deterrent Effect of Antitrust Enforcement', 89 *Journal of Political Economy* (1981), 429–45.

34 With respect to the effects of an increase in fines, Whinston remarks that such a step should, ceteris paribus, lead to an increase in the level of effectiveness at which firms find it worthwhile to cartelise. As a consequence, the price effects of detected cartels should be more fundamental. See M. Whinston, *Lectures on Antitrust Economics* (MIT Press 2006), p. 45.

cost mark-up by the cartel firms. The reduction in price is solely caused by the deterrent effect of antitrust enforcement.

Deterrence-optimal fines – Extended model framework

Taking the basic mechanics of optimal fines into account, Buccirossi and Spagnolo (2005)[35] present a richer model set-up for a derivation of deterrence-optimal fines. In a non-cartelised market, they assume that the profits π are given by π=qcm, with q being individual quantity demanded at the competitive price, c being (constant) marginal cost and m standing for the competitive mark-up (leading to a competitive price of $p=c(1+m)$). If a cartel is implemented and the price increases from p to p^m, each firm sells a quantity $q^m=q(1-\varepsilon k)$, with ε being the absolute value of the demand elasticity at the competitive price and k representing the percentage price increase reached by the cartel, i.e. $p^m=p(1+k)$ is the collusive price. The collusive profits are then given by $\pi^m=qc(1-\varepsilon k)[k(1+m)+m]$. The increase in a firm's profit due to the collusive agreement can then be expressed so:

$$\pi^m - \pi = qkc\left[(1+m)(1-\varepsilon k)-\varepsilon m\right] \quad (1)$$

As the revenues in the affected market at the collusive price are

$$qc(1+m)(1+k)(1-\varepsilon k), \quad (2)$$

the expected fine can be expressed as

$$\alpha fqc(1+m)(1+k)(1-\varepsilon k). \quad (3)$$

A minimum fine with deterrence effects has to remove the expected gain from participating in a cartel, i.e. the increase in profits minus the expected fine must be equal to zero. In the model framework of Buccirossi and Spagnolo, such a minimum fine with deterrence effects f^* can be calculated as follows:

$$f^*(\alpha,k,\varepsilon,m) = \frac{k\left[(1+m)(1-\varepsilon k)-\varepsilon m\right]}{\alpha(1+m)(1+k)(1-\varepsilon k)} \quad (4)$$

As shown by equation (4), the minimum fine depends on the four variables α, k, ε and m. By simply studying the equation, we can already say that the minimum fine shrinks as α increases (since α appears in the denominator only). But since further insights are more difficult to gain from simply studying equation (4), the following paragraphs provide simple simulations in which we fix two variables and calculate the minimum fines for various combinations of the remaining two variables.

In the upper left chart in Figure 3, we plot the respective minimum fine against various values for market demand elasticity and competitive mark-up based on the assumption that k=0.1 and α=0.15. The areas shown in the chart delineate corresponding minimum fine levels. For example, the small area in the top right corner of the chart delineates minimum fines between 0% and 20% of the sales in the affected market. For instance, one data point that lies in this small area would be ε=2 and m=0.5 (with an exact fine of f^*=0.101, or 10.10%). It is easy to see the effects of a change in either ε or m. If we keep m constant at m=0.5 and reduce demand

[35] P. Buccirossi and G. Spagnolo, 'Optimal Fines in the Era of Whisleblowers – Should Price Fixers Still Go to Prison?', *Lear Research Paper 05-01* (Rome 2005).

elasticity starting from $\varepsilon=2$, the minimum fine increases because we reach areas in the chart reserved for higher minimum fines. For instance, if $\varepsilon=1$ (with $m=0.5$), the corresponding minimum fine now falls in the 20%–40% area (the exact value can be calculated to be $f^*=38.16\%$). The same exercise can be repeated for a fixed elasticity, say $\varepsilon=2$, and a decreasing competitive mark-up m. Not surprisingly, the smaller m is, the higher the corresponding minimum fine that must be chosen to deter infringement. For example, if $\varepsilon=2$ and $m=0.25$, the minimum fine can be calculated to be $f^*=30.3\%$.

Fig. 3. Minimum fines against market demand elasticity and competitive mark-up

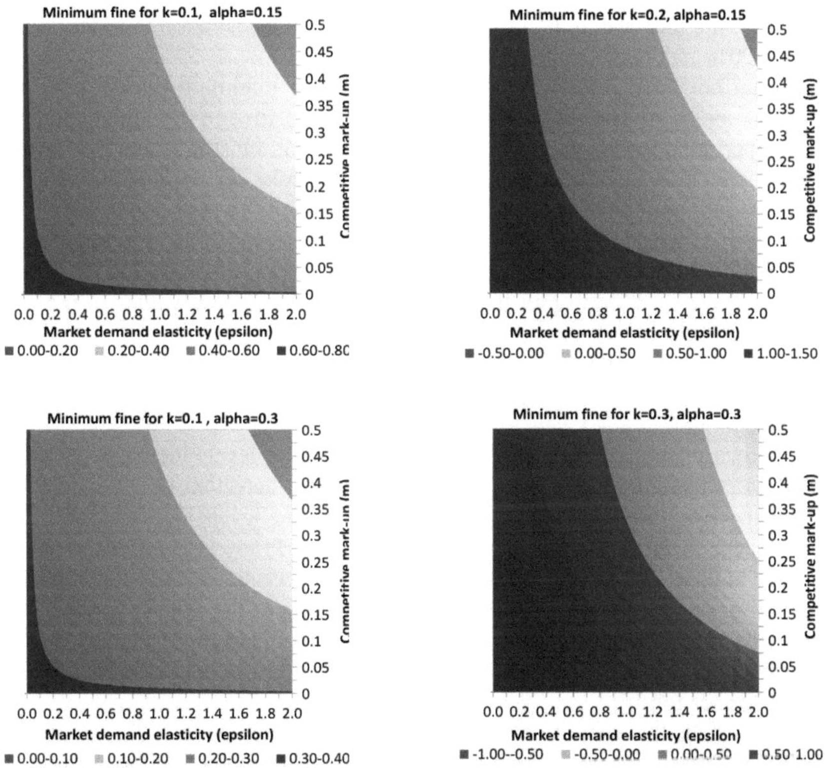

In addition to the study of a single chart, simple simulation exercises also provide insights on the effects of discrete changes in either k or α. The upper right chart in Figure 3 shows the effect of an increase in k from 0.1 to 0.2. This means that the cartel-related percentage price increase rises from 10% to 20%. When comparing both upper charts, it becomes apparent that, while the general pattern stays similar, the minimum fine values increase substantially. While the $\varepsilon=1$ and $m=0.5$ combination leads to a minimum fine in the 20%-40% area (exact value: $f^*=38.2\%$), the corresponding data point in the $k=0.2$ world is located in the 50%-100% area (exact value: $f^*=64.8\%$). It can therefore be concluded that larger cartel overcharges must lead to increases in the minimum fine if the desired deterrence effect is to be reached.

The lower left chart in Figure 3 again plots the minimum fines for various market demand elasticities and competitive mark-ups. In this chart, we leave the cartel-related percentage price increase unchanged at k=0.1 and increase the probability of detection from α=0.15 to α=0.30. Taking the functional form of equation (4) into account, it is not surprising to find a pattern identical to the one in the upper left chart. The only change in the chart is the legend, which reflects that minimum fine levels decrease as values of α increase. For example, while the ε=*1* and m=0.5 combination originally leads to a minimum fine in the 20%-40% area (exact value: f^*=38.2%), the increase in the probability of detection leads to a minimum fine in the 10%-20% area (exact value: f^*=19.1%).

Last but not least, the lower right chart shows the minimum fines if both parameters k and α are tripled/doubled (k=0.3, α=0.3) relative to the initial situation in the upper left chart (k=0.1, α=0.15). We can see that the shapes and the respective minimum fine areas look quite similar. For example, for ε=1 and m=0.25, we receive a minimum fine of 47% in the 'k=0.1, α=0.15' world and 55% in the 'k=0.3, α=0.3' world. For ε=0.5 and m=0.5, the corresponding minimum fines would be 38% and 40%, respectively.

It is an easy exercise to plot the minimum fines for various values of α and k and to assume specific parameter values for the remaining two variables m and ε. Figure 4 shows the respective simulation results. The upper left chart presents the reference situation for comparison with parameter value changes. This chart shows the minimum fine levels for m=0.1 and ε=1.

As shown in the upper left chart, the minimum fine levels increase as cartel-related percentage price increases and probabilities of detection decrease. If market demand elasticity is reduced from ε=1 to ε=0.5, fine levels increase (while the shapes of the different fine level areas stay similar). If, however, market demand elasticity is increased to ε=1.5, the lower left chart reveals not only the expected reduction in fine levels but also a change in the shapes of the respective fines areas. Finally, if m is increased to m=0.3 while ε=1, a comparison of the lower right with the upper left chart reveals that minimum fine levels are reduced with increasing values for m.

In a nutshell, this section has shown that a deterrence-optimal fine generally depends on the gain (or alternatively harm) of the infringement and the probability of detection. In an extended model framework, the gain is determined by three factors: the cartel-induced percentage price increase, the competitive mark-up and market demand elasticity. Hence: the higher the cartel-induced price increase is, and the lower competitive mark-up and market demand elasticity are, the larger the respective minimum fine becomes.

Fig. 4. Minimum fines against probability of detection and cartel percentage price increase

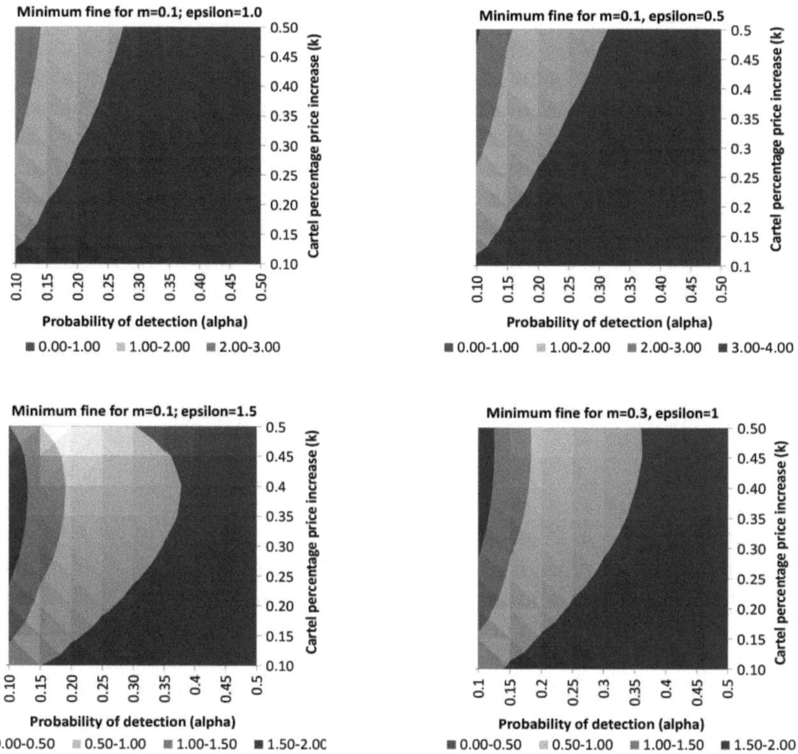

2.2.2 The Role of Leniency Programmes

A recently rediscovered way of increasing the probability of detection – and strengthening the deterrence effect – is the use of leniency programmes. Generally speaking, a leniency programme promises the first cartel member that reports its involvement in the cartel to the competition authority either partial or total exemptions from any imposed fines. However, in practice, leniency programmes are much more complex: they must provide appropriate incentive structures for corporations and individuals[36] to come forward with hard facts while preventing abuses to the programme.

---

[36] As price-fixing is a criminal offence in the US, leading cartel managers may be given (and are given) jail terms of up to three years. Following Gallo *et al.*, 53% of convicted managers have been sent to prison since 1970. The threat of incarceration might be an important incentive for managers to come forward without necessarily wanting to convince the whole company to apply for leniency as a corporate act. See J. Gallo, K. Dau-Schmidt, J. Craycraft and C. Parker, 'Department of Justice Antitrust Enforcement, 1955–1997: An Empirical Study', 17 *Review of Industrial Organization* (2000), 75–133, p. 53. Hence, the reaction to the situation in the US was the implementation of a separate leniency programme for individuals. See G. Werden and M. Simon,

From a theoretical perspective, the general idea behind leniency programmes is that they 'may destabilise organised crime by undermining internal trust with the increased risk that one of the involved parties unilaterally reports to enjoy the benefits of the leniency programme'[37]. In other words, leniency programmes intend to reinforce the prisoner's dilemma situation that exists in every cartel agreement.

The plausibility of this fundamental argument in favour of leniency programmes as a way to destabilise collusion is disputed among economists. For instance, Ellis and Wilson[38] ask why cartel members ought to abandon their profitable cartel agreement in exchange for a reduction in fines. Intuitively, applying for leniency would only make a difference to them if the cartel is at the verge of disbanding anyway. In other words, firms only apply for leniency when the cartel is already detected and the probability of punishment is sufficiently high. The influence of a leniency programme on the probability of detection can therefore be expected to be small or even negligible.

Aubert *et al.*[39] study the effects of leniency programmes on collusive agreements in a simple theoretical model. They assume two Cournot firms playing an infinitely repeated game in which the firms decide at the beginning of each period whether to collude or compete (deviate). The payoffs are defined as follows: π^M is the per-period firm profit if both firms decide to collude, π^D is the profit for a firm that deviates, π^S is the profit of the firm that decides to collude while the other firm deviates, and π^C is the profit if both firms compete on the market. It is reasonable to assume that firms gain from collusion and that the deviating firm benefits at the expense of the other firm, so $\pi^S<\pi^C<\pi^M<\pi^D$ as well as $\pi^S+\pi^D<2\pi^M$. The model also assumes that if one firm deviates, both firms play the competitive strategy in each of the coming (infinite) number of periods.

Aubert *et al.* introduce a competition authority that can either collect evidence by auditing the industry or rely on a leniency programme. Industry audits are assumed to take place with probability ω. If a leniency programme is implemented, each firm can decide to inform the authority of the existence of the collusive agreement. The agency can impose a maximum fine F, but this is not large enough to deter collusion, so $\pi^M-\pi^C>\omega F$.

In the absence of a leniency programme, period profits are $\pi^M-\omega F$ in case both firms collude, $\pi^D-\omega F$ for a firm that competes while the other colludes (and thus only realises a profit of $\pi^S-\omega F$), and simply π^C if both firms compete. Aubert *et al.* show that the most profitable strategy is to collude in every period and punish de-

'Why Price Fixers Should Go to Prison', 32 *Antitrust Bulletin* (1987), 917–37, for a general assessment of why price-fixers should go to prison.

37 G. Spagnolo, 'Optimal Leniency Programs', *Working paper* (Fondazione Eni Enrico Mattei, Milan 2000), p. 3.

38 C. Ellis and W. Wilson, 'What Doesn't Kill us Makes us Stronger: An Analysis of Corporate Leniency Policy', *Working Paper* (University of Oregon 2001), p. 3.

39 C. Aubert, W. Kovacic and P. Rey, 'The Impact of Leniency and Whistle-blowing Programs on Cartels', 24 *International Journal of Industrial Organization* (2005), 1241–66.

viations by returning to the competitive equilibrium. Collusion is sustainable if the gains realised when deviating are lower than the discounted gains from colluding:

$$\pi^D - \omega F + \frac{\delta}{1-\delta}\pi^C \leq \frac{1}{1-\delta}\left[\pi^M - \omega F\right] \tag{5}$$

or equivalently

$$\pi^D - \pi^M \leq \frac{\delta}{1-\delta}\left[\left(\pi^M - \omega F\right) - \pi^C\right] \tag{6}$$

If, however, the competition authority implements a leniency programme that rewards reporting firms with a reduction of the fine from F to f, a deviating firm will denounce its competitor when the reduced fine is lower than the expected fine it would have to pay in the case of an audit. In this case, collusion is sustainable if

$$\left(\pi^D - f\right) - \left(\pi^M - \omega F\right) \leq \frac{\delta}{1-\delta}\left[\left(\pi^M - \omega F\right) - \pi^C\right] \tag{7}$$

It follows that a leniency programme has a deterrence effect on collusion only if

$$\pi^D - \pi^M \leq \frac{\delta}{1-\delta}\left[\left(\pi^M - \omega F\right) - \pi^C\right] \leq \pi^D - \pi^M + \omega F - f \tag{8}$$

In this model, leniency programmes do not influence the profitability of collusion and they affect its sustainability only by giving deviating firms the opportunity to avoid a fine in case the competition authority investigates. 'Leniency programs can therefore be effective only when the expected fine … is large, that is, when collusion would already be fragile without any leniency program'[40]. In other words, leniency programmes are likely to raise the probability of punishment (as defecting firms have an incentive to apply for leniency and to provide hard evidence about the conspiracy), but are unlikely to have much influence on the probability of detection.[41] However, a refinement of the basic model shows that leniency programmes become better at detection and deterrence as soon as the competition authority is allowed to pay rewards to reporting cartel members (especially individuals) instead of just offering fine exemptions.[42] Such an approach, however, might be in conflict with moral considerations, insofar as it allows lawbreakers to receive rewards for cheating on an illegal agreement they profited from.

---

40 Aubert *et al.*, *supra* note 39, p. 12.

41 Scepticism about the ability of leniency programmes to influence the probability of detection is expressed by Harrington as follows: '[I]t is an open question … as to how effective leniency programs have been in discovering cartels. I am convinced by their role in prosecution as the evidence is much stronger when it is provided by one of the cartel members.' See J. Harrington, 'Detecting Cartels', in P. Buccirossi (ed.), *Handbook in Antitrust Economics* (MIT Press, 2008).

42 Spagnolo, *supra* note 37, models another, more courageous form of leniency programme allowing reporting firms to be rewarded. Optimally designed leniency programmes for undetected cartels can be a very powerful detection instrument. While the reporting firm receives rewards, the costs for competitors are raised by the fines imposed.

Motta and Polo[43] present another model for leniency programmes. In it, they analyse the effects of leniency programmes on the incentives of firms to collude and to reveal information that helps the competition authority prove illegal behaviour. One important result of their model is that leniency programmes can induce firms to collude more often, as leniency programmes reduce the expected fines in the event of detection. Consequently, preventing collusion by setting optimal fines is a competition authority's first best option. However, if the optimal fine solution is not feasible, the introduction of leniency programmes may be the second-best option. As Motta and Polo point out[44], '[f]ine reductions, inducing firms to reveal information once an investigation is opened, increase the probability of ex-post desistence and save resources of the antitrust authority, thereby raising welfare'.

There have been some promising attempts to clarify the ambiguous results found in game theory literature on the impact of leniency programmes. In the most promising attempt, Miller[45] develops a theoretical model of cartel behaviour that provides empirical predictions and subsequently applies the model to a dataset of information reports issued by the US Department of Justice (DOJ). The results from reduced-form statistical tests are consistent with the notion that leniency programmes positively affect deterrence and detection capabilities. The direct estimation of the model yielded a 59% lower cartel formation rate and a 62% higher cartel detection rate due to leniency programmes. Brenner[46] conducted an empirical study of the European corporate leniency programme and finds strong evidence that the programme provides incentives to reveal information on conspiracies, i.e., competition authorities are better informed about cartel conduct with the programme than without. With respect to the role of deterrence, Brenner neither finds that the leniency programme stabilises cartels (through facilitating punishment strategies) nor does he find that cartels are destabilised (as defecting from the cartel agreement becomes less costly).

In a nutshell, it is unlikely that leniency programmes in their current design will have a big impact on the probability of detection, at least in the EU. However, leniency programmes may contribute significantly as an integral part of a competition authority's overall strategy for detecting hard-core cartels. The competition authority has structural and behavioural tools for screening industries. If something suspicious is found – which is to say, if the probability of detection increases significantly – cartel members might decide to come forward and apply for leniency. This step, in turn, typically provides the competition authority with the hard

---

43 M. Motta and M. Polo, 'Leniency Programs and Cartel Prosecution', 21 *International Journal of Industrial Organization* (2003), 347–79.

44 Motta and Polo, see note 43 above, p. 26.

45 N. Miller, 'Strategic Leniency and Cartel Enforcement', 99 *American Economic Review* (2009), 750–68.

46 S. Brenner, 'An Empirical Study of the European Corporate Leniency Program', 27 *International Journal of Industrial Organization* (2009), 639–45.

evidence it needs to prevail in court. As Harrington observes[47], 'the presence of an active leniency programme makes the case for screening more, not less compelling because they are complements'.

3 Empirical Evidence from EC Cartel Enforcement (2000–2011)[48]

In this section, we present several basic empirical findings on cartel enforcement by the EC between 2000 and 2011. In particular, we describe the dataset and the corresponding descriptive statistics in section 3.1, followed by a discussion of time series of selected enforcement characteristics in section 3.2. Finally, section 3.3 tries to answer the question whether current EU fines levels are deterrence-optimal.

3.1 Dataset and Descriptive Statistics

The dataset applied in this article contains information on all cartel cases decided by the European Commission between 2000 and 2011. The data were collected from decisions and press releases published by the EC in the course of its investigations and combine case-specific as well as firm-specific information. On the case level, information such as cartel type, cartel duration, number of cartel members, affected industry, relevant geographic market(s) and imposed overall fines are available. Regarding firm-specific data, we include information on the individual length of cartel participation, the level of fines imposed by the EC, whether the firm applied for leniency or not and the value of fine reductions following a successful leniency application. Furthermore, specific factors that are relevant for the calculation of the fine are included such as aggravating and mitigating circumstances or repeated offenders. In sum, the dataset combines information on 73 EC cartel cases and 471 cartel members.[49] Table 1 displays an excerpt of the descriptive statistics of the dataset.

---

47 J. Harrington, 'Behavioral Screening and the Detection of Cartels', in C.D. Ehlermann and I. Atanasiu (eds.), *European Competition Law Annual 2006: Enforcement of Prohibition of Cartels* (Hart Publishing 2007).

48 This section draws partly on K. Hüschelrath, U. Laitenberger and F. Smuda, 'Cartel Enforcement in the European Union: Determinants of the Duration of Investigations', *European Competition Law Review* (2013).

49 It is worth noting that each cartel member is not necessarily represented by a single firm in the dataset. In cases in which several firms are jointly liable for the infringement, the 'group of companies' is treated as one observation.

Table 1. Descriptive statistics

	Mean	Median	Std. dev.	Min	Max
Number of firms	6.45	5	3.90	2	17
Cartel duration (total, in months)	105.73	72	84.75	5	408
Cartel duration (firm specific, in months)	93.66	68	69.23	4	408
Total fine per case (m €)	228.04	109.90	283.95	0.45	1383.90
Individual fine per firm (m €)	35.39	10.64	78.87	0	896
Fine reduction per firm	0.21	0.01	0.31	0	1
Share of leniency cases	0.88	1	0.33	0	1
Leniency collaboration rate per case	0.51	0.50	0.33	0	1

As shown in Table 1, the average number of cartel firms is 6.45 and the average overall cartel duration is 106 months (8.81 years). The median values of both factors are 5 firms and 72 months (6 years), respectively. The average firm-specific length of cartel participation is 94 months (7.81 years), which is close to the overall cartel duration and suggests that cartels are generally stable in terms of membership losses during cartelisation. Interestingly, plotting cartel duration against the number of firms reveals a positive relationship, i.e., cartel duration increases with the number of firms in the cartel (see Figure 5).

Fig. 5. Cartel duration vs. number of firms

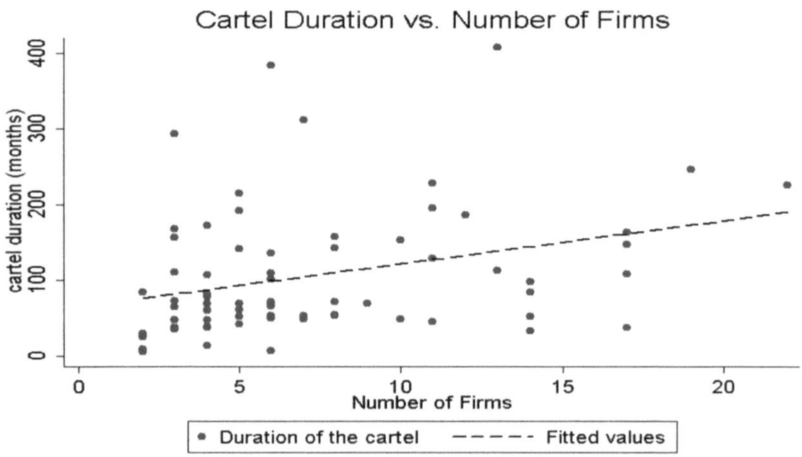

On the surface, this finding contradicts the theoretical industrial organisation literature, which suggests that the larger the number of cartel members, the more difficult it is to reach consensus on an agreement (and its subsequent monitoring).

However, case-study related evidence suggests that particular types of cartel agreements (market division agreements, in particular) are workable even with larger numbers of cartel members. Furthermore, as soon as industry associations or comparable organisations support members in their coordination activities (e.g., by providing detailed industry-specific datasets), larger numbers of cartel members can be organised effectively.

Regarding cartel fines, the average fine per case imposed by the European Commission between 2000 and 2011 was €228 million. It varies between the €450,000 fine imposed in the Luxembourg brewer case and the €1.38 billion fine imposed in the Carglass cartel. 88% of the cases show leniency applications and, on average, 51% of the firms in each case applied for fine reductions as part of the programme. The average fine reduction per firm – which might also be because of a company's inability to pay larger fines – is 21% of the initial base fine.

3.2 Discussion of Selected Enforcement Characteristics over Time

In addition to the presentation of the descriptive statistics in the preceding section, a discussion of selected enforcement characteristics over time can create further insights on cartel enforcement in the European Union.

3.2.1 Number of Decided Cases and the Role of Leniency

The usual starting point of studies on cartel enforcement is a basic analysis of the number of decided cases over time. Figure 6 illustrates the number of cases decided by the European Commission between 2000 and 2011.

Fig. 6. Number of cases and the role of leniency (2000–2011)

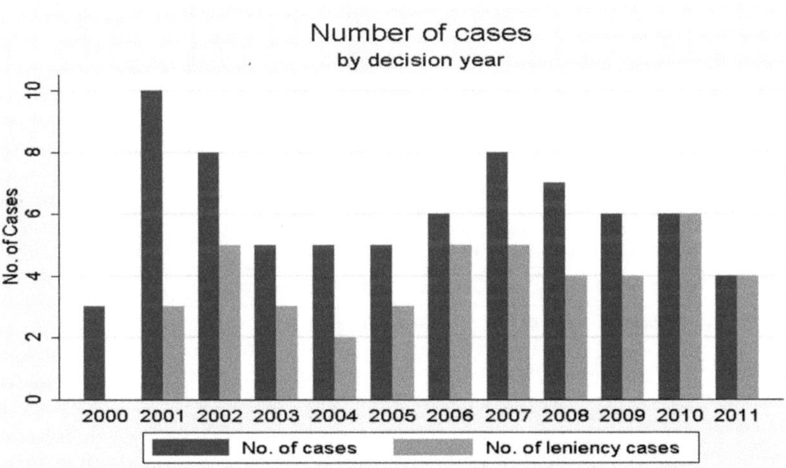

As Figure 6 shows, the number of decided cases varies between a minimum of only 3 cases in 2000 and a maximum of 10 cases in 2001. In most years, between five and eight cases were decided by the Commission. Figure 6 also shows that the number of leniency cases has increased substantially in recent years. While none of the 3 cases decided in 2000 involved any leniency application, all cases decided by the Commission over the last two years show at least one leniency application by a cartel member.

Although not displayed in Figure 6, the database allows a further characterisation of the decided EC cartel cases. With respect to the affected industries, about 75% of all cartels in our database refer to the manufacturing industry while the remaining 25% largely belong to either wholesale trade or transport and storage. Within manufacturing, roughly 40% of the cartel cases occurred in the subcategory 'chemicals and chemical products'. Turning to types of agreements, cartel decisions by the Commission involved the cartel type 'information exchange' in 60 cases, followed by 'market division' in 38 cases, 'quantity fixing' in 20 cases and 'price fixing' in 19 cases.[50] Interestingly, 'bid-rigging' only played a minor role and was mentioned as a type of collusion in only 3 decided cases.

3.2.2 Sum of Fines and Average Fines per Firm

In addition to an analysis of the number of cartel cases, an analysis of the sum of fines imposed together with the average fine per firm can add value. Figure 7 below displays the respective time series.

Fig. 7. Sum of fines and average fine per firm (2000–2011)

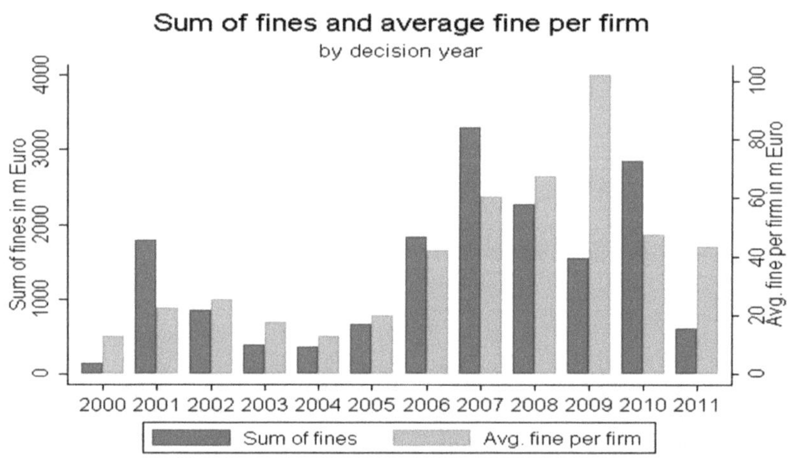

[50] It is important to mention here that many cartel cases involved more than one type of collusion.

As shown in Figure 7, the sum of fines fluctuates substantially in the period under investigation. While the year 2000 shows the smallest fine total, with a sum of €149.46 million, 2007 shows the largest, with a sum of €3294.30 million. As already mentioned above, the sum of fines is often driven by just a few very large cartels (in terms of revenue), which receive proportionately large fines.

In addition to the sum of fines imposed by the EC in the respective years, Figure 7 also displays the average fine per firm on a yearly basis. We see that the average fine stayed at a relatively low level until 2004, but then experienced a substantial increase in the following years. Interestingly, the years 2010 and 2011 show a remarkable drop in the average fine (compared with its all-time high in 2009). One reason for this development was the larger fine reductions granted by the EC.

3.2.3 Share of Leniency Applicants and Average Fine Reductions

As already shown in section 3.2.1, the share of leniency cases increased substantially in the EU from 2000 to 2011. As leniency programmes do not only offer fine exemptions or reductions for the first firm that discloses its participation in a cartel but also aims at incentivising other cartel members to come forward and cooperate, an interesting question is how the share of leniency applicants apart from the chief witness changed over time. Figure 8 below presents the respective time series.

Fig. 8. Average reduction of cartel fines for firms (2000–2011)

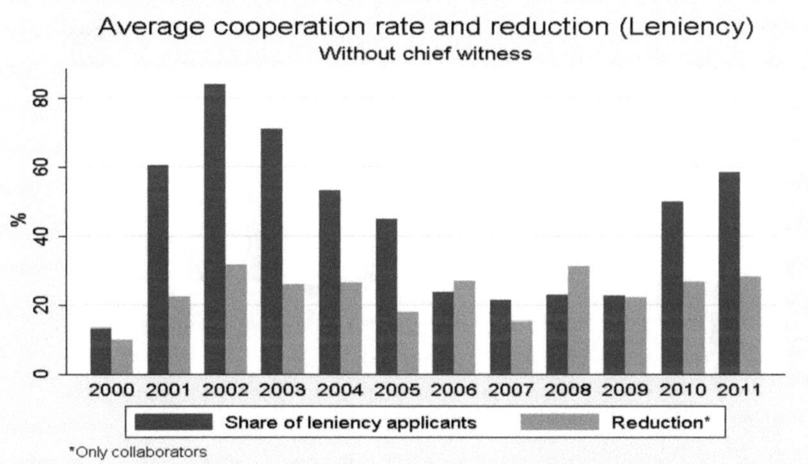

As shown in Figure 8, after a very small share of leniency applicants in the year 2000, a substantial increase was observed from 2001 to 2003, with values exceeding 60%. Interestingly, the following years experienced a constant decrease of leniency shares, with a minimum of less than 20% in 2007. In recent years, the share of leniency applicants in the respective cases increased again, reaching a value of almost 60% in 2011. Although it is generally difficult to draw any meaningful conclusions from these isolated empirical observations, one possible explanation for the observed time trend is the increased transparency on how the leniency programme is applied together with observations that fine levels decrease significantly when a cartel member decides to fully cooperate with the Commission.

In addition to the share of leniency applicants, Figure 8 also shows the average percentage reduction for firms collaborating with the competition authority under the leniency programme. As revealed by the time series, the average reduction fluctuates between 10% and 30%, with the year 2000 showing the lowest value (about 10%) and the year 2002 showing the highest value (about 33%).

3.2.4 Duration of Cartel Investigations

In formal investigations of competition policy cases in general and cartel cases in particular, several enforcement periods can be differentiated. First, there is the time span between the end of the cartel and the beginning of the investigation. Generally, one would expect the competition authority to detect a cartel and start an investigation shortly afterwards. As shown in Figure 9, this expectation is only met in several years of the investigation period.

Fig. 9. Time span between cartel end and beginning of investigation (2000–2011)

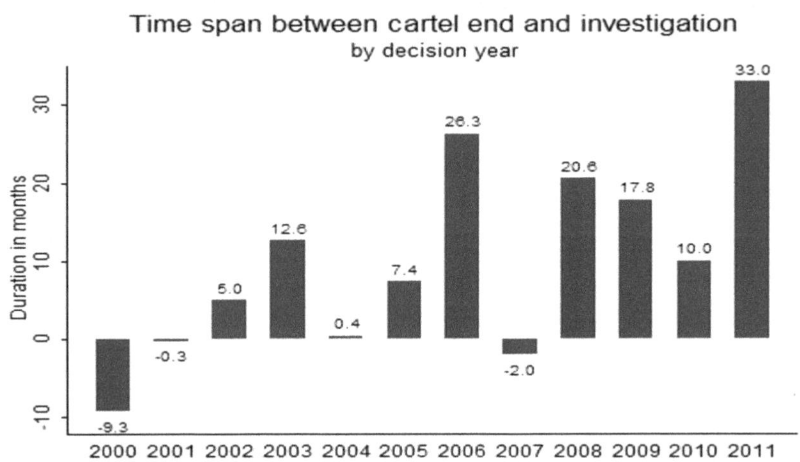

Although several years show, as expected, a short duration from the end of the cartel to the beginning of the investigation, the last few years in the dataset show a substantial increase in the average time span. One explanation for this development might be the increase of cartels reported by involved firms long after they were actually terminated. Such behaviour might be rational when a newly installed management would like to start off with a clean record and therefore decides to report old infringements of competition law. The possibility of applying for leniency further motivates such behaviour. The time series might also reflect an increase in the 'passive' detection of cartels by the leniency programme and a corresponding decrease in 'active' cartel detection activities (or successes) of the Commission.[51]

A second enforcement period of potential interest is the time span between the beginning of the investigation and the decision by the competition authority. Figure 10 shows the EC's development for the period from 2000 to 2011. As shown in Figure 10, the time span between the beginning of the investigation and the decision fluctuates from on average 93.3 months (about 7.7 years) in the year 2000[52] to 32.8 months (about 2.7 years) in the year 2003. On average, a cartel investigation lasted about 50.8 months (4.2 years) for the entire period from 2000 to 2011 and 46.6 months if the (exceptional) year 2000 is excluded from the analysis.[53]

Fig. 10. Time span between beginning of investigation and decision (2000–2011)

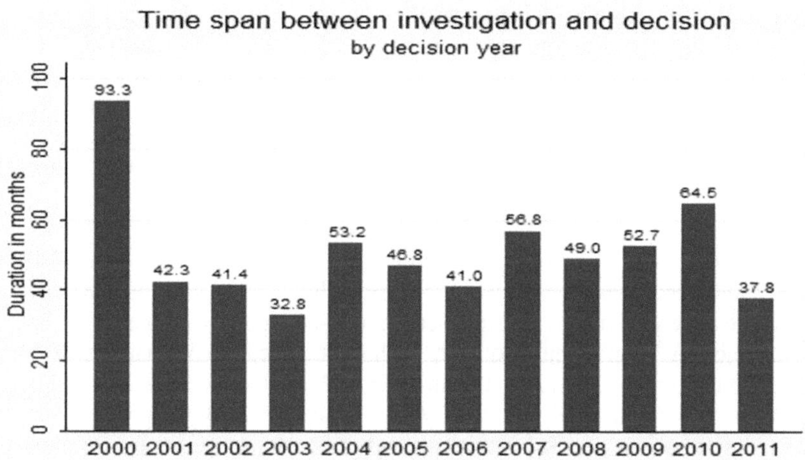

51 The negative values in 2000, 2001 and 2007 indicate that in some cases, investigations already started before the actual cartel breakdown. This might be due to the fact that either the EC already attracted attention in such cases or the chief witness in the course of the leniency programme collected further evidence in coordination with the EC while the cartels were still active. Furthermore, there might be cases in which it is legally unclear whether the collaboration is an infringement of competition law and firms thus decide to continue their cooperation after the investigation has been opened.

52 The long time span in the year 2000 was mostly caused by a single cartel case with an exceptionally long investigation length.

53 In addition to the two enforcement periods discussed here, further periods could be identified. For example, the time span between the decision of the Commission and a first court decision could be analysed. Another option would be to investigate the full time span from the beginning of the investigation until a final decision is reached.

3.3 Are Current EU Fine Levels Deterrence-Optimal?

In general, any kind of evaluation of the successfulness of cartel enforcement faces an identification problem. If only a few cartels are detected, this could indicate a successful deterrence policy of the competition authority. Alternatively, it could be interpreted as evidence that the competition authority is ill-equipped to detect cartels or has insufficient resources to exercise its duties effectively. Vice versa, an increase in the detection of cartels could indicate that certain policy changes have been beneficial. It might also indicate that the number of cartels has risen and the competition authority detected some of them more or less accidentally.

Despite these apparent problems with identification, economists have developed and applied several methods for collecting evidence on the effectiveness of cartel enforcement activities such as optimal corporate fines, the impact of cartel enforcement on post-cartel prices and attempts to measure the deterrent effect of cartel enforcement.[54] In the remainder of this section, we concentrate on the implementation of optimal corporate fines by focusing on whether the fines actually collected by the EC come anywhere near the optimal fines we identified (signalling to firms that cartelisation does not pay). To answer this question, Veljanovski[55] collected data on duration, fines imposed, sales, overcharges and consumer losses for several detected and prosecuted hard-core cartels in the EU. He then calculated optimal fines largely based on the respective cartel overcharge estimate (the measure for 'harm caused') and on an (optimistic) probability of detection for cartels of 33%.

As shown in Table 2, the fines collected by the Commission largely 'under-deter' price-fixing.[56] As shown by the multiplier in the last column, the optimal fine would have been between 1.6 and 115.5 times higher than the fines actually imposed. The general result of the significant under-deterrence of price fixing has been confirmed by Combe and Monnier,[57] who concluded from a sample of 64 cartels convicted by the Commission from 1975 to 2009 that the fines imposed by the Commission were generally too low (whatever the assumed probability of detection). Furthermore, a detailed empirical study of cartel sanctions by Bolotova

---

54 See Hüschelrath and Weigand, *supra* note 4.

55 C. Veljanovski, 'Cartel Fines in Europe: Law, Practice and Deterrence', 30 *World Competition* (2007), 65–86.

56 In a recent paper, Connor (*supra* note 30) reaches the same conclusion albeit using an alternative approach. He concludes that in order to 'ensure optimal deterrence of global cartels, total financial sanctions should be four times the expected global cartel profits (the overcharge). In the case of followers, deterrence would require penalties in all geographic regions to be equal to eight times global cartel overcharges. Even in cases widely regarded as exemplary prosecutions, antitrust sanctions historically have failed to approach optimal levels' (p. 30).

57 E. Combe and C. Monnier, 'Fines Against Hard-core Cartels in Europe: The Myth of Overenforcement', 56 *Antitrust Bulletin* (2011), 235–276.

and Connor[58] using a sample of international cartels suggests that modern antitrust policy is unlikely to be effective in their deterrent function. One key reason is the weak link between the concept of optimal fines (based on the net harm to others) and the fine calculation methods actually applied by competition authorities (typically based on a percentage of affected sales during the last full calendar year of cartel operation). Interestingly, Bolotova and Connor[59] find that the relationship between cartel fine and cartel overcharge is negative, implying that cartels imposing higher overcharges (i.e., cartels harming customers more) tend to pay smaller fines. Based on the theoretical model sketched above, Buccirossi and Spagnolo[60] conclude that past EU fines appear to have been too low to have sufficient deterrence effects.

Table 2. Estimates of consumer losses and optimal fines

Cartel	Duration	Fine	Sales	Overcharge	Consumer loss	Fine	Optimal fine	
							Fine	
	years	€m	€m	€m	€m		€m	Multipl.
Lysine	4	110	164	121	181	61%	549	5,0
Vitamin A	9	132	150	275	413	32%	1.251	9,5
Vitamin E	9	203	250	459	688	30%	2.085	10,3
Vitamin C	5	114	120	112	168	68%	510	4,5
Vitamin D3	4	41	20	15	22	184%	67	1,6
Graphite Electr.	6	219	420	481	722	30%	2.188	10,0
Citric Acid	4	135	320	236	353	38%	1.071	7,9
Food Flavor Enh.	9	21	12	22	33	62%	100	4,9
Organic Peroxides	25	70	250	1.694	2.649	3%	8.029	115,5
Copper Plumbing	13	222	1.151	3.311	4.967	4%	15.052	67,7
Rubber Chemicals	5	76	200	188	282	27%	854	11,3

Note: Optimal fines calculations are based on a probability of detection of 0.33. 'Sales' refers to annual sales in the preceding year.
Source: Table largely follows Veljanovski[61]; own calculations.

Although these results may indicate significant under-deterrence, it is important to note that the fines imposed by the EC are often supplemented by other payments that can be interpreted as additional fines by cartel members. For example,

58 Y. Bolotova and J. Connor, 'Cartel Sanctions: An Empirical Analysis', *Working Paper* (University of Idaho, Moscow, 2008).

59 Bolotova and Connor, *supra* note 59.

60 Buccirossi and Spagnolo, *supra* note 35. See also F. Smuda, 'Cartel Overcharges and the Deterrent Effect of EU Competition Law', *Journal of Competition Law and Economics,* forthcoming.

61 Veljanovski, *supra* note 55, p. 80.

in some EU Member States, courts are not only entitled to impose (pecuniary) fines on undertakings for proven infringements of competition law; they can also punish the responsible individuals for (specific) infringements of competition law with either pecuniary fines and/or prison sentences. *Individual punishment* is normally not limited to the prison term as such but is often extended by the reduced employability of the manager afterwards. Furthermore, the loss of the respective manager can have an additional punitive effect on the firm, especially if the manager was important for the business success and cannot be replaced easily. Although the legal system of the EU does not foresee individualised sanctions at this time, the legal situation in several Member States such as the UK and Germany allows individualised sanctions for specific serious infringements such as cartelisation in general (UK) or bid-rigging specifically (Germany).

An additional component in calculating overall negative consequences of hardcore cartels is *private damage claims*. Although damages generally aim to compensate affected private parties for the harm caused by price-fixing conspiracies, they can also be interpreted as an additional punitive weapon. For example, in the US, damages are an important cornerstone of the entire enforcement strategy and damaged parties are entitled to sue for up to three times the damages. Furthermore, class actions are permitted to bundle interests against cartelists. In the EU, private damage claims have not played a huge role so far, but recent initiatives taken by the Commission lead us to expect this situation to change in the coming years. In Table 2 above, a comparison of the values for corporate fines and overcharges shows that the addition of both categories lead to a significant increase in the overall fine, reducing the specific multiplier (based on the optimal fine in each case).

The court trials of detected cartels have to be considered as a further component of the entire fine package. These procedures not only incur direct costs such as litigation costs and counsel fees but also cause substantial in-house costs, as employees need to invest part of their working time in the provision of information for the investigation or trial. These costs might be complemented by contract renegotiation costs if it turns out that contracts including anticompetitive practices are void and therefore need to be renegotiated. The actual size of litigation costs and counsel fees depends mostly on the type and size of the case. For the EU, Neven[62] reports that the costs and fees spent by Airtours in the Commission merger investigation of *Airtours/First Choice*[63] add up to more than €2.2m overall, with about 80% of these costs going to lawyers and the remaining 20% to economists. Although merger cases tend to be more complex and therefore need more resources than cartel cases – in the latter illegal conduct is easier to prove – litigation costs and counsel fees can still become quite significant if, first, the costs of trials in multiple jurisdictions are taken into account[64] and, second, private damag-

---

62 D. Neven, 'Competition Economics and Antitrust in Europe', 21 *Economic Policy* (2006), 741–91.

63 Case No IV/M.1524 – Airtours/First Choice.

64 A survey by PriceWaterhouseCoopers found that a typical multi-jurisdictional merger deal generates on average €3.3m in external merger review costs. However, the sur-

es actions follow the imposition of public fines, thereby demanding the investment of substantial additional resources in measures such as the calculation of 'true' damages caused by the cartel agreement.

Further, the calculation has to take into account the *effects on stock prices*. Generally, the stock price of a firm changes as a result of market forces. It is an indicator of the perceived value of the firm. Profits and profit expectations affect stock price and the value of a company. The existence of a detected cartel reduces profits and profit expectations. Accordingly, a drop in the stock price is to be expected post detection. Ceteris paribus, such a development must be considered as an additional negative consequence of detected hard-core cartels. With respect to quantification, Langus and Motta[65] use an event-study approach to investigate the impact of various events of EU cartel enforcement on a firm's stock market value. Their results show that dawn raids reduced the firm's stock market value by 2.2% on average on the day of the raid. Furthermore, the formal announcement of the Commission that a cartel was detected led to another loss of 3.0% on average of the firm's stock market value.

In most cases it is hard to keep the detection of hard-core cartels secret. Accordingly, another, final component of the entire fine package is *negative effects on firm reputation*. The knock-on effects of such a decrease in reputation can be multifaceted. For example, in addition to a general reduction in future business opportunities, public sector customers may exclude the firm from doing business with them. Furthermore, a damaged reputation may complicate the process of hiring high potential employees and may thus adversely affect future firm performance. Additionally, the payment of substantial fines and damages can cause a competitive disadvantage due to reduced possibilities to undertake investments in the firm's operations or research and development. Depending on the general financial situation of the firm and the competitive situation in its given markets, the competitive disadvantages might become so severe that the firm's existence is put in jeopardy, fortifying the negative effects on firm reputation.

In sum, given the absence of a complete empirical assessment of the various cost components of detected hard-core cartels, the question whether price-fixing in the EU is really under-deterred continues to remain open.

---

vey also shows that a few major deals with at least one in-depth review by a competition authority incurred costs of more than €10m. See PriceWaterhouseCoopers, *A Tax on Mergers? Surveying the Time and Costs to Business of Multi-jurisdictional Merger Reviews* (London 2003), p. 4.

65 G. Langus and M. Motta, 'The Effect of Antitrust Investigations and Fines on the Firm Valuation', *Working Paper* (European University Institute, Florence 2006).

4 Conclusion

The desire of firms to ease competitive pressures and increase joint profits through the implementation of cartel agreements has long been recognised by academics. Although Adam Smith's[66] famous statement on the social harmfulness of (price) coordination among competitors is usually seen as the foundation of a large literature on the economics of cartel agreements, the general concept of cartelisation and the need for state intervention was already expressed quite clearly in the works of Greek philosophers such as Aristotle.[67]

Nowadays, the prohibition of hard-core cartels lies at the heart of antitrust policy and competition authorities are consequently given the task of enforcing anticartel laws. In this article, I assessed these public enforcement activities from both theoretical and empirical perspectives. The first central insight of the theoretical discussions was that competition authorities can generally apply ex ante and ex post tools to fight hard-core cartels. Ex ante tools include blacklisting, regulation of communication, market design and merger control and aim at avoiding the formation of cartels in the first place. But as it is unlikely that such instruments alone will deter cartelisation in an economically optimal fashion, policy makers have to implement ex post tools.

Based on a differentiation between detection and intervention, I showed that competition authorities can choose from a variety of pro- and reactive tools to detect cartel agreements – tools such as market screening, industry monitoring, complaints or leniency applications. These activities need to be combined with optimal fines for detected infringements. In a simple framework, it was shown that a deterrence-optimal fine depends on the gain (or alternatively harm) of the infringement and the probability of detection. In the extended model framework, the minimum fine that deters cartelisation was found to increase as the cartel-induced price increases and decrease with competitive mark-up, the probability of detection and market demand elasticity.

As part of the discussion of empirical evidence on EC cartel enforcement activities, a dataset of 73 EC cartel cases – decided between 2000 and 2011 – was used to present and interpret selected enforcement characteristics over time. Among other things, it was discovered that the number of decided cases varied between a minimum of only 3 cases in 2000 and a maximum of 10 cases in 2001. The sum of fines also showed substantial fluctuation during the observation period. While the year 2000 shows the smallest fine total, with €149.46 million, 2007 shows the largest, with 3294.30 million. It was also discovered that the number of leniency cases increased substantially in recent years. With respect to the central question whether current EC fine levels are deterrence-optimal, empirical studies mostly suggest that current fine levels are too low to reach optimal deterrence. However, as these studies mostly fail to take further components of the entire fine package into account – individual punishments, private damage claims, effects on stock

66 A. Smith, *An Inquiry into the Nature and Causes of the Wealth of Nations* (London 1776).

67 Aristotle, *Politica* (347 BC), Part XI.

prices, effects on firm reputation – the question whether price-fixing in the EU is really under-deterred continues to remain open.

In the light of the key findings of this article, it is important to recall from a more general perspective that the public enforcement of anti-cartel laws is only one specific area of the public enforcement of competition law. As a consequence, a more general approach of public enforcement must also include other parts of competition law. Furthermore, in many countries public enforcement is complemented by a system of private enforcement. While public enforcement means that antitrust rules are enforced by state authorities, private enforcement is based on the actions of private parties – such as competitors, suppliers, customers or consumers – who can bring antitrust lawsuits based on the private damages caused by forms of anticompetitive behaviour. The private system has the central advantage that private enforcers often have greater incentives, information and resources to take enforcement actions than public enforcers do. As McAfee *et al.*[68] argue, this might lead to additional benefits for society through additional deterrence. However, the downside is – in addition to the general costs incurred by an additional private system – that private enforcers also have greater incentives to (ab)use antitrust rules strategically and might therefore cause harm to society.[69] In any case, the co-existence of public and private enforcement suggests the need for a harmonisation of both systems in order to avoid problems of under- or overdeterrence.[70]

---

68 P. McAfee, H. Mialon and S. Mialon, 'Private v. Public Antitrust Enforcement: A Strategic Analysis', 92 *Journal of Public Economics* (2008), 1863–75.

69 See P. McAfee and N. Vakkur, 'The Strategic Abuse of Antitrust Laws', 1 *Journal of Strategic Management Education* (2004), 1–17.

70 See, for instance, D. Rubinfeld, 'An Empirical Perspective on Legal Process: Should Europe Introduce Private Antitrust Enforcement?' in P. Nobel and M. Gets (eds.), *New Frontiers of Law and Economics* (Schulthess 2006), p. 143.

Leniency Programmes and the Structure of Cartels – Remarks from an Economic Perspective

Ulrich Schwalbe[1]

1 Introduction

In the last two decades, leniency programmes have been established as a new instrument to fight cartels in almost all legal systems. They complement the traditional instruments – fines – and, in some jurisdictions, criminal prosecution. Leniency programmes were established in the US as early as 1978.[2] They were introduced in Europe in 1996, with Germany's 'Bonusregelung'system being enacted in 2000. Within a short period of time, these programmes have become major 'case generators' for cartels. More than two thirds of all cartel cases in the EU and about 50% of all cartel detections in Germany are based on statements from key witnesses.[3] But more important than destabilizing existing cartels (desistance) is the ability of leniency programmes to deter the formation of new cartels.

Over time, most leniency programmes have been modified and adapted multiple times. Though a certain degree of harmonization between jurisdictions has been observed – as demonstrated by the master leniency programme of the ECN[4] –leniency programmes continue to vary in certain respects, such as the question of candidate eligibility for leniency, or what fine reductions to grant to which per-

---

1 I am grateful to Jan Höft, Morten Hviid, Wouter Wils and the participants of the conference Public and Private Enforcement of Competition Law at the Mannheim Centre for Competition and Innovation on 10–11 March 2011 for their valuable suggestions and comments.

2 The regulations of the first leniency programme in the US were equivocal, leaving firms with substantial levels of uncertainty. Only after their revision, in 1993, there was a sharp increase in the number of cartel detections.

3 It might be automatically assumed that with the number of cartel detections also the detection rate has increased, but it could also be the case that the number of cartels as such has risen. Empirical investigations, however, suggest that leniency programmes have indeed succeeded in increasing the detection rate. See N.H. Miller, 'Strategic Leniency and Cartel Enforcement', 99 *American Economic Review* (2009), 750–768.

4 The ECN-leniency regulation model, available at http://ec.europa.eu/competition/ecn/model_leniency_de.pdf.

sons. For example, in Germany and in the US, ringleaders are excluded from leniency. In Great Britain, by contrast, leniency is refused only if the firm has coerced other firms to take part in the cartel, or to remain in an existing cartel (coercer test). In the US, only the first firm that applies for leniency is eligible for a fine reduction.[5] The differences in the leniency programme reflect disparities in the legal systems. For instance, the 'winner-takes-all' principle practised in the United States probably results from the better options for US competition authority to acquire information compared with those available in Europe or Germany.

The success of a leniency programme depends crucially on its interrelation with damage enforcement. Several authors point out that both public and private enforcement must be coordinated to prevent them from counteracting each other.[6] This raises questions about the transmission of information the authority receives from the leniency applicant to third parties, about the quantification of damage caused by the cartel and about the passing-on defence or cartel regress.

Economists have been analysing leniency programmes for more than ten years. A number of models have been developed that analyse the effects of leniency programmes on destabilizing existing cartels as well as on deterring new ones. But a major drawback in all these models is that they do not, or do not fully, take into account the legal systems underlying the leniency programmes.[7] Often, moreover, they assume that cartels do not consider the existence of competition authorities or leniency programmes with regard to their organization and activity. In most cases, a simple model is assumed to describe cartel behaviour: cartels determine prices and produce quantities in such a way as to maximize joint profits. Only recently have studies factored in the possibility that cartels might modify their behaviour when a competition authority is present or that cartels might respond to detection measures.

This essay analyses the possible reactions of cartels to the existence of competition authorities and leniency programmes. It is unreasonable to assume that cartels will simply ignore competition authorities or passively accept the existence of leniency programmes. More likely, cartels adapt their behaviour and internal structure to existing institutions and instruments. Harrington has pointed out that a cartel behaves differently when a competition authority is in place from when one is not.[8] In the former case, a newly formed cartel will not immediately set the profit

---

5 The willingness to cooperate could be rewarded as part of the plea bargaining process.

6 See U. Schwalbe, 'Kronzeugenregelungen und Kartelle', in J. Ramser,and M. Stadler (eds.), *Marktmacht* (Mohr-Siebeck, 2010), 99–129; U. Schwalbe, 'Kronzeugenregelungen und die Struktur von Kartellen – Anmerkungen aus ökonomischer Sicht', in Studienvereinigung Kartellrecht (ed.), *Festschrift für Cornelis Canenbley* (C.H. Beck 2012), 423–439; U. Schwalbe and J. Höft, 'Ausgestaltung von Kronzeugenprogrammen und private Kartellrechtsdurchsetzung', in S. Bechtold, J. Jickeli and M. Rohe (eds.), *Festschrift für Wernhard Möschel* (C.H. Beck 2011).

7 *Ibid.*

8 See, e.g., J. E. Harrington, 'Cartel Pricing Dynamics in the Presence of an Antitrust Authority', 35 *RAND Journal of Economics* (2004), 651–673; J. E. Harrington, 'Op-

maximizing cartel price, since such a sudden and substantial increase in price within a short period of time would arouse the suspicion of the authority and the cartel's customers. This essay primarily deals with the question whether cartels are likely to change their internal structure – the number of contacts, their specification, the connections between its members – when a leniency programme is in place, and if so, what kind of changes are to be expected. In the second section of the essay, the economic principles of leniency programmes are sketched. Then, the two possible reactions of a cartel with respect to leniency programmes are described in more detail, i.e. the possible changes in the cartel's behaviour as well as in its internal structure. Especially the latter aspect has hardly been dealt with in the economic literature. To analyse this question, concepts from the theory of organized crime are employed. Finally, the effects on competition policy are discussed. It turns out that a probable reaction to leniency programmes is the increased formation of 'hub-spoke cartels'. This finding serves as further justification for the increased attention cartel authorities have paid to vertical restrictions as of late. Accordingly, the extension of leniency programmes to vertical structures – as has been enacted in the UK – should be considered.

2 Leniency Programmes

From an economic point of view, the main difference between fines (the conventional instrument of public competition law enforcement) and the relatively measure of leniency programmes is that the former aims at the profitability of a cartel, while the latter affects the incentive of a firm to remain a member of the cartel, or to form a cartel and participate in it in the first place. A fine reduces or eliminates cartel profit, and may even exceed the economic damage caused by the cartel.[9] That is, a fine ex post eradicates the very purpose of the cartel. Yet this is the case only if the cartel is detected by an authority. Thus the relevant variable considered by a cartel firm is the extent of the fine weighted by the probability of detection. If the probability of detection is sufficiently high, even a low fine may undercut the profitability of the cartel.

In contrast to fines, leniency programmes leave the profitability of a cartel untouched. Instead, they decrease the incentive to remain a cartel member, or to form a cartel in the first place. As mentioned above, leniency programmes have two effects. First, the promise of amnesty encourages firms to quit existing cartels that

timal Cartel Pricing in the Presence of an Antitrust Authority', 46 *International Economic Review* (2005), 145–169; J.E. Harrington and J. Chen, 'Cartel Pricing Dynamics with Cost Variability and Endogenous Buyer Detection', 24 *International Journal of Industrial Organization* (2006), 1185–1212.

9 According to the Oxera study, about 7% of all cartels do not have an economic effect. See Oxera, *Quantifying Antitrust Damages – Towards Non-Binding Guidance for Courts, Study prepared for the European Commission* (Publications Office of the European Union 2009), pp. 90 *et seq.*

would have otherwise remained active, allowing greater detection.[10] Each cartel member fears that another member may be the first to quit, inform the competition authority and receive amnesty, clearly reducing the stability of the cartel.[11] Further, leniency programmes contribute to preventing cartels *a priori* because potential cartel members expect other members to defect in the future. Unlike the detection effect, which is mostly short term, the deterrence effect works in the medium and long run. The latter effect is significantly more important, since fewer cartels will be formed in the future. This deterrence effect is invisible, however, whereas the detection effect often yields spectacular cases.

The economic arguments for leniency programmes stem primarily from the theory of cartels, a field of the theory of industrial organization,[12] where methods from game theory are used to derive conditions for the existence and the stability of cartels.[13] These arguments also have roots in the economic theory of crime and punishment.[14] This approach examines how an optimal combination of penalties and law enforcement may prevent potential offenders from committing a crime. The literature usually assumes that a penalty, when combined with a positive probability that the crime will be detected, shall prevent only a single agent from committing a crime. In the case of cartels (and organized crime), however, several agents are involved in illegal activities. Here it is possible to play off the members against each other by offering incentives for individuals. Hence, leniency programmes make sense only in the case of illegal activities that are jointly committed by the members of criminal organizations and cartels.[15]

Economic theory shows that the conditions under which an illegal cartel agreement may arise and exhibit stability are comparatively weak. If the members of a cartel interacted only once, or a finite number of times, a cartel agreement would be unstable since each member would face an incentive to set lower prices, which will attract more customers provided that the other cartel members stick to

---

10 Provided that the cartel is not detected by an independent investigation of the cartel authority, or is not tipped off by affected customers.

11 In all leniency programmes, full amnesty is granted only to the first whistleblower. In some jurisdictions, such as in the US, only the first applicant has a right to claim a fine reduction.

12 For a survey on the economic literature on leniency programmes, see Schwalbe (2009) or Spagnolo (2008).

13 A survey on this literature can be found in contemporary textbooks on industrial organization. See, for instance, P. Belleflamme and M. Peitz, *Industrial Organization – Markets and Strategies* (Cambridge University Press 2010), 335–372; S. Martin, *Industrial Organization in Context* (Oxford University Press 2010), 179–211; and L. Pepall, D. Richards and G. Norman, *Contemporary Industrial Organization – A Quantitative Approach* (Wiley 2011), 234–281.

14 The classical article on this topic is G.S. Becker, 'Crime and Punishment – An Economic Approach', 76 *Journal of Political Economy* (1960), 169–217.

15 This is why leniency programmes play a certain role in criminal law. Thus, Art. 46 b of the German Penal code (StGB) introduces an extensive leniency programme.

the agreement.[16] Such a situation where interaction between cartel members takes place for a finite number of periods is a prisoners' dilemma: sticking to the agreement would be in the collective interest of all cartel members, but each individual firm has an incentive to deviate from the agreement and seek higher profits.[17] All firms are aware of this problem and, as a consequence, are unwilling to form a cartel in the first place. A different situation will arise if the firms in the market interact without any predetermined last period. As there is always a chance for an additional interaction, firms may react to their co-members' present behaviour in the future. For instance, adhering to the agreement may be rewarded in the next round of interaction by all firms' sticking to the agreement in the next period as well. Likewise, if a firm deviates from the agreement in one period, the other cartel members will punish it later, for example by aggressive pricing behaviour in subsequent periods. Hence, each potential cartel member must weigh the immediate profit from deviating against the loss in future cartel profits due to punishment.

By contrast, if a firm sticks to the agreement, it will receive the cartel profit in each period. That is, in each period, each firm has to decide whether to stick to the agreement or to deviate. A cartel will be stable if the present value of the steady stream of cartel profits exceeds the one-time profit from deviating plus the lower profit received during the subsequent punishment phase. The condition for a stable cartel is:

$$\frac{\pi^c}{1-\delta} \geq \pi^d + \delta\left(\frac{\pi^*}{1-\delta}\right). \qquad (1)$$

Here, $\pi^c/(1\text{-}\delta)$ denotes the present value of the profits received by each cartel member when all members stick to the agreement; and δ is the common factor used to discount future profits to the present period.[18] The cartel will be stable if this value exceeds the profit a firm will earn if it deviates once. The deviation profit consists of the one-time higher profit in the period of deviation, π^d, plus the present value of the profits received in the following periods when the firm is being punished by other cartel members. This value is given by $\delta(\pi^*/(1\text{-}\delta))$, where π^* denotes the profit received under competitive behaviour.[19]

16 Leniency programmes rely on the existence of explicit agreements among cartel members, as leniency applicants must provide concrete proof of collusion. In the case of tacit collusion, such proof is impossible. This is the only difference between equilibria in tacit collusion and in collusion by explicit agreement. In either case, the same incentives are at work, and even explicit cartel agreements must be self-enforcing or incentive compatible.

17 The same argument holds true when the number of interactions is finite and known to all agents.

18 As in most models that involve leniency programmes, it is assumed that firms employ a so-called 'grim-trigger' strategy. A one-time deviation from the cartel agreement will be punished by permanent competitive behaviour in the future.

19 This is not profit earned under perfect competition; it is profit earned in the oligopolistic market without collusion.

This approach allows for fines to be taken into account by reducing the profits by the amount of the fine. Yet the competition authority detects a cartel agreement only with a certain probability. For this reason, the relevant variable is the fine weighted by the probability that it will occur. This probability is composed of the probability of cartel detection combined with the probability of conviction. The latter probability is assumed to be exogenous and is denoted by ρ, while b denotes the fine. Accordingly, the short-term profit from deviating from a cartel is given by

$$\left(\pi^d - \rho b\right) - \left(\pi^c - \rho b\right) = \pi^d - \pi^c . \tag{2}$$

The expected fine ρb reduces the profitability of remaining in a cartel. However, the incentive to stick to the agreement remains unchanged; the short-term profit from deviating is independent of the fine. Introducing a leniency programme reduces the expected fine when a member deviates from the agreement. In this case, the fine is reduced to f when $0 \leq f \leq \rho b$, where the amount of the expected fine f depends on the design of the leniency programme. In the case of full amnesty, the expected fine will be zero. The short-term profit from deviating is

$$\left(\pi^d - f\right) - \left(\pi^c - \rho b\right) = \pi^d - \pi^c + \left(\rho b - f\right) . \tag{3}$$

Since the last term is positive, the incentive to deviate has increased. This shows that leniency programmes increase the incentive to deviate from a cartel agreement, or not to join a cartel in the first place. However, competition authorities must continue to investigate even when leniency programmes are in effect; otherwise the probability of detection and conviction would be equal to zero, and no member would want to apply for leniency.

This simple approach underlying most economic models of leniency programmes make two sorts of assumptions. First, conventional economic models assume that, after a cartel has been formed, it will immediately seek to maximize profit, and market price will shoot up from the competitive level to the cartel price (which usually corresponds to the monopoly price).[20] Secondly, it is assumed that each member of the cartel is perfectly informed about the cartel, its members, the agreements, the meetings, etc., and that each member is able to communicate this information to competition authorities, and provide proof of collusion. If a cartel wants to minimize the probability of being detected, however, it is unlikely that the cartel will behave in the way presumed by economic theory. Instead, the cartel will try not to arouse suspicion with the authorities. This could be achieved by increasing the price slowly, instead of immediately adopting the monopoly price. In other words, the cartel would change its behaviour to prevent detection and sanctions by the authorities.

---

20 In the following sections, price competition is assumed throughout. In the case of quantity competition, the cartel immediately reduces competitive quantity to cartel quantity.

The introduction of a leniency programme causes another problem for the cartel: the amnesty granted to a leniency applicant increases the incentive to deviate from the cartel agreement. This will destabilize existing cartels, and prevent the formation of new ones. But a condition for claiming leniency is that the leniency applicant is able to provide information on the cartel to authorities. The better the information, the higher the likelihood of obtaining amnesty. This is why cartels are anxious to minimize information of each member on agreements and other incriminating evidence. Cartels can achieve this by changing the internal structure such that information is decentralised. In this case, the incentive to claim leniency is reduced, as any member is able to provide only limited information to the authorities.

All in all, then, one might expect a twofold reaction by cartels to the instruments used by the competition authorities. First, cartels will adapt their pricing behaviour in order to reduce the probability of detection, thereby increasing the external stability of the cartel. Second, the cartel can modify its internal structure such that each member has limited information on other members and on the agreements. This will enhance the internal stability of the cartel when threatened by the presence of leniency programmes. In the next sections, both these reactions are analysed in more detail.

3 Reactions of Cartels to the Competition Authority and its Measures

3.1 Adjustments in Cartel Behaviour

Most economic analyses of cartels are based on the assumption that the price is raised to the monopoly level immediately after a cartel has been established. Yet the assumption of a sudden price rise, or the reduction of supply, from the competitive level to the monopolistic one is not convincing for several reasons. First, this assumption contradicts empirical studies, which show that prices tend to rise gradually rather than leap to monopoly level all at once.[21] This is because a sudden price jump would rouse the suspicion of both the cartel authority and the customers, which would considerably increase the probability of detection. Clearly, a sudden price rise is not in a cartel's interest because every cartel wants to remain undetected by competition authorities. To date, few economic studies have taken into account cartel behaviour when a competition authority is present. The early work of von Harstadt and Phlips shows that, in certain circumstances, a cartel is

21 Such price paths are noted in J.M. Connor, *Global Price Fixing* (Springer, 2nd ed. 2006) and M.C. Levenstein & V.Y. Suslow, 'What Determines Cartel Success?', 44 *Journal of Economic Literature* (2006), 43–85.

able to behave in such a way that detection is impossible.[22] The cartel pretends competitive behaviour, albeit on a higher price level. As a consequence, the cartel authority is unable to detect the cartel agreement by means of existing data. In this case, it is impossible to distinguish competitive behaviour from that of a cartel.

To reach the higher price level, it is necessary to adapt the price from the level that prevailed before the formation of the cartel. The adaptation continues until the level desired by the cartel is reached. Here the cartel faces a trade-off between rapidly reaching the higher price and minimizing the probability of detection. Harrington provides several theoretical analyses of this kind of cartel behaviour.[23] He assumes that the probability of detection depends on the pace of the price increase. The faster the price increase, the higher the risk that the cartel authority will become suspicious and start to investigate. The problem faced by the cartel is to raise the price in such a way that the ratio between higher profits and higher detection probability remains constant. Harrington concludes that it is optimal for the cartel to raise its price rather slowly as not to rouse the suspicion of the cartel authority. This has been confirmed by empirical studies. The precise progression of the price path depends on the design of the fine system. If the fines are correlated to the duration and severity of the infringement, even periods of decreasing prices may occur. This will not be the case with a lump-sum fine. In another contribution, Harrington and Chen analyse the effects of leniency programmes on the cartel's optimal price path.[24] They show that, in the presence of a leniency programme, the price path will always remain below the one without the programme. In other words, the price increase is slower with leniency programmes than without. Further, Harrington and Chen prove that the maximum price set by a cartel is lower in the presence of a leniency programme. As a result, leniency programmes have a welfare increasing effect. If a cartel is not deterred by the leniency programme, the price will increase at a lower rate, and the maximum price will be lower relative to situations without the programme. The findings indicate that authorities should take this strategic behaviour into account.

Of course, however much cartels try to simulate competitive behaviour at a higher price level, their behaviour must differ from real competition in at least some respects. The reason is that, in order to reap cartel profits, price adjustments have to be coordinated between the cartel members, and the firms must be able to

---

22 See R.M. Harstad and L. Phlips, *Informational Requirements of Collusion Detection: Simple Seasonal Markets* (European University Institute, Florence 1994). As Louis Philips writes, 'That is, the industry is able to fill in the authority's report with false but indisputable data that make even joint profit maximising behaviour appear to be static Cournot behaviour. Of course, such indistinguishability renders implementation of antitrust policies that are dependent on detection of tacit collusion a farce.' L. Phlips, *Competition Theory: A Game-Theoretic Perspective*, (Cambridge University Press 1995), pp. 125 *et seq*.

23 Harrington (2004, 2005), Harrington/Chen (2006), *supra* note 8.

24 See J. Chen and J.E. Harrington, 'The Impact of Corporate Leniency Programs on Cartel Formation and the Cartel Price Path', in V. Ghosal & J. Stennek (eds.), *Political Economy of Antitrust* (North-Holland 2006), 59–80.

observe other members' pricing behaviour. Such deviations from competitive behaviour are identified through 'collusive markers'.[25] Thanks to the cartel's coordination efforts, price adjustments occur less frequently, and there is a more significant positive correlation between prices and less market share variation than under conditions of normal competition.

Existing models still assume that the cartel authority is unaware of the strategic behaviour of the firms. That is, they assume that the competition authority does not act strategically, which implies an asymmetry between the cartel members and the government. But it stands to reason that the competition authority is well aware of the fact that cartels aim at hiding its existence from the authority by raising their prices slowly. The competition authority will anticipate this and modify its behaviour accordingly, while firms, in turn, will respond with yet another strategy. This requires an approach that models both the cartel and the competition authority as strategic players. But the issues involved here are complex and have yet to be analysed in detail.

In the next section it is argued that competition authority and leniency programmes affect not only a cartel's behaviour but also its internal structure.

3.2 Adjustments in the Internal Structure of a Cartel

Another way in which a cartel may react to leniency programmes is to reduce the information available to its members. Information may include information on the members of the cartel, the existing contacts between them, the arrangements made and the organisation of the cartel (e.g. frequency of interactions, participants at meetings). The less information a cartel member has, the smaller will be its incentive to apply for leniency, since such a claim requires that the applicant be able to provide evidence to the authority. An applicant that is able to provide little information stands a small chance of receiving leniency and fine reductions.

One way for a cartel to reduce available information is to decentralize its structure as much as possible. To date, no systematic analysis of internal cartel structures has been provided. While Harrington provides a study of how cartels work, he focuses on the levels of hierarchy of a firm that take part in the cartel, not on the connections between the cartel members.[26] In this area, there is substantial need for further research.

In what follows, the internal structure of a cartel will be understood as the information of its members on the involvement of other firms in the cartel and the agreements made between them. The theory of economic and social networks will be used to describe such structures. This approach analyses the structure and the

---

25 See J.E. Harrington, 'Detecting Cartels', in P. Buccirossi (ed.), *Handbook of Antitrust Economics* (MIT Press 2008), 236–248.

26 See J.E. Harrington, *How Do Cartels Operate?* (Now Publishers 2006). The study uses decisions made by the commission between 2000 and 2004 to analyse the operating mode of detected cartels. The problem with this approach is that cartels with a different structure may not have been detected.

emergence of networks between economic agents by using concepts from graph theory.[27] The firms are interpreted as the nodes of a graph, while the connections between them correspond to the links between the nodes. For instance, the situation that each member is perfectly informed about all other members is described by a complete graph. In this situation, each member is connected to each other member by a link. If a member wants to apply for leniency in this situation, it will be able to provide comprehensive information to the authority, which in turn increases the probability of attaining a fine reduction. Economic theory implicitly assumes that this is the relevant structure of a cartel, with each member possessing the same, complete information on all relevant aspects of the cartel.

In reality, however, this assumption is not justified. A cartel is an illegal institution that is interested in preventing disclosure either externally by the competition authority or internally through a member's use of a leniency programme.

Similar problems with respect to internal and external stability arise in the area of organized crime, where leniency programmes were first introduced. A criminal organization has to exhibit external stability against law enforcement as well as internal stability with respect to the deviation of individual members. This requires a structure that allows little information to be held by each single member so as not to jeopardize the internal or external stability of the entire organization.[28]

Recently, a number of studies have been presented that rely on the theory of social and economic networks to analyse organized crime. These studies show a trade-off between the stability of a criminal organisation, on the one hand, and the information held by each member, on the other. A criminal organisation will work more effectively if each member has complete and precise information on the organisation. At the same time, however, such complete information enables a member to apply for leniency if he is arrested, which in turn jeopardizes the entire organisation. Hence, the criminal organisation has to find a structure that achieves the best possible compromise between the stability of the organisation and the amount of information held by individual members.

Obviously, there are strong similarities between criminal organisations and cartels. In both cases, the organisation relies on illegal agreements, with a minimum of fixed structures, and mutual commitment to a common purpose. Thus, the theoretical approaches to organised crime carry over to cartels. Except for two studies, however, the theory of social and economic networks has been applied only to criminal organisations, although the methods may well be applied to the structure of cartels.[29]

---

27 A survey on the theory of social and economic networks is provided by S. Goyal, *Connections - An Introduction to the Economics of Networks* (Princeton University Press 2007) and M.O. Jackson, *Social and Economic Networks* (Princeton University Press 2008). An introduction to graph theory is provided by Bollobás, *Modern Graph Theory* (Springer 1998).

28 A similar problem arises in the case of resistance organisations in totalitarian regimes. I am grateful to Thomas Ehrmann for this observation.

29 The only works that apply the theory of social and economic networks to the analysis of cartels are P. Belleflamme and F. Bloch, 'Market Sharing Agreements and Collu-

The studies that draw on social and economic network theory found that the structures that are robust against prosecution and punishment by state-owned institutions are characterized by a minimum number of connections between the agents. This is in contrast to the implicit assumption that each cartel member is perfectly informed about all other members and about all agreements and meetings, as economic studies of leniency programmes assume. The structures that possess the smallest number of connections so that all members are connected either directly or indirectly are either line shaped or star shaped. In a line network, each member is connected to at most two other members. The members at both ends of the line are connected only to one member each. In a star-shaped network, a central agent is connected to all members, while the members themselves are not connected to each other. Their connections are only indirect, through the central agent.

Such structures have been detected in several instances such as the DRAM cartel (COMP/38511):[30]

> The members of the cartel form a network of contacts and exchange secret information on a bilateral basis in order to coordinate the prices of DRAMs (Dynamic Random Access Memory), a prevalent model of dynamic semi conductor storage device for personal computers, servers, and work stations that are sold to big original equipment manufacturers of PCs or servers in EWR.

Similar structures have been observed in the vitamin cartel (COMP/E-1/37.512), the banana cartel (COMP/39188), and the calcium carbide cartel (COMP/39396). It has to be kept in mind that these were cartels that had been detected. Probability is high that similar structures prevail in cartels that have escaped the attention of the authority.

In this context, one specific arrangement should be mentioned that prevails in several leniency programmes. This is the exclusion of ringleaders from leniency. It has been pointed out in the literature that the efficacy of leniency programmes is reduced by excluding ringleaders since this means that there are fewer agents eligible as leniency applicants.[31] This also applies in the event that the ringleader gets a higher share of the cartel profit as compensation for the role as a coordinator and for exclusion from leniency.[32] Thus, a star-shaped cartel structure with ringleader exclusion may turn out to be particularly attractive. The individual members possess only limited information on other members and on the agreements, since each

sive Networks', 45 *International Economic Review* (2004), 387–411 and J. Fischer, *On Collusive Behaviour – Models of Cartel Formation, Organizational Structure, and Destabilization* (PhD thesis, University of Hohenheim, 2011).

30 Press statement, DRAM-Kartell (COMP/38511).

31 See, e.g., C. Aubert, W.E. Kovacic, and P. Rey, 'The Impact of Leniency and Whistleblowing Programs on Cartels', 24 *International Journal of Industrial Organization* (2006), 1241–1266; Ch.R. Leslie, 'Antitrust Amnesty, Game Theory, and Cartel Stability', 31 *Journal of Corporation Law* (2006), 453–488.

32 J. Herre and A. Rasch, *The Deterrence Effect of Excluding Ringleaders from Leniency Programs* (mimeo, University of Cologne 2009).

member's direct contact is restricted to the ringleader. Hence, each member is able to provide only limited information to the authority, and thus facing little incentive to apply for leniency. The ringleader, by contrast, has perfect and precise information on all cartel members, but he cannot apply for leniency. It is obvious that this structure enhances the stability of a cartel. For this reason, it may be advantageous to switch from the ringleader concept to the coercer test, which permits exclusion from leniency only if a firm has coerced another cartel member by threat of punishment to remain in the cartel.

Another, probably even more attractive version of a star-shaped cartel structure is when a common supplier or customer of the cartel acts as an organizer, rather than a firm that operates in the relevant market. This structure is known as a 'hub-spoke cartel' with a vertical structure where the hub is the organizer or ringleader of the cartel that operates at another stage of the supply chain. The role of the organizer is to arrange indirect contacts between the members of the cartel, who in turn compensate the organizer through purchase guarantee or higher prices. Such a vertical structure implies that there is no contact between the individual members of the cartel, as each member interacts only with the organizer. Thus, each member holds limited information, and the incentive to apply for leniency is marginal.[33]

As a non-member, the organizer is unable to claim leniency since a cartel is usually defined by an agreement or coordination between two or more competitors, rendering the cartel fairly stable even in the presence of a leniency programme. This suggests an increase in hub-spoke cartels with the introduction of leniency programmes. This change in the internal structure of cartels justifies the increased attention competition authorities have paid to vertical structures between firms as of late.

4 Conclusions for Competition Policy

All in all, these considerations show that cartel members will not passively accept the introduction of new instruments such as leniency programmes. Instead, they will adapt both their behaviour and their internal structure to the new circumstances. As shown by Harrington and Chen, a cartel will not immediately raise the price to the desired level; they will opt for a slow process of incremental adjustments to provide as little evidence as possible to both the authorities and the customers. In the presence of a leniency programme, this process will be even slower, and the price will remain at a lower level.

Furthermore, a cartel is likely to change its internal organisation to minimize the destabilizing and deterring effects of leniency programmes. Without leniency programmes, the information held by the individual cartel members is of little im-

---

33 A further advantage of this structure is that, in the case of an investigation, there is no evidence of any horizontal agreements – all arrangements are made through the organizer.

portance. If, however, a leniency programme is introduced, cartels, above all new ones, will organize themselves in a way that reduces member incentives to request leniency. The resulting cartel structure may depend on the specific design of the leniency programme. When the ringleader is excluded from leniency, a star-shaped structure has proved to be particularly stable. This is why the ringleader concept should be replaced by the coercer test.

The introduction of leniency programmes will probably give rise to an increase in the number of hub-spoke cartels with a vertical structure. As a rule, both the European and the German leniency programme assume that cartel members are competitors, and accordingly only offer leniency to firms that operate in the same market. Firms that act as cartel organizers but operate at a different stage of the value chain do not qualify as competitors and are thus excluded from leniency. But such vertical structures need to be taken into account. The UK leniency programme, which already does so, states: [34]

> Where vertical behaviour might be said to be facilitating horizontal cartel activity, leniency is available in principle, as a facilitator can be a party to the cartel activity and as a result be exposed to significant sanctions.

Altogether, the analysis has shown that cartels will usually refuse to passively accept alterations in competition law. Instead, they adapt their behaviour as well as their internal structure to these measures. These reactions have to be considered by the cartel authority. This, however, heralds the next round in the analysis.

---

34 See Office of Fair Trading (2008), *Leniency and No-Action – OFT's Guidance Note on the Handling of Applications*, available at: http://www.oft.gov.uk/OFTwork/ competition-act-and-cartels/cartels/confess#named1, p. 70. I am grateful to Wouter Wils for pointing this out to me.

The Role of Fines in the Public Enforcement of Competition Law

Wolfgang Bosch[1]

1 Introduction

There is consensus that the prohibition of hard-core cartels is one of the pillars of free and undisturbed trade, and that prosecution of cartels is necessary to ensure undisturbed competition. Dissenting opinions could only come from members of working and undiscovered cartels, but such opinions do not count.

But the fines imposed by the Commission have reached a very high level, and there are doubts whether the fining practice of the Commission is on firm legal ground.[2]

2 The Commission's Basis for Imposing Fines and the 'Rule of Law' Principle

a) Art. 23 Reg. 1/2003 is the European Commission's legal basis for the imposition of fines on undertakings. Art. 23 (2) Reg. 1/ 2003 says that fines can be imposed for intentional or negligent behaviour, and that the fine shall not exceed 10% of the participating undertakings turnover in the preceding business year. Pursuant to Art. 23 (3) Reg. 1/2003, the fine must consider gravity and duration of the infringement.

These very broad provisions raise the legitimate question whether Art. 23 Reg. 1/2003 complies with the 'essential decisions' doctrine, an overriding principle

---

[1] The article was prepared for the MaCCI Conference 'Public and Private Enforcement of Competition Law' in March 2011. As a consequence, the article is unable to take cases decided after that date into account (such as, e.g., Otis and Schindler).

[2] Many of the thoughts outlined in this short article rely on a more-detailed study of deficiencies in European Community Competition Law. See Schwarze, Bechtold and Bosch, *Deficiencies in European Competition Law*, 2008 (available at http://ec.europa.eu/competition/consultations/2008_regulation_1_2003/gleiss_lutz_en.pdf).

derived from Art. 249b of the Treaty of Lisbon and which says, 'All essential elements of any area shall be reserved for the legislative act and accordingly shall not be subject for delegation of power.' This essential decisions doctrine is a special form of the rule of law principle, which says that important governmental decisions need to be based on law and requires that law provides for sufficient detail of what the requirements for such governmental decisions are, and what kind of governmental decision is possible.

Art. 23 (2) and (3) 1/2003 do not say much more than that gravity and duration have to be considered in setting the fine. Furthermore, these provisions refer not only to violations of Art. 101 TFEU, but also to violations of Art. 102 TFEU. The failure to differentiate between punishment of anti-competitive agreements and unilateral abusive behaviour may already be a stand-alone problem. The 10%-turnover threshold in Art. 23 (2) Reg. 1/2003 is no sufficient boundary because it is a ceiling, or cap, but it does not determine a range within which a fine should be determined. Thus, the wide discretion determined by Art. 23 (2) and (3) Reg. 1/2003 does not provide sufficient detail for setting fines as required under the rule of law principle.

The true basis for the imposition of fines is the Commission's 2006 Guidelines of the Method of setting fines[3] (hereinafter: 'Fining Guidelines'). The Fining Guidelines would certainly pass the test of sufficient detail according to the rule of law principle. But the Fining Guidelines have been issued by the Commission. Thus, the Fining Guidelines are not legitimized by the Member States, the Council or the European Parliament, and cannot be a legitimate basis for the setting of fines.

b) In the *Degussa* judgment, the CFI held that according to the case law of the Community courts, 'the principle that penalties must have a proper legal basis is a corollary of the principle of legal certainty, which constitutes a general principle of Community law and requires, inter alia, that any Community legislation, in particular when it imposes or permits the imposition of sanctions, must be clear and precise so that the persons concerned may know without ambiguity what rights and obligations flow from it and may take steps accordingly'.[4]

Since the principle of clear and unambiguous legal basis applies to any sanction, including both administrative and criminal sanctions, the question as to the nature of the fines imposed by the Commission can be left open. Thus, the legal basis for the imposition of fines – Art. 23 (2) Reg. 1/2003 – has to be 'clear and unambiguous'. This requirement of clarity not only relates to the legal basis of the sanction but also to the extent of sanction itself, i.e. the provisions that define the consequences.[5]

---

3 2006 OJ C 210/2 *et seq.*

4 Case T-279/02, *Degussa v. Commission* [2006] ECR II-897, para. 66.

5 CFI, loc. cit., para. 67.

Even though the infringement of the principle of a clear and unambiguous legal basis seems to be very obvious, the General Court held in recent decisions that the Commission's discretion is not unlimited and that Art. 15 (2) Reg. 17 itself, as the predecessor of Art. 23 (2) Reg. 1/2003, limits the scope of discretion. According to the General Court:[6]

> Firstly, by specifying that 'the Commission may by decision impose on undertakings or associations of undertakings fines of from [EUR] 1,000 to 1,000,000 ... or a sum in excess thereof but not exceeding 10% of the turnover ... it provides for a ceiling on fines, based on the turnover of the undertakings concerned, that is to say, based on an objective criterion. Thus, although ... there is no absolute ceiling applicable to all infringements of the competition rules, the fine that may be imposed is nevertheless subject to a quantifiable and absolute ceiling calculated by reference to each undertaking in respect of each infringement, so that the maximum amount of the fine which may be imposed on a given undertaking is determinable in advance. Secondly, that provision requires the Commission to fix fines in each individual case having regard ... both to the gravity and to the duration of the infringement.

This decision was confirmed by the ECJ on 22 May 2008.[7] These limiting factors, however, do not work: sanctions need to be pre-determined in a reasonably precise manner protecting the individual from random decisions by way of legislation. It is not sufficient for the administrative body to safeguard the necessary degree of transparency and predictability. Therefore, Reg. 1/2003 itself must meet the standards and clearly define the limiting factors, and it is of no relevance whether the Commission's fining principles are sufficiently clear and unambiguous or not.

In sum, the two limiting criteria in Art. 23 Reg. 1/2003 that may serve as parameters to set the fine – duration and gravity – are not capable of mitigating the lack of clarity since these parameters are not sufficiently determined. According to the case law of the Community courts, there is no list of criteria that have to be taken into consideration regarding the gravity of the case.[8] Therefore, contrary to the current decision practice of the CFI, Art. 23 (2) Reg. 1/2003 infringes on the principle of a clear and unambiguous legal basis.

The infringement on the principle of a clear and unambiguous legal basis can only be remedied by limiting the scope of discretion of the Commission in determining the fine amount, but this would require amending Art. 23 Reg. 1/2003.

c) There is another argument that the Commission's 2006 Guidelines of the Method of setting fines are not even in line with Art. 23 Reg. 1/2003. The Guidelines clearly say that fines should aim at a sufficiently deterrent effect in the sense of special deterrence and general deterrence. But the idea of deterrence seems to contradict Art. 23 Reg. 1/2003. According to Art. 23 (5) Reg. 1/2003, the fines imposed under Art. 23 are not of a criminal character. This provision may be read in the way that fines imposed by the Commission for cartel infringements may not

---

6 CFI, loc. cit., para. 75 *et seq.*

7 Case C-266/06 P, *Evonik Degussa v. Commission*, para. 36 *et seq.*

8 Case T-9/99, *HFB v. Commission* [2002] ECR II-1487, para. 443.

reach the level of criminal sanctions. One important criterion for deciding whether a sanction is a criminal sanction or just an administrative sanction is deterrence. Therefore, Art. 23 (5) Reg. 1/2003 may limit the Commission's discretion in imposing fines to the extent that concepts of deterrence or general prevention might not play a decisive role in the determination of the fine amount. Therefore, it could already be concluded under existing rules that the Commission may not impose fines that consider deterrence or general prevention as prevailing aspects. This, in turn, raises the question whether the Commission's 2006 Guidelines are compatible with Art. 23 Reg. 1/2003.

3 Proposals for a New Approach to Fines

3.1 Turnover-Based Assessment of Fines Must Be Reviewed

A better balance is needed between the advantages of infringement, damage claims and fines. To this end, the assessment of fines must consider the damage caused or the benefits obtained as a result of infringement and private enforcement. In an ideal world, the infringer should be aware that he will be punished with a fine in addition to giving back the advantages he gained by cartelizing. But this means that a concept that starts with a fine of up to 30% of the revenue, as currently applied by the Fining Guidelines, may not be the right one. If the current level of fines is maintained, a concept must be developed that reserves at least part of the fines to compensate those who have actually been damaged. The US system, which operates with modest fines compared with those imposed by the Commission, relies much more on the litigation exposure cartelists receive.

3.2 Compliance Efforts Must Be Considered

a) Fining practice must also consider the responsibility of the infringers, especially whether the infringer is a compliant corporate citizen or not. The Fining Guidelines do not even mention compliance efforts as relevant for setting the fine, and more recent case law shows that compliance efforts might even be considered an aggravating factor.

Clearly, compliance efforts are in a company's best interest, because compliance is designed to safeguard against infringements. But what happens if there is an infringement despite state-of-the-art compliance efforts? Art. 23 (2) Reg. 1/2003 allows the imposition of fines for negligent and intentional infringements of Art. 101 TFEU. Accordingly, negligent and intentional infringement would also have to be determined when imposing fines. Correctly applied, Art. 23 (2) Reg. 1/2003 necessitates that individuals who participated in the infringement be identified. In the next step, the Commission would then have to determine whether the actions of these individuals can be attributed to the undertaking. This is only the case when the individuals in question are the statutory representatives of the undertaking, or because the acting individuals were not sufficiently supervised by the statutory representatives of the undertaking.

This approach would allow for the consideration of compliance efforts of currently overlooked undertakings. If an undertaking has done all that can be reasonably expected of it to avoid committing infringements, the imposition of sanctions may not be justified.

b) This approach to compliance efforts is not consistently shared by the decision practices of the European courts and the Commission:

aa) In re *Parker Pen*, the Court of First Instance[9] approved the position of the Commission that compliance programmes can be considered mitigating factors if the compliance programme already existed before the infringement was discovered and prosecuted.[10] In other cases, the Commission found that the existence of a compliance programme could be taken as a mitigating factor, even if the compliance programme had been introduced after the infringement had been discovered, but only in cases in which the infringement did not constitute a hard-core infringement.[11]

bb) In later cases, the Commission has refused to consider a compliance system a mitigating factor.[12] In re *electrical and mechanical carbon and graphite products* the Commission decided:[13]

> ... However, the Commission considers that it is not appropriate to take the existence of a compliance programme into account as an attenuating circumstance for a cartel infringement, whether committed before or after the introduction of such a programme ".

In more recent cases, the Commission has confirmed its negative standpoint with respect to the consideration of compliance programmes.[14] The Commission said that it approved the existence of compliance programmes, but affirmed that infringements need to be sanctioned.

cc) There are also cases in which the existence of a compliance programme has been considered an aggravating factor. In re *British Sugar*, the Commission took

9 Case T-77/92, *Parker Pen/Kommission* [1994] ECR II-549, para. 93.

10 Commission, decision of July 16, *Viho/Parker Pen*, 1992 OJ L 233/27, para. 24.

11 Commission, decision of June 5, 1991, *Viho/Toshiba*, 1991 OJ L 287/39, para. 28.

12 Commission, decision of Juni 7 2000, *amino acids*, 2001 OJ L 152/24, para. 312.

13 Commission, decision of December 3, 2003 - C.38.359 - para. 313.

14 Commission, decision of December 21, 2005 - F/38.443, *rubber chemicals*, para. 345; Commission, decision of May 31, 2006 - F/38.645, *Methacrylates*, para. 386; Commission, decision of February 21, 2007 - E-1/38.823, *elevators and escalators*, para. 754.

this position.[15] The Commission had fined British Sugar for the abuse of a market dominating position in 1988, and had found that compliance programme put in place by British Sugar can be considered a mitigating factor.[16] In 1998, when British Sugar was fined again as a cartel instigator, the Commission considered the programme an aggravating factor with the explicit reason that the programme had been considered a mitigating factor in the earlier decision. One may regard this decision as being unique, a response to a very special situation. Neither before nor after has the Commission considered a compliance system that was unable to prevent infringement an aggravating factor. One may conclude that the aggravation was provoked by the earlier infringement, and the fact that the compliance system had been unable to prevent the company from the new infringement.[17]

The European Courts seem to agree with the current practice of the Commission, which does not consider compliance programmes a mitigating factor. In re *Degussa*, the Court of Justice found:[18]

> As regards the second of those considerations, it is settled case-law that, whilst it is indeed important that the applicant took steps to prevent fresh infringements of Community competition law from being committed by members of its staff in the future, that circumstance does not alter the fact that an infringement was found to have been committed. It follows that the mere fact that in certain cases the Commission took the implementation of a compliance programme into consideration as a mitigating factor does not mean that it is obliged to act in the same manner in any given case. …
>
> According to that case law, the Commission is therefore not required to take a circumstance such as that into account as an mitigating factor, provided that it adheres to the principle of equality of treatment, which requires that it should not assess the matter differently for any undertaking addressed by the same decision … .

c) This decision practice does not correctly take into account the value of compliance programmes. In order to properly remunerate compliance, compliance efforts should be considered as a mitigating factor in the assessment of fines. Compliance efforts can and must be considered under European Law. Art. 23 (2) Reg. 1/2003 allows for the imposition of a fine only if the undertaking intentionally or negligently infringes on Art. 101 or 102 TFEU. The gravity of the infringement must be considered as well. If Art. 23 (2) Reg. 1/2003 applies, then it must be determined whether the company has acted negligently or intentionally; if the infringement is not found to involve at least a negligence, a fine cannot be imposed.

The reasons why the Commission and the European courts have difficulties finding the right approach for dealing with compliance efforts is the failure to con-

15 Commission, *Napier Brown/British Sugar,* 1988 OJ L 284/41, para. 86.

16 Commission, *British Sugar*, 1999 OJ L 76, 1, para. 208.

17 See Bechtold, Bosch, Brinker & Hirsbrunner (eds.), *EG-Kartellrecht* (C.H. Beck, 2nd ed. 2009), Art. 23 VO 1/2003, para. 65; Weitbrecht and Tepe, 'Erste Erfahrungen mit den neuen Bußgeldleitlinien der Europäischen Kommission', *Europäisches Wirtschafts- und Steuerrecht* 2001, 220, p. 228; and Dannecker and Biermann, in Immenga/Mestmäcker (eds.), *Wettbewerbsrecht: EG* (C.H. Beck, 4th ed. 2004), Art. 23 VO 1/2003, para. 163.

18 Case T-279/02, *Degussa/Kommission* [2006] ECR II-897, paras. 350 f.

sider the responsibility of companies for acts on the part of their employees. Pursuant to the case law of European courts, acts of an individual can be attributed to the undertaking that has employed such individual, regardless whether there has been an instruction, or an omission to instruct or control, by a statutory representative of the company. In order to attribute the act of an individual to the undertaking, it is sufficient that a person entitled to act on behalf of the company commit the infringement.[19] This concept ignores the condition that the infringement must be committed intentionally or at least negligently. The first question to be answered is whether the statutory representative of the company or somebody acting on its behalf has committed an infringement or neglected his duty to organize or supervise employees. If there is a working compliance system in place, then the statutory representative need do no more to prevent competition law infringement. Hence, the Commission must examine whether the infringement can still be viewed as being 'negligent' or 'intentional'. It goes without saying that the compliance system has to meet very high standards in order to rule out a negligent infringement.

But if the breach has been committed by employees despite a compliance system, Art. 23 (2) Reg. 1/2003 requires the compliance efforts to be accounted for as a mitigating factor. If a company operates a fundamentally effective compliance system, the existence of such system must be taken into account while considering the gravity of the infringements. This is even more true when the infringement was committed by one or more non-compliant employees. A compliance programme is the only means for a company to prevent employees from violating competition law. Even if a programme fails and infringements take place despite such programmes, the compliance programme has an effect. The compliance programme reduces the risk of non-compliance and documents the intentions of management to fulfil its obligations concerning organization and control.[20] No compliance programme can entirely prevent infringements committed within an undertaking. But an effective compliance programme creates structures in the company that minimize the possibility of infringements committed by employees. What is more, such programmes allow infringements to be detected at a very early stage and countermeasures to be taken against them.

If compliance systems are ignored when assessing the fine, a company's preventive measures and their effect on fighting cartels are overlooked.[21] Compliance systems prevent cartels before they come into existence. This has even been acknowledged by the Court of First Instance in its decision in re *Degussa*: the assessment of fines without sufficient consideration of special preventive elements is inadequate.[22]

---

19 Joined Cases C-100 to 103/80, *Musique Diffusion Francaise*, [1983] ECR 1825, para. 97.

20 Moosmayer, 'Die neuen Leitlinien der Europäischen Kommission zur Festsetzung von Kartellgeldbußen', *wistra* 2007, 91, p. 94.

21 Schwarze, Bechtold & Bosch, *Deficiencies in European Community Competition Law* (2008), p. 63.

22 Case T-279/02, *Degussa/Kommission* [2006] ECR II-897, para. 361.

There is another reason why the existence of compliance programmes needs to be considered. Under the Commission's Leniency Notice,[23] undertakings which cooperate with the Commission can apply for immunity or reduction of a fine under the Leniency Notice. Currently, companies need not have compliance programmes in place for immunity or fine reduction. The result is that companies with working compliance programmes may suffer significant disadvantages in leniency cases in comparison with companies that do not have a compliance system. If a company applies a working compliance system, it will sanction employees who contravene legal provisions. Competition law infringements in compliant companies are often hidden and secretive, and are only discovered by accident. Therefore, a company with a compliance system may have difficulties finding out whether its employees infringe on the law. Employees violating competition law in compliance companies will not voluntarily cooperate with their employer due to the sanctions they may face. Therefore, a compliant company will have difficulties contributing 'added value', let alone unveiling an infringement that has not been previously known by the authority. The purpose of leniency programmes should not be to remunerate companies without a working compliance system.

Because of the preventive effect of compliance programmes, the inconsistencies with the effects of the Commission's leniency practice compliance programmes have to be regarded as a mitigating factor in the assessment of fines. Only then can costs and efforts of compliance companies be remunerated. Other competition authorities, as for example those in the US, acknowledge compliance systems.[24]

3.3 The Concept of Parent Company Liability Needs to Be Reviewed

A concept of imposing fines based on responsibility would also require that the current system of parent company liability be reshaped. The current system is based on the concept of an economic unit between the parent company and a subsidiary. The prerequisites for the assumption of an economic unit are mainly based on the amount of shareholding and potential influence. This has little to do with the 'piercing the corporate veil' requirements as developed in the Member States' jurisdictions with respect to the requirements under which a parent company can be held liable for debts incurred by a subsidiary. It does not consider that 100% or

---

23 See *Commission Notice on Immunity from Fines and Reduction of Fines in Cartel Cases*, 2006 OJ C 298/17.

24 See *United States Sentencing Commission*, Guidelines Manual, Chapter 8: 'The two factors that mitigate the ultimate punishment of an organization are: (i) the existence of an effective compliance and ethics program; and (ii) self-reporting, cooperation, or acceptance of responsibility', available under http://www.ussc.gov/2006 guid/gl2006.pdf; *Office of Fair Trading* - OFT's guidance as to the appropriate amount of a penalty, Step 4, section 2.16: 'Mitigating factors include: ... adequate steps having been taken with a view to ensuring compliance with Art. 81 and 82 and the Chapter I and Chapter II prohibitions', available at www.oft.gov.uk.

majority shareholding does not allow influence in all cases; influence depends on the corporate structure along with many other factors. The concept of parent company liability needs to shift to a system that looks at whether the parent company has negligently or intentionally participated in the infringement, either by acting actively or by omitting obligations to supervise the conduct of its subsidiary. In such a system, compliance efforts of the parent company would play a major role.

4 Conclusions

The approach to fines against competition law infringements in the European law ought to be revised. First, there needs to be a sufficient legal basis in Reg. 1/2003, and it might be a good first step to incorporate the current Fining Guidelines into Reg. 1/2003. Second, turnover as a basis for the calculation of fines does not seem to be the right approach, especially because the earnings from the cartel should be given back to those who have suffered. Third, compliance efforts of companies need to be considered when setting the fine. And finally, the current concept of parent company liability needs to be reviewed.

The Interaction of Public and Private Antitrust Enforcement – The Calculation of Fines and Damages

Thomas Ackermann

1 Introduction

During the last decade, the enforcement of EU antitrust law has been characterized by two trends: on the one hand, there has been a significant increase of fines imposed by the Commission and by National Cartel Authorities (NCAs) for the violation of Articles 101 and 102 TFEU; on the other hand, the Commission has vigorously strengthened private damages actions, which, according to the European Court of Justice, Member States are required to grant to everyone who is harmed by antitrust infringements.[1] While both developments have been dealt with separately in numerous studies, the interaction of public and private sanctions has received less attention. Basically, there are two issues that merit closer attention. The first question is what the calculation of fines and the calculation of damages have in common, and what separates them. Such a comparison between the goals and the methods of calculating fines and damages will help us find out whether and to which extent the relatively recent private enforcement of EU antitrust law can learn from the experience made in the area of public enforcement. The second question is how the calculation of damages and the calculation of fines affect each other. As the significance of private damages claims grows in the EU, it is becoming more important to understand the interaction between damages and fines, in particular how increasingly successful damages claims can be factored into the calculation of fines. This article will address both issues. Its emphasis will, however, be on the first question, the answer to which will help us address the second question, if somewhat more briefly.

My analytical starting point is fairly simple. Monetary sanctions for antitrust infringements can aim at compensation or at deterrence or at both. Compensation relates to the losses caused by infringement. A compensatory sanction has to put the victims of the infringement in the position they would have been in without the infringement. Deterrence relates to the gains made due to infringement. The *ex ante*

1 Case C-453/99, *Courage* v. *Crehan* [2001] ECR I-6297, para. 60; Joined Cases C-295 to C-298/04, *Manfredi and Others* v. *Lloyd Adriatico Assicurazioni and Others* [2006] ECR I-6619, para. 60.

expected amount of a deterrent sanction must exceed the *ex ante* expected profit from infringement. Hence, both compensatory and deterrent sanctions require an idea of the hypothetical world that would exist but for the infringement. This counterfactual scenario is the baseline for the assessment of infringement-related gains and losses. As is well known, however, counterfactual market scenarios are notoriously difficult to assess. It is virtually impossible to determine with absolute certainty the state the world would have been in without a given infringement. Any legal system that provides for compensatory and/or deterrent sanctions for antitrust infringements must find a solution to this problem.

Turning to the EU and its Member States, public enforcement is entrusted with the task of deterring antitrust violations by the imposition of fines, while private enforcement mainly performs a compensatory function (with deterrent side-effects) by ordering infringers to pay damages to antitrust victims. There are of course instances where private enforcement performs a straightforward deterrent function by providing for over-compensatory damages,[2] and where public enforcement measures include the compensation of victims.[3] Taking a broader view, one may of course question the wisdom of having a dualistic instead of a monistic enforcement structure.[4] Yet, for the time being, the dualistic enforcement structure seems to be firmly in place, with (deterrent) fines and (compensatory) damages as the archetypes of public and private enforcement in the European context, all the more so since the Commission seems to have no intention to overcome the resistance of many Member States against the introduction of any kind of over-compensatory damages, and there is no inclination to replace private damages actions by public measures.

The typical allocation of tasks between public and private antitrust enforcement has important implications for the calculation of fines and damages. While both

2 The most famous examples are of course US treble damages. At the present time, the EU Commission does not seem to plan an initiative for the introduction of over-compensatory damages as a sanction for the violation of EU antitrust rules. See *Commission Staff Working Document: Accompanying document to the White Paper on Damages actions for breach of the EC antitrust rules*, COM(2008) 165 final, para. 154.

3 See Ariel Ezrachi and Maria Ioannidou, 'Public Compensation as a Complementary Mechanism to Damages Actions: From Policy Justifications to Formal Implementation', *Journal of European Competition Law & Practice* 2012, Advance access, published 21 June 2012. For German perspective, see Andreas Fuchs, 'Die Anordnung von Wiedergutmachungszahlungen als Inhalt kartellbehördlicher Abstellungsverfügungen nach § 32 GWB?', *Zeitschrift für Wettbewerbsrecht* 2009, 176. In the 8th reform of the German Act against Restraints of Competition (ARC), which was still pending when this essay was being written, cartel authorities are explicitly authorized under section 32(2a) ARC to order the recovery of benefits received from an infringement. See *Entwurf eines Achten Gesetzes zur Änderung des Gesetzes gegen Wettbewerbsbeschränkungen*, BR-Drs. 176/12 of 30 March 2012.

4 See, for instance, Hans Jürgen Meyer-Lindemann, 'Durchsetzung des Kartellverbots durch Bußgeld und Schadensersatz', *Wirtschaft und Wettbewerb* 2011, 1235, at p. 1246.

types of sanctions refer to the same counterfactual scenario, they do so in pursuing different goals, and as they typically belong to different branches of the law, the legal instruments applied to determine the counterfactual scenario differ as well. Only if these differences are fully appreciated, can the question be answered of how the calculation of fines and the calculation of damages affect each other.

This article will explore these differences in two steps. First, I briefly look at damages and fines in a hypothetical world without taking account of the problem of determining counterfactuals. Second, I examine in somewhat more detail the German experience with calculating damages and fines to illuminate the different ways of dealing with counterfactuals in the real world.

2 Compensatory Damages and Deterrent Fines in a Hypothetical World: The Example of Horizontal Price-Fixing

If we consider the example of horizontal price-fixing between all suppliers in a market where competition would otherwise prevail, it can easily be seen how damages and fines should ideally be calculated.

Ideal damages require the full compensation of the *damnum emergens*, i.e. of the actual loss suffered by the victim of a wrongful act, and of the *lucrum cessans*, i.e. of the profit the victim would have made but for the wrongful act. Only if these two elements are covered is the victim put into the position he would have been in but for the wrongful act, which is the universally accepted baseline for damages.[5] The *damnum emergens* caused by a cartel is the overcharge paid by the customers of cartel members. This is the difference between the actual cartel price paid by the customers and the hypothetical market price they would have paid but for the cartel (the 'but-for' price), multiplied by the quantity of goods sold by the cartel members (the cartel quantity). In order to assess the overcharge, it is therefore necessary, but also sufficient to determine one element of the counterfactual scenario. Regarding the *lucrum cessans*, a more demanding assessment is necessary. In cartel cases, the total profit forgone by the victims of the cartel is defined by the consumer share of the deadweight loss caused by the cartel. This requires information not only about the price effect, but also about the quantitative effect of a cartel in terms of an output reduction that amounts to the difference between the hypothetical quantity that would have been sold but for the cartel (the 'but-for' quantity) and the cartel quantity.

Ideal fines presuppose the same information, but for a different purpose. As has already been mentioned, the *ex ante* expected fine must exceed the *ex ante* expected profit from the infringement in order to effectively deter market partici-

---

5 As far as damages for the breach of EU antitrust law are concerned, this has explicitly been held by the ECJ, Joined Cases C-295 to C-298/04, *Manfredi and others* v. *Lloyd Adriatico Assicurazioni and others* [2006] ECR I-6619, para. 95.

pants from forming cartel agreements.[6] To put it more precisely, the reference point for the calculation of a deterrent fine is the expected amount of the cartel-based net gain, i.e. of the overcharge paid by cartel members' customers less the cartel members' share of the deadweight loss caused by the cartel. Again, knowledge of the but-for price and of the but-for quantity is necessary as a basis for the calculation.

So if, for the sake of simplicity, we make the somewhat unrealistic assumption that but-for prices and but-for quantities are known elements of the counterfactual scenario, compensatory and deterrent sanctions can be separately set at an appropriate amount. However, even if each of these sanctions is calculated in accordance with the rules that have just been set out, their combined effect is sub-optimal if both sanctions are imposed for the same infringement: an optimal deterrent fine plus the award of fully compensatory damages will inevitably lead to over-deterrence. As denying damages to victims of an infringement for which a fine has already been imposed is not a viable option under EU law,[7] this effect can only be avoided by taking into account the amount of damages in the calculation of the fine so that not the fine by itself, but the combination of the fine with the award of damages constitutes an optimal deterrent sanction. How exactly this should be done is a question that can be answered easily if we stick to a hypothetical scenario where all information about the effects of an infringement, including but-for prices and but-for quantities, is available for public authorities and private plaintiffs alike once the infringement has been discovered, and where both sanctions will follow the discovery of the infringement (though not necessarily the infringement itself) with 100% probability. Under these circumstances, from an ex ante perspective, fines and damages are imposed with the probability of an infringement being discovered so that optimal deterrence is achieved if the expected sum of the fine plus damages exceeds the expected net gain from the infringement. To put it differently, if damages were awarded for antitrust violations with the same probability as fines are imposed, the amount of damages can be simply deduced from the amount of the fine, as calculated on the basis of the expected net gain from the infringement, in order to reconcile the goals of compensation and deterrence.[8]

---

6 See, for instance, Wouter Wils, *Efficiency and Justice in European Antitrust Enforcement* (Hart Publishing 2008), para. 184.

7 According to the ECJ in Manfredi (cited *supra* note 5), para. 95, 'it follows from the principle of effectiveness and the right of any individual to seek compensation for loss caused by a contract or by conduct liable to restrict or distort competition that injured persons must be able to seek compensation not only for actual loss (*damnum emergens*) but also for loss of profit (*lucrum cessans*) plus interest.'

8 To put it more formally, if an infringement is detected with probability $p \leq 1$ and the detection always leads to the imposition of a fine amounting to F and, in addition, to an award of damages amounting to D, while in case of a non-detection (with probability $1 - p$), the infringer gains an amount G, then the expected value of the combination of fine and damages would be $p\ (F + D)$, while the expected value of the infringement-related gain would be $(1 - p)\ G$. Optimal deterrence would require p (F +

Moving one step closer to the real world, one can easily assess the combination of damages and fines if the *ex ante* probability of an award of fully compensatory damages is only a fraction of the probability of the imposition of a fine. If we assume that the fraction of the (potential) amount of damages would be known, the fine would only have to be reduced by this fraction in order to avoid over-deterrence.[9] So if e.g., successful follow-on suits could only be expected with a probability of 20% after the imposition of a fine, the amount of the fine, as calculated on the basis of the expected net gain, would only have to be reduced by 20% of the (potential) amount of damages.

3 Calculating Damages and Fines in the Real World: The German Experience

The main problem encountered in the real world when it comes to calculating damages and fines is the difficulty of ascertaining counterfactual scenarios. But-for prices and but-for quantities that are required for the calculation set out above are normally neither known nor can they be found with absolute or near-absolute certainty. As a consequence, such a requirement would likely cause serious under-enforcement. If cartel authorities and private plaintiffs had to prove but-for prices and but-for quantities beyond reasonable doubt, damages and fines would most probably either be too low, or not be imposed at all. I will illustrate the problem of under-enforcement by referring to experiences under the German Act against Restraints of Competition, which in its former version, in force until 2005, made it necessary to rely on counterfactuals in the imposition of fines (section 3.1).

D) $\geq (1 - p)$ G. It follows that $F \geq (1 - p)/p \times G - D$. That is to say, the amount of damages must be deducted from an 'isolated fine', i.e. a fine that is exclusively calculated by taking into account the gain derived from the infringement and the probability of detection (and, when applicable, non-detection).

9 If we consider the sequence of events in follow-on scenarios, there is a more formal explanation. After the infringement was committed in the first stage, the second stage that occurs with probability $p_1 \leq 1$ is its detection and the imposition of a fine amounting to F. So the expected value of the fine, as seen from the first stage, is $p_1 \times F$. On the other hand, the expected value of the gain G the infringer receives in case of a non-detection is $(1 - p_1)$ G. After the second stage, the payment of damages amounting to D follows in a third stage with probability p_2. So the expected value of the damages to be paid, as seen from the first stage, is $p_1 \times p_2 \times D$. 3. Optimal deterrence (for a single infringer) demands that in stage one, the minimum expected sum of F and D at least equals the expected amount of G, i.e. $p_1 \times F + p_1 \times p_2 \times D = (1 - p_1)$ G. The effect that D has on the amount of F in an ideal world can simply be assessed by rewriting this formula: $F = (1 - p_1)/p_1 \times G - p_2 \times D$. In plain words, if a fine is followed by damages with probability p_2, the optimal amount of an isolated fine should be reduced by the amount of damages multiplied by the probability of damages being awarded after the imposition of the fine (p_2).

But there are solutions to this problem. A legal system may either provide means to facilitate findings about the counterfactual scenario, or it may introduce alternative criteria that serve as proxies for the counterfactual scenario and that are easier to ascertain than but-for prices and but-for quantities. While the latter method has been applied by the present EU and German guidelines on the calculation of fines (section 3.2), the former path has been chosen for private antitrust enforcement in Germany (section 3.3). Having examined the different approaches taken in the area of fines and in the area of damages, I will now address the question of how under real-world conditions a solution that avoids over-deterrence caused by the combination of damages and fines can be found (section 3.4).

3.1 Calculating Fines on the Basis of Counterfactuals: Lessons from the Application of Former Section 81(2) ARC

The intricacies of enforcing antitrust rules by relying on fines that are based on the assessment of counterfactual market scenarios became apparent in the application of former section 81(2) of the German Act against Restraints of Competition (ARC) that was in force until 2005. Section 81(2) ARC provided that fines could amount to 'up to three times the additional proceeds obtained as a result of the violation', adding that '[t]he amount of the additional proceeds may be estimated.' In order to estimate the additional proceeds, the cartel authorities, namely the Federal Cartel Office (FCO), and the courts (that have full jurisdiction to review the fines)[10] must form a judgment about the but-for price and the but-for quantity as elements of the counterfactual market scenario. In the *Paper Wholesaler* judgment of 19 June 2007,[11] the Bundesgerichtshof (BGH; Federal Supreme Court) gave some guidance about the estimation required by former section 81(2) ARC. The advice can be summarized in four points:

- The BGH granted judicial discretion regarding the estimation of the additional proceeds resulting from an antitrust violation, but only insofar as the requirements of criminal procedure are met is the estimation conclusive, and the results economically feasible.
- As to the method of assessing the counterfactual market scenario, the BGH regarded a 'comparative market analysis' (a 'comparator-based approach' in the terminology of the Oxera study for the Commission)[12] as generally superior.

---

10 Under German law, a fining decision by a cartel authority is only preliminary in the sense that if the addressee of the fine appeals against the decision, the decision merely serves as indictment in the proceeding before the court, and the court is free to set the fine without being bound by any legal or factual assessment in the administrative stage. See Rainer Bechtold, in Rainer Bechtold (ed.), *Kartellgesetz* (C.H. Beck, 6th ed. 2010), Art. 81, para. 6.

11 BGH, Case KRB 12/07, judgment of 19 June 2007, *WuW/E* DE-R 2225 – *Papiergroßhandel (Paper Wholesaler)*.

12 *Oxera, Quantifying antitrust damages: Towards non-binding guidance for courts* (Study prepared for the European Commission, 2009), pp. 46 *et seq.*

But the court also accepted an 'overall economic analysis' (a 'financial-analysis-based approach' in the terminology of the Oxera study)[13] as an alternative.

- In order to carry out the assessment required under former section 81(2) ARC, the BGH suggested expert support.
- Even if, with the help of experts, the additional proceeds have been calculated correctly on the basis of the methods accepted by the BGH, a safety margin must be discounted in order to satisfy the principle *in dubio pro reo*.

The consequences of this approach for the calculation of fines can be observed in the *Cement Cartel* case. Following a fining decision by the FCO, this case was under review before the *Oberlandesgericht* (OLG; Higher Regional Court) Düsseldorf.[14] Adhering to the guidance given by the BGH, the court appointed an expert for estimating the cartel's effects on prices and quantities in the relevant market. As far as the assessment of the price effect was concerned, the expert chose a temporal approach (during/after) with the consent of the court because comparisons with other geographic or product markets were not feasible. However, a problem that occurred in the application of the during/after comparison was that after the breakdown of the cartel, a price war started between the former members of the cartel so that it was difficult to say at which point in time after the end of the infringement a price could be found that could serve as a reference point for the but-for price. The court overcame this obstacle by accepting a periodization, which the expert regarded as robust and as comparatively favourable to the cartel members. Regarding the quantity effect of the cartel, the expert did not provide his own empirical study of the price elasticity of demand in the relevant market, but merely based his estimation on a review of other studies, again reaching a result that was relatively favourable to the cartel members. Having approved the expert's results, the court then proceeded by granting a discount of 25% as a safety margin required by the principle *in dubio pro reo*.

It is easy to see that this approach falls short of the goal of optimal deterrence. In the first step of the assessment of fines in the *Cement Cartel* case, estimates of counterfactuals are required that have to be either robust or, if within a plausible range, favourable to cartel members. This means that estimates may be rejected even if they are reasonably probable, but not the most favourable to cartel members within a range of similarly probable estimates. As a consequence, estimates will more likely than not be too low. To put it differently, if estimates with a probability of more than 50% are rejected because they are not robust and not favourable enough to the infringers, then there is an equally high probability that the resulting fine is an under-deterrent, as the assessment of the profit resulting from the infringement tends to be too low. This tendency becomes even stronger in the second step of the assessment, in which any remaining uncertainty is taken account of in a margin that is deducted from the result of the original calculation. Even if, despite the shortcomings just mentioned, the original calculation came close to a re-

---

13 Oxera (op.cit. *supra* note 12), pp. 62 *et seq.*

14 OLG Düsseldorf, Case VI-2a Kart 2-6/08 OWi, judgment of 26 June 2009 (on appeal before the Federal Supreme Court).

sult that could achieve optimal deterrence, the discounted amount would almost certainly be too low. Considering that the resulting amount may only be multiplied with a maximum factor of 3, which would only be sufficient under the assumption that the *ex ante* probability of being caught was not lower than 25%,[15] which does not seem to be realistic in the case of hard-core cartels, the gap between an optimal fine and a fine that follows from the application of former section 81(2) ARC under the relevant rules of procedure becomes even bigger in the final step of the calculation. The upshot is that, due to the impact of procedural rules that demand robust estimates and follow the principle *in dubio pro reo*, fines that require an assessment of counterfactual scenarios are bound to be under-deterrent.

3.2 Calculating Fines on the Basis of Proxies: The Present EU and German Guidelines

In view of the German experience with counterfactuals under former section 81(2) ARC, the question is how under-deterrence can be avoided in the calculation of fines. Theoretically, there are three options, but only one of them seems viable. The most obvious way to solve the problem would be to try harder to find the 'right' counterfactuals. But due to constraints in terms of time and money, making estimates more robust so that smaller discounts are required is only feasible within narrow limits. Relaxing the standards for the assessment of counterfactuals is not a viable option either because of constitutional limits in criminal procedures, namely *in dubio pro reo*, that apply to antitrust fines and that do not allow for lowering the standard of proof. So the only way out of this dilemma is the introduction of alternative criteria that serve as proxies for a direct assessment of counterfactuals.

This is the path taken by the Commission's 2006 Guidelines and, in a similar way, by the FCO's Guidelines that followed the reform of section 81 ARC in 2005.[16] In a nutshell, the calculation set out by the EU Guidelines starts from a basic amount of up to 30% of the value of infringement-related sales, multiplied by the years of participation, topped up by an entrance fee, and adjusted on account of aggravating or mitigating circumstances.[17] The German Guidelines

---

15 If the probability of an infringement being detected is 25%, the expected value of the fine is 25% of its nominal amount, while the expected value of the gain derived from the infringement is 75% of its nominal amount. Hence, a fine is only deterrent if its amount is at least three times higher than the amount of the infringement-related gain.

16 EU Commission, *Guidelines on the method of setting fines pursuant to Art. 23(2)(a) of Regulation No 1/2003*, O.J. 2006, C 210/2; FCO, *Notice no. 38/2006 on the imposition of fines under Section 81 (4) sentence 2 of the German Act against Restraints of Competition (GWB) against undertakings and associations of undertakings* (English version available under http://www.bundeskartellamt.de/wEnglisch/Legal_bases/Legal_basesW3DnavidW2627.php (last visit: 10 October 2012).

17 See the EU Guidelines (cited *supra* note 16), paras. 12–26 for the basic amount and paras. 27–31 for the adjustments.

roughly follow the same pattern.[18] They also start from a basic amount of up to 30%, but this is calculated on the basis of turnovers for the whole duration of participation in the infringement.[19] Moreover, while there is no separate 'entrance fee', the German Guidelines provide for aggravating and mitigating circumstances, and they single out a separate 'deterrence factor' that allows for an increase of the basic amount of up to 100%.[20]

As opposed to the calculation required under the German law that was in force until 2005, the criteria used by the EU and by the German Guidelines neither contain any direct reference to the gain from the antitrust violation, nor do they require the use of a multiplier that is equal to the inverse of the probability of being caught to achieve optimal deterrence. This does not mean that fines that follow the methodology of the Guidelines do not aim at deterrence. Although deterrence as such is not explicitly mentioned in the EU and German legal bases, it is clear that fines must be determined in the light of the deterrent effect the imposition of the fine is meant to achieve.

As the General Court held with regard to fines imposed by the Commission, 'the deterrent effect of a fine is one of the factors which, according to the case-law, must be taken into account in determining the gravity of the infringement… the taking into account of the deterrent effect of the fines forms an integral part of weighting the fines to reflect the gravity of the infringement'.[21] This reflects the position taken earlier by the ECJ that the 'gravity of the infringements must be assessed in the light of numerous factors, such as the particular circumstances of the case, its context and the dissuasive effect of fines'.[22] More specifically, the General Court stressed that 'if the fine were set at a level which merely negated the profits of the cartel, it would not be a deterrent.'[23]

Similarly, there seems to be a consensus that German antitrust fines serve the purpose of deterring infringements, and even though this is not uncontroversial, deterrence is rightly regarded as an aspect that forms an integral part of the assessment of all factors that are relevant for the calculation of fines, and not as a separate factor.[24]

---

18 See the FCO Guidelines (cited *supra* note 16), paras. 4–13 for the basic amount and paras. 14–17 for the adjustments.

19 See on this aspect and other differences between the FCO Guidelines and the EU Guidelines Andreas Mundt, 'Die Bußgeldleitlinien des Bundeskartellamts', *Wirtschaft und Wettbewerb* 2007, 458, at 469–70.

20 See the FCO Guidelines (cited *supra* note 16), para. 15.

21 Joined Cases T-109/02, T-118/02, T-122/02, T-125/02, T-126/02, T-128/02, T-129/02, T-132/02 and T-136/02, *Bolloré and Others* v. *Commission* [2007] ECR II-947, para. 540 (with further references to the case law).

22 Joined Cases C-189/02 P, C-202/02 P, C-205/02 P to C-208/02 P, and C-213/02 P, *Dansk Rørindustri and Others* v. *Commission* [2005] ECR I-5425, para. 241.

23 Case T-329/01, *Archer Daniels Midland Co.* v. *Commission* [2006] ECR II-3255, para. 141.

24 See Gerhard Dannecker and Jörg Biermann, in Ulrich Immenga and Ernst-Joachim Mestmäcker (eds.), *Wettbewerbsrecht, Vol. 2: GWB – Kommentar zum Deutschen Kartellrecht* (C.H. Beck, 4th ed. 2007), Art. 81, para. 362 (with further references).

With this in mind, the actual calculation of a fine on the basis of the Guidelines published by the Commission and by the FCO must be seen as an approximate calculation of an optimal deterrent fine that is carried out on the basis of surrogate criteria. These criteria relate to general observations about infringement-related profits and the probability of the infringement not being discovered. So for example, with regard to the German Guidelines, the basic amount of up to 30% – which due to the 'deterrence factor' may be increased to up to 60% – has been explained with reference to estimates of average infringement-related gains ranging between 15% and 20%, an amount which must be increased to reflect the risk that infringements may not be detected.[25] As far as the EU Guidelines are concerned, it has rightly been said that the reason for the use of the value of sales as a starting-point 'is that harm or expected gains are in principle related to the value of sales affected by the infringements'.[26] Moreover, the assessment of the gravity of the infringement, on which the proportion of the value of sales of up to 30% that forms the basic amount of the fine depends, is clearly related to the deterrent nature of the fine. As can be seen from para. 23 of the Guidelines, the Commission regards horizontal price-fixing, market-sharing and output-limitation agreements as the most harmful restrictions of competition as they 'are usually secret' This reflects the idea that the lower the probability of detection is, the higher the fine for the infringement must be in order to achieve deterrence.

This being said, it cannot be denied that the ultimate amount of a fine is not exclusively founded on concerns of deterrence. In particular, the limitation of a fine to a maximum of 10% of the total turnover of the undertaking concerned[27] is not based on this rationale. The amount of an optimal fine may well exceed the 10% threshold. But as a matter of proportionality, it is also important to take account of the size of the undertaking that is fined and its ability to cope with the fine without being forced out of a market. Beyond individual cases where companies plead their inability to pay, the 10% threshold generally safeguards these interests. Therefore, if the calculation of a fine on the basis of criteria such as infringement-related sales, years of participation etc. that serve as proxies for the calculation of expected gains from the cartel leads to a higher amount, the 10% threshold serves as a cap. This has clearly been recognized by the ECJ.[28] Regrettably, in Germany, a consensus on this interpretation has not yet been reached. According to the OLG Düsseldorf in the *Cement Cartel* case, the 10% threshold that the German legislature copied from EU law has to be read as a definition of the upper limit for the calculation of a fine and not merely as a cap on fines that, if calculated according to the proper criteria, may otherwise be higher.[29] If this reading prevailed, the deterrent effect of antitrust fines would be severely disturbed.

---

25 See Andreas Mundt (op.cit. *supra* note 19), at p. 461.

26 Fernando Castillo de la Torre, 'The 2006 Guidelines on Fines: Reflections on the Commission's Practice', 33(3) *World Competition* (2010), 359, at p. 367.

27 Art. 23(2) Reg. 1/2003; section 81(4) ARC.

28 Joined Cases C-189/02 P, C-202/02 P, C-205/02 P to C-208/02 P, and C-213/02 P, *Dansk Rørindustri and Others* v. *Commission* [2005] ECR I-5425, paras. 280–283.

29 OLG Düsseldorf (cited *supra* note 14), para. 627.

3.3 Calculating Damages on the Basis of Counterfactuals: Facilitating Devices in German Law

While the calculation of fines under EU and German law dispenses with the need to determine counterfactual scenarios, hypothetical prices and quantities remain relevant for the assessment of antitrust damages. As a starting point, the calculation of antitrust damages follows the general rule set out in section 249(1) of the Bürgerliches Gesetzbuch (BGB, German Civil Code), according to which the aggrieved party must be put into the position she would have been in but for the event the injurer is held responsible for. Therefore, courts generally have to deal with counterfactuals if confronted with damages claims. However, in contrast to criminal law, rules that apply to damages litigation facilitate the assessment of counterfactuals to a considerable degree.

The main instrument provided by German law is a lowering of the standard of proof with regard to findings concerning the amount of damages. According to the normal standard under section 286(1) of the Zivilprozessordnung (ZPO, German Code of Civil Procedure), 'the court is to decide, at its discretion and conviction, and taking account of the entire content of the hearings and the results obtained by evidence being taken, if any, whether an allegation as to fact is to be deemed true or untrue'. While absolute certainty is not required, the court may not have serious doubts as to the existence of a certain fact. This standard of proof is relaxed with regard to the assessment of damages. Under section 287(1) ZPO, a court is granted discretion as to whether evidence is taken concerning the existence and the amount of damages, and the standard of proof applied in this area is akin to the preponderance of evidence required in common law jurisdictions. Moreover, as far as lost profits are concerned, section 252 of the BGB allows courts to base their findings on an estimation of how profits would probably have developed in the regular course of events.

It has been suggested that under these rules, courts should be permitted to rely on perfect competition as a counterfactual scenario so that but-for prices and but-for quantities would not necessarily have to reflect the market conditions that would have existed if the infringement had not taken place.[30] But this position has not been taken by German courts in antitrust damage decisions, which so far have aimed at a concrete assessment of hypothetical prices that would have existed but for the infringement.[31] Considering that even without cartel arrangements between market participants real markets would rarely meet the conditions of perfect competition, such a definition of the counterfactual scenario would indeed be unrealis-

---

30 Gerhard Wagner, 'Schadensersatz bei Kartelldelikten', in Thomas Eger and Hans-Bernd Schäfer (eds.), *Ökonomische Analyse der europäischen Zivilrechtsentwicklung* (Mohr Siebeck 2007), 605, at p. 626.

31 See Heike Schweitzer, 'Kartellschadensersatz – rechtlicher Rahmen', in Kai Hüschelrath, Nina Leheda, Kathrin Müller and Tobias Veith (eds.), *Schadensermittlung und Schadensersatz bei Hardcore-Kartellen* (Nomos 2012), 39, at p. 55. See also Roman Inderst and Ulrich Schwalbe, 'Das kontrafaktische Szenario bei der Berechnung von Kartellschäden', *Wirtschaft und Wettbewerb* 2012, 122, at p. 124.

tic. Moreover, this would make infringers responsible for all existing market imperfections. As accountability is limited to harms caused by infringement, infringers must be allowed to rely on market conditions that would plausibly have led to supra-competitive prices without infringement. Last but not least, it is doubtful whether such a simplification would really help antitrust plaintiffs to overcome the problem of convincing a court of a particular hypothetical price (and the quantity sold at such a price) as the criterion of marginal cost that determines the price in the theoretical world of perfect competition is not readily available, and often very hard to establish. If under-compensation is to be avoided, the main solution available under German law seems to be a comparably low standard of proof (roughly speaking, a probability threshold of more than 50%) combined with economic expertise. If reasonably probable estimates are allowed, this is an important step towards avoiding the detrimental consequences of the difficulties of establishing counterfactuals that could be seen in the context of antitrust fines calculated under former section 81(2) ARC, where such a relaxation of the standard of proof is not permitted for constitutional reasons.

This being said, it cannot be denied that setting the standard of proof at a minimum probability of 50% may not be a sufficient answer to the problem of underenforcement. Even if an infringement is established and it is clear that it caused losses to market participants, it may not be possible to pinpoint any particular amount for which the probability exceeds 50%. However limited the German experience with antitrust damages may be, the length of ongoing litigation, as with the pioneering *Cement* case, indicates that it may be exceedingly difficult for courts to come to reasonable estimates of the damages to be awarded.[32] Considering that the Federal Supreme Court has accepted in its path-breaking ORWI judgment that indirect purchasers are also entitled to damages and that infringers may raise a passing-on defence against direct purchasers (albeit under limited circumstances),[33] there is an additional risk that effective enforcement may suffer from the complexity of the assessment required. This is a reason to find additional facilitating devices for assessing antitrust damages.

First, it can be observed that successful follow-on actions have largely relied on estimates based on facts available from preceding decisions by the Commission or by the Federal Cartel Office.[34] But in contrast to findings on the infringement as

---

32 The claims collected and brought forward by the Belgian company CDC were held admissible by the OLG Düsseldorf in a judgment from 14 May 2008, Case VI-U (Kart) 14/07, *WuW/E* DE-R 2311 – *Belgisches Kartellklageunternehmen*, but as of October 2012 there has yet to be a judgment on damages.

33 BGH, Case KZR 75/10, judgment of 28 June 2011, *Gewerblicher Rechtsschutz und Urheberrecht* 2012, 291 – *ORWI* (annotated by Thomas Ackermann and Jens-Uwe Franck).

34 See LG (District Court) Dortmund, Case 13 O 55/02, judgment of 1 April 2004, *WuW/E* DE-R 1352, at 1354 – *Vitaminpreise Dortmund (Vitamin Prices Dortmund)*; Kammergericht (Higher Regional Court Berlin), Case 2 U 10/03 Kart, judgment of 1 October 2009, *WuW/E* DE-R 2773, at 2278 *et seq.* – *Berliner Transportbeton (Berlin Ready-Mix Concrete)*.

such,[35] the authorities' findings on these facts are not binding on courts, and it seems that they are becoming less frequent.

Second, a profit-based estimation of damages may help antitrust plaintiffs. Somewhat ambiguously, the third sentence of section 33(3) ARC provides that the assessment of the damage 'may take into account, in particular, the proportion of the profit which the undertaking has derived from the infringement'. While the wording of this provision, which was introduced in 2005 and has not been applicable in the cases that have so far been decided by German courts, is less than perfectly clear, the preferable interpretation (from the perspective of effective enforcement) seems to be that if a but-for price is not available, damages may be estimated on the basis of the part of the total profit that is apportionable to the sales made to the plaintiff.[36]

Third, presumptions on the amount of the *damnum emergens* and/or of the *lucrum cessans* would undoubtedly increase the success of private enforcement. However, in its ORWI judgment, the Federal Supreme Court was cautious about the formulation of presumptions. In particular, the court rightly rejected a presumption about the causation of losses to indirect purchasers.[37] Moreover, while it can be said (and has been held by German courts)[38] that cartel arrangements on prices or quota generally lead to a price increase and thus to losses suffered by direct customers of the cartel members, there seems to be no empirical basis that would allow a German court to accept a presumption as to the extent of the loss caused by a cartel. This would require rather broad generalizations and is therefore a task for the legislature. One may object that statutory presumptions on the amount of the overcharge (such as the presumption of a 10% overcharge in Hungary) or of the deadweight loss seem arbitrary. But if other measures fail to achieve a sufficient level of enforcement, this may be a viable tool.

3.4 How to Take Account of Damages in the Calculation of Fines

As we have seen, in a hypothetical world where antitrust infringement is followed by fines and damages with the same probability (or where damages are obtained with a known fraction of the probability of the imposition of a fine), optimal enforcement requires a reduction of the fine by the amount of damages (or, respectively, by a fraction of this amount that reflects the lower probability of obtaining damages). Turning to the real world, a much more complex relationship emerges. If we consider the normal case of a follow-on damages action, it is not known at the time of the imposition of the fine whether or with which probability damages will be awarded in the case at hand. So the idea of adjusting the amount of the fine

35 See section 33(4) ARC.

36 On this disputed interpretation see Gero Meeßen, *Der Anspruch auf Schadensersatz bei Verstößen gegen EU-Kartellrecht* Mohr Siebeck 2011), p. 424–5.

37 Case KZR 75/10 (cited *supra* note 33), para. 45.

38 See, for instance, Kammergericht (Higher Regional Court Berlin), Case 2 U 10/03 Kart (cited *supra* note 34), at 2777.

by deducting the expected amount of damages would normally not be feasible. Once damages have been awarded, one may of course think of an ex-post adjustment: the infringer could be permitted to reclaim the amount of damages or rather a fraction of it (in order to reflect the fact that the ex-ante probability of a successful follow-on action was less than 100%) as a rebate on the fine. But this would obviously create incentives for collusion between cartel members and their victims as cartel members would be able to pass on the amount of damages (or at least part of it) to the authority that fined them. There is hardly a way to avoid this dilemma. Therefore, it seems there is only a second-best solution: if it eventually turns out that private enforcement is a success, the general criteria for the calculation (such as the basic amounts) should be adjusted to reflect the contribution of damages awards to the deterrence of antitrust infringements. This would certainly not exactly result in an optimally deterrent sum of fines and damages. Then again, the calculation of fines according to the German and European guidelines as such is merely an approximation, and not a perfect implementation of the concept of deterrence.

4 Conclusion

Despite their different aims, both optimal damages and optimal fines ideally require knowledge of counterfactuals (but-for prices and but-for quantities). Since establishing but-for prices and but-for quantities beyond reasonable doubt would be exceedingly difficult, ways must be found to overcome the problem of under-enforcement that follows from this obstacle. As the example of the German legal system shows, the law of damages and the law of fines differ with regard to the instruments they apply in order to cope with the risk of under-enforcement resulting from uncertainty about counterfactuals. While the assessment of fines relies on substitute criteria, the assessment of damages relies on facilitating devices. The instruments used so far in the sphere of damages, namely the application of a comparably low standard of proof, may not yet be sufficient to make private damages claims a seizable contribution to the enforcement of antitrust law. However, the more effective private enforcement by means of damage becomes, the more significant the need to factor this into fine calculation.

The Interaction of Public and Private Enforcement – The Calculation and Reconciliation of Fines and Damages in Europe and Germany

Thorsten Mäger and Thomas B. Paul

1 Introduction

While public and private enforcement of competition law are sometimes heralded as two sides of the same coin, the developments in Germany and Europe in recent years have made it abundantly clear that there are in fact numerous sources of conflict and friction. Understandably, much of the discussion has been focused on the exposure of leniency applicants in private follow-on litigation and on methods that could alleviate this exposure. For various reasons, whistleblowers seem to have become a primary target in civil damage lawsuits, and this is seen as one of the greatest threats to the effectiveness of leniency programmes as a means of public enforcement. Apart from the special case of leniency applicants, however, one may also pose the somewhat broader question whether the principles that are applied in calculating the level of fines and those applied for calculating the amount of damages are in need of reconciliation. Indeed, the rapid growth of civil litigation in Europe has already led to the perception, particularly prevalent in the mainstream media, that cartel offenders will now face a second 'payday', leading to additional financial burdens that come on top of what is already considered severe punishment through fines. Examples of such 'double exposure' abound. For instance, the cement cartel in Germany received fines that run in the hundreds of million euros and soon became the target of private claimants demanding damages on the same order of magnitude. In a similar manner, members of the hydrogen peroxide cartel, after having received significant fines from the Commission, are now being sued for several hundred million euros in damages. Other prominent lawsuits have followed or are underway (such as with the Carglass cartel and the German rail cartel).

While the sheer aggregate amount of 'double exposure' is certainly not the right yardstick for addressing the issue, the development of a new competition litigation culture in Germany and Europe still raises a fundamental question: Is it still justified to calculate the fines according to the same principles that were applicable when civil enforcement was still dormant? Put another way: Were fines too low back then, or are they too high now? And to what extent can one justify rules on private enforcement (i.e. the tort laws of the Member States) being attuned to the overarching goal of deterrence when most damage cases are, in fact, follow-on cases?

In this article, we provide an overview of the recent discussion about the interaction between liability in fines and liability in damages. While we will devote some attention to the special case of leniency applicants, our special focus will lie on the broader question of reconciling the level of fines and damages, because this topic has been somewhat overshadowed by the debate about leniency cases and is therefore still underdeveloped. To this end, we will consider reconciliation both from economic and legal angles. Not surprisingly, from the viewpoint of the economic theory of optimal deterrence, it is ultimately an empirical question whether the aggregate burden imposed by fines and damage awards is too high or too low (or just right). However, it seems clear that, in principle, reconciliation between these two elements of competition law enforcement should be possible and can only occur at the expense of fine levels.

2 Interaction Between Fines and Damages – Economic Principles

2.1 The Optimal Deterrence Framework

To appreciate the interaction between public and private enforcement from the economic angle, it seems appropriate to begin by briefly reviewing the principles of optimal deterrence that have long become familiar to competition law practitioners. Obviously, the 'double burden' for cartel offenders through fines and damages is no cause for concern *per se* because of the arguably significant percentage of cartels that go undetected. Indeed, standard economic models of deterrence in competition law suggest that, in order to achieve a socially optimal degree of deterrence, the *expected burden* arising from the infringement, taking into account the combined likelihood of detection and conviction, should outweigh the 'net harm' caused by it.[1] Put another way:

$$E(B) > H,$$

where H denotes the net harm, B denotes the burden in case of detection and $E(\cdot)$ is a function that reflects the (perceived) combined probability of detection and conviction.

[1] See W.M. Landes, 'Optimal Sanctions for Antitrust Violations', 50 *The University of Chicago Law Review* (1983), 652–678.

Although it is not critical to our present discussion, it should perhaps be mentioned that the latter component of this inequality – the net harm – is still subject to some controversy, which mainly stems from the question whether it is desirable to prevent even 'efficient' antitrust infringements. While the pioneers of the economic theory of optimal deterrence, Gary Becker and William Landes, have advocated for allowing such efficient breaches,[2] others prefer to calibrate the expected burden to the benefit that accrues to the infringer, because this would 'sanction' violations, whereas the net harm approach would merely put a 'price' on the violation and force the infringer to internalize the harms caused to society.[3] We will not delve into this discussion here – suffice it to say that the instances in which the offender gains more than the victims – and society as a whole – lose, leading to an *increase* rather than a decrease in total welfare, will be rare indeed.[4]

What is important here is the rather straightforward insight that the endeavour of optimizing the level of deterrence requires us to consider both the expected level of fines and the expected level of damages. In fact, from the standpoint of the economic theory of optimal deterrence, the amount of fines imposed and the amount of damages awarded are simply part of the same variable[5] – the expected burden in case the infringement is detected (and successfully prosecuted). This means that the economics of competition law enforcement would advise for an optimization of the aggregate expected burden imposed by fines *and* civil damages in light of their respective likelihoods.[6]

Needless to say, optimization of deterrence requires us to consider both ends of the spectrum: while under-deterrence might lead to excess cartel activity, which is obviously harmful, over-deterrence can lead to socially inefficient suppression, which is to say, to an '*under*supply' of cartel infringements. The latter might seem counter-intuitive in hard-core cartel cases, but is certainly easy to understand in cases of vertical restraints that involve legal boundaries that are blurry and diffi-

2 See G.S. Becker, 'Crime and Punishment: An Economic Approach', 76 *Journal of Political Economy* (1968), 169–217, and W.M. Landes (*supra* note 1).

3 See W.P.J. Wils, 'Optimal Antitrust Fines: Theory and Practice', 29 *World Competition* (2006), 345–366.

4 In most real-world cases, the benefits-oriented approach would actually lead to *lower* sanctions, because most competition law infringements cause economic losses that do *not* correspond to a gain on the part of the offender (most notably, the deadweight loss). It is therefore somewhat misleading to suggest that the net-harm approach would 'merely' price the infringement and that the benefits approach would provide a more stringent sanction.

5 This is somewhat of an overstatement. Obviously, one would need to attach different probabilities of conviction to the respective burdens from public and private enforcement, so that it is necessary to keep both variables mathematically separated.

6 Indeed, from a purely economic point of view, one may argue that the distributive part of private enforcement, i.e. the wealth transfer that is achieved through a successful civil lawsuit, has little intrinsic meaning besides lending credibility to the deterrent effect of private enforcement. In other words, since it is only the deterrent effect that counts, a system that relies exclusively on public enforcement (but provides the same level of deterrence) would seem perfectly equivalent to a mixed system which also allows private damage claims.

cult to identify by courts and companies alike. In these cases, excessive sanctions would increase the economic risks arising from Type 1 errors (i.e., over-enforcement) and could therefore stifle economically productive market behaviour.[7] And even in hard-core cartel cases, the dangers associated with over-deterrence should not be underestimated. This becomes more apparent if one employs a somewhat more refined economic analysis that takes account of the fact that a company is not a uniform economic actor and that cartel infringements are rarely orchestrated by its shareholders (i.e., its economic beneficiaries). If one keeps in mind that cartel infringements are often the work of a small group of employees, sometimes in spite of extensive corporate compliance programmes, it becomes clear that an increase of the financial burden levied upon the company does not always translate into an increase in deterrence for individual actors. In fact, the marginal increase in deterrence may be *zero*. This is because, for the individuals involved in the infringement, even an 'average' company fine – 50 million euros, say[8] – would most likely suffice to trigger personal insolvency if the company were to seek redress for this financial burden. But such redress is rarely sought as most companies who are subject to competition law investigations will try to take advantage of the leniency rules enacted by the respective competition authorities (or at the very least prepare an appropriate defence against the allegations), and this will require the cooperation of the involved individuals. Experience shows that most companies would rather ensure such cooperation and forego the opportunity of seizing the limited personal assets of the responsible individuals.

Admittedly, the various complications that arise when considering the incentive structure of the responsible individuals are still largely unexplored, and there may be other factors to consider. For example, most behavioural economists would point out that high company fines are nonetheless necessary to convey a clear message that competition law infringements are indeed *detrimental* to the company, as this would deprive the responsible individuals of the sense of moral righteousness that may persist if their company were to retain a net benefit from the infringement.[9] Besides, in some jurisdictions, it may be legally difficult to seek

---

7 Many economists associated with the Chicago antitrust tradition have even argued that Type 1 errors might be more harmful to economic welfare than Type 2 errors (i.e., under-enforcement), because monopoly and/or cartel profits accruing from under-enforcement will incentivize potential competitors to enter into the monopolized/cartelized market and will therefore, over time, be dissipated through new competition. On the other hand, so the argument goes, over-enforcement by competition agencies that prevents economically beneficial market behaviour is not subject to the same kind of competitive erosion. See, e.g., F.H. Easterbrook, 'The Limits of Antitrusts, 63 *Texas Law Review* (1984), 1–40.

8 In the period from 1 January 2008 to 5 December 2012, the European Commission levied a total of €8.7 billion in fines (adjusted for subsequent Court judgments) on 196 undertakings for cartel infringements under Art. 101 TFEU, leading to a per-company-average of roughly €44.4 million.
See http://ec.europa.eu/competition/cartels/statistics/statistics.pdf.

9 This argument has its limits. Most people would judge the profitability of an infringement by its outcome (i.e., from an *ex post* perspective), so that even a moderate

redress from the responsible individuals if the claimant company did in fact achieve a net gain from the infringement.[10] More importantly still, high company fines would arguably reinforce efforts to ensure compliance. On the other hand, compliance mechanisms are costly and significant over-enforcement may cause companies to incur excessive expenditures.

In any event, it should be clear from the above discussion that over-deterrence is indeed a concern, *even in hard-core cartel cases*, and that there may be instances where an increase of the burden imposed on a company does not provide additional benefits in terms of additional deterrence for potential offenders but may cause economic harm. Most economists would therefore agree that the socially optimal level of competition law infringements is probably low, but certainly not zero, and that, correspondingly, both under- and over-deterrence are undesirable.

While the principle message from the economic literature is clear, the development of concrete recommendations on the appropriate level of deterrence is notoriously difficult, mainly because of the extraordinary intricacies involved in procuring and assessing relevant empirical data. To begin with, most empirical investigations on the average cartel overcharge are meta-analyses of studies that use a wide range of diverging – and sometimes questionable – methods. Also, the resulting averages from these meta-analyses may be subject to a certain selection bias due to the higher attention that extensive cartels with significant overcharges typically receive. And to the extent the empirical studies rely on court decisions in damage cases, one needs to consider the possibility of positive feedback effects which can arise when courts employ presumptions of loss or reversals of the burden of proof.

The European Commission has recently tried to address some of these problems when it presented its own research in its 2013 practical guide on quantifying harm in damage actions.[11] However, even the Commission's estimates are still subject to significant time-lag problems resulting from the rapid development in

---

fine that only slightly exceeds the illicit gains from the infringement could suffice to convey the necessary moral message. In other words, few people would regard an infringement that led to illicit gains of 100 but to a fine of 200 as 'profitable', even if the probability of detection was below 0.5.

10 See H. Fleischer, 'Kompetenzüberschreitungen von Geschäftsleitern im Personen- und Kapitalgesellschaftsrecht', *Deutsches Steuerrecht* 2009, 1204, p. 1210, for a recent discussion of the situation under German law, where the principles of 'adjustment of damages for benefits received' (*Vorteilsausgleichung*) would arguably limit or exclude personal liability of the responsible individuals vis-à-vis their employer when the infringement resulted in a net benefit. Note, however, that this argument is subject to similar objections as those pointed out in note 9.

11 See *Communication from the Commission on quantifying harm in actions for damages based on breaches of Article 101 or 102 of the Treaty on the Functioning of the European Union*, O.J. 2013, C 167/19, and *Guidance to national courts: Quantification of harm caused by infringements of the EU antitrust rules* (11 June 2013), paras. 139 et seq., available at http://ec.europa.eu/competition/antitrust/actionsdamages/quantification_guide_en.pdf. See also Oxera *et. al.*, *Quantifying antitrust damages – Toward non-binding guidance for courts* (2009), pp. 89 *et seq.*, available at http://ec.europa.eu/competition/antitrust/actionsdamages/index.html.

antitrust enforcement efforts around the world. For instance, if we look at the status of antitrust enforcement in Europe in the 1980s or the early 1990s and consider the level of fines prevalent at that time,[12] it becomes clear that the average duration and average overcharge achieved by cartels in Europe during that time is a very imperfect yardstick to the current situation. For example, the absence of any cartel-destabilizing leniency policy[13] would suggest that cartels could be organized and maintained in a more efficient manner. Since the level of deterrence through public and private enforcement needs to be calibrated to the *current* situation, the time-lag problem implies that progress in competition law enforcement is insufficiently accounted for and that an unmodified application of the existing empirical data may lead to over-enforcement (and *vice versa*).[14]

Even more complicated is the issue of assessing the rates of detection and applying them in an appropriate manner. This is not only a problem of estimating how big the proverbial 'tip of the iceberg' is in relation to the hidden remainder.[15] Even if one settles on a specific number (say a 15% probability of annual detection),[16] it is not clear how this number should be used in the calculation to account for the various dynamic effects at play.[17]

---

12 The Commission's study actually considers cases from the 1960s onwards. See para. 121.

13 The first Commission Notice on the non-imposition or reduction of fines in cartel cases dates from 1996. See OJ C 207 of 18 July 1996, pp. 4–6.

14 See, e.g., E. Combe, C. Monnier & R. Legal, 'Cartels: The Probability of Getting Caught in the European Union', *BEER paper n° 12* (March 2008), who find that the annual cartel detection rate in the European Union increased sharply from 1.64 cartels per year in the period between 1969 and 1996 – i.e., the period before the introduction of the first leniency notice (note 13) – to roughly 5 cartels per year thereafter.

15 While it is impossible to calculate the *actual* probability of detection when the *actual* number of cartels is unknown, one of the most popular surrogate methods consists of inferring the instantaneous probability of detection for cartels that are eventually detected, see e.g. P.G. Bryant & E.W. Eckard, 'Price Fixing: The Probability of Getting Caught', 73 *Review of Economics & Statistics* (1991), 531–536. With this method, one can calculate annual probabilities of detection, but always with the important proviso that the figures only hold for cartels that are eventually detected. See also G. J. Werden & M. J. Simon, 'Why Price Fixers Should Go to Prison', 32 *Antitrust Bulletin* (1987), 917–937.

16 The study by Bryant & Eckard (*supra* note 15) estimated the probability of cartel detection for a sample of cartels prosecuted by the US Department of Justice (DoJ) between 1961 and 1988. They arrived at an annual probability of detection of 13–17%. Using the same technique for all European cartels detected and convicted between 1969 and 2007, Combe, Monnier and Legal recently estimated the annual probability of detection to be between 12.9% and 13.2% (see E. Combe, C. Monnier & R. Legal, cited *supra* note 14).

17 For a discussion of the existing literature, see M.-L. Allain, M. Boyer, R. Kotchoni & J.-P. Ponssard, 'The Determination of Optimal Fines in Cartel Cases – The Myth of Underdeterrence', *CIRANO Working Papers* 2011s-34, available at http://www.cirano.qc.ca/pdf/publication/2011s-34.pdf. Their calculation of the optimal fine is not based on the simple annual probability of detection but rather on the probability in the

In sum, it would seem overly optimistic to expect any kind of mathematical precision from the economic theory of optimal deterrence any time soon. The existing body of research can only provide rough clues and indications that leave ample leeway for competition authorities to exercise their discretionary judgment about the required levels of deterrence. All this, however, does not affect the validity of the principle message that the economic literature provides about the *internal relationship* between public and private enforcement. *If* a particular level of deterrence through fines and damage awards was considered sufficient and appropriate at a time when private enforcement was still underdeveloped, economic logic would suggest that, all other things being equal, an increase in private enforcement would need to be compensated in order to avoid over-deterrence. In short, unless new empirical evidence shows that what was previously considered a sufficient amount of deterrence was in fact insufficient, economic theory would suggest that reconciliation between public and private enforcement is indeed necessary.

2.2 Leniency Cases

Even more pronounced is the case for coordination between public and private enforcement when the impact of damage claim exposure on the effectiveness of leniency programmes is considered. This is particularly apparent if one considers a hypothetical counterfactual in which leniency applications are possible but private enforcement is completely absent. In such a situation, the incentives set by the historical build-up of potential liability in fines alone could be expected to drive cartel offenders into the arms of leniency programmes. Because fines increase proportionally over time, all cartel members will eventually stand to gain more from filing for leniency than from continuing the cartel – even when fines are extremely moderate. To make this more concrete, assume that a company derives an annual profit of 100 from the cartel, and that the annual probability of detection is 0.2. Assume further that fines are merely 'restitutionary', i.e. equivalent to the cartel offender's illicit gains. In such a setting, after five years of having successfully operated a cartel, the expected (gross) burden from fines in case the cartel is continued for another year would be 5 x -100 x 0.2 = -100, whereas the expected (gross) gain is only 100 x 0.8 = 80. Assuming, for the sake of simplicity, that the cartel consists of two symmetric participants, one can see that filing for leniency would be the *dominant* strategy for both participants:

nth year, which suggests that the existing level of fines provides a significantly higher degree of deterrence than previously thought.

Fig. 11. Simplified illustration of a scenario without private enforcement

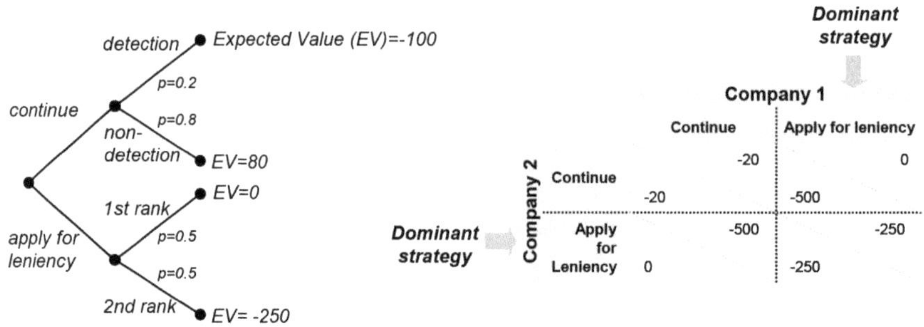

Although our example serves merely as an illustration, the underlying logic seems to be quite robust. In other words, many cartels will eventually reach a point where the build-up of potential liability in fines outweighs the expected incremental gains from continuing the cartel. Following the game-theoretic logic of backward induction, one might even conclude that an effective leniency programme should prevent the formation of cartel agreements in the first place. Of course, all this depends on rather stringent assumptions about the rationality of the individual actors and their time horizon,[18] but the extraordinary success of leniency programmes around the world provides a strong indication that the incentives set by these programmes are by and large effective.[19]

All this changes when significant liability for damages comes into play. Since private enforcement makes it costly for cartel participants to come forward and make use of leniency programmes, it effectively works as a mechanism that eliminates or at least reduces the cartel-destabilizing incentives of these programmes. Building upon the example used above, one can easily see why this is so. Assume, for the sake of simplicity, that private enforcement would eliminate all illicit gains if the cartel is detected. This means that the net financial effect of filing for leniency would be -500 for the first successful applicant. The net expected effect from continuing the cartel (assuming that both participants do so) would be -120.[20] From a game-theoretic perspective, filing for leniency in this case would still constitute a Nash equilibrium, but so would the continuation of the cartel!

---

18 To fully appreciate the incentive effects of leniency policies, one would need to extend the analysis to the responsible individuals and consider the fact that their incentives may differ substantially from what would be rational/optimal from the viewpoint of their respective company. For example, if the time horizon of the individual involved is rather short, all participants may expect to escape the sanctions that are eventually bound to occur.

19 See *supra* note 14, on the sharp increase in the annual rate of detection in the European Union after 1996 (the year of the introduction of the first leniency notice).

20 To keep the presentation simple, we will ignore the fact that detection can happen at any point during the sixth year and that the illicit profits that have accrued up to this point – and the additional liability in fines and damages – would need to be considered as well.

Fig. 12. Simplified illustration of a scenario with private enforcement

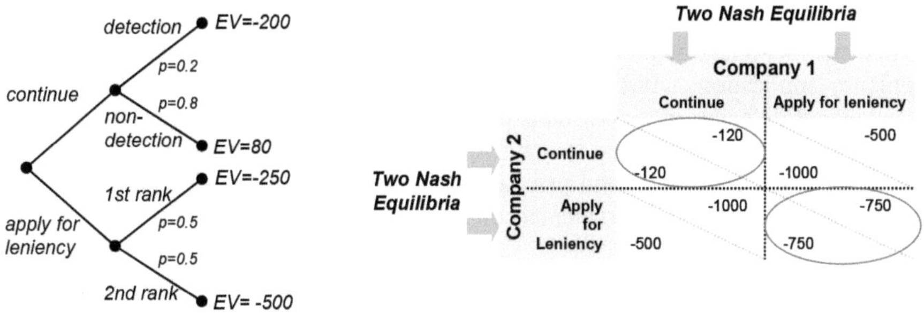

Again, the results are to a certain extent dependent on some fairly stringent assumptions, and the real-world effects of private enforcement on the effectiveness of leniency programmes may not be quite as dramatic as in our example.[21] Nonetheless, experience shows that the potential exposure from damage claims has become an important factor in the decision process that precedes a leniency application. This is all the more so given that recent developments in European cases have shown a particular vulnerability of leniency applicants in follow-on lawsuits (see 3.1).

3 Interaction of Fines and Damages – The Legal Perspective

With this in mind, the remainder of this article will explore the legal perspective, which is a good deal more complicated. While economic theory is only concerned with setting the appropriate incentives to induce lawful behaviour in a cost-efficient manner and does not attach significance to the ways this is achieved – be it fines or damages, or a mixture of both – the legal perspective differs significantly, not least because claims for compensation are considered as a proprietary right of the victim. In principle, the calculation of fines and the calculation of damages are therefore completely decoupled. Fines are determined on the basis of turnover figures and are adjusted for attenuating and aggravating circumstances.[22] Damag-

---

21 Interestingly, a study of the immediate effects following the introduction of the US Antitrust Criminal Penalty Enhancement and Reform Act 2004 – which limits the civil liability of leniency applicants (more on this *infra* sub 3.3.1.) – did not show a statistically significant increase in cartel discoveries. See N.H. Miller, 'Strategic Leniency and Cartel Enforcement', 99 *American Economic Review* (2009), 750–768.

22 See sec. 1 and 2 of the 2006 Commission Guidelines on the method of setting fines imposed pursuant to Art. 23(2)(a) of Regulation No 1/2003 (OJ C 210 of 1 September 2006, p. 2) and paras 8 et seq. of the corresponding notice by the German Federal

es, however, are assessed on a case-by-case basis, and a successful claimant under German law is entitled to a (monetary) restitution of the 'but-for situation' (including any profits lost due to the infringement and interest), regardless of whether the infringement was intentional or merely due to negligence. And of course, successful leniency applications will limit or exclude liability in fines, but are not part of the recognized defences in a civil damage lawsuit. Nonetheless, the legal discussion has long identified the need to achieve a certain amount of coordination and reconciliation between public and private enforcement.[23] This is particularly evident in leniency cases, but by no means confined to them.

3.1 Leniency Cases

As explained in the introductory remarks, the discussion about coordination between public and private enforcement has so far been mostly focused on leniency cases, since leniency programmes have proven to be the most effective enforcement tool at the disposal of competition authorities. At the same time, the exposure of leniency applicants in private follow-on litigation seems to be rather high. Indeed, recent experience in the UK (in particular in the graphite products case[24] and in the paraffin wax case[25]) and in Germany (in the Carglass cartel case[26]) confirms the suspicion that leniency applicants might be particularly prone to becoming 'sitting ducks' in a follow-on lawsuit. The reasons for this are manifold, but two stand out as particularly crucial. First, successful leniency applicants will have little reason to contest the Commission's decision, whereas other participants will often file an appeal to the General Court. Under the *Masterfoods* doctrine, a pending appeal means that the national court trying the damage case would need to either stay the proceedings until the appeal in the European courts has been finally decided, or consider referring the matter to the ECJ.[27] This creates an asymmetry between the leniency applicant and other cartel participants and sets a specific incentive for civil claimants to target the leniency applicant in order to bypass time-consuming quarrels about the binding effect of the Commission's decision and to

Cartel Office *Leitlinien für die Bußgeldzumessung in Kartellordnungswidrigkeitenverfahren (25 June 2013).*

23 See, e.g., W.P.J. Wils, 'The Relationship between Public Antitrust Enforcement and Private Actions for Damages', 32 *World Competition* (2009), 3–26.

24 See *Emerson Electric Co and others v. Morgan Crucible Company plc*, [2007] CAT 30.

25 On 31 July 2009, Hausfeld launched a High Court damages action on behalf of several European candle manufacturers specifically against Shell and Exxon Mobil, who had received full and partial immunity from fines on account of their respective leniency applications in the Commissions proceedings.

26 See *Frankfurter Allgemeine Zeitung*, 24 January 2011, No. 19, p. 15.

27 Case C-344/98, *Masterfoods Ltd. v. HB Ice Cream Ltd.* [2000] ECR I-11369, para. 57.

avoid a stay of the proceedings.[28] Second, the nature and extent of the leniency applicant's participation in the infringement is often particularly well documented and therefore easier to prove in a damage lawsuit. Although the Commission still rejects requests from private claimants for access to its files under the Transparency Regulation[29] and grants particular protection to leniency documents,[30] the ECJ's judgment in re *Pfleiderer*[31] has cast some doubt on this policy. Instead of affording absolute protection from discoverability, the ECJ advocated a case-by-case weighing of interests,[32] which seems to indicate that there may be cases in which the information interest of private claimants outweighs the interests of the leniency applicant in safeguarding confidentiality.[33]

In the US, the conflict between private enforcement and leniency programmes has been significantly alleviated by the Antitrust Criminal Penalty Enhancement

---

28 See, e.g., D.Zimmer & J.Höft, 'Private Enforcement im öffentlichen Interesse?', *Zeitschrift für Unternehmens- und Gesellschaftsrecht* 2009, 662, p. 716.

29 The Commission is currently fighting various pending requests for access under the Transparency Regulation before the European Courts, as in the *Gas-insulated switchgear* case, in which it denied the request for access to the entire case file in re COMP/F/38.899. This case is pending before the ECJ after the General Court (Case T-344/08) had quashed the Commission's denial, arguing that it was obligated to carry out a concrete, individual examination of the content of the documents covered by the request for access. Similarly, in the *Bitumen* case, the Commission denied a request for access to the confidential version of its decision in COMP/F/38.456; this case is now pending before the General Court (Case T-380/08). In the *Hydrogen Peroxide and Perborate* case, the Commission did not appeal the decision by the General Court (Case T-437/08), which only granted access to the full statement of contents of the Commission's case file in re COMP/F/38.620 and was thus rather limited in scope.

30 See *Commission Notice on Immunity from Fines and Reduction of Fines in Cartel Cases* (OJ C 298 of 8 December 2006, p. 17), para. 40, and *Commission Notice on the Cooperation between the Commission and the Courts of the EU Member States in the Application of Art. 81 and 82 EC* (OJ C 101 of 27 April 2004, p. 1) para. 26: '[T]he Commission will not transmit to national courts information voluntarily submitted by a leniency applicant without the consent of that applicant.'

31 Case C-360/09, *Pfleiderer v. Bundeskartellamt* [2011] ECR I-0000 (not yet published). See also T. Mäger, D.J. Zimmer & S. Milde, 'Konflikt zwischen öffentlicher und privater Kartellrechtsdurchsetzung', *Wirtschaft und Wettbewerb* 2009, 885 *et seq.*

32 See *Pfleiderer v. Bundeskartellamt* (*supra* note 31), para. 30 *et seq.*

33 In Germany, the courts have so far indicated that such weighing of interest generally leads to the conclusion that leniency applications are not subject to discovery by potential claimants. See Higher Regional Court of Düsseldorf, Decision of 22 August 2012 – Case V-4 Kart 5 + 6/11 (OWi), *Kaffeeröster*; County Court of Bonn, Decision of 18 January 2012 – Case 51 Gs 53/09. See, however, Higher Regional Court of Hamm, Decision of 26 November 2013, ref. 1 Vas 116/13, *Betriebs-Berater* 2014, 526, which denied any special protection for leniency documents contained in the files of a state prosecutor's office and ordered the handing-over of such documents to the civil court deciding over damage claims.

and Reform Act that was passed by Congress in January 2004.[34] This Act limits the damages recoverable from a corporate leniency applicant to the portion of the actual damage sustained by the claimant that is attributable to the commerce done by the applicant in the goods or services affected by the violation – thereby 'de-trebling' the amount that could otherwise be collected under sec. 4 of the Clayton Act –, provided that the leniency applicant also *cooperates* with private claimants in their damage actions against the other cartel members (see Title II, sec. 213).

In Europe, however, proposals have so far remained at the level of policy considerations. In its 2005 Green Paper, the Commission identified one procedural protection mechanism – the exclusion of leniency material from discoverability – and two options concerning substantive law. Both substantive law options strongly resembled the US solution in that they would either grant the leniency applicant a 'rebate on any damages claim facing him in return for helping claimants bring damages claims against all cartel members' or limit his civil liability 'to the share of the damages corresponding to the applicant's share in the cartelised market'.[35] In the 2008 White Paper, the Commission gave a refined version of the latter option and proposed limiting the leniency applicant's civil liability 'to claims by his direct and indirect contractual partners'.[36] In the Commission's view, this would contribute to making the scope of damages to be paid by successful leniency applicants more predictable and more limited, without providing undue relief from liability. This is also the approach the Commission has taken in Article 11(2) of its proposal for a directive on cartel damage claims, albeit with the additional twist that leniency applicants would remain liable if injured parties show they are unable to obtain full compensation from the other undertakings that were involved in the same infringement.[37] However, the Commission proposal would still work at the expense of victims, e.g. if the other undertakings are not unable to provide full compensation, but merely farther removed from the injured party (e.g., domiciled in another country, whereas the leniency applicant could be sued in the home jurisdiction of the injured party), which seems questionable. It is thus not entirely surprising that the European Parliament has been hesitant to adopt this approach.[38]

34 H.R. 1086 [108th]. The bill was originally to a five-year 'sunset' provision. On 27 May 2010, Congress then passed a bill extending the civil leniency provisions for another ten years.

35 *Green Paper – Damages actions for breach of the EC antitrust rules*, COM(2005) 672, p. 10 (available at http://eur-lex.europa.eu/LexUriServ/LexUriServ.do?uri=COM:2005:0672:FIN:EN:PDF)

36 *White Paper on Damages actions for breach of the EC antitrust rules*, COM(2008) 165 final, p. 10 (available at http://eur-lex.europa.eu/LexUriServ/LexUriServ.do?uri=COM:2008:0165:FIN:EN:PDF).

37 *Proposal for a Directive of the European Parliament and of the Council on certain rules governing actions for damages under national law for infringements of the competition law provisions of the Member States and of the European Union*, COM(2013) 404, 11 June 2013.

38 See Opinion of the Committee on Legal Affairs for the Committee on Economic and Monetary Affairs, 2013/0185(COD), 27 January 2014, p. 21, which proposes to delete Article 11(2) from the directive.

In the German discussion, other ideas have been developed in the meantime, and one of the most noteworthy suggestions is the concept proposed by Kersting[39] and Meeßen.[40] Under this concept, successful leniency applicants would indeed receive a favourable treatment in damage lawsuits, but only in their *internal recourse actions* vis-à-vis other participants. Under German law, the extent of such recourse claims is determined by sec. 426(1) of the German Civil Code (*Bürgerliches Gesetzbuch* 'BGB'), and the open wording of this section makes it possible to consider a variety of different criteria. Apart from the share in causing the damage (which in turn may be assessed according to affected turnover or market shares), the level of fault or blameworthiness on the part of the individual participants can also be taken into account.[41] It is thus not inconceivable to modify the criteria that determine the recourse claim in cartel damage cases in such a manner that the share of the total damage that is borne by the leniency applicant would be alleviated so as to account for his 'redeeming' act of coming forward. Nonetheless, such a solution would most likely require a basis in statutory law, and the most natural place for such a statutory amendment would be sec. 33 of the German Act Against Restraints of Competition (Gesetz gegen Wettbewerbsbeschränkungen, 'GWB'), i.e. the general provision for cartel damage claims in German law. It is therefore somewhat unfortunate that this issue was not even on the agenda for the recent 8th GWB Reform Act, which has entered into effect on 30 June 2013.

However, one may take consolation in the fact that a purely national solution would suffer from severe shortcomings in European cases, where internal recourse actions are typically subject to a range of different national laws. Indeed, most Member States would determine the laws applicable to recourse claims in accordance with principles substantially similar to the ones set forth in Articles 15 and 16 of the Rome I Regulation for contractual claims,[42] under which the law governing the debtor's obligation towards the creditor also governs the debtor's right to claim recourse from the other debtors. For instance, a French cartel participant who paid damages to cartel customers under French law would not be barred from seeking recourse against the German leniency applicant, even if German law contains rules that would limit the latter's exposure. One can therefore make a strong argument that coordination of liability in fines and damages in leniency cases can only be achieved through a harmonized European approach.

39 See C. Kersting, 'Perspektiven der privaten Rechtsdurchsetzung im Kartellrecht', *Zeitschrift für Wettbewerbsrecht* 2008, 252, p. 266 *et seq.*

40 See G. Meeßen, *Der Anspruch auf Schadensersatz bei Verstößen gegen EU-Kartellrecht* (Mohr Siebeck, 2011), p. 552 *et seq.*

41 See C. Grüneberg, in *Palandt – Bürgerliches Gesetzbuch* (C.H. Beck, 73rd ed. 2014), sec. 426, para. 14.

42 Regulation (EC) No 593/2008 of the European Parliament and of the Council of 17 June 2008 on the law applicable to contractual obligations (Rome I), OJ L 177 of 4 August 2008, p. 6.

3.2 Reconciling the Level of Fines and Damages

If we turn to the broader question of reconciling the level of fines and damages more generally, we encounter a complex and multi-layered picture. The relationship between fines and damages can be considered under a multitude of possible approaches, none of which currently offers a broad-scale reconciliation. The situation under German law, which allows reimbursement claims under which cartel offenders could receive a refund for the profit-disgorging part of the sentence if and to the extent they pay damages to victims, would certainly come nearest to the economic ideal, but this has so far remained largely theoretical.

3.2.1 Recognition of Previous Compensation Payments as Attenuating Circumstances

Since in many cartel cases, public enforcement precedes any talks about possible compensation, defendants will rarely be able to invoke such payments before the competition authorities. Nonetheless, there are cases in which defendants had already made such payments and successfully argued before the European Commission that they should be taken into account as attenuating circumstances. For example, in the *Pre-Insulated Pipe Cartel* case, cartel-ringleader ABB had made substantial payments to Powerpipe, who was the only competitor of the cartel and was subject to several concerted exclusionary practices by cartel-members. In recognition of this element, the Commission applied a reduction of ECU 5 million to the basic amount (which was set at ECU 70 million).[43] Similarly, in the *Nintendo* case, the Commission granted a reduction of the fine on account of the fact that Nintendo offered compensation to third parties identified in the Statement of Objections as having suffered financial harm as a result of the infringement.[44]

In Germany, traditional doctrine also supports the notion that compensation payments can be a relevant factor in calculating the appropriate fine. In fact, sec. 46a of the German Penal Code (*Strafgesetzbuch*, 'StGB') explicitly states that in criminal cases, the judge may consider it a mitigating circumstance if the perpetrator seeks to provide compensation to his victim. Although there are as of yet no prominent competition law cases, recital 17 of the 2006 fining guidelines[45] by the Federal Cartel Office (FCO) seemed to indicate that similar principles would apply to competition law infringements. The 2013 fining guidelines do not use the

---

43 Case No IV/35.691/E-4 *Pre-Insulated Pipe Cartel*, OJ L 24 of 30 January 1999, p. 1, 64 para. 172. This was later confirmed by the CFI, Case T-31/99, *ABB Asea Brown Boveri Ltd v. Commission* [2002] ECR II-1881, para. 254.

44 Case No COMP/35.587 *PO Video Games*, OJ L 255 of 8 October 2003, p. 33, 96 para. 440.

45 *Bekanntmachung Nr. 38/2006 über die Festsetzung von Geldbußen nach § 81 Abs. 4 Satz 2 des Gesetzes gegen Wettbewerbsbeschränkungen (GWB) gegen Unternehmen und Unternehmensvereinigungen.*

same wording, but there are no indications that this was motivated by a conscious decision against recognizing compensation payments as an attenuating factor.[46]

There are, however, important limitations to these principles. As already mentioned above, recognition as an attenuating circumstance can work only if the compensation payment *precedes* the decision by the competition authority or, in case of an appeal, the decision by a court that has full competence to hear new facts. This means that, in European cases, a compensation payment must be made before the General Court rendered its decision,[47] whereas in Germany, the appeal decision by the Higher Regional Court would be the latest point in time when damage payments might be considered (see sec. 84 GWB, 79(3) OWiG[48], 337 StPO). Also, recognition of damage payments as an attenuating factor seems to be dependent on whether or not the payment reflects a deliberate and genuine effort to make amends for the infringement, which means that a judgment from a civil court ordering the defendant to pay damages would normally not be sufficient.[49] And finally, the geographical scope of compensation payments plays a crucial role. Thus, the European courts have on several occasions rejected the proposition that damage payments in the US, in particular treble damages, should be considered – thereby echoing a consistently held position on the application of the *non bis in idem* principle in cases where the US authorities had already imposed fines.[50]

3.2.2 Claims for Reimbursement Under Sec. 34(2) GWB and Sec. 99(2) OWiG

Until the entry into force of the 7th GWB Reform Act in July 2005, the calculation of fines for competition law infringements in Germany was based on an estimation of the actual illicit profit that accrued to the infringer. Since this system had proven tedious and cumbersome, and was also out of step with the turnover-based calculation employed elsewhere (in particular at the European level), the 7th GWB Reform Act put the system on completely new footing and adopted the 10% worldwide turnover ceiling familiar from Article 23(2) of the Procedural Regula-

---

46 See *supra* note 22.

47 Although Art. 31 of the Procedural Regulation seems to endow the ECJ with 'unlimited jurisdiction to review decisions whereby the Commission has fixed a fine', it is settled case law that the ECJ will only consider 'points of law' under Art. 256(1) subpara. (2) TFEU.

48 Act on Administrative Offences (Ordnungswidrigkeitengesetz, 'OWiG').

49 In the *Citric acid* case (Case T-59/02, *Archer Daniels Midland Co. v. Commission* [2006] ECR II-3627), the CFI made it clear that the Commission is not required to take (any) damage payments into account as an attenuating factor (although the court apparently overlooked the Nintendo decision, arguing that 'it is not possible to establish the existence of a Commission practice on the basis of one case alone [i.e., the ABB case]' [at para. 354]).

50 See, e.g., CFI, *Archer Daniels Midland Co. v. Commission* (*supra* note 49), paras. 70–72.

tion 1/2003.[51] Nonetheless, the idea that fines should skim off the profit derived from the infringement was not abandoned. The FCO retained the power to either

- integrate the disgorgement into the new turnover-based calculation of the fine (under sec. 81(5) 1st sentence GWB);
- issue a disgorgement order in a separate administrative proceeding that is conducted in parallel or after a fining decision has been rendered (under sec. 34 GWB); or
- make use of a separate profit-disgorging sentencing instrument instead of the fine ("*Verfall*", see sec. 29a OWiG and sec. 82a(2) GWB).

In all cases, however – and this is where reconciliation between fines and damages comes into play – the disgorgement of profits can be *reversed* if the cartel offender later pays damages to victims. For disgorgements under sec. 34 GWB and sec. 29a OWiG, this is explicitly set forth in sec. 34(2) GWB and sec. 99(2) OWiG, respectively; and the same principles would arguably apply if the FCO chooses to integrate the disgorgement into the calculation of the fine under sec. 81(5) GWB.[52] Even though sec. 34(2) GWB and 99(2) OWiG still fall conspicuously short of their counterpart in German criminal law (sec. 73(1) 2nd sentence StGB), where the mere *existence* of a private damage claim would be sufficient to rule out a disgorgement, both sections seem to have all the makings for a universal mechanism of reconciliation between fines and damages in the form of a reimbursement claim.

In practice, however, both provisions have achieved little, if any, relevance. The main reason for this is that the FCO has been extremely reluctant to make use of either sec. 34 GWB or sec. 81(5) GWB, let alone sec. 29a OWiG, which means that there is at present no reported case under the new law (after the 7th GWB Re-

51 Note, however, that the German Federal Court of Justice has made it clear that the 10% threshold is not to be seen as a cap. Instead, the threshold also provides substantive orientation for determining the fine in individual cases in the manner that a fine equal to the 10% threshold should only apply in the most severe cases. See Decision of 26 February 2013, ref. KRB 20/12, *Wirtschaft und Wettbewerb – Entscheidungssammlung* DE-R 3861.

52 For this case, most authors seem to endorse a *mutatis mutandis* application of sec. 99(2) OWiG. See e.g. H. Achenbach, in H. Hahn, W. Jaeger, P. Pohlmann, H. Rieger & D. Schroeder (eds.), *Frankfurter Kommentar zum Kartellrecht* (Otto Schmidt, 61st ed. 2006), sec. 81 GWB para. 308; G. Dannecker & J. Biermann in U. Immenga & E.-J. Mestmäcker (eds.), *GWB* (C.H. Beck, 4th ed. 2007), sec. 81 para. 458; K. Rogall in L. Senge (ed.), *Karlsruher Kommentar zum OWiG* (C.H. Beck, 3rd ed. 2006), sec. 30 para. 127; P.H. Müther, *Die Vorteilsabschöpfung im Ordnungswidrigkeitenrecht in § 17 Absatz 4 OWiG unter Berücksichtigung des deutschen und europäischen Kartellrechts* (Peter Lang, 1999), p. 70; and R. Raum, in G. Müller, E. Osterloch & T. Stein (eds.), *Festschrift für Günther Hirsch*. (C.H. Beck 2008), p. 301, 308. This has important ramifications for the question whether compensation payments based on *settlements* could be eligible for reimbursement. In principle, sec. 99(2) OWiG only considers payments based on unappealable court judgments (and arguably court settlements), whereas sec. 34(2) GWB takes a broader approach and considers any form of compensation payments.

form Act) in which illicit profits were explicitly calculated. Instead, the FCO has simply adopted the same principles used by the European Commission and issued 'purely punitive' fines calculated on the basis of the affected turnover.

This practice has already attracted a fair share of criticism from prominent authors, who have argued that constitutional law – in particular the principle of equal treatment (Article 3(1) of the Basic Law) – would normally *require* the FCO to explicitly disgorge the illicit profits.[53] The situation is further complicated by the obscure wording of sec. 81(5) 2nd sentence GWB, which stipulates that in cases where the FCO issues a purely punitive fine, it shall be required to 'take this into account when calculating [the fine]'. Neither the wording of this provision nor its legislative materials provide any reliable clue whether this should be taken to mean that a 'purely punitive' would be lower than a fine which includes a disgorgement, or, on the contrary, that the calculation of the fine would then somehow make up for the lack of an explicit disgorgement (perhaps on the basis of a rough estimate of the illicit gains that is then translated into an appropriate increase of the basic amount).[54] So far, the FCO has not openly addressed this point in its published decisions, which is in itself a legally questionable practice as it makes it difficult for the addressee to appreciate how sec. 81(5) 2nd sentence GWB is in fact interpreted. The development of the general level of fines certainly shows no signs of a decrease,[55] which may be taken as an indication that the FCO follows the latter interpretation. In any event, it seems clear that reimbursement claims under sec. 34(2) GWB and 99(2) OWiG will, for the time being, remain without practical relevance.

3.2.3 Application of the *non bis in idem* Principle

Another mechanism of reconciliation that has recently come into focus is based on the *non bis in idem* principle. This principle is enshrined in Article 4 of Protocol No. 7 to the European Convention for the Protection of Human Rights and Fundamental Freedoms and also in Article 50 of the Charter of Fundamental Rights of the European Union; it is therefore regarded as a fundamental principle of Union law.[56] In its purest form, it acts as an absolute defence against new proceedings

53 See H. Achenbach, op. cit. (*supra* note 52), sec. 81 GWB para. 323; H. Achenbach & C. Wegner, 'Probleme der „reinen Ahndungsgeldbuße" im Kartellrecht (§ 81 Abs. 5 GWB)', *Zeitschrift für Wettbewerbsrecht* 2006, 49 *et seq.*; and J. Kühnen, 'Mehrerlös und Vorteilsabschöpfung nach der 7. GWB-Novelle', *Wirtschaft und Wettbewerb* 2010, 16, p. 28.

54 See R. Bechtold, *GWB* (C.H. Beck, 7th ed. 2013), sec. 81, para. 44.

55 The average fine per company increased from slightly below €6 million in the period between 2002 and 2005 to slightly over €12 million between 2006 and 2009. In total, the Federal Cartel Office issued fines amounting to €1.046 billion between 2006 and 2009, up from €943.4 million in the period from 2002 through 2005. These numbers should be treated with caution as not all decisions in the period from 2006 through 2009 were made under the new turnover-related calculation principles.

56 See ECJ, Joined Cases 18/65 and 35/65, *Gutmann v. Commission of the EAEC* [1966] ECR 103, 119, and Joined Cases C-238/99 P, C-244/99 P, C-245/99 P, C-247/99 P,

brought against the same undertaking on the same set of facts (in respect of which it has already been penalized or declared not liable by a previous unappealable decision) in order to protect one and the same legal interest.[57] *Non bis in idem* can, however, also take the form of a 'set-off mechanism' which requires one competition authority to take account of the penalty already imposed by another – although the ECJ has so far preferred to speak of 'a general requirement of natural justice'[58], apparently to hold this somewhat diluted version of *non bis in idem* apart from the more stringent procedural defence which prevents any new trial.

Since the ECJ did not limit the scope of application of *non bis in idem* – or the aforementioned 'general requirement of natural justice' – to criminal or administrative punishments, but spoke more broadly of any kind of sanction ('already been penalized', 'a été sanctionnée', 'mit einer Sanktion belegt', 'ha sido sancionada'), many authors are convinced that these principles would also require a reconciliation of the fine imposed on an undertaking and a damage award against it if and to the extent the latter was punitive in nature.[59] The case law of the European courts does not contradict this proposition, and may even be interpreted as providing some superficial and indirect support. In three major cases in which the payment of treble damages under US law were put forward under the heading of *non bis in idem* (*Graphite Electrodes*, *Vitamins*, *Citric Acid*), the CFI rejected the argument, but did so on the basis that the geographical scope of the judgments in the US and the Commission's proceedings were different and that the objective of deterrence pursued by the Commission related to the conduct of undertakings within the Community or the EEA.[60]

Further support for this proposition can be found in the famous *Devenish* ruling by the English High Court, which resulted from the *Vitamins* cartel. In this case, Lewison J came to the conclusion that the Community principle of *non bis in idem* would preclude the award of exemplary damages if the defendants had already been fined (or if fines had been imposed and then reduced or commuted) by the European Commission.[61] Following this decision, it has become the prevailing

C-250/99 P to C-252/99 P and C-254/99 P, *Limburgse Vinyl Maatschappij and Others v. Commission* [2002] ECR I-8375, para. 59.

57 See ECJ, *Limburgse Vinyl Maatschappij* (*supra* note 56), para. 59.

58 Case 14-68, *Walt Wilhelm* [1969] ECR I-1, para. 11.

59 See G. Dannecker & J. Biermann in U. Immenga & E.-J. Mestmäcker (eds.), *EG-Kartellrecht* (C.H. Beck, 4th ed. 2007), Vorbem. zu Art. 23 VO 1/2003, para. 249; H. Dreier, *Kompensation und Prävention* (2002), p. 511 *et seq.*; M.-P. Weller, 'Die Anrechnung pönaler Schadensersatzleistungen gemäß § 33 GWB auf Kartellgeldbußen', *Zeitschrift für Wettbewerbsrecht* 2008, 173, p. 182 *et seq.*

60 Joined Cases T-236/01, T-239/01, T-244/01 to T-246/01, T-251/01 and T-252/01, *Tokai Carbon Co. Ltd v. Commission* [2004] ECR II-1181, para. 348; Case T-15/02, *BASF AG v. Commission* [2006] ECR II-497, paras. 192 and 269; Case T-59/02, *Archer Daniels Midland Co. v. Commission* [2006] ECR II-3627, paras. 70–72.

61 *Devenish Nutrition Ltd & Ors v. Sanofi-Aventis SA (France) & Ors* [2007] EWHC 2394 (Ch), paras. 40–55.

opinion in Britain that exemplary damages would not be available in follow-on cases.[62]

Whether or not reconciliation on the basis of *non bis in idem* could also play a role in cartel damage claims under German law, is a difficult question. Although there are no openly 'punitive' elements in German tort law, the applicable rules on competition law damage claims still offer several features that may be seen in a punitive light:

Passing-on defence: Until recently, the treatment of the passing-on defence was certainly one of the prime examples for such 'hidden' punitive elements in German cartel damage law. Despite the high incidence of pass-on in many markets, several judgments from Higher Regional Courts[63] and the prevailing opinion among legal scholars[64] rejected this defence on the basis that it would undermine the effective enforcement of competition law and lead to an unjustified discharge from liability on the part of the defendant. Further support for this proposition could arguably be drawn from sec. 33(3) 2nd sentence GWB, which was introduced in 2005 and expressly states that 'the occurrence of damage is not excluded on account of the fact that the respective goods or services have been resold'. Yet the Federal Court of Justice, in a somewhat unexpected move, overturned this case law in 2011 and explicitly allowed the passing-on argument both as a 'shield' and as a 'sword'.[65] Although most observers expect the standard of proof for a successful passing-on defence to remain fairly high – which means that the defence will most likely only succeed in clear-cut cases – the general admissibility of the defence has arguably taken the 'punitive edge' out of the issue. Future cases will now view the treatment of pass-on as a simple evidentiary issue and as part of the damage estimation under sec. 287 ZPO, which provides the judge with a broad discretion in appraising the relevant facts.

Calculation of damages on the basis of the defendant's (entire) profits: Another provision that was introduced in 2005 with the intention of fostering private damage claims can be found in sec. 33(3) 3rd sentence GWB, which allows the judge

---

62 Note, however, that the Competition Appeal Tribunal has recently decided not to strike out a claim for exemplary damages in a case that did not involve a previous decision by the European Commission (see *Albion Water Ltd v. DŴR Cymru Cyfyngedig* [2010] CAT 30).

63 See Higher Regional Court of Berlin, Decision of 1 October 2009 – Case 2 U 10/03 Kart.; Higher Regional Court of Karlsruhe, Decision of 11 June 2010 – Case 6 U 118/05 (Kart.); Higher Regional Court of Düsseldorf, Decision of 16 May 2007 – Case VI-2 U (Kart) 10/05.

64 See, e.g., V. Emmerich in U. Immenga & E.-J. Mestmäcker (eds.) *GWB* (C.H. Beck, 4th ed. 2007), ‚sec. 33 para. 53 *et seq.*; J. Topel in G. Wiedemann (ed.), *Handbuch Kartellrecht* (C.H. Beck, 2nd ed. 2008), Chapter 50 para. 133 *et seq.*

65 Federal Court of Justice, Judgment of 28 June 2011 – Case KZR 75/10, *ORWI, Entscheidungssammlung des Bundesgerichtshofs in Zivilsachen (BGHZ)* 190, 145.

to take account of the profits derived from the infringement when estimating damage. This might be seen as containing punitive elements in two different regards:

- First, the provision is interpreted by some as allowing the claimant to disgorge a *pro rata* share of the defendant's profits even if it exceeds his losses. While this position bears some resemblance to cases of infringements of intellectual property rights (where it is settled case law to allow a claimant to calculate his claim on the basis of the profits derived by the infringer), this does not mean that what is compensatory in one situation (IP rights) can also be considered compensatory in another (competition law infringements). Since IP rights are, by definition, property rights, the infringer's profits can be interpreted as 'belonging' to the claimant; and this interpretation provides his claim with firm *compensatory* underpinnings. The same is *not* true for competition law infringements,[66] which means that a disgorgement of profits that goes beyond the claimant's losses would almost automatically acquire a certain punitive element.

- The second potentially 'punitive' aspect of sec. 33(3) 3rd sentence GWB concerns the way the defendant's profits may be calculated. According to a widely held opinion amongst legal scholars[67] – which finds explicit support in the legislative materials[68] – fixed and overhead costs are not deductible when considering the defendant's profit. Again, this principle was derived from IP infringement cases, where it seems perfectly compatible with compensatory damages to consider the infringer's entire gross margin, as otherwise the infringer would keep part of the margin that he extracted from the claimant's IP right to cover his own fixed and

66 In this context, it is worth noting that in cases concerning unfair competition, claimants can calculate their damage on the basis of the defendant's profit only if the infringement affected a proprietary right. See H. Köhler in H. Köhler & J. Bornkamm (eds.), *UWG* (C.H. Beck, 30th ed. 2012), sec. 9, para. 1.36b.

67 See J. Bornkamm in H. J. Bunte (ed.), *Kommentar zum Deutschen und Europäischen Kartellrecht, Vol. 1: Deutsches Kartellrecht* (Heymanns/Luchterhand, 11th ed., 2010), sec. 33, para. 133; R. Bechtold, op. cit. (*supra* note 54), sec. 33, para. 34; E. Rehbinder, in U. Loewenheim, K.M. Meessen & A. Riesenkampff (eds.), *Kartellrecht*, (C.H. Beck, 2nd ed. 2009), sec. 33, para. 38; T. Lübbig in G. Hirsch, F. Montag & F.J. Säcker (eds.), *Münchener Kommentar zum Europäischen und Deutschen Wettbewerbsrecht, Vol. 2: GWB*, (C.H. Beck 2007), sec. 33, para. 111; M. Schütt, 'Individualrechtsschutz nach der 7. GWB-Novelle', *Wirtschaft und Wettbewerb* 2004, 1124, p. 1130; G. Meeßen, op. cit. (*supra* note 40), p. 424 *et seq.*; H.P. Logemann, *Der kartellrechtliche Schadensersatz* (Duncker & Humblot 2009), p. 466 *et seq.*; and C. Alexander, *Schadensersatz und Abschöpfung im Lauterkeits- und Kartellrecht* (Mohr Siebeck 2010), p. 401. F.-W. Bulst, *Schadensersatzansprüche der Marktgegenseite im Kartellrecht* (C.H. Bec, 2006), p. 140) and W. Tilmann, in R.M. Hilty, J. Drexl & W. Nordemann (eds.), *Festschrift für Loewenheim*, (C.H. Beck 2009), 571, p. 574) disagree, arguing that sec. 33(3) 3rd sentence GWB can cover only the difference between the actual (cartelized) price and the but-for price.

68 BT-Drucksache 15/3640, p. 54.

> overhead costs. Since this line of thinking is yet again rooted in the proprietary aspect of IP rights and has no equivalent in competition law, it could lead to significant overcompensation in the latter context. For example, in a typical price-fixing case, the aforementioned interpretation of sec. 33(3) 3rd sentence GWB would seem to require the cartel offender to hand over not only the illicit gain (the difference between the cartelized price and the competitive but-for price) but also any mark-up on pure variable costs, thereby putting the customer in a position as if he had been able to buy at prices *below average total costs* for the entire duration of the infringement. In industries with high fixed and overhead costs (e.g. pharmaceuticals, computer software), this would have major consequences on the amount recoverable by claimants and would obviously endow the claims with a significant 'punitive' dimension.

In sum, it would seem that, in cases involving damage claims under German law, reconciliation on the basis of *non bis in idem* or the 'general principle of natural justice' might have *some* scope of application,[69] but it will certainly not lead to the kind of general re-calibration of fines and damages advocated by economic theory. Also, given that German tort law does not contain an express dedication to punitive elements it will certainly be harder for defendants to invoke *non bis in idem* than it is in the case of exemplary damages under English law.

Moreover, one may wonder if *non bis in idem* could ever lead to the conclusion that the level of *fines* needs to be reduced, given that public enforcement usually precedes private claims and that *non bis in idem* would normally require the second proceeding to take account of the first. Unlike German law, European law does not provide a legal basis for reimbursement claims, although Weller[70] has argued that the general European claim for repayment of fines under Article 266 TFEU (ex-Article 233 EC)[71] should apply *mutatis mutandis*. To that effect, he proposed combining the *Walt Wilhelm* decision and the statement in *Manfredi*, according to which the national jurisdictions should award punitive damages for breaches of EU competition law if such damages may be awarded pursuant to similar actions founded on domestic law,[72] into an implicit acknowledgement that the award of damages in national courts, to the extent it contains punitive elements, takes precedence over the collection of EU fines. However, this proposition, while certainly original, may be seen as too much of a doctrinal sleight of hand. *Non bis in idem* was apparently not raised as an argument in the *Manfredi* case, and it dealt with a decision by the Italian competition authority (AGCM) that was based ex-

69 For a more extensive discussion of other potentially 'punitive' elements in the German rules on competition law damage claims, see M.-P. Weller, *Zeitschrift für Wettbewerbsrecht* 2008, 170–193.

70 Op. cit. (*supra* note 69).

71 See Case T-48/00, *Corus UK Ltd. v. Commission* [2004] ECR II-2325, para. 222 *et seq.*

72 Joined Cases C-295/04 to C-298/04, *Manfredi* [2006] ECR I-6619, para. 92.

clusively on Italian competition law.[73] Besides, the ECJ explicitly added that Community law does not prevent national courts from taking steps to ensure that the protection of the rights guaranteed by Community law does not entail the unjust enrichment of those who enjoy them.[74] Against this background, a fair reading of *Manfredi* would probably come to the conclusion that the decision does not provide any indication regarding a possible reconciliation of fines and punitive damages on the basis *non bis in idem*.

3.2.4 The Principle of Proportionality

From the principles of *non bis in idem* and the 'general requirement of natural justice' cited in Walt Wilhelm, it is only one step further to the overarching principle of proportionality. Although this principle is notoriously vague and leaves ample room for interpretation, it seems like the most natural place to consider reconciliation between fines and damages. Indeed, the European courts have consistently held on numerous occasions that any fine imposed on an undertaking under European law must 'at least' be proportionate in relation to the factors that are capable of entering into the assessment of the gravity of the infringement.[75] Since the achievement of a sufficient and appropriate amount of deterrence is one of the preeminent factors in this assessment, it seems not far-fetched to postulate that the principle of proportionality would require competition authorities to take account of the developments in private enforcement when exercising their discretion about the appropriate amount of public enforcement through fines. In the German legal tradition, additional support may also be found in the prohibition of a 'double burden' (*Verbot der Doppelbelastung*)[76] that underlies the aforementioned sec. 34(2) GWB and 99(2) OWiG (as well as sec. 73(1) 2nd sentence StGB).

Obviously, there are important counter-arguments, most notably the 'different purpose argument', i.e. the proposition that private enforcement is concerned with compensation whereas public enforcement is concerned with punishment. This argument has occasionally been used by the European Commission,[77] and is also evident, in slightly different form, in the prevalent legal distinction between sentences that include an explicitly quantified profit disgorgement and 'purely punitive' sentences. Moreover, income and corporate tax laws in Germany and in some oth-

73 See decision No 8546 (I377) of 28 July 2000 (Bolletino 30/2000 of 14 August 2000).

74 ECJ, *Manfredi* (cited *supra* note 72), para. 94.

75 Joined Cases T-202/98, T-204/98 and T-207/98, *Tate & Lyle and Others v. Commission* [2001] ECR II-2035, para. 106; Case T-229/94, *Deutsche Bahn v. Commission* [1997] ECR II-1689, para. 127.

76 See E. Rehbinder, op. cit. (*supra* note 67), sec. 34 para. 8; W. Joecks in W. Joecks & K. Miebach (eds.), *Münchener Kommentar zum StGB* (C.H. Beck, 2nd ed. 2012), sec. 73 para. 54.

77 See Commission, Case COMP/E-1/36.490 – *Graphite electrodes*, para. 183: 'Finally, the possibility that undertakings may have been required to pay damages in civil actions is of no relevance. Payments of damages in civil law actions which have the objective of compensating for the harm caused by cartels to individual companies or consumers cannot be compared with public law sanctions for illegal behaviour.'

er Member States consider a fine that is 'purely punitive' non-deductible, whereas a fine that includes a profit disgorgement would be treated as a tax-deductible operating expense (on a *pro rata* basis). Against this background, one may argue that even high levels of private enforcement cannot call into question the proportionality of a fine that is 'purely punitive' because such a fine serves an entirely different purpose.

The argument certainly has some intuitive appeal, but is, in our view, nonetheless debatable. Most modern legal theories of punishment would agree that punishment is not a legitimate purpose *per se*,[78] but only insofar as it is necessary and appropriate to induce future lawful behaviour (both in the subject receiving the punishment and in other potential offenders). This is especially true in the context of corporate fines, which are borne by the economic owners of the company (usually the shareholders), even though they are seldom directly responsible in a meaningful sense. Accordingly, the severity of the penalty (even a 'purely punitive' one) that can be justified under the principle of proportionality would seem to decrease if and to the extent other areas of law already provide for a certain amount of deterrence.[79]

This is all the more so when the calculation of the fine is specifically tuned to ensure that, at least *on average*, it exceeds the illicit gains and provides an additional deterrent surcharge to account for the chance of escaping detection.[80] Since the calculation of the fine on the basis of the affected turnover has been expressly endorsed by the European courts as using 'an objective criterion which gives a proper measure of the harm which the offending conduct represents for normal

---

78 Kantian philosophy famously disagreed by taking a retributive approach according to which even the last murderer in an island society that is about to disband and leave the island should be punished. See *Metaphysik der Sitten (Metaphysics of Morals)*, A 199; B 229.

79 Admittedly, our argument has its limitations. In the German legal literature, many authors view criminal and administrative sentences as being concerned with the 'damage to the validity of the norm' (*Normgeltungsschaden*) that was caused by the offence (see, e.g., G. Freund & E.G. Carrera, 'Strafrechtliche Wiedergutmachung und ihr Verhältnis zum zivilrechtlichen Schadensersatz', *Zeitschrift für die gesamte Strafrechtswissenschaft* 2006, p. 76 *et seq.*). Such 'damage to the norm' does not necessarily decrease if private enforcement becomes more prevalent and could therefore provide a justification for holding the level of fines constant. In our view, however, this is at least partially due to the elusiveness of the concept. For example, in a society with extremely low levels of unlawful behaviour, one might argue that the 'damage to the norm' caused by the occasional offence is extremely high (and *vice versa*: a society with high levels of crime would experience little 'damage to the norm' from an additional offence). This would mean that a peaceful society would be *forced* to employ draconian punishments to account for this immense 'damage to the norm' – a conclusion that runs counter to most conventional theories of punishment and is certainly debatable. So far, German case law has not picked up on the concept.

80 See, e.g., A. Mundt, 'Die Bußgeldleitlinien des Bundeskartellamtes', *Wirtschaft und Wettbewerb* 2007, 458, p. 461.

competition',[81] it seems somewhat simplistic and perfunctory to deny any intrinsic relationship between fines and damages. Besides, the 'different purpose argument' is conspicuously at odds with the ECJ's decisions in *Courage* and *Manfredi*, where the Court explicitly considered private damage claims as a means of effective enforcement of European competition law.

Nonetheless, one cannot fail to notice that proportionality is a highly abstract principle and usually applied with great caution by European courts and courts in Germany alike.[82] It is most compelling when competition authorities fail to consider recognized attenuating factors, but loses significant force when one attempts to use it as a tool for the adjustment of the general level of fines. Therefore, the proposition that competition authorities should consider the level of private enforcement from the perspective of proportionality when they set the level of fines certainly lies on the boundary between what can still be considered a legal rule and what is merely a *policy recommendation*. Moreover, as we said earlier, the discussion about a broad-scale adjustment of the level of fines may still be somewhat premature given that the development of a private litigation culture is still in the early stages and that the economic dispute over the appropriate levels of deterrence is still in full swing. One would certainly need significantly higher levels of activism from private litigants before cartel offenders can expect to raise concerns of proportionality as a *legal* argument with any prospect of success.

3.2.5 Reduction of the Amount of Damages

So far, our discussion has been limited to mechanisms that require an adjustment of the level of fines. However, as we have seen in the context of *non bis in idem*, one may also contemplate a reconciliation that works in the other direction. Indeed, the situation in the UK seems to be developing in precisely this direction. Whereas Devenish[83] effectively ruled out exemplary damages in EU follow-on cases, the CAT's decision in Albion[84] seems to suggest that in other cartel damage cases (not involving a prior Commission decision) exemplary damages could still be available.

For cases involving damage claims under German law, as we have seen above, the scope for such a reduction would be rather limited. Although there are some rules that may be interpreted as having a punitive side, this is more the result of inconsiderate 'legal transplants' from the case law on IP infringements than an

81 Case T-151/94, *British Steel v. Commission* [1999] ECR II-629, para. 643; Case T-220/00, *Cheil Jedang* v. *Commission* [2003] ECR II-2473, para. 91; Case T-224/00, *Archer Daniels Midland and Archer Daniels Midland Ingredients* v. *Commission* [2003] ECR II-2597, para. 196.

82 The German Constitutional Court has drawn the line where the severity of the sentence would seem 'plainly unreasonable'. See BVerfG, Case 2 BvM 2/86, *Neue Juristische Wochenschrift* 1987, p. 2156 ('Eine Strafandrohung oder Verurteilung darf nach Art und Maß dem unter Strafe stehenden Verhalten nicht schlechthin unangemessen sein.')

83 See *supra* note 61.

84 See *supra* note 62.

outspoken commitment to punitive components in cartel damage claims. Of course, this does not change the fact that sec. 33(3) GWB would significantly exceed pure compensation if it were to be interpreted in such a way that, for example, fixed and overhead costs are not recognized in the assessment of the defendant's illicit profits. Rather, it seems that these deviations from pure compensatory damages are better addressed by a general rethinking as to whether they are really compatible with established principles of German tort law, and not by a (limited) correction through *non bis in idem*.

As regards an even further reduction of the recoverable amount of damages (i.e., a reduction that goes beyond the punitive element), it suffices to say that this would come into direct conflict with the constitutional right to property (Article 14 of the Basic Law). Although such a reduction would certainly not amount to an 'expropriation' in the technical sense but merely to a regulation of 'contents and limits' (*Inhalt und Schranken*) of a property right, it would still require a public welfare justification that pays due regard to the constitutional idea of private property and to the principle of proportionality – and such justification is evidently missing. After all, the avoidance of a double burden that results primarily from the imposition of a fine by a government agency can hardly justify a reduction in the amount of damages afforded to the victim of the infringement.

3.2.6 Evaluation

Summing up, one can say that reconciliation between fines and damages is a complicated and multi-faceted issue – and that the current state of affairs may seem unsatisfactory, at least from an economic standpoint. Recognition of damage payments as an attenuating factor in the calculation of the fine has an obviously narrow scope of application, because of time constraints and because it seems to require voluntary payments. The same holds true for the *non bis in idem* principle. One may also question the wisdom of having a reconciliation mechanism that only accounts for 'punitive' elements in damage awards, when in fact the entire financial burden from private damage claims contributes to the overall level of deterrence.

As for sec. 34(2) GWB and 99(2) OWiG, these provisions have been rendered practically meaningless due to the decision practice of the FCO to issue only fines that are 'purely punitive'. It is certainly noteworthy that, at the precise moment when private damage claims became a reality, the existing statutory provisions that would allow broad-scale reconciliation in the form of a reimbursement claim were bereft of their scope of application. Still, one may take some comfort in the fact that, from a practical angle, a claim for reimbursement has its drawbacks. In particular, one should not underestimate the ramifications on the incentive structure of the parties and the practical difficulties arising from a reimbursement scheme. The fundamental problem is that, between claimant and defendant, any form of reimbursement for damage payments would provide what economists sometimes call a 'free lunch'. Since the reimbursement effectively provides an additional source for settlement compensations that is cost-free for claimants and defendants alike, both may have a shared incentive to *maximize* the amount of the refund.[85] Thus, it is not difficult to image negotiations where the cartel offender would willingly agree to a fairly high amount of damages in exchange for the implicit (or even explicit[86]) promise of favourable terms in future dealings (e.g. the conclusion of a new long-term delivery contract). In other words, under a legal regime that grants reimbursement claims, settlement arrangements would be an efficient tool for the parties to siphon off parts of the fine and redistribute the proceeds amongst them.[87]

Obviously, the severity of this manipulation problem is inversely correlated with the general level of private enforcement. If the cartel-offender expects to be confronted with claims from the majority of his customers (or at least a significant share), this would certainly reduce his incentives to agree to overly generous settlement payments as the aggregate financial burden from these settlements may well exceed the amount eligible for reimbursement.

In this context, it is worth pointing out that sec. 99(2) OWiG – one of the two explicit statutory bases for reimbursement claims under German law – actually limits the reimbursement to cases in which the offender has been ordered to pay damages by an unappealable court judgment (whereas sec. 34(2) GWB does not). This is not a satisfactory solution, however; it simply shifts the problem elsewhere and may arguably exacerbate it. It is obvious that this rule, taken at face value, would provide a strong disincentive for defendants to ever agree to settlement talks. And since court judgments in private damage litigation are an extremely inefficient and time-consuming way of dispute resolution, such a rule has the potential to severely hamper the effectiveness of private enforcement.[88] Although some authors have proposed the consideration of compensation payments made on the

---

85 One may object that this problem could be avoided by limiting the reimbursement to a *pro rata* share of the disgorged illicit profits so that, for example, damage payments to a customer that accounts for 5% of the entire business of the offender can only lead to a maximum reimbursement of 5% of the entire disgorgement. This interpretation, however, does not seem possible on the basis of the clear wording of both sec. 34(2) GWB and sec. 99(2) OWiG (according to which the entire amount of a verified payment would count). More importantly still, this solution breaks down in cases with several cartel members because joint and several liabilities arguably imply that any cartel member would be liable for any damage that accrued to the customers of any of his co-conspirators.

86 Explicit promises might be made in another agreement concluded on the same day.

87 In light of the foregoing, it seems clear that it would be even harder to limit the reimbursement to those elements of a damage claim that are punitive in nature, as Weller proposed (*Zeitschrift für Wettbewerbsrecht* 2008, 170, p. 188 *et seq.*). While it might be possible to distinguish and quantify those elements in the rare case where damages are being awarded through a court judgment, it would be next to impossible for a competition authority to make such a distinction – and for the defendant to prove it – in a reliable way on the basis of a settlement.

88 Even in the US, most cases are resolved through settlements and very few go beyond the pre-trial discovery stage. See J.M. Connor, 'Forensic Economics: An Introduction With Special Emphasis on Price Fixing', 4 *Journal of Competition Law & Economics* (2008), p. 31 *et seq.*, who estimates the settlement rate in treble damage cases at roughly 90%.

basis of a court settlement (*gerichtlicher Vergleich*) to be equally eligible for reimbursement under sec. 99(2) OWiG,[89] this does not really improve matters, because (a) it would once again provide opportunities for manipulation[90] and (b) court settlements are public and therefore of limited value in most competition lawsuits.[91]

Nonetheless, despite all practical difficulties that may arise, the overall concept embodied by sec. 34(2) GWB and 99(2) OWiG does have some redeeming virtues, particularly compared with a general downward adjustment of the level of fines. Most importantly, it would avoid the kind of windfall profits that are bound to accrue when an individual offender escapes civil liability (such as when nobody comes forward to assert claims). Although from an economic perspective such windfall profits are not necessarily a cause for concern – it is the *expected* burden through fines and damages that provides the required deterrence – they certainly run counter to common notions of justice. Finally, the reimbursement solution would provide a much higher degree of transparency.

4 Conclusion

In this article, we presented an overview of the various strains of discussion regarding the interaction of liability in fines and liability in damages, both from an economic and from a legal point of view. Although the debate is in many respects still in its infancy, a number of points are worth noting:

1. While the economic theory of optimal deterrence is not yet able to provide more than rough and imperfect clues about the socially optimal level of deterrence, economic logic nonetheless suggests that reconciliation between public and private enforcement is important, as both contribute to the aggregate deterrent effect of competition law.
2. This is especially apparent in leniency cases, as private enforcement is particularly susceptible to being abused by cartel participants as a 'commitment mechanism' that eliminates or at least reduces the cartel-destabilizing incentives set by leniency programmes.

---

89 See e.g. W. Mitsch in L. Senge (ed.), *Karlsruher Kommentar zum OWiG* (C.H. Beck, 3rd ed. 2006), sec. 99 para. 8; H. Seitz in: Göhler (ed.), *Ordnungswidrigkeitengesetz* (C.H. Beck, 16th ed. 2012), sec. 99 n. 5.

90 While court settlements need to be publicly *recorded* – either in the trial transcript under sec. 794(1) No. 1 of the German Civil Procedure Code ('**ZPO**') or through a court decision (*Beschluss*) under sec. 278(6) ZPO – the entire negotiations can take place outside of the court, allowing the parties to present only the end result of their negotiations to the court for recording. This means that the court will not be in a position to effectively prevent a joint maximization of the amount eligible for reimbursement under sec. 99(2) OWiG.

91 Since most competition lawsuits involve several defendants, the claimant has a strong interest in being able to settle individually and on confidential terms.

3. The need for reconciliation between fines and damages goes beyond leniency cases, however. Given that over-deterrence is as much a concern as under-deterrence, rational policy-making would imply that a substantial increase in private enforcement should be reflected in a reduction of the level of fines unless new evidence suggests that previous *aggregate* levels of deterrence were insufficient.
4. Measured against these standards, the current legal status at the European level and in Germany may seem unsatisfactory, both with regard to leniency cases, where possible solutions have not progressed beyond the stage of policy discussions, and with regard to the general reconciliation of the level of fines and damages, where existing legal mechanisms are rudimentary at best:

    a) At the European level, the interaction between fines and damage has so far mostly been viewed through the lens of *non bis in idem*, which is questionable as it confines the issue to punitive damages when in fact the entire amount of private damage claims contributes to the aggregate level of deterrence. In some cases, previous damage payments were also considered to be attenuating factors, but obviously this has a limited scope of application.
    b) In Germany, sec. 34(2) GWB and 99(2) OWiG contain what could, in theory, be a universal reconciliation mechanism in the form of reimbursement claims. But the current practice of the FCO to issue only fines that are 'purely punitive' has rendered these claims practically meaningless. This is a legally questionable development, at least insofar as the FCO's decisions do not give a proper account as to how sec. 81(5) 2nd sentence GWB should be interpreted.
    c) It is also possible to frame the economic argument for broad-scale reconciliation in terms of proportionality considerations. Given that proportionality is a highly abstract concept and applied with some caution by the courts, such an argument nevertheless lies on the boundary between what can still be considered a legal rule and what is merely a policy recommendation.

Disgorgement and Private Enforcement as Mitigating Circumstances for the Determination of Fines in Antitrust Law

Gerhard Dannecker and Ursula Kern

1 Recent Developments

The European Commission currently pursues a high-fine policy in the area of antitrust law.[1] This is possible due to enhanced levels of sanctioning, with fines of up to 10% of turnover of the entire corporate group now permissible. The European Commission has attempted to strengthen private enforcement by encouraging consumers and business rivals to claim damages,[2] and it drafted a whitepaper[3] to this effect on a variety of topics, from individual damage claims[4] to the extension of passing-on damages.[5] But high fines together with strict private enforcement can create a disproportionately high burden for affected companies and ultimately violate Art. 49 para. 3 of the EU's Charter of Fundamental Rights. Accordingly, it is

---

1 For a critical view of EU policy and fine classification, see Schwarze J., 'Europäische Kartellbußgelder im Lichte übergeordneter Vertrags- und Verfassungsgrundsätze', *Zeitschrift Europarecht* 2009, 171–199, p. 184, 187.

2 Case C-295/04 to C-298/04, *Vincenzo Manfredi et. al v. Lloyd Adriatico Assicurazioni SpA et al* [2006] ECR I-6619, para. 61; White Paper on Damages Actions for the Breach of the EC Antitrust Rules, COM (2008) 165, p. 2 *et seq.* Drexl J., Gallego B., Enchelmaier S., Mackenrodt O. and Podszun R., 'Comments of the Max Planck Institute for Intellectual Property, Competition and Tax Law on the White Paper by the Directorate-general for Competition of April 2008 on Damages Actions for Breach of the EC Antitrust Rules', *International Review of Intellectual Property and Competition Law* (2008), 799–811, p. 800.

3 See the Commission's White Paper on Damages Actions for the Breach of the EC Antitrust Rules, COM (2008), p. 165

4 For a critical view of cooperation between European courts and competition authorities and indirect purchasers claims, see Cengiz F., 'Antitrust Damages Actions: Lessons From American Indirect Purchasers Litigation', *International and Comparative Law Quarterly* 2010, 39–63, p. 58 *et seq.*

5 For more, see Kießling E., 'Neues zur Schadensabwälzung', *Gewerblicher Rechtsschutz und Urheberrecht* 2009, 733–739, p. 734 *et seq.*

important to rethink the relationship between fines, disgorgement and private enforcement, especially because the Commission's enthusiasm for private proceedings has yet to receive careful analysis.[6]

The situation has been exacerbated by Regulation 1/2003, which decentralizes prosecution and punishment, delegating responsibility to the Member States to prosecute and punish violations to Art. 101, 102 TFEU. Because the sanctioning procedure is now left for each Member State to decide, provisions vary widely, especially those concerning non-fine-related punishments such as disgorgement, the disqualification of directors and managers, and private enforcement proceedings. The use of disgorgement – the confiscation of illegal profits – is widespread in many countries that have an Anglo-American tradition but requires that specific individual benefits be identified. In New Zealand, for example, the profit minus compensation payments remains with the company, resulting in the perception that enforcement brings with it minimal deterrence,[7] which increases the likelihood of a new cartel infringement.[8]

The Commission has seen no need to harmonize antitrust sanctions. Yet creating a common – genuinely European[9] – approach is needed to ensure just and proportionate sanctions, all the more so given the enormous consequences of cartel offences for society. The following analysis examines the prerequisites required for such sanctioning and proposes a balanced solution. We first address the definition and elements of profit in the context of levies. Then we consider possible sanctions in antitrust crimes, including the relationship between the current legal situation in Germany and the EU. Finally, we assess these models with regard to purpose and efficiency.

---

6 See the Ashurst study Conditions of Claims for Damages of Infringement of EC Competition Rules, Comparative Report (31 August 2004), p.1.

7 New Zealand is in the process of introducing criminal sanctions for hard-core cartel behaviour (report due 14/5/2013). See New Zealand Ministry of Economic development, http://www.med.govt.nz/business/competition-policy/cartel-criminalisation/draft-regulatory-impact-statement-cartel-criminalisation.pdf/view and New Zealand Parliament http://www.parliament.nz/en-NZ/PB/Legislation/Bills/3/a/d/00DBHOH_BILL11153_1-Commerce-Cartels-and-Other-Matters-Amendment-Bill.htm (last accessed 29/10/2013). The legislation has received much criticism. See, for instance, Bellgully http://www.bellgully.com/resources/resource.02514.asp; BusinessNZ http://www.med.govt.nz/business/competition-policy/pdf-docs-library/business-nz-exposure-draft-bill.pdf; and business round table http://www.med.govt.nz/business/competition-policy/pdf-docs-library/nzbr-submission-on-exposure-draft-bill.pdf (last accessed 29/10/2013).

8 See Scholz U. and Haus F., 'Geldbußen im EG-Kartellrecht und Einkommensteuerrecht', *Europäische Zeitschrift für Wirtschaftsrecht* 2002, 682–688, p. 684.

9 See White paper (*supra* note 2), p. 3.

2 Profit and Sanctioning

Because levies must stand in relation to company profit, it is important to define profit in the context of sanctioning and determine the elements involved.

2.1 Gross Principle

To begin with, profit consists of all earnings of a company arising from specific transactions.[10] This 'gross principle' (or pre-tax principle) includes primary/direct financial benefits as well as other aspects that affect earnings such as growing market share and weakened business rivals. These indirect factors can affect the number of players in a specific market and shape future trade and development, especially when the company or group is listed on the stock market.

2.2 Net Principle

After determining the pre-tax profit it is necessary to subtract all relevant expenditures, leading to the net profit. In this calculation only the profit is considered that was actually made. There are two main problems arising from net-profit calculation. The first has to do with determining which expenditures are appropriate; the second with how to assess expenditures.

2.2.1 In General

Generally speaking, all expenditures should be deducted, provided they are related to the profit of the specific transaction in question. This narrowing is essential as it is otherwise possible to further reduce profits – and levies – when other projects are cross-calculated. Costs per piece, excluding the general production costs like lightning, water and employment, provide a good indication.

2.2.2 Compensation and Profit

The crucial question is how to deal with private enforcement proceedings and the resulting compensation payments when it comes to disgorgement. Basically there are two options. First, compensation could be excluded from the calculation of the profit. The compensation proceedings would then be seen as fully independent from the calculation for disgorgement. But this would overlook the fact that compensation payments are closely related to the profit in question because they derive from the same actions. While damage claims are mainly based on comparing

---

10 On the gross principle in German forfeiture, see Lackner K. and Kühl K., Commentary on the German Criminal Code (StGB)(C.H. Beck, 27th ed. 2011), Art. 73, para. 4 *et seq.*

prices before and after the creation of an alleged cartel,[11] the profit depends on the amount of compensation paid on account of infringement proceedings. The resulting minimization of profit requires that compensation payments are subtracted as related expenditures.

2.2.3 Estimation

It is not always possible to assess the full profit exactly, and in some cases it is permissible to estimate. Judges and governmental authorities have considerable discretion in assessing profit, but a basic framework is necessary to secure a consistent application throughout the Member States.[12] Estimations need to be transparent and as accurate as possible for taxation purposes. At the same time, the formulas for estimation and calculation should not be disclosed publicly to prevent artificial stimulation of the compensation proceedings.

2.2.4 Problem Relating to the Succession of Private and Public Proceedings

Though it is possible to estimate the profit as a whole, assessing the amount of compensation payments is more complicated. While it is easy to fix the amount of compensation payments after the private enforcement proceedings are finished it is not possible to estimate them beforehand. This is particularly problematic because the amount of the disgorgement needs to be reported for the purposes of taxes and certainty. In this context it is also necessary to factor in compensation for the sake of justice and fairness.

One possible solution is the introduction of a system similar to the legal institution of forfeiture in German law.[13] If no fine or a too low fine is imposed so that profit exceeds the fine, the gains can be declared as forfeited (Art. 29a Administrative Offences Act [OWiG]; Art. 34 Restriction of Competition Act [GWB]). But compensation claims of consumers and business rivals are prioritised and diminish the amount of forfeiture. This principle can be transferred to EC law. In antitrust cases it is necessary to modify this principle, however. The profit should be reduced only if the compensation has already been paid. If the profit is being forfeited earlier than the imposition of compensation, the company has to be repaid

---

[11] For more on empirical models quantifying damages, see Friederiszick H. and Röller L.-H., 'Quantification of Harm in Damages Actions for Antitrust Infringements: Insights from German Cartel Cases', *Journal of Competition Law and Economics* (2010), 595–618, p. 604 *et seq.*

[12] See Kießling E. (*supra* note 5), p. 737.

[13] In contrast to the German system, the benefits gained from the illegal action must be specified as set out in part 5 of the Proceeds of Crime Act 2002 and Civil Recovery. See Olliers Solicitors, 'United Kingdom: Civil Recovery – Who Needs a Conviction?' http://www.olliers.com/articles/90-civil-recovery-who-needs-a-conviction.html (last accessed 29/10/2013) Because it is regarded as a civil matter, the costs are recovered from the target.

(Art. 73 s. 1 ss. 2 German Criminal Code [StGB]). All compensation payments that have already been made need to be deducted from the profit. As compensation payments are subtracted from the profit, they do not have any influence on additional fines and the possible subtraction is limited by the profit. If the fine, including the disgorgement, has not yet been paid, the amount of compensation is subtracted from the disgorgement. If the disgorgement has already been paid, it is necessary to create a legal basis for a repayment of the disgorgement up to the amount of the compensation payment. This can be arranged analogously to German forfeiture law. Although the amount is not exactly fixed, the repayment is foreseeable for all parties involved. The difficulties associated with calculating the compensation arise prior to determining the sanction; hence, compensation payments are taken into account only after they are clearly fixed by the outcome of the corresponding private proceedings. As a result, it is not essential for sanctioning reasons *how* the compensation is calculated. This procedure leads to fair and just results for the company itself as well as for competitors and consumers.

2.2.5 Tax and Profit

The statement of the exact profit is particularly relevant for tax reasons, although tax issues of Member States are generally excluded from consideration when assessing the fine on EC level.[14] This regulation does not lead to fair and just results when comparing different tax practices in the EU. Because the profit functions as the basis of taxation the estimation of the profit needs to be clearly displayed.[15] It is necessary, therefore, to adjust the taxation when compensation proceedings precede public proceedings and the amount can be set immediately. When the compensation is set later, taxation needs to be changed twice: once when the profit is calculated without the compensation when the profit to be disgorged needs to be subtracted from the taxable profit; and again when compensation payments are later included and the taxable profit has to be increased by the amount of the compensation payments made because of the decline of deductible profit.

3 Elements of Fine, Disgorgement and Compensation

Besides disgorgement and compensation there is the (criminal or administrative) sanctioning of antitrust law infringements. These three elements each have a different focus and varying significance throughout the EU and the Member States.

The first element in the sanctioning of antitrust offences is the imposition of a fine. It serves mostly preventive purposes by trying to scare company owners from

---

14 See Case C-44/69, *Buchler & Co v. Commission* [1970] ECR 733, para. 51; for the relationship between fine, profit and tax, see Scholz U and Haus F (*supra* note 8) p. 683 *et seq*.

15 Art. 4 (5) No. 8 German Income Tax Act (EStG) only allows the deduction for tax reasons of the disgorgement, not the fine.

committing cartel offences.[16] The fine is set by public authorities and should be higher than profit if it is to have a deterrent effect.

The second element is the disgorgement of illegally gained profit. The purpose is to deter companies from recommitting the offence, as there is no financial advantage left. In the United Kingdom a specific gain must first be identified before setting the fine. In other parts of Europe, by contrast, an estimation of the advantage is sufficient to set the fine.[17]

The third element, which has received increased attention from the European Union as of late, is creating a deterrent effect by strengthening private enforcement proceedings. An inevitable part of private proceedings are verifiable damages for consumers or business rivals: without damages there cannot be a claimant demanding compensation.

4 The Legal Situation

4.1 In the European Union

Through the strengthening of private proceedings the EU aims to complement existing public enforcement with the aim of full compensation as a guiding principle.[18] It sees the detection of antitrust law infringements as more likely to occur when effective compensation proceedings are offered.[19] Accordingly, the compensation does not intend to replace public proceedings.[20]

The European fines primarily serve determent purposes.[21] They are meant to operate in a preventive manner to prevent responsible people from committing the offence.[22] The infringer can be sued for the whole harm caused in the EU before the courts of his domicile.[23] EU guidelines stipulate that fines should at least equal the profit, but when fixing the basic amount of the fine they consider the fine on

16 For a critical view of criminal sanctions, see Schwarze J. (*supra* note 1), p. 183; for a critical view of high fine policy with regard to community budget, see Völcker S., 'Rough Justice? An Analysis of the European Commission's New Fining Guidelines', *Common Market Law Review* (2007), 1285–1320, p.1285.

17 See Joined Cases T-25/95, T-26/95, T-30/95 to T-32/95, T-34/95 to T-39/95, T-42/95 to T-46/95, T-48/95, T-50/95 to T-65/95, T-68/95 to T-71/95, T-87/95, T-88/95, T-103/95 and T-104/95 *Cimenteries CBR and Others v. Commission* [2000] ECR II-491, para. 4881.

18 White Paper (*supra* note 2) p. 3.

19 *Ibid.*

20 *Ibid.*

21 On deterrence and increasing fines, see Schwarze J. (*supra* note 1), p. 175.

22 See Guidelines, http://ec.europa.eu/competition/antitrust/legislation/fines_en.pdf (last accessed 29/10/2013), para. 30.

23 See Art. 2 s. 1 of Regulation 44/2001/EC, OJ, L-12/1, 3.

group turnover with regard to the gravity and the duration of the infringement.[24] The starting point is usually not the actual profit but the sales of goods or services made by the undertaking during the business year prior to its participation in the infringement generally, even though in principle a direct or indirect connection to the infringement is required.[25] The European Commission has great discretion with regard to the weighting of these elements.[26] This is partly due to the fact that identification of the exact amount of profit related to the infringement faces enormous difficulties. For this reason, concern about using it as a determining factor of the fine is understandable since estimations are indispensable.[27] The guidelines refer to the gains improperly made only in respect to the possibility of increasing the fine for deterrence purposes when actual gains can be estimated and are lower than the calculated fine.[28] In practice it is possible to adjust the fine in relation to the benefits.[29] The difficulty arises in assessing the proper adjustment because the actual profit is determined by different, non-IFRS accounting standards inside the European Union. Furthermore, the profit is reduced for taxes with the result that a fine adjusted only to benefits can sometimes be less effective than intended.[30] This means that the gains have no influence on the calculation of the basic amount of the fine and serve only as a reason for later adjustment, even though the benefits play an underlying role when assessing the length of the infringement (leading to higher gains in particular) and when evaluating the intensity of the infringement.[31] The amount of the fine is in total limited to 10% of the group turnover. This leads to problems if the benefits exceed the maximum amount of the possible fine. Moreover, the fine can be reduced by 10% of what the company normally would have to pay even in addition to reductions granted under the leniency programme

24 For a critical view on the implementation of these criteria in their first introduction in 1998, see Korthals C. & Bangard A., 'Die neuen Leitlinien der Kommission zur Bußgeldbemessung in Kartellverfahren – eine Kritik', *Betriebsberater* 1998, 1013–1016, p. 1015 *et seq.*

25 Guidelines (*supra* note 22), para. 13.

26 Case T 17/99, *Kelit v. Commission* [2002] ECR II-1647, para. 127.

27 Guidelines (*supra* note 22), para. 18

28 Guidelines (*supra* note 22), para. 31, Case C-100-103/80, *Musique diffusion francaise v. Commission* [1983] ECR 1825, para. 109; Case T-9/99, *HFB v. Isoplus*,[2002] ECR II-1487, paras. 453 *et seq.* On the extensive interpretation of the 10% upper limit, see Case C-308/04, *Carbon v. Commission* [2006] I-5977, para. 82. Scholz U. & Haus F. (*supra* note 8), p. 686 argue that benefits are regularly considered when determining the fine but are not disclosed. Yet the disgorgement has a different intention than the fine even if the equation of the latter must factor in the illegal gains. This is because the disgorgement amount is based on a factual dimension, not a moral one.

29 See Case C-100-103/80, *Musique diffusion francaise v. Commission* [1983] ECR 1825, para. 108; Case C-13/89, *ICI v. Commission* [1992] ECR II-1021, para. 385; and Case T 14/89, *Montedipe SpA v. Commission* [1992] ECR II-1155, para. 346.

30 See Korthals C. & Bangard A. (*supra* note 23), p. 1015.

31 See Scholz U. & Haus F. (*supra* note 8), p. 685.

if the requirements of the settlement procedure are fulfilled.[32] But it needs to be demonstrated that this reduction is appealing enough for settlement, especially because the Commission may decide to revert to the usual procedure.[33]

The other significant question – the relationship between private and public enforcement – is not adequately addressed by the guidelines, which do not consider the compensation of consumers and business rivals to be a mitigating circumstance when setting the fine. The Commission, however, agrees that compensation diminishes profit. Currently, though, compensation payments can only be regarded when they are fixed prior to public proceedings, and European law lacks a provision to change the fine retrospectively, with the result being that later compensation cannot be included in the calculation. This produces an unjust outcome, as the order of proceedings is crucial.

As the fine does not actually include the repayment of illegally obtained gains it is impossible for the company to change their tax statement to reflect the loss.[34] This missing element makes it hard to prove the reduction of profits in the tax return. Of course, it makes sense not to make the profit margin or expected gains public to protect affected companies from unrealistically high compensation claims.

4.2 In Germany

German law has a different approach regarding the relationship between disgorgement and fines. Similar to European antitrust law, German law sanctions offences with administrative fines. But in Germany the focus is less on the turnover than on the specific gain. The economic advantage is determined by a factual view, the underlying quantification based solely on economic grounds. This results in the application of the net principle. Included are all benefits gained by the infringement – primary benefits such as remuneration and earnings as well as secondary benefits such as an enhanced market share. Conversely, all expenditures of the infringing company are excluded. As a consequence, the economic advantage consists of pure profit. Because the assessment of profit faces problems similar to those faced by the assessment of turnover, estimations must be used.

---

32 See the Commission Notice from 2.7.2008 on the conduct of settlement procedures in view of the adoption of decisions pursuant to Art. 7 and Art. 23 of Council Regulation (EC) No. 1/2003 in cartel cases, OJ C 167, p. 1, 5, para. 32, 33, http://eur-lex.europa.eu/LexUriServ/LexUriServ.do?uri=OJ:C:2008:167:0001:0006:EN:PDF (last accessed 29/10/2013).

33 See MacLennan J. & Rogers A., 'Recent Trends in EC Competition Law', *White & Case publications Nov. 2008* [http://www.whitecase.com/files/Publication/a9c7c62b-aaa6-44a3-b34d-9abfa5e4f15c/Presentation/PublicationAttachment/2b2c5c29-f46a-4c17-91b2-9cce1c80c3bc/Recent_Trends_in_EU_Competition_Law.pdf (last accessed 29/10/2013)], p. 1, 2.

34 On the necessity of disclosing the fine calculation algorithm for tax reasons, see already Wegner C., 'Keine umfassende Begründungspflicht der Kommission für Kartellgeldbußen in Millionenhöhe?', *Wirtschaft und Wettbewerb* 2001, 469–477, p. 476.

Unlike the EU method of sanctioning, fines imposed in Germany include a portion of the disgorged gains. Since each component serves different purposes, it is necessary to disclose if and to what extent the economic gains are disgorged. The competent authority must distinguish between the portion of the sanction dependent on the profit and the portion that reflects a repressive function. While the repressive part will not be changed by later events, the disgorgement will still depend on the actual profit calculation. This is immediately relevant for the taxation of the company. Even if the tax burden is already assessed conclusively for the relevant period, it must have a strong reducing effect on the disgorgement. If the tax assessment can be corrected, the profit can be disgorged, and the deduction becomes an operating expenditure. By contrast, the repressive part cannot be deducted. This approach is based on the equality-before-the-law principle required by the German Constitutional Court and set out in Art. 3 para. 1 GG. The court ruled the simultaneous disgorgement and full taxation of pre-tax profit unconstitutional. Such a double inclusion through fine and taxation violates the tenets of the German constitution.

As in the European Union, the fines in Germany are supposed to exceed profits, but no duty to do so exists. The cartel authority has four possibilities: first, a fine can be imposed that disgorges a portion of the profit; second, a fine can be imposed that disgorges all the profit but has no repressive element; third, a fine can be imposed that disgorges the profit and has an exceeding repressive element; and fourth, a fine can be imposed with a repressive element while disgorgement occurs based on a separate administrative decision. In private proceedings, disgorgement was first introduced in Germany in the German Act Against Unfair Practices (UWG) with additional and (in part) narrower requirements. This was highly and controversially discussed. It was then decided to pay the confiscated profit to the federal budget (see Art. 34a GWB) but not to the claimants.[35] The differences between European and German Law brought out in this section emphasise the need for a harmonized approach in the EU.

---

35 See Alexander C., 'Marktsteuerung durch Abschöpfungsansprüche', *JuristenZeitung* 2006, 890–895, p. 891 for further references.

5 The Relationship between Public and Private Enforcement

5.1 Advantages and Disadvantages

Historically, European countries have relied on public enforcement rather than private.[36] The advantage of this approach is that the limits inherent in private enforcement are respected, especially with regard to future competition, by avoiding the abuse of confidential information gained through private proceedings. The underlying considerations between the initiation of public proceedings and the pursuit of private claims are inevitably at odds. While the public prosecution is partially bound by the principle of reasonability and the consideration of unemployment, consumer or environmental issues, the initiation of private enforcement is determined by a risk-cost-analysis of competitors or consumers.[37] Private enforcement by consumers is widely accepted in the public; what must be addressed is the danger of abusive behaviour by competitors, e.g. from unsubstantiated claims for the purpose of gaining information or dissuading the alleged culprit from continuing their behaviour even if pro-competitive.[38] Legislation needs to ensure that private enforcement is not used against the consumer and the interests of competition.[39] This is why claimants must have access only to the relevant data and strict rules must be in place for data disclosure in private proceedings.[40]

---

36 See Drexl J., Gallego B., Enchelmaier S., Mackenrodt O. and Podszun R. (*supra* note 2), p. 800. On the lack of development of private enforcement (only 60 reported cases sued for violations of competition law and only 18 cases with allegations against EC competition law),see Waelbroeck D., Slater D. and Evan-Shoshan G., Study on the Conditions of Claims for Damages in Case of Infringement of EC Competition Rules (31 Aug 2004), http://ec.europa.eu/competition/antitrust/actionsdamages/comparative_report_clean_en.pdf (last accessed 29.10.2013).

37 See Weber N., 'Claims under Sec. 1 of the German Act Against Unfair Competition for Cases of Infringement of EC Antitrust Law', *International Review of Intellectual Property and Competition Law* 2003, 920–932, p. 930.

38 The likeliness exists especially in the US, as the costs for private proceedings are high and even the small chance of treble damages can induce the defendant to abandon his behaviour. See Ginsburg D., 'Comparing Antitrust Enforcement in the United States and Europe', *Journal of Competition Law and Economics* (2005), 427–439, p. 436.

39 McAfee R., Mialon H. and Mialon S., 'Private v. Public Antitrust Enforcement: A Strategic Analysis', *Journal of Public Economics* (2008), 1863–1875, p. 1864.

40 The white paper (*supra* note 2), p. 5, proposes a similar approach to the Intellectual Property Directive (2004/48/EC). This gradualist practice depends on the plausibility of the claim and the proportionality of the requested disclosure. On disclosure in the settlement procedure, see Hirnsbrunner S., 'Settlements in EU-Kartellverfahren', *Eu-*

This approach arose in the Anglo-American system and is more or less alien to the prior state of civil proceedings in most continental European countries.[41] In particular, the relationship between disclosed data during the leniency programme and private action needs to be considered more closely as the former will prove ineffective if claimants of private actions have access to data.[42] Furthermore, public interest can be taken into account more closely in public proceedings.[43] By contrast, the disadvantage of the public approach is that individual consumer interests and the need for compensation of individual damages may be neglected.[44] Private enforcement has great potential to augment the governmental resources devoted to deterring and remedying the effects of anticompetitive conduct.[45] Often, private enforcement can be a useful instrument for raising awareness of the importance of antitrust law.[46] But if only small damages occur, the likelihood of private enforcement proceedings decreases dramatically.[47] A recent tendency in Germany is to shift emphasis towards private enforcement in competition proceedings, with a higher number of damages claims predicted over the coming years.[48] As both approaches have crucial weaknesses, an equitable, fair combination must be found for satisfying the standards of proportionate sanctioning set out in Art. 49 para. 3 of the EU's Charter of Fundamental Rights. Such a solution is also seen to offer the greatest benefit to society.[49] To achieve fair and just results, it should make no difference in the outcome which proceedings and which decisions are made first: damage claims do not rely on infringement in public enforcement proceedings.[50]

ropäische Zeitschrift für Wirtschaftsrecht 2011, 12–16, p. 15. For instance, in the UK, documents are commonly disclosed pre-trial.

41 See Burrichter J. & Logemann H., 'Evaluation of Evidence in National Courts: Reflection from the German Perspective', in Ehlermann C. &Marquis M. (eds.), European Competition Law Annual 2009, 683–696, *passim*.

42 See MacLennan J. & Rogers A. (*supra* note 33), p.1, 7.

43 See Drexl J., Gallego B., Enchelmaier S., Mackenrodt O. and Podszun R. (*supra* note 2), p. 800.

44 See Kießling E. (*supra* note 5), p. 735.

45 See Ginsburg D. (*supra* note 38), p. 435, which contains a critical evaluation of the US experience on private enforcement claims.

46 See Weber N. (*supra* note 37), p. 930.

47 See Kießling E. (*supra* note 5), p. 739.

48 See Burrichter J. & Logemann H. (*supra* note 41), *passim*.

49 For mathematical and economic calculations on public and private enforcement proceedings and their ideal combination, see McAfee R., Mialon H. and Mialon S. (*supra* note 39), p. 1868 *et seq*.

50 See the aims set out in the white paper (*supra* note 2), p. 3.

5.2 Theoretical Models

There are a few basic variables that arise from the relationships between public and private proceedings and between disgorgement and fine: the profit-minimizing effect of compensation, fair and just taxation, and privacy concerns. It is crucial that a balance is found between the variables and that their combination is adequate and proportionate.

5.2.1 The Relationship Between Private and Public Enforcement

Public and private enforcement are generally separate processes. This is due to the differing goals of sanctioning and compensation. Private proceedings are based on damage recovery for consumers and business rivals. But private enforcement of antitrust law rules may do more than serve civil reconciliation: it can also be seen to contribute to the deterrent effect of sanctioning.[51] If, on the contrary, private enforcement is viewed as an independent element, it will be seen to serve only compensation between individuals.[52]

5.2.2 Exemplary Damages

Problems arise when Member States use exemplary damages: it is a rare practice, of course, and even in British Courts the awarding of exemplary damages is becoming more restricted.[53] It is limited to specific situations, such as when 'the defendant's conduct has been calculated by him to make a profit for himself which may well exceed the compensation payable to the plaintiff'.[54] If exemplary damages are awarded in an antitrust case the compensation will already consist of a repressive and a compensatory element, as the aim of exemplary damages is to punish the offender, which is usually the objective of criminal courts.[55] Things can become complicated if there is more than one damage claim and the amount of damages to be awarded is already exhausted. This is because when subtracting the compensation from the disgorgement only the pure compensation can be deducted. The amount of the damages awarded for exemplary reasons must be considered with respect to the appropriate sanction if legal violations are to be avoided. Furthermore, subsequent private proceedings have to take the earlier decisions into account and forgo the imposition of exemplary damages.

---

51 See Drexl J., Gallego B., Enchelmaier S., Mackenrodt O. and Podszun R. (*supra* note 2), p. 801.

52 *Ibid*.

53 See*Rookes v. Barnard* (1964) AC 1129 and*Cassel and Co. Ltd. v. Broome* (1972) AC 1027; *AB v. South West Water Services Ltd* (1993) 1 All ER 609 (CA).

54 *Cassell and Co. Ltd v. Broome* (1972) AC 1027.

55 The Law Commission, Item 2 of the sixth programme of Law Reform: Aggravated, Exemplary and Restitutionary Damages, *passim*.

5.2.3 Restriction to Pure Restitution

The most obvious solution would be to restrict compensation payments to the pure restitution of damages even though compensation may have a deterrent effect.[56] The aims of sanction and compensation differ and it is not possible for the private claimant to replace the public authority and collect the disgorged profit.[57] The guidelines for public and private enforcement are too contrary. The purpose of compensation is to revert the company to the situation prior to committing the infringement, and the inclusion of repressive elements would mix the dogmatic and structural differences between public and private enforcement. This distinction is especially important when discussing collective actions.[58] The use of punitive damages must be restricted to antitrust law and public proceedings. A widening of damage compensation would violate the requirement that sanctioning must be proportionate in pursuant to Art. 49 s. 3 of the EU's Charter of Fundamental Rights. This is only feasible if the repressive element and the compensatory element are fixed independently yet related. This link is made possible by calculating the underlying profit. If profit and disgorgement are reduced by compensation, the resulting system will avoid double payment and an unjust outcome.

5.2.4 Advantage of a Flexible System

By considering only the paid compensation (based on judgments or compromise settlement) and not the undefined claims, the proposed system of disgorgement does not interfere with civil liability law in the Member States. Especially for the passing-on defence and claims of indirect purchasers, damages cannot be estimated properly in advance. According to Art. 33 para. 1 s. 3 GWB it is only necessary to be a miscellaneous market participant who is negatively affected by the cartel infringement; hence, the legislation dismisses the limitation on the target-orientation of the infringement.[59] The consideration of the claim alone as in German forfeiture law (Art. 73 para. 1 s. 2 StGB)[60] would lead to incalculable uncertainties for the companies and huge difficulties in the accounting process when possible damage payments must be included. The determination of damages and the determination of interdependences between a decision of the national competition authority (NCA) and the courts on factual questions is extremely challenging.[61] This also applies to issues concerning the conflict of law,[62] as only the final

---

56 See Drexl J., Gallego B., Enchelmaier S., Mackenrodt O. and Podszun R. (*supra* note 2), p. 805. For the deterrent effect of compensation, see Lange & Schiemann, Schadensersatz(3rd ed. 2003), p. 9 *et seq.*

57 See Drexl J., Gallego B., Enchelmaier S., Mackenrodt I. and Podszun R. (*supra* note 2) p. 806.

58 *Ibid.*, p. 802.

59 See the government draft on the 7th Amendment to the Restriction of the Competition Act, BR-Drs 441/04, 59 *et seq.*, p. 92; and Kießling E. (*supra* note 5),p. 735.

60 In relation to forfeiture, see Lackner K. & Kühl K. (*supra*note 10),Art. 73 para. 6.

61 For more on the dependence of factual questions regarding infringements decisions made by NCAs and civil proceedings, especially in pan-European cases, see white

amount after a judgement or settlement is taken into account, leading to more certainty in the sanctioning and confiscation procedure. If the problem from sanctioning proceedings and preserving the independence of repressive elements is omitted, legal certainty can be achieved. Hence, the fear of an intrusion is unwarranted and the complex harmonization of the civil liability systems of the Member States can be postponed.

5.2.5 Relation between Confiscation and Fine

The imposition of fines and the confiscation of illegal profits can either be separate processes or a single combined one. In the first option, two different public authorities are responsible for imposing the sanction; in the second, one authority does both.

Separate systems
Separate systems have the advantage of decentralisation and decriminalisation, as the confiscation of profits is not connected with the fine, though in all likelihood the amount of the fine is higher than in a single system. While the fine itself would be just as high as the fine being imposed by the criminal or administrative authority, the non-consideration of the profit excludes the possibility of a reduction from compensation payments. Even if the compensation payments equal the profit they cannot be taken into account. Hence, disproportionate and unjust practices result without a connection between fine, compensation and disgorgement.

Single system
A single system is when one authority both imposes the fine and disgorges the illegal profits. In this case, it does not suffice to add up fine and illegal profit and impose the total amount. As shown above, it is necessary to identify true profits for tax reasons, so that confiscation reconstitutes the status prior to the infringement. Moreover, the fine needs to exceed the illegal profit if it is to have a repressive effect. This approach ensures separate treatment of fine and profits but also supplies the certainty required for sanctioning by making foreseeable which part is due to mere earnings and which part is due to wrongdoing. As mentioned above, the exact calculus should not be considered publicly to safeguard privacy and competition.

paper (*supra* note 2), p. 6 *et seq.*; and Drexl J., Gallego B., Enchelmaier S., Mackenrodt O. and Podszun R. (*supra* note 2), p. 803.

62 See Art. 6 s. 3 lit a,b Rome II Regulation 864/2007/EC, OJ L-199/40.

6 Conclusion

To reach a conclusion private enforcement and public enforcement must be independent yet connected, while fine and disgorgement need to be connected but independent. In this way it is possible to secure adequate and proportionate sanctioning. This connected system leads to the result that the non-enforcement of compensation claims does not benefit the offender, and the private enforcement achieves a higher significance as willingness to pay damages increases because of the minimal financial consequences (except taxes). The proposed system is also consistent with harmonization, as it leaves the compensation of damages and the underlying dogmatic structures to the Member States. As the specific calculation of the compensation payments is irrelevant for disgorgement and as the compensation payments can also be taken into account later than the proceedings, this solution offers a flexible and just system for sanctions against cartels. Accordingly, the Commission's work on creating more uniform rules for private damage claims arising from the infringement of Community antitrust rules and their efforts to facilitate private enforcement for companies should be continued. Only if the sanctioning systems of the EU and the Member States are harmonized, and disgorgement and the proposed relationship between private and public proceedings throughout the EU are standardized, can a just, proportionate and homogenous system be created.

Quantifying Antitrust Damages – Economics and the Law

Gunnar Niels and Robin Noble[1]

1 Introduction

Enforcement of competition law across the EU has moved at a steady pace in the last years. Some of the hefty fines imposed by the European Commission have grabbed the headlines, raising awareness of competition law among business communities and the general public. In the 1990s, cartel fines imposed by the Commission totalled only around €615m. In 2012 alone, total cartel fines were €1.9 billion; in 2011 the fines amounted to €600m and in 2010 they came to €2.9 billion.[2] In addition, Microsoft was fined €899m in 2008 and Intel €1.1 billion in 2009, both for abuse of dominance.[3] Many national competition authorities have uncovered cartel and abuse cases as well.

But fines are not the end of the story for infringers of competition law. Parties harmed by anti-competitive conduct, usually customers or competitors, can claim compensation before a national court. For example, manufacturers of car tyres may initiate a damages action against members of a cartel among synthetic-rubber producers;[4] a small airline may claim damages after its dominant rival has been

---

1 This article draws on a study prepared for the European Commission by Oxera and a multi-jurisdictional team of lawyers led by Dr. Assimakis Komninos titled 'Quantifying Antitrust Damages: Towards Non-binding Guidance for Courts', dated December 2009, copyright European Union, published at http://ec.europa.eu/competition/antitrust/actionsdamages/. We bear the responsibility for any modifications of the content.

2 See the European Commission document 'Cartel Statistics', available at: http://ec.europa.eu/competition/cartels/statistics/statistics.pdf.

3 European Commission, 'Antitrust: Commission Imposes €899 Million Penalty on Microsoft for Non-compliance with March 2004 Decision', press release, IP/08/318, 27 February 2008; and European Commission, 'Antitrust: Commission Imposes Fine of €1.06 Bn on Intel for Abuse of Dominant Position; Orders Intel to Cease Illegal Practices', press release, IP/09/745, 13 May 2009.

4 A cartel among five oil and chemical companies to fix the price of synthetic rubber was fined by the European Commission in 2006. European Commission,

found guilty of making anti-competitive loyalty payments to travel agents.[5] 'Follow-on' damages claims under competition law are increasingly common in many jurisdictions. In Europe alone in the last ten years, there have been damages actions against cartels in vitamins, sugar, gas-insulated switchgear, asphalt, cement, lysine, car insurance, car glass, driving schools, liquid crystal displays, cathode ray tubes, methionine, synthetic rubber, carbon and graphite products, air cargo services, hydrogen peroxide, industrial copper tubes, lifts, escalators and football shirts.

The European Commission has been actively trying to promote private actions for damages, as reflected in its 'White Paper on Damages Actions for Breach of the EC Antitrust Rules' of April 2008 and in its February 2011 consultation on mechanisms for collective redress.[6] One of the obstacles discussed in the 2008 White Paper is the uncertainty about the quantification of the harm suffered. Specifically, how does one best assess what would have happened but for the infringement? Which methods are acceptable? Which methods are feasible? In June 2011 the Commission issued a draft guidance paper on the quantification of damages with the aim of assisting courts and parties.[7] A first step towards this guidance was taken with the publication of a report by Oxera and a team of legal and academic experts in January 2010 titled 'Quantifying Antitrust Damages: Towards Guidance for Courts'. This article discusses some of the aspects of that report.

2 Policy Principles Behind Damages Claims

Damages actions brought before courts by harmed parties are a form of private enforcement of competition law, complementing public enforcement by competition authorities. In the US, more than 90% of antitrust cases have been private actions.[8] Elsewhere, the majority of cases tend to be taken on by competition authorities, but the importance of private actions has grown. There is a distinction between original (or stand-alone) private actions, where infringement and damages must be established by the court, and follow-on private damages actions, which are brought before a court after an infringement decision by a competition authority.

'Commission Fines Producers and Traders of Synthetic Rubber €519 Million for Price Fixing Cartel', press release, IP/06/1647, 29 November 2006.

5 The Competition Tribunal in South Africa found South African Airways to have engaged in anti-competitive loyalty payments in Case No. 80/CR/Sep06, *Nationwide Airlines (Pty) Ltd and Comair Ltd v. South African Airways (Pty) Ltd*, decision of 17 February 2010. We advised one of the two claimants in this case.

6 European Commission, 'Towards a Coherent European Approach to Collective Redress', February 2011.

7 European Commission, 'Quantifying Harm in Actions for Damages Based on Breaches of Art. 101 or 102 of the Treaty on the Functioning of the European Union', draft guidance paper, June 2011.

8 C.A. Jones, *Private Enforcement of Antitrust Law in the EU, UK and USA* (Oxford University Press 1999).

There are various reasons why policy-makers find private actions attractive, and hence seek to facilitate them. One is that they save taxpayers' money. Competition authorities have limited budgets, and must prioritise their enforcement actions. As economists would say, there is scope for an efficient division of labour here: business-to-business disputes on vertical and horizontal agreements and exclusionary behaviour seem to lend themselves to private actions, as businesses will be willing to pay for litigation if the stakes are sufficiently high. In the US, treble damages are awarded to parties harmed by antitrust infringements, providing an extra incentive to bring private actions. Competition authorities can then deal with the rest – in particular, cases involving end-consumers or cartel cases where private parties are less likely to initiate a lawsuit because they lack the investigative powers of competition authorities.

Another reason for policy-makers to encourage private damages actions is that they contribute to the deterrence of anti-competitive practices. Effective deterrence enhances competition without costing taxpayers much money. Nowadays, hefty fines, and possible prison sentences for individuals, already constitute a strong deterrent (though apparently still not sufficiently strong, judging by the number of cartels still being uncovered every year). The prospect of having to pay damages on top of the fines may further dampen any enthusiasm to form cartels.

A third policy principle behind damages actions, and one that is embedded in EU law, is that of compensation. As stated in the European Commission's White Paper and its accompanying Commission staff working paper:

> Any citizen or business who suffered harm as a result of a breach of EC antitrust rules (Articles 81 and 82 of the EC Treaty [now Articles 101 and 102 TFEU]) must be able to claim reparation from the party who caused the damage. This right of victims to compensation is guaranteed by Community law, as the European Court of Justice recalled in 2001 and 2006.
>
> Victims of an EC competition law infringement are entitled to full compensation of the harm caused. That means compensation for actual loss (*damnum emergens*) and for loss of profit (*lucrum cessans*), plus interest from the time the damage occurred until the capital sum awarded is actually paid.[9]

We discuss in this article how the compensation principle can be made to work in practice. If followed to the letter it would imply a certain degree of precision in the determination of the harm, avoiding both under-compensation and over-compensation. It would also mean that compensation should reach the victims of an infringement regardless whether they operate in the supply chain. If the cartel's direct customers have passed on the cartel overcharge, their own customers are the ones who should be compensated (unless those customers have also passed it on further downstream). We show how economics can help with these legal principles.

---

9 The Court of Justice rulings referred to are Case C-453/99, *Courage Ltd. v. Bernard Crehan* [2001] ECR I–6297 and Joined Cases C–295/04 to C–298/04 *Vincenzo Manfredi and others v. Lloyd Adriatico Assicurazioni SpA and others* [2006] ECR I–6619.

3 Searching for the Right Answer Within Practical and Legal Limits

Any damages assessment needs to strike a balance between two objectives: first, finding the most accurate answer possible – the desire to determine the real damage value as closely as possible, which is how an economist would naturally seek to approach quantification problems; and second, using approaches that are clear and easy to apply and that fit within the existing legal frameworks.

Calculating the exact damage arising from an infringement of competition law requires complete information about what would have happened in a parallel world where the infringement did not take place. This is commonly referred to as the 'but-for' situation, or counterfactual. Because complete information does not exist, one has to describe the counterfactual scenario with a model containing simplified assumptions. (Here, 'model' does not necessarily imply complicated equations; any abstract projection of a counterfactual world would be considered a 'model' in economics.) The aim of the model should be to produce an estimate of what would have happened 'but for' the infringement.

All models are necessarily simplifications of the real world. They can vary in the degree to which they take into account all possible factors that may influence the counterfactual; this variation is often driven by data or time (or budgetary) constraints. Nonetheless, despite the 'unknowability' of the exact damages value, the aim is to approximate the answer as accurately as possible. This normally requires the use of established economic and financial methods (as described in this article), and therefore introduces an element of complexity to the legal analysis. To the dismay of some competition lawyers, perhaps, a degree complexity in the quantification of damages is inevitable because the way markets and businesses work is complex. But economists shouldn't be blamed for this.

At the same time, any area of law benefits from simple approaches that are easy to understand and apply. In this regard, many jurisdictions have developed rules addressing matters such as the distribution of burden of proof and the required level of proof. Several EU Member States have in place rules dealing with the degree of freedom that judges have in calculating damages in special cases or, more generally, when exact quantification is impossible or very difficult. Such rules may reflect to a lesser or greater extent principles of equity, justice, and procedural efficiency. For example, the Italian Supreme Court, in a follow-on damages claim regarding a car insurance cartel, confirmed that when the exact harm is difficult to prove, the Italian courts can rely on Article 1226 of the Italian Civil Code and award an equitable amount of damages (*ex aequo et bono*).[10] In that regard, the Supreme Court considered the case 'a textbook example' of where the Italian courts should make use of such a power because it was difficult for the claimant to prove the precise value of the actual loss (the cartel overcharge, essentially) that it had suffered. Another example of such a rule is section 287 of the German Code of Civil Procedure, which provides that a court has a degree of discretion to estab-

---

10 See *Fondiaria SAI SpA v. Nigriello*, judgment of 17 February 2007.

lish the amount of loss based on its best judgment and by assessing all the circumstances of the individual case. All these rules mean that the amount of damages does not have to be proven to the last cent, giving courts a more efficient and feasible means of awarding damages.

Courts have long recognised that the counterfactual is 'unknowable'. And yet this has not deterred them from setting damages awards (both in competition law and other fields of law), nor from relying on economic analysis. One US court stated, 'The antitrust cases are legion which reiterate the proposition that, if the fact of damages is proven, the actual computation of damages may suffer from minor imperfections.'[11] Another US court ruled that 'the vagaries of the marketplace usually deny us sure knowledge of what the plaintiff's situation would have been in the absence of the defendant's antitrust violation.'[12]

4 Main Stages in the Damages Estimation

Compensatory damages awards seek to put a claimant back into the financial position that it would have been in but for the breach of competition law. Tyre manufacturers are entitled to be compensated for the cartel overcharge they paid on rubber. The small airline is entitled to compensation for the harm caused to it by the anti-competitive loyalty payments by the dominant airline.

Any damages estimation has two main stages. The first stage involves determining the counterfactual scenario. What would the price of rubber have been in the absence of the cartel? What market position and profits would the small airline have achieved in the absence of the exclusionary conduct? This is often the central stage in any damages estimation, and certainly the one that tends to attract most attention (and disagreement between parties) in these cases. The second stage involves moving from the factual–counterfactual comparison to a final damages value. One step is to ensure that the damages estimate covers the relevant time period. If the counterfactual analysis has estimated the average annual overcharge of the synthetic-rubber cartel and the cartel infringement lasted five years, the estimate needs to be aggregated over those five years. The analysis usually requires converting the aggregated figures (cash flows) over time into one value, expressed as the current value of all those cash flows combined. This requires cash-flow discounting and uprating, a standard method in financial analysis. The question of interest (a standard component of compensatory damages in Europe, as mentioned in the quote from the Commission above) is addressed as part of this stage. As we discuss below, this final stage has received relatively little attention in the debates about quantifying damages, and is an area where the economics and the law are not always well aligned. The application of interest can make a substantial difference to the damages estimate, especially if long time periods are involved.

---

11 *South-East Coal Co. v. Consolidation Coal Co.,* 434 F.2d 767, 794 (6th Cir.1970).

12 *J. Truett Payne Co., v. Chrysler Motors Corp.*, 451 U.S. 557, 565, 101 S.Ct. 1923, 68 L.Ed.2d 442 (1981).

5 Harm from Hard-Core Cartel Agreements

The archetypal cartel agreement is one in which firms collectively fix higher prices. The harm arising from this type of competition law infringement is that parties further down the supply chain pay more for the product than they would have in a non-cartelised market. The higher price would normally also result in existing customers purchasing lower volumes or in customers who would have purchased the product at the non-cartelised price not purchasing at all.

Figure 13 shows the overcharge paid on all the units actually sold (rectangle A), and the reduction in volume (triangle B). Triangle C represents consumer surplus in this market (the difference between what consumers are willing to pay for each of the units bought, and what they actually pay). Note that the counterfactual price here is not necessarily the same as the price in perfect competition (markets are rarely perfectly competitive), and the cartel price is not necessarily the same as the monopoly price (not all cartels manage to set prices at the profit-maximising monopoly level).

Fig. 13. Stylised illustration of the main effects of a price-fixing cartel

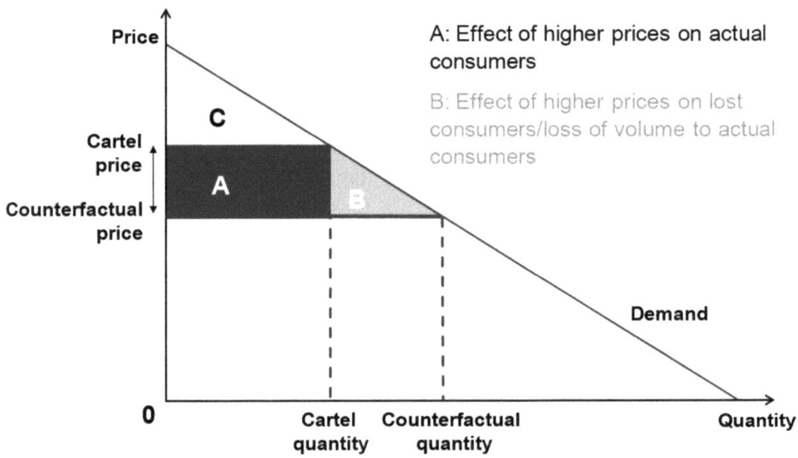

The overcharge, A, is the quantity of actual unit sales by the cartel multiplied by the difference between the actual cartel price and the counterfactual price (i.e., the price that would have been charged in the absence of the cartel). It is convenient to express the overcharge A as a percentage of the actual price, or actual cartel revenue. If the cartel price is €125, and the counterfactual price is €100, the overcharge would be 20%. (€25 is 20% of €125.) The overcharge is sometimes expressed as a percentage of the counterfactual price (in this case 25%). This is equally valid, but it is important to be clear about which basis for the percentage calculation is used. Expressing the overcharge as a percentage of the actual price makes it easy (and intuitive) to calculate the total amount of overcharge by applying the percentage to the amount that the buyer actually paid for its purchases. For example, if the cartel sold 1m units at a price of €125 each, the total overcharge would be €25m. If one specific claimant filed a successful damages action, and it could demonstrate that its total purchases from the cartel amounted to, say, €15m over the relevant period, the amount it was overcharged is 20% of €15m, i.e. €3m.

The lost-volume effect (as represented by triangle B above) is known in economic theory as a deadweight welfare loss; it represents an inefficiency to the economy as a whole. This deadweight loss is greatest if the counterfactual price is equal to the price under perfect competition, but also arises if the counterfactual represents some other form of competitive, non-cartel interaction, such as oligopoly (where price is higher than under perfect competition). From an economic perspective, this is inefficient because the cartel does not serve those customers who would be willing to pay the price under more competitive conditions.

Follow-on actions for damages in cartel cases are typically brought by parties that were direct or indirect purchasers of the cartel during the infringement period, and will most frequently focus on the harm caused to them by the overcharge (area A in Figure 13). Damages for different types of harm caused by the cartel, including the volume reduction (area B), negative effects on quality and choice, and possible other effects on cost levels, are generally more difficult to prove than the overcharge harm.

As regards damages from volume reduction, it may be difficult to identify the harmed parties. This may be less of a problem in the case of an existing customer purchasing lower volumes; it applies particularly to potential customers who did not purchase at all during the infringement period and yet would have purchased the product at the non-cartelised price. To take a hypothetical example based on a real case, in the private schools cartel case in the UK, those who could no longer afford to send their children to private schools at the inflated school fees may have been more harmed than those who paid the higher fees and did send their children to those schools.[13]

Those direct purchasers that are themselves producers or distributors may seek to link the reduction in volume of purchases from the cartel to a reduction in their own sales (and hence reduced profit) in a market downstream, and claim this as a separate type of harm from the cartel overcharge. In the example of the synthetic-rubber cartel, tyre manufacturers would first claim a cartel overcharge harm. However, to the extent that they have passed this overcharge on through their tyre prices (and hence passed the harm on to their customers), they may still, in theory, have suffered harm from lost sales of tyres, as customers buy fewer tyres at the higher price.

Figure 13 above shows the overcharge and lost-volume effect of a cartel on direct purchasers. These can be either sellers themselves (intermediate producers or distributors located one level further downstream in the supply chain) or end-consumers. But the ultimate harm caused to particular direct and indirect customers by the overcharge (and also the volume effect) will depend on the extent to

13 Office of Fair Trading, 'Independent Schools Agree Settlement: Competition Investigation Resolved', press release, 19 May 2006.

which the price increase caused by the cartel is passed along the supply chain. This is a significant and complex issue with any damages claim. The question of pass-on does not affect the calculation of the overcharge in itself, only the distribution of that harm along the supply chain. The question of whether to allow the passing-on defence – according to which a defendant can dispute a damages claim by a direct purchaser on the basis that the latter has passed on cost increases further downstream – has been (and still is) the subject of much policy debate both in the US and Europe.[14]

6 A Classification of Methods and Models for the Quantification of Damages

The economics and finance literature has developed a wide array of methods and models for quantifying damages. The classification presented in Figure 14 is divided into three levels. The first identifies the approach. The second level identifies the basis for the counterfactual that underlies each of the approaches. The third level then summarises the estimation techniques that can be used within each approach. In principle, each of these approaches can be used for quantifying damages for any type of antitrust infringement (cartels, other restrictive agreements and abuse of dominance). They are not mutually exclusive and in fact often complement each other, as discussed below.

Comparator-based approaches use data from sources that are external to the infringement to estimate the counterfactual. This can be done in three ways: cross-sectional comparisons (comparing different geographic or product markets); time-series comparisons (analysing prices before, during and/or after an infringement); or a combination of these in 'difference-in-differences' models (e.g. analysing the change in price for a cartelised market over time, and comparing that against the change in price in a non-cartelised market over the same timeframe). Various techniques can be used to analyse this comparator data, ranging from the simple such as comparing averages, to the more sophisticated such as panel data regression. These are discussed in more detail in the next section.

14 For an overview of the recent debates in the USA, see Antitrust Modernization Commission, 'Report and Recommendations', April; and European Commission (2008), 'White Paper on Damages Actions for Breach of the EC Antitrust Rules', COM(2008) 165, April 2007.

Fig. 14. Classification of methods and models

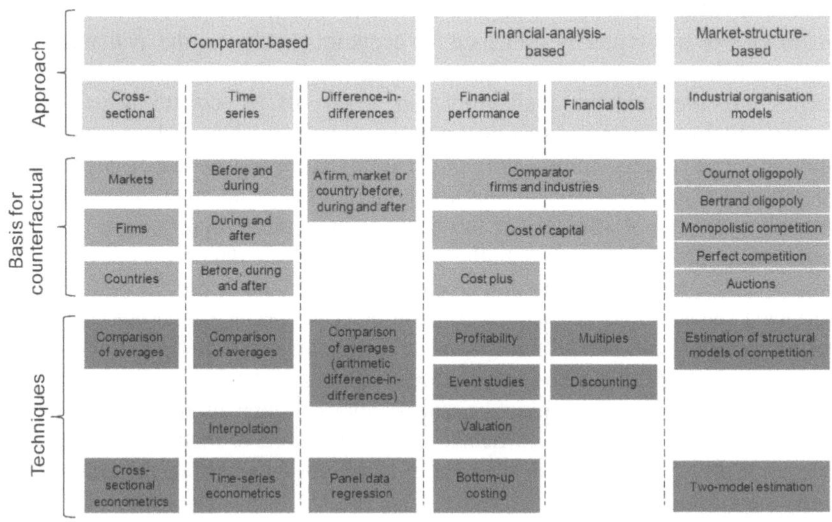

Source: Oxera *et al.* (2009).

Financial-analysis-based approaches have been developed in finance theory and practice.[15] They use financial information on comparator companies and industries, benchmarks for rates of return and cost information on defendants and claimants to estimate the counterfactual. There are two types of approach that use this information. The first are those that examine financial performance. These include assessing the profitability of defendants or claimants and comparing this against a benchmark, and bottom-up costing of products. The second type is a group of more general financial tools, such as discounting and multiples, which can be used alongside the other categories of methods and models.

Market-structure-based approaches are derived from industrial organisation (IO) theory and use a combination of theoretical models, assumptions and empirical estimation (rather than comparisons across markets or over time) to arrive at an assessment of the counterfactual.[16] These approaches involve identifying models of competition that best fit the relevant market, and using them to provide insight into how competition works in the market concerned and to estimate prices or volumes in the absence of anti-competitive conduct.

15 The European Commission's draft guidance paper of June 2011 (referred to above) defines this category slightly more narrowly as 'cost-based methods'.

16 The European Commission's draft guidance paper of June 2011 (referred to above) refers to this category as 'simulation models'.

7 Selecting which Methods or Models to Use

Two main factors will typically influence the economist's choice: the availability and quality of data and information (more data usually makes a greater range of approaches possible) and the availability and quality of the counterfactual. In some cases a high-quality cross-sectional comparator is available, such as a closely matching cross-country comparator for a cartelised market, where it is likely that no similar infringement exists in the comparator country. In other instances, a close match is either not available or the nearest comparator country shows evidence of similar infringement, potentially 'contaminating' the data.

In any given case it may be possible to apply more than one approach using different models, assumptions and data. Furthermore, both claimants and defendants may offer differing estimates, perhaps using different approaches. Ultimately, however, a court needs to decide on the specific amount of damages (if any) to be awarded. Methods and models cannot be ranked a priori. The main question in any particular case would normally be whether specific methods or models have been applied reasonably and robustly to the case at hand, not whether one approach is inherently superior to another.

The economics literature has found two solutions for deciding between multiple estimates of the same variable: identify a preferred approach (e.g. one unique combination of modelling and data) or 'pool' a selection of reasonable approaches. Pooling involves combining the results of two or more of the methods and models into a single value. One approach that empirical studies have shown to work quite well is that of simply taking the mean average of the available forecasts.[17] This is often used for macroeconomic forecasts. For example, if three robust models predict that the damages award should be €10.1m, €11.2m and €12.0m, the pooled model result, using a simple mean average, would be €11.1m. This combined value can then be used as the best estimate of the actual harm. It is not always appropriate to use estimates of the damages in such an averaging process, particularly if there are reasons to prefer one group of estimates over another. Indeed, when pooling modelling results it is standard practice to remove approaches that have significant weaknesses (a process sometimes referred to as 'trimming'), and to take steps to avoid double-counting of similar approaches. Pooling was recently accepted in a judgment by the Court of Session in Scotland in relation to a contractual damages dispute.[18]

---

17 See, for example, D.F. Hendry and M.P. Clements, 'Pooling of Forecasts', 7 *Econometrics Journal* (2004), 1–31, p. 1, which notes that 'the combination of individual forecasts of the same event has often been found to outperform the individual forecasts'.

18 See *Tullis Russell Papermakers Limited v. Inveresk Limited* , 2010 CSOH 148. Oxera acted as economic experts for the pursuers (Tullis Russell) in this matter. See Oxera, 'Damages and Customer Portfolio Valuation: A Case on Paper', *Agenda*, February 2011.

8 Comparator-Based Approaches

Comparator-based approaches estimate the counterfactual using data from sources that are not affected by the specific infringement or any other similar infringement. This comparator class of models is intuitively appealing in that they use information from actual transactions in markets where there is no infringement. A possible problem with comparator models is that they effectively assume that all of the difference between the factual and estimated counterfactual relates to the presence of the infringement. This assumption might bias the estimated effect of the infringement if there are other factors that coincide with the presence of the infringement but that are not accounted for. This bias can be mitigated by including other causes as additional explanatory variables in the model.

Once appropriate comparators have been selected, a comparison can be made between the factual (i.e. data from the market involved in the infringement) and the counterfactual (data from unaffected markets). Figure 15 provides an example. The price in the cartelised market is €12, while the average price in comparator markets is €10, implying that the overcharge is around €2.

Fig. 15. Example of a cross-sectional comparison

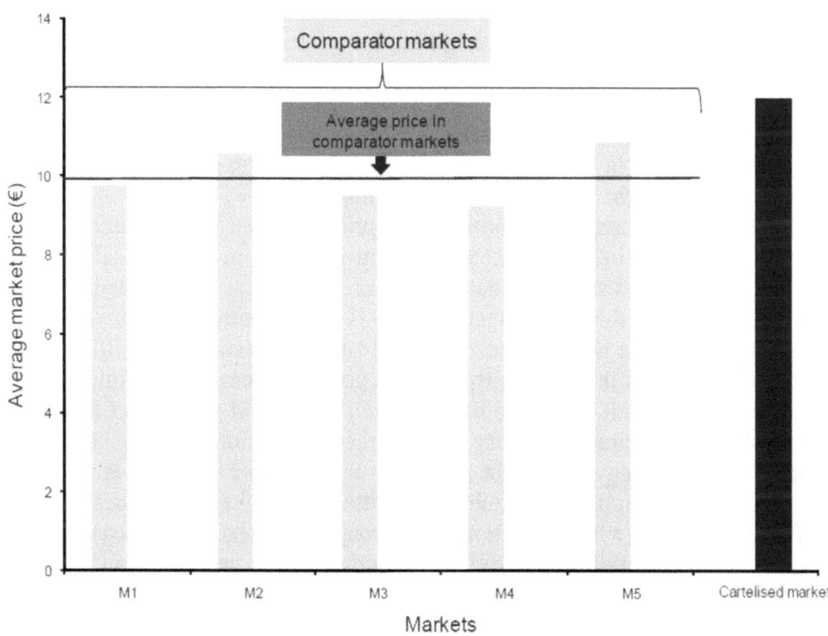

Source: Oxera *et al.* (2009).

Cross-section comparisons can be made between companies, between product markets or between geographic areas. In *Conwood v. US Tobacco*, a US monopolisation case in moist snuff (dipping tobacco), the plaintiff's expert compared market shares in different US states where no exclusionary practices had taken place, and in the related market for loose-leaf tobacco, in which the defendant was not active.[19] In *Apollo Theater Foundation v. Western International*, an expert for the plaintiff used a range of past exclusive trademark licence fees from other firms and markets to estimate reasonable royalty rates in patent disputes, which were then used to calculate the counterfactual licence fees.[20]

The ideal cross-sectional comparison includes data from only the relevant market and data from unaffected groups that are otherwise similar. If a regional infringement had the effect of increasing prices nationally, comparing data from two regional markets within the country would give a biased estimate of the damage since the comparator groups would be 'contaminated' by the effect of the infringement. In a case relating to a German paper wholesaler cartel, both the higher regional court and the German Federal Court of Justice felt unable to use cross-sectional comparisons between cartelised and other regional markets for paper wholesaling for the purposes of estimating the overcharge because they were concerned that there was some evidence of cartels existing in all or most of the regional markets, and that these markets were therefore possibly affected by the cartel as well.[21]

Several estimation techniques can be employed to derive the counterfactual price using cross-sectional comparators, ranging from the simple to the more sophisticated. A relatively simple comparison of averages uses the average price in an unaffected comparator group as an estimate for the counterfactual price. If there are five comparator markets with an average price of €10 (as in Figure 15), €10 is a simple estimate of the price that would have prevailed in the relevant market in the absence of the infringement. This price can then be compared with the actual price charged in the relevant market – €12, say – to estimate the overcharge (€2, or 16.7% of the cartel price in this example).

Whichever metric is used, the counterfactual price can then be compared with the actual price charged in the market with the infringement in order to calculate the overcharge. If there is sufficient data on prices, a statistical test can be undertaken to check whether the counterfactual price is significantly different (in the statistical sense) from the actual price charged. Testing for statistical significance and making the results of the tests transparent are good practices in economics and statistics. To continue with the above illustration, if the factual price was €12 and the average of the comparator markets was €10 then the overcharge may be estimated to be €2. However, the weight placed on this estimate of the overcharge may depend on the uncertainty surrounding the estimate of the counterfactual. If the confidence interval (which is determined through the t-test and indicates the range that contains the true value with 95% certainty) ranges from €5 to €15, less weight might be placed on the analysis than if the confidence interval suggests a range of €9 to €11.

---

19 *Conwood Co. v. US Tobacco Co.*, 290 F.3d 768 (6th Cir. 2002).

20 *Apollo Theater Foundation Inc. v. Western International*, United States District Court of New York, 02 Civ 10037 (DLC), 5 May 2005.

21 *Paper wholesalers cartel*, judgment of 19 June 2007.

Regression (econometrics) techniques are a more sophisticated statistical method that can explain the variation in data using other factors. These techniques address one of the main shortcomings of simple comparisons of averages – finding markets that are sufficiently similar – by controlling for differences in market or firm characteristics in the relevant and comparator markets.

The alternative – and perhaps most commonly used – source of a comparator is data over time. Although this approach is often described generically as 'before and after', it is appropriate to make an explicit distinction between three types of comparison that can be made using time-series data. First, before and during – an unaffected period before the infringement can be compared with the period of the infringement. Second, during and after – an unaffected period after the infringement can be compared with the period during which the infringement took place. Third, before, during and after – both comparisons can be made if data before and after the infringement is available. These variants have been used in many damages cases. In two German rulings, the courts used the price after the termination of the cartels to estimate the overcharge and the consequent loss incurred by the claimants.[22] In *Apollo Theater Foundation v. Western International*, the costs and advertising revenue trends from a period before the infringement were used to calculate projected revenues and costs for the infringement period, in order to estimate damages for lost profits. (This case also used cross-section comparisons, as discussed above.)[23]

Time-series data has the advantage that the comparison involves like-for-like companies or markets because it refers to the same companies or markets in both the factual and counterfactual cases. A possible problem with time-series models is that they effectively assume that all of the unexplained differences between the time periods can be attributed to the infringement. As with the cross-sectional comparators, other drivers of the variable under consideration should be controlled for to ensure that the difference between the periods is not biased by any external factors (see below).

Time-series comparisons can sometimes be used by claimants to provide support for their argument when a clear pattern is observed. For example, in the *LePage's* monopolisation case in the USA, the court found that the 'impact of 3M's discounts was apparent from the chart introduced by LePage's showing that LePage's earnings as a percentage of sales plummeted to below zero – to negative 10% – during 3M's rebate programme', and was satisfied that LePage's had 'introduced substantial evidence that the anti-competitive effects of 3M's rebate programmes caused LePage's losses'.[24] Another relatively simple during-and-after comparison was made in a damages action before the Regional Civil Court of Graz in Austria that had followed on from a 2005 judgment by the Austrian Cartel

---

22 LG Dortmund 0 55/ 02 Kart *Vitaminkartell III*, Decision, 1 April 2004, and Oberlandesgericht Düsseldorf, *Berliner Transportbeton I*, KRB 2/05, Decision, 28 June 2005.

23 *Apollo Theater Foundation Inc. v. Western International*, United States District Court of New York, 02 Civ 10037 (DLC), Decision, 5 May 2005.

24 *LePage's, Inc. v. 3M, 324 F.3d (3d Cir. 2003).*

Court, which imposed fines of €75,000 on five driving schools for price fixing.[25] The Cartel Court found that, for a period of two months, the schools had charged identical prices for the most popular driving courses, which was an infringement of the Austrian Cartel Act. The claim was brought by the Bundesarbeitskammer (the Federal Chamber of Workers) on behalf of customers of the driving schools who had suffered damage as a result of the cartel. The Bundesarbeitskammer argued that the loss suffered by customers could be quantified as the 22% difference between the price charged by the driving schools for the two months of the cartel's duration (which was identical for the cartel members) and the lower price once the cartel had ended (based on an average price calculated at that time). The court accepted this calculation.

Interpolation involves joining the price points before and after the relevant period to indicate what the prices would have been in the intervening period. In its simplest form the connecting line will be linear, as in the example in Figure 16, which is based on a cartel damages case we have worked on. The top line shows the development of actual prices paid by the claimant. The starting point of the cartel is the date at which, according to the European Commission's infringement decision, the first meeting between cartel members was held. The starting price for the interpolation is based on an average actual price in the months before this start date. The end price is an average actual price in the months after the Commission's dawn raids took place and the cartel was broken up. (The actual price plummets at about that time.) The dashed line between these points shows the counterfactual price according to the interpolation exercise. More sophisticated versions of interpolation can incorporate seasonal patterns if that is a feature of the market. Figure 16 incorporates a different adjustment, namely one for exchange rate movements, since in this case the cartel fixed prices in one European currency and the claim related to prices in another currency that had devalued during the cartel period. This results in a new counterfactual line, as shown in the figure. It can be seen that the price increase (and later decrease) due to the exchange rate movement explains a small part of the price increase that took place at the start of the cartel, but there is still a significant overcharge effect.

25 *Bundesarbeitskammer v. Powerdrive Fahrschule Andritz GmbH*, judgment of 17 August 2007.

Fig. 16. Example of interpolation to determine the counterfactual (prices before, during and after the cartel)

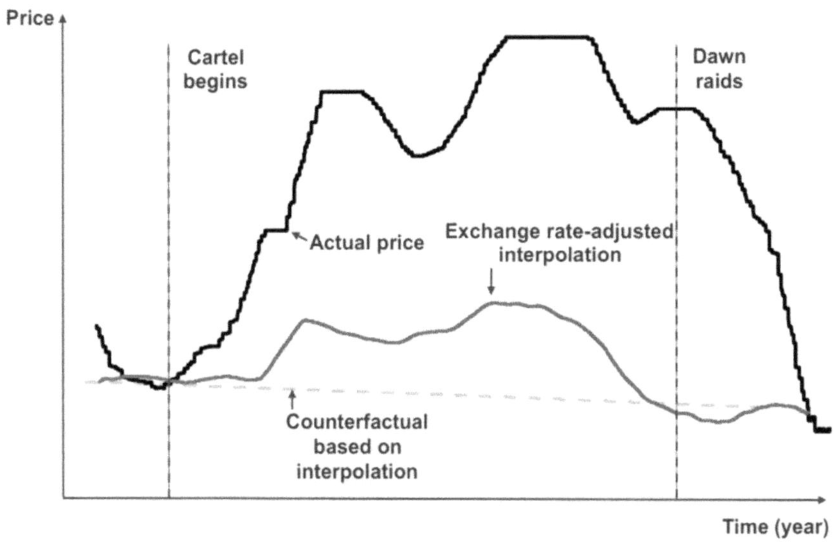

The difference-in-differences technique aims to avoid some of the shortcomings of cross-sectional and time-series approaches, in particular the assumption that any unexplained difference is due solely to the infringement. Difference-in-differences estimators control for what would have happened without the infringement by examining what changed over time for the infringement and non-infringement markets, followed by a comparison of those differences. This technique requires data both over time and across infringement and non-infringement markets.

The estimation techniques for panel data are similar to those often used for evaluating clinical trials and the effect of policy choices, in that one group has a 'treatment' applied to it (the infringement) while another that is not treated is used as a control group.[26] The difference-in-differences analysis then compares what happens to each group before, during and after the treatment. By using the control group, the analysis removes the impact of any changes that affect both treatment and control groups. Such changes would have introduced a bias in the time-series-based damages estimate.

26 See, for example, H. Krum, E.L. Conway, J.H. Broadbear, L.G. Howes, and W.J. Louis, 'Postural Hypotension in Elderly Patients Given Carvedilol', 309 *British Medical Journal* (1994), 775–76 and D. Card & A.B. Krueger, 'Minimum Wages and Employment: A Case Study of the Fast-food Industry in New Jersey and Pennsylvania', 84(4) *American Economic Review* (1994), 772–93.

Figure 17 illustrates how the difference-in-differences estimator can be determined. This technique uses the average price in the treatment group (i.e. the infringement market, A) in the period before the infringement, and the corresponding averages for B (infringement market during the infringement), C (non-infringement market before) and D (non-infringement market during). The difference (B – A) reflects the change in prices in the market concerned before and during the infringement, while (D – C) reflects that in the comparator market. Not all of (B – A) may be due to the infringement, since the prices may have changed even without the infringement. This change can be assumed to be equal to that in the comparator market as reflected by (D – C). The difference in the differences in the average prices, i.e. (B – A) – (D – C), is therefore used to identify the change in prices in the relevant market due to an infringement.

Fig. 17. Example of difference-in-differences model (prices for the treatment and control groups, before and during the cartel)

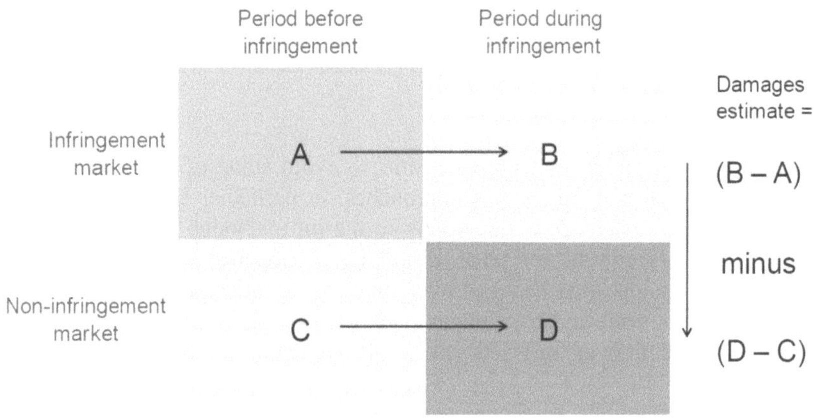

Source: Oxera *et al.* (2009).

9 Interest and Discounting: Why Things Are not Always Simple

A competition law infringement may have lasted many years. The counterfactual analysis may have generated an overcharge estimate in monetary terms for each year, and the yearly cash flows would have to be added up. From an economic perspective, this involves uprating and discounting cash flows to take into account the time value of money. For this you use a discount rate. Furthermore, part of the harm may be suffered even after the anti-competitive practice has ceased. Depending on the legal rules and the facts of each case, those future losses may need to be included in the damages calculation, again using discounting.

From a legal perspective, the uprating of cash flows is closely related to the application of interest to damages estimates. As noted at the start of this chapter, the compensation principle in EU law means that damages awards should also include interest. This requires moving cash flows between time periods in accordance with the legal rules (for example, from the year in which a harm occurred to the year in which the damage is paid), which in essence is a form of uprating. The principles of uprating and discounting, as set out here, also capture the application of interest, and are therefore in line with the compensation principle.

Legal rules and practices regarding the award and calculation of interest vary significantly across jurisdictions and across cases within jurisdictions. They also tend to be somewhat at odds with economic principles. One specific issue is whether the interest is simple or compound (interest on interest). Another is that various jurisdictions require statutory rates of interest rather than market rates for certain periods of uprating. Some jurisdictions give greater weight to the economic principles of uprating and discounting than others. In this section we set out those principles and explore some of the differences between law and economics.

From an economic perspective, any summation or movement of cash flows over time needs to take account of the time value of money – €1 today is worth more than €1 tomorrow. This is a fairly standard approach to valuation and investment appraisal, and requires the use of an appropriate discount rate, as explained in any standard text on corporate finance.[27] Conceptually, the discount rate should take into account the time value of money, inflation and risk. Inflation means that prices rise over time and hence the same nominal amount of money decreases in value. Future expected profits are uncertain. When calculating the value of the damage today for expected lost profits in the future, this uncertainty needs to be accounted for through the risk component of the discount rate (at least according to economic principles).

The logic of the time value of money is also captured in the legal principle of compensation. As the European Commission notes:

> With regard to the payment of interest, the Court refers to its earlier judgment in the 1993 Marshall case. In that judgment, the Court stated that 'full compensation for the loss and damage sustained … cannot leave out of account factors, such as the effluxion of time, which may in fact reduce its value. The award of interest, in accordance with the applicable national rules, must therefore be regarded as an essential component of compensation'. The Court's objective is thus clearly to ensure that the victim is given the real value of the loss suffered. The reference in Manfredi to the payment of interest should therefore be understood as covering the whole period from the time the damage occurred until the capital sum awarded is actually paid.[28]

---

27 For example, see R.A. Brealey, S.C. Myers and F. Allen, *Principles of Corporate Finance* (McGraw Hill, 9th ed. 2008).

28 European Commission, 'Staff Working Paper Accompanying the White Paper on Damages Actions for Breach of the EC Antitrust Rules', SEC(2008) 404, April 2008, para. 187. The cases referred to in this quote are Case C-271/91, *Marshall v. Southampton and South West Hampshire Area Health Authority* [1993] ECR I-4367, pa-

Applying interest on damages is one form of uprating cash flows in the quantification of damages. In simple terms, if an infringement has caused the victim a loss of €100 during each of the past five years, each year's loss needs to be uprated using the discount rate to determine the current value of this harm suffered. Suppose that the discount rate is 10% per year. The harm from the first of the five years (i.e. the first €100) needs to be uprated five times, which is comparable to paying cumulative interest on that amount for five years. The current value of that amount is €161.05 (€100 times 1.10 to the power of 5). The harm from the second year needs to be uprated for four years (€100 times 1.10 to the power of 4, which equals €146.41), and so on. The present value of the total harm over these five years is €671.56. For simplicity's sake, this example assumes that the cash flows occur on 1 January of each year. Another assumption is that the interest rate is compounded – i.e. the calculation includes interest on accumulated interest from prior periods (see below).

If it is demonstrated, and accepted by the court, that the infringement, even if it has ceased, will still cause losses to the victim in the subsequent three years (say, because the victim cannot immediately recover the market position it would have had in the absence of the infringement), those future losses form part of the harm suffered. They need to be added to the present value of the harm over the first five years. Suppose the losses are €75, €50 and €25, and the same discount rate applies. The €75 occurs in the current year, so does not require uprating or discounting. The €50 occurs next year, so needs to be discounted once, and is worth €45.45 in present terms (€50 divided by 1.10). The €25 in two years' time is worth €20.66 in present terms (€25 divided by 1.10 to the power of 2). The present value of the total harm over the whole eight years (five past years, the current year and the two future years) is now €812.68.

From the above example it follows that the choice of discount rate can have a significant influence on the damage value. If the discount rate was 5% instead of 10%, the present value of the damage from the five past years would be €580.19 instead of €671.56. If it was 15% the value would be €775.37. The higher the discount rate, the greater the present value of the past losses when uprated at the discount rate, but the smaller the present value of the future losses when discounted at this rate. Various jurisdictions require statutory rates of interest – generally prescribed by civil or contract/tort law provisions – to be used for certain periods of uprating, i.e. moving a sum of money from an earlier period to a later period, such as for late payment of the damages.

Economic and finance theories have developed a range of principles on how to determine the discount rate. In the context of damages valuation, it may be appropriate to use the cost of capital for the claimant as the discount rate for future expected losses. This discount rate takes into account the time value of money and the business risk of the claimant (i.e. the fact that future factual and counterfactual scenarios, and hence estimates of losses, are uncertain). Discounting expected future losses would provide an estimate of their value at the award date.

ra. 31, and Joined Cases C–295/04 to C–298/04 *Vincenzo Manfredi and others v. Lloyd Adriatico Assicurazioni SpA and others* [2006] ECR I–6619.

There are several possible approaches to uprating past losses. The first is the cost of capital from the claimant. During the period in which the damages were incurred, a claimant earning 'normal' returns would have earned profit consistent in the long run with the cost of capital. Thus, damages uprated at the cost of capital would capture the expected return that the claimant could have earned on the amounts lost had they been available for investment, compensating investors for the use of their capital. The second approach is the risk-free rate, which is usually approximated by taking the rate of a virtually risk-free investment such as a government bond. The rationale for this is that the repayment of damages is certain once awarded (unless the defendant is unable to pay), thus ensuring that the claimant is compensated for the time value of money without risk component, which is conceptually equivalent to paying interest.

Interest (and discount) rates can be applied as simple interest or compound interest. When the interest rate is compounded, the calculation includes interest on accumulated interest from prior periods. For example, 10% is applied to €100 in the first year, yielding €110, in the second year the 10% is applied to that €110 from the first year, yielding €121. From an economic perspective, compounding interest is the usual, and conceptually correct, approach to discounting. When you put your money in the bank, you expect interest to be paid on the whole balance, which includes past interest as well. And yet there are many instances where the legal framework requires the simple interest to be applied (i.e. interest calculated solely as a percentage of the principal sum). For example, 10% is applied to €100 in the first year, yielding €110; and in the second year the 10% is again applied to the €100, yielding a total of €120. In this example the difference between the two methods is only €1. However, for longer time periods and higher interest rates the differences become substantially greater.

EU case law seems to have used both approaches, depending on the specifics of the case. In 2001 the European General Court stated that:

> Regarding the rate of interest, it should be pointed out that, according to a principle generally accepted in the domestic law of the Member States, in an action for the recovery of a sum unduly paid based on the principle prohibiting unjust enrichment, the claimant is normally entitled to the lower of the two amounts corresponding to the enrichment and the loss. Furthermore, where the loss consists of the loss of use of a sum of money over a period of time, the amount recoverable is generally calculated by reference to the statutory or judicial rate of interest, without compounding.[29]

But the General Court also found that, in that particular case, the actual amount to be calculated would be better reflected by applying a compound interest rate, and it therefore applied the latter approach. A more recent UK House of Lords ruling, in *Sempra Metals*, contains a useful discussion of these points.[30] It notes several comments made by legal representative bodies: 'The obvious reason for awarding compound interest is that it reflects economic reality.' And: 'Computation of the time value of the enrichment on the basis of simple interest will inevitably fall short of its true value.' And finally: 'The virtue of simple interest is its

29 Case T-171/99, *Corus UK Ltd v. Commission* [2001] ECR II-2967, para. 60.

30 *Sempra Metals Ltd v. Revenue & Anor* [2007] UKHL 34, 18 July 2007.

simplicity. That cannot be said of compound interest, which can be calculated in different ways leading to different results.' Increasingly, case law in the UK recognises that the use of the statutory interest rate as opposed to a commercial interest rate is not necessarily aligned with business reality. In a case outside competition law the court held that:

> The Judgments Act [statutory] rate is fixed for the benefit of unpaid judgment creditors. It is not normally an appropriate rate of interest to award in the context of a dispute between two businesses … If Claymore or a company such as Claymore, had sought to borrow £750,000.00 over the period since June 2004, Claymore would have had to pay interest at more than 1% over base rate.[31]

Once the principle is acknowledged that the interest rate should reflect the commercial opportunity costs of borrowing, and hence that commercial interest rates should be used, it is a relatively small step towards using the cost of capital. Companies do not finance themselves solely by borrowing – they have debt and equity capital, and hence the opportunity cost of raising capital contains both the cost of debt (interest) and the cost of equity.

All in all, plenty of room exists for economics and the law to move closer in the area of discounting and interest in damages cases. Until then, however, the last stage in the damages calculation will remain far from simple.

31 *Claymore v. Nautilus* [2007] EWHC 805 (TCC).

Best Practices for Expert Economic Opinions – Key Element of Forensic Economics in Competition Law

Arndt Christiansen and Christian Ewald[1]

1 Introduction

In October 2010 the Bundeskartellamt, the independent German federal competition authority, published for the first time a formal notice that sets forth binding quality standards for expert testimony provided by economists.[2] The publication of these 'Best Practices' signifies the increasing importance of economic reasoning and methods in German competition law enforcement. The Best Practices are first and foremost intended to make sure that the interaction between economic experts drawn upon by the parties to a case, competition authorities and the courts contributes effectively to sound decision making. Studies prepared by experts are one important source of theoretical insights and empirical analysis to guide competition law proceedings. A detailed analysis of the Bundeskartellamt's Best Practices

1 Christian Ewald is Chief Economist of the Bundeskartellamt (German Federal Cartel Office). Arndt Christiansen is an economist in the Unit G3 - Economic Issues of the Bundeskartellamt. All opinions in this article are those of the authors and do not necessarily represent the official position of the Bundeskartellamt. This article draws on a presentation given by Christian Ewald at the ZEW Conference 'Public and private enforcement of competition law' in March 2011 as well as a presentation given by Arndt Christiansen at the 4th St. Martin Conference of the Office for the Protection of Competition at Brno in November 2010, which was later published in modified form (see A. Christiansen, 'The "Best Practices for Expert Economic Opinions" by the Bundeskartellamt in international Context', *Antitrust: Revue of Competition Law* (2/2011), p. 66–73; published by Sdružení Kairos, Prague). The authors would like to thank participants at both conferences for valuable comments and suggestions as well as their colleague Sara Buccino for excellent editorial assistance.

2 Bundeskartellamt, Best Practices for expert economic opinions, 20 October 2010, available at http://www.bundeskartellamt.de/wEnglisch/download/pdf/Merkblaetter/Bekanntmachung_Standards_Englisch_final.pdf. In case of contest only the German version is valid, which is available at http://www.bundeskartellamt.de/wDeutsch/download/pdf/Merkblaetter/Merkblaetter_deutsch/Bekanntmachung_Standards_final.pdf.

and in particular a comparison with similar guidance documents and principles applied in other jurisdictions provides valuable insights. This article seeks outline core principles that should inform the effective integration of economic analysis in competition law enforcement.

The article is structured as follows: Section 2 sketches the main issues and challenges surrounding the effective integration of economic arguments and methods into competition law enforcement. Section 3 specifies the rationale for quality standards in producing economic assessments, describes key elements of the Bundeskartellamt's Best Practices and provides a comparison with similar documents published by competition authorities in other jurisdictions. Section 4 analyzes the quality standards developed and applied within the U.S. adversarial enforcement regime for (economic) expert testimony in court. Section 5 concludes.

2 Forensic Economics in Competition Law

The single most important recent trend in competition law and policy has been the rising significance of economic analysis.[3] On the EU level this development has often been labelled 'the more economic approach', taking a cue from certain statements made by European Commission representatives.[4] This new approach has been debated with particular intensity in reaction to the European Commission's reform initiatives in virtually all areas of competition law since the late 1990s.[5] Very pronounced criticism has come from German scholars and practitioners, albeit from somewhat different perspectives and with different reform proposals.[6] Presumably, some if not most of the criticism is based on the perceived normative and policy implications of the Commission's new approach.[7]

---

3 See inter alia C. Ewald, Ökonomie im Kartellrecht: Vom more economic approach zu sachgerechten Standards forensischer Ökonomie, 9 *Zeitschrift für Wettbewerbsrecht* (2011), p. 15–47 with regard to Germany and A. Christiansen, *Der More Economic Approach in der EU-Fusionskontrolle. Darstellung, konzeptionelle Grundlagen und kritische Analyse* (Peter Lang 2010) with regard to the EU.

4 For example, then Commissioner for Competition Policy Mario Monti said in 2002: 'I should like to underline that an increased economic approach in the interpretation of our rules was, indeed, one of my main objectives [...]. And we have already substantially increased our economic approach in all areas of competition policy.' (See M. Monti, EU Competition Policy, 31.10.2002, available at http://ec.europa.eu/ competition/speeches/, p. 7).

5 See the overviews provided by the two former Chief Competition Economists Damien Neven and Lars-Hendrik Röller (D. Neven, Competition economics and antitrust in Europe, 21 *Economic Policy* (2006), p. 741–791 and L.-H. Röller, Economic analysis and competition policy enforcement in Europe, in P. van Bergeijk and E. Kloosterhuis (eds.), *Modelling European Mergers: Theory, Competition Policy and Case Studies* (Edward Elgar 2005), p. 13–26).

6 See inter alia U. Böge, Der 'more economic approach' und die deutsche Wettbewerbspolitik, 54 *Wirtschaft und Wettbewerb* (2004), p. 726–733; O. Budzinski, Mono-

Irrespective of these more abstract debates, the cardinal relevance of economics as a scientific discipline for competition law and policy seems beyond any reasonable doubt.[8] Economics heavily influences competition law at distinct stages – namely, in the formulation of rules (including guidelines) and in the analysis of individual cases.[9] This article focuses on the analytical refinement of assessment techniques through the introduction of economic concepts and the greater use of quantitative analysis. Such refinement closely mirrors advances in industrial economics (or industrial organization, as it is called in the US), the field of economic science most closely related to competition law and policy. Economic research has greatly expanded the range and sophistication of available theoretical concepts and empirical tools.[10] Great advances in empirical research have also been enabled by the increasing availability of quantitative data, the improvement of statistical software packages and growing computer power. The challenges associated with integrating scientific concepts and methods into different aspects of the legal process is, however, by no means unique to competition law. On the contrary, such challenges can arise in many if not all areas of law enforcement, and can probably best be summarized under the term 'forensic science'. Broadly defined: [11]

> [...] forensic science (often known as forensics) is the application of a broad spectrum of sciences and technologies to investigate and establish facts of interest in relation to criminal or civil law. The word *forensic* comes from the Latin *forēnsis*, meaning 'of or before the forum.' In Roman times, a criminal charge meant presenting the case before a group of public individuals in the forum. Both the person accused of the crime and the accuser would give speeches based on their sides of the story. The individual with the best argument and delivery would determine the outcome of the case.

---

culture versus Diversity in Competition Economics, 32 *Cambridge Journal of Economics* (2008), p. 295–324; W. Möschel, 'European Merger Control', 34 *European Competition Law Review* (2013), p. 283–286; I. Schmidt, 'The suitability of the more economic approach for competition policy: dynamic v. static efficiency', 28 *European Competition Law Review* (2007), p. 408–411.

7 These debates relate, for example, to the ultimate goals and possible intermediate targets of competition law and policy. See also J. Haucap, Irrtümer über die Ökonomisierung des Wettbewerbsrechts, 114 *Orientierungen zur Wirtschafts- und Gesellschaftspolitik* (2007), p. 12–16.

8 For the sake of a focused discussion it seems advisable to separate normative or policy issues from the analytical question of the integration of economics in competition law enforcement (see also Ewald, *supra* n 3, 21 et seq. and Christiansen, *supra* n 3, 285 et seq.). This separation will be adhered to in this article.

9 On this distinction and its implications, see generally A. Christiansen and W. Kerber, 'Competition Policy with Optimally Differentiated Rules Instead of "Per se Rules vs. Rule of Reason"', 2 Journal of Competition Law and Economics (2006), 215–244.

10 See overviews by P. Buccirossi (ed.), *Handbook of Antitrust Economics* (MIT Press 2008); P. Davis and E. Garcés, *Quantitative Techniques for Competition and Antitrust Analysis* (Princeton 2010); P. Davis, 'On the role of empirical industrial organization in competition policy', 29 *International Journal of Industrial Organization* (2011), 323–328.

11 Quoted from wikipedia at https://en.wikipedia.org/wiki/Forensic_science.

Accordingly, the issues and challenges associated with the effective integration of economic concepts and methods in competition law enforcement seem best subsumed under the heading 'forensic economics in competition law'.[12]

There is, however, no generally accepted definition for forensic economics. In fact, the term has traditionally received a quite narrow interpretation with respect to the kind of activities it designates. As Zitzewitz[13] aptly puts it: 'Traditionally, forensic economics has referred to the application of economics to the detection and quantification of harm from behaviour that has become the subject of litigation, and has been practiced by experts who are paid by the court or one of the parties.' Especially in the US, economists testify regularly in cases concerned with determining liability – for example, following traffic accidents, industrial accidents or commercial litigation. This subfield has its own organization, the National Association of Forensic Economics (NAFE),[14] and its own journal, the Journal of Forensic Economics.[15]

In recent years the term forensic economics has come to be used in a somewhat broader sense. In particular, academic papers employing this term have been published on a diverse range of subjects, including trading on financial markets, teaching, surgery, traffic control and real estate brokerage.[16] However, this broader conception does not conform to the specific meaning attributed to the term in our context of competition law enforcement. Here, the focus is not exclusively on the identification of damage and the calculation of its magnitude (although this is one specific task in private competition law enforcement). Rather, the task of forensic economics in public competition law enforcement is to assess the competitive effects of firm behaviour against the backdrop of relevant theoretical and empirical knowledge, as well as to identify behaviour harmful to competition, as opposed to behaviour that is neutral or benign.

In this way, forensic economics should be defined more specifically in relation to the subfield in which it is used. For example, according to Schinkel,[17] forensic economics in competition law is the 'application of theoretical and empirical in-

---

12 See also Ewald, *supra* n 3, and M. P. Schinkel, 'Forensic Economics in Competition Law Enforcement', 4 *Journal of Competition Law and Economics* (2008), 1–30.

13 E. Zitzewitz, 'Forensic Economics', 50 *Journal of Economic Literature* (2012), 731–769, p. 731.

14 See the website of the NAFE at http://www.nafe.net/.

15 For a recent survey among members of the NAFE, see F. Slesnick, M. Luthy and M. Brookshire, 'Survey of Forensic Economists: Their Methods, Estimates, and Perspectives', 24 *Journal of Forensic Economics* (2013), 67–99. Among the responding NAFE members the mean time of practicing forensic economics amounts to 25.48 years (p. 91). Moreover, the survey noted a shift of income sources away from academic salaries to consulting which may hint at an increasing detachment from academia (p. 92).

16 See examples in J. Ritter, 'Forensic Finance', 22 *Journal of Economic Perspectives* (2008), 127–147; D. Schap, 'Forensic Economics: An Overview', 36 *Eastern Economic Journal* (2010), 347–352 and Zitzewitz, *supra* n 13.

17 See Schinkel, *supra* n 12, p. 3.

dustrial organization economics in one or more of the various stages of the legal process of competition law enforcement. It is close to antitrust economics, which is concerned with the economics underlying competition law generally.' This understanding has the merit of stressing the fact that the application of economics in competition law is not confined to supporting decision-making in individual cases, but that it is also necessary for the development of general rules and for the setting of priorities for investigation and enforcement. Moreover, it is not limited to empirical analyses, whether quantitative or econometric.[18] Although empirical evidence is of course important and economists are especially capable of developing it, the implementation of quantitative and econometric analysis is sensible only as the second logical step. Indeed, the more important first logical step is the conceptual analysis of a given case,[19] particularly the development of a consistent and testable theory of harm. The term 'theory of harm' refers to a conceptual framework that specifies the way in which competition is actually harmed (or is likely to be so if future conduct is concerned) by a given behaviour. This framework is used to organize the facts of the case in question. Only when a sound conceptual framework has been established, it is possible to devise an appropriate investigation and assess the empirical evidence.[20] This may include the collection of quantitative data, which can then be used for an econometric analysis. But in many cases simpler types of empirical analysis may also suffice. In a recent paper, Bishop[21] quite rightly stated that '[it] is a common fallacy to equate the use of empirical evidence with the use of econometric analysis. Econometric analysis represents only one method for analyzing observed data.'

Furthermore, the fact that forensics in general marks the interface between science and the legal process of law enforcement constitutes an important difference between forensic economics in competition law proceedings and economic research in the academic context.[22] In the latter, the use of sophisticated models and

18 See A. Italianer, 'Quantity and quality in economic assessments', Speech at Charles River Associates Annual Conference, 7 December 2011, available at http://ec.europa.eu/competition/speeches/text/sp2011_15_en.pdf.

19 The current Director-General at the Directorate-General for Competition of the European Commission ('DG COMP'), Alexander Italianer, offered a description of the task of the economists at DG COMP in the much the same way by saying: 'The contribution of our in-house economists is not limited to quantitative econometric work. Our economists are now fully involved in the development of conceptual frameworks for our cases and our overall policy-making.' A. Italianer, 'The interplay between law and economics', Speech at Charles River Associates Annual Conference, Brussels, 8 December 2010, available at http://ec.europa.eu/competition/speeches/index_ speeches_by_the_dg.html.

20 See also K.-U. Kühn, '"Good economics" in administrative proceedings: Three challenges', *Concurrences* (3/2013), 1-3, pp. 2 et seq.

21 S. Bishop, 'Snake-Oil with Mathematics is Still Snakeoil: Why Recent Trends in the Application of So-Called 'Sophisticated' Economics is Hindering Good Competition Policy Enforcement', 9 *European Competition Journal* (2013), 67–77, p. 68 (fn. 5).

22 See also D. Evans, 'Economics and the Design of Competition Law', in: ABA Section of Antitrust Law, *Issues in Competition Law and Policy, Vol. 1* (ABA Publishing

complex quantitative techniques is apparently valuable for its own sake, because it demonstrates the researcher's capabilities or because the novelty of a piece of research may precisely depend on the method(s) employed. Moreover, it seems to be common practice to demonstrate the theoretical possibility of a certain outcome based on a specific set of assumptions. This, in turn, leads to additional research based on a slightly modified set of assumptions, which in turn stimulates further study, and so on. In this process, time constraints are not of foremost importance.[23] In fact, a long-standing criticism of game theory-based modern industrial economics is that it produces too many theoretically possible results, and too few insights as to their empirical relevance and applicability to real-world cases.[24]

By contrast, in competition law enforcement, the capabilities of the analyst and the novelty of the method(s) applied are not as important. Neither is the mere theoretical proof of the possibility of a certain outcome. Rather, any economic analysis put forward in the context of competition law proceedings must produce robust and reliable results that help to decide a specific case within a given, often very tight, time-frame. This means that it is not enough to merely state that a certain behaviour possibly leads to a certain effect. Rather, it is necessary to offer a reasoned assessment as to whether this is likely in the case at hand.

Further challenges result from the character of forensic economics as the interface between economic science and the legal process of competition law enforcement. These relate to the practical interaction between law and economics, i.e. between practitioners with a legal background and those with an economics

2008), 99–123, p. 114 and pp. 119 et seq.; F. Fisher, 'Games Economists Play: A Noncooperative View', 20 *Rand Journal of Economics* (1989), 113–124.

23 They certainly do not (or at least should not) matter with regard to the economic 'science' viewed as a whole but they likely do matter with regard to individual scholars who pursue an academic career, the success of which depends above all on articles published in highly ranked journals over a finite period of time. On that matter, see G. Ellison, 'The Slowdown of the Economics Publishing Process', 110 *Journal of Political Economy* (2002), 947–993.

24 See O. Budzinski, 'Modern Industrial Economics: Open Problems and Possible Limits', in J. Drexl, W. Kerber and R. Podszun (eds.), *Competition Policy and The Economic Approach. Foundations and Limitations* (Edward Elgar, 2011), 111–138; Bishop, *supra* n 20; and Fisher, *supra* n 21. Fisher contributed an already famous and particularly outspoken specimen of this criticism, and even more interestingly, in one of the top journals in the field (Rand Journal of Economics). For example, he wrote (p. 188): 'Returning to my main subject, it should be plain that (with or without game theory) the status of the theory of oligopoly is that of exemplifying theory. We know that a lot of different things can happen. We do not have a full, coherent, formal theory of what must happen or a theory that tells us how what happens depends on well-defined, measurable variables.' Or, at a later point in his article (p. 123): 'There is a strong tendency for even the best practitioners to concentrate on the analytically interesting questions rather than on the ones that really matter for the study of real-life industries.'

background.[25] Properly understood, forensic economics does not intend to replace but to effectively support an ultimately legal assessment of a given case. Therefore, in order to be effective, economic insights – whether in the form of conceptual knowledge, or empirical findings – must be sufficiently accessible and comprehensible to legal practitioners and, perhaps foremost, to judges.[26] Accordingly, the current Director-General at DG COMP, Alexander Italianer,[27] correctly noted in a recent speech:

> However we must all bear in mind that we ultimately have to prove our cases before a court. And when we prove our cases we do not do it to an economic standard, but to a legal one. The key point here is that we are in fact using economic analysis to support the construction of legally robust cases.

With regard to the role of economists, the primacy of the 'rule of law' in competition law enforcement has important implications not only for the final form taken by economic analyses, but also for decisions concerning which analyses to perform in the first place. The relevance for the case at hand and the robustness of the results are particularly important. The same holds for the accessibility and comprehensibility of economic assessments submitted to legal practitioners and judges.[28]

However, the operation and effectiveness of any interface crucially depend on the quality of the connection and the responsiveness of both sides. Accordingly, legal practitioners, for their part, have an obligation to acquire at least a sufficient understanding of economics to assess the adequacy and relevance of a piece of analysis in a given case. In this context, economic experts commissioned or appointed by courts or the parties to a case are by no means a cure-all for remedying communication problems between practitioners with a legal background and those

---

25 See also Italianer, *supra* n 19; A.-L. Sibony, 'Limits of Imports from Economics into Competition Law', in I. Lianos and D. Sokol (eds.), *The Global Limits of Competition Law* (Stanford University Press 2012), 39–53; P. Pohlmann, 'Ökonomische Normtatsachen im Kartellzivilprozess – Am Beispiel der Kosten-Preis-Schere', in A. Bruns, C. Kern, J. Münch, A. Piepenbrock, A. Stadler and D. Tsikrikas (eds.), *Festschrift für Rolf Stürner zum 70. Geburtstag*, (Mohr Siebeck 2013), 435–454.

26 On that matter, see J. Nothdurft, 'Ökonomie vor Gericht. Richterliche Überprüfung wirtschaftlicher Fragen im deutschen und europäischen Kartellverwaltungsprozess', in G. Müller, E. Osterloh and T. Stein (eds.), *Festschrift für Günter Hirsch zum 65. Geburtstag* (Beck, 2008), 285–300; D. Wood, 'Square Pegs in Round Holes: The Interaction between Judges and Economic Evidence', 5 *Competition Policy International* (2009), 50–64; and also the OECD Competition Policy Roundtable on Presenting Complex Economic Theories to Judges, 2008, DAF/COMP(2008)31, available at http://www.oecd.org/daf/competition/abuse/ 41776770.pdf.

27 See Italianer, *supra* n 19, p. 5.

28 For example, Bishop, *supra* n 20, p. 76 put it that way: 'If economists cannot explain and demonstrate the relevance of their results, and show how their predictions about economic effects are drawn from a body of work that is consistent with observed industry facts, it is not clear why they should be taken seriously by the ultimate decision-makers.'

with an economics background. In order to avoid being supplanted by economic experts when it comes to assessing the merits of a case, lawyers and judges should acquire the basic economic knowledge necessary to 'separate the wheat from the chaff', i.e. to evaluate the relevance and adequacy of expert opinions provided by economists. This ability is all the more necessary in cases in which adjudicators are confronted by contradictory economic assessments from opposing parties. At the same time, this serves to make sure that the level of complexity of an analysis does not fall below the adequate level.

3 Minimum Quality Standards for Expert Opinions

3.1 Purpose and Rationale

Assessing the quality of an expert opinion in competition law proceedings is in fact equal to evaluating its probative value. Against this backdrop, and also taking into account the most recent developments in enforcement practice, several reasons strongly militate in favour of the development and implementation of minimum quality standards.

Since the primary objective of forensic economics is to contribute to high-quality decision making,[29] poor economic arguments and analyses of weak probative value should generally be avoided. This is additionally true because economic analyses of a specific case also have to satisfy the ancillary condition of procedural efficiency.[30] Considering the famous assertion attributed to William Gladstone that 'justice delayed is justice denied', the fact that different expert opinions may come to different conclusions or even contradict each other should not lead to a deadlocked battle over who can make the most sophisticated argument, with attendant delays in case resolution. Yet by the same token, the objective of ensuring procedural efficiency should not undermine the due assessment of the probative value of potentially contradictory expert opinions. Any assertion should be avoided that contradictory expert opinions 'neutralize' each other, and do not have to be assessed in terms of their relative quality and/or probative value. In this context,

---

29 In a decision-theoretic framework, the objective of increased decision quality corresponds to a reduction in the cost of erroneous decisions, i.e. of over-enforcement (false positives, type-1 error) or under-enforcement (false negatives, type-2 error) of the legal provisions at stake. See Christiansen and Kerber, *supra* n 9, pp. 223 et seq. and Ewald, *supra* n 3, pp. 18 et seq.

30 In a decision-theoretic framework, this aspect is covered by the implementation cost of any attempt to reduce the cost of erroneous decisions by a more sophisticated and elaborate analysis of the relevant facts of a case. At the margin, any further reduction in the cost of error (marginal benefit) should be only aspired to if the (expected) reduction exceeds the additional implementation cost (marginal cost) associated with a more sophisticated assessment of facts.

quality standards for expert opinions may facilitate efficient and transparent debate over the merits and demerits of expert opinions submitted in parallel.

The experiences gathered in recent years in German competition law enforcement clearly indicate that assessing the relative probative value of expert opinions has become an increasingly relevant challenge. Since the creation of the economics unit at the Bundeskartellamt in mid-2007, the number of expert opinions submitted has risen steadily.[31] Expert opinions are submitted on the initiative of the parties to a case or in reaction to the economic arguments and empirical analyses advanced by the Bundeskartellamt. Taken together, the number of expert opinions submitted since July 2007 exceeds sixty. In the year 2012 alone a total of 14 studies were submitted and evaluated. In principle, they concern all areas of competition law enforcement. The majority of studies were compiled by specialist economic consultancies, some of which focus their practice on Germany and some of which belong to international consultancy firms.[32] A noteworthy number of opinions were prepared by individual academic economists.

Looking at absolute numbers, merger control is a key issue. However, this would appear to simply reflect the high number of merger cases compared to other areas of competition law. Indeed, the relative importance of economic studies appears to be at least as high in other areas, such as cartel enforcement and sector inquiries. Generally, expert opinions are only submitted with regard to more complex cases. In terms of methods, most of the studies contain quantitative analyses, while practically all opinions contained references to theoretical research. Purely theoretical analyses are, however, the exception.

3.2 The Bundeskartellamt's 'Best Practices for Expert Economic Opinions'

In light of the growing number of expert opinions being submitted, in October 2010 the Bundeskartellamt for the first time published a formal notice that sets forth binding quality standards for expert opinions. The notice is titled 'Best Practices for expert economic opinions'. Although formally addressed only to expert opinions submitted to the Bundeskartellamt, these Best Practices have wider implications. To begin with, their content is equally relevant to economic arguments put forward by the parties to a case, and not just by economic experts. As corporate lawyers and outside counsel may also use economic arguments, it would appear that their arguments will be assessed according to the same standards set

31 See A. Christiansen and L. Locher, 'Die neuen Standards des Bundeskartellamts für ökonomische Gutachten in der Kartellrechtsanwendung', 61 *Wirtschaft und Wettbewerb* (2011), 444–453, pp. 446 et seq.; Christiansen, *supra* n 3, pp. 9 et seq.; Ewald, *supra* n 3, 39 et seq.

32 For an overview of the economic consultancies active internationally see Global Competition Review, 'The Economics 20', in *GCR 100. A Guide to the world's leading competition law and economics practices*, 13th annual edition (London, 2013), 227–236.

forth in the Best Practices. Furthermore, the notice also implicitly sets standards for economic analyses conducted by the competition authority itself. However, mainly because of confidentiality requirements, especially with regard to empirical analyses, a certain asymmetry with regard to data disclosure is inevitable. This is, however, not fundamentally different from other pieces of evidence. Information gathered by the authority in the course of market investigations is generally not disclosed to the parties completely.

In line with the general rationale for minimum quality standards set out above, the Best Practices explicitly state that '[the] Bundeskartellamt expects that common and transparent procedures for evaluating expert economic opinions will allow for a fair and efficient application of this type of evidence to the specific competition law proceedings'.[33] Focusing on the probative value of submitted assessments, the document furthermore stipulates that the 'arguments, results and conclusions of economic opinions which do not comply with these standards can only be considered to a lesser extent, if at all' [*sic*].[34] The aim of the document is thus not to discourage the submission of expert opinions. Rather, the aim is to discourage parties from submitting studies of low quality or with little or no relevance to the case at hand. The reason is that such studies cannot contribute to a high-quality decision making, but only result in additional costs and effort for all parties concerned.

The detailed structure of the Best Practices (see table 3 below) clearly indicates that more room is devoted to substantive issues, while procedural steps are addressed in less detail. This weighting reflects not least the fact that – from a legal point of view – expert opinions are in principle subject to the same procedural rules as other documents submitted by the parties. Accordingly, the Best Practices do not set out binding procedural steps, and are not meant to establish a universally applicable course of action for dealing with expert opinions. Consultation with the Bundeskartellamt prior to submitting an opinion is nevertheless advised.[35] Moreover, the necessity of a timely submission is stressed repeatedly in order to enable the authority to examine the study adequately.[36]

33 Best Practices, *supra* n 2, p. 2.
34 Best Practices, *supra* n 2, p. 2.
35 Best Practices, *supra* n 2, p. 9.
36 Best Practices, *supra* n 2, pp. 2 and 9.

Table 3. Contents of the Bundeskartellamt's Best Practices

Note: page numbers at the right-hand side

With regard to substance, the notice sets forth several basic requirements:[37] Above all, the analyses conducted have to be relevant for the competition issues of the case at hand. Should the submission contain several different pieces of analysis with regard to the same competition issue, an additional requirement is that the results should be consistent. The requirement that results must be robust is elaborated in the Best Practices both with regard to theoretical and empirical analyses (sections 2.3 and 3.4, respectively). If a certain theoretical model proves to be highly sensitive to small modifications in underlying assumptions, then the Best Practices call for less probative value to be ascribed to the results compared to more robust models. The same applies to empirical results if they prove to be highly sensitive to minor changes in the dataset or the included variables.

37 Best Practices, *supra* n 2, pp. 2 et seq.

Furthermore, submissions must be complete and comprehensible; assumptions have to be transparent and should be discussed with respect to their compatibility with the market conditions underlying the specific case. An expert opinion can only be considered complete if the Bundeskartellamt is able to replicate the relevant arguments and quantitative analyses in each and every detail. Where relevant details are missing, an expert opinion is regarded as incomplete and will, depending on the level of incompleteness, not be considered at all or only to a lesser degree. With regard to quantitative analyses, the requirement of completeness includes in particular the submission of relevant (raw) data (including documentation of the process for data gathering and validation), programme codes as well as explanations needed to follow and replicate the empirical results.[38]

In addition, the Best Practices clearly state a preference for established and tested theories and methods that have been published in scientific journals and have thus undergone peer review. Ideally, methods have been used in competition law proceedings before, and have thus been examined with regard to their informative value and limitations in this specific context. On the other hand, the Best Practices do not rule out the possibility of applying relatively new and untested concepts and methods.[39] In order to be accepted, however, new theories and methods require more elaborate explanation and reasoning, including explanation as to why established theories or methods are thought to be unsuited to the case at hand.

Concerning the presentation of the results, the Best Practices require the inclusion of a non-technical summary, which should be comprehensible to a lay audience, and a complete list of references.[40] As regards the content of the non-technical summary, the Best Practices require five aspects to be covered: (1) purpose: issues addressed by the opinion and their relevance; (2) methodology: reasons for the method(s) chosen; (3) specification of the theoretical model and/or empirical method; (4) presentation of main results and their implications for the competitive assessment; and (5) a discussion of the robustness of the results.

In summary it can be said that the Best Practices essentially stipulate and further elaborate the following core evaluation criteria for the quality of expert opinions:

- relevance to the case at hand,
- reliability/robustness of the results,
- replicability/transparency of all steps of analysis and
- accessibility/comprehensibility, also for lay readers.

Beyond expressing a preference for established and tested theories and methods, the Best Practices abstain from detailed prescriptions with respect to the substantive content or methodologies used in expert opinions.

[38] Best Practices, *supra* n 2, p. 9.

[39] Best Practices, *supra* n 2, p. 4.

[40] Best Practices, *supra* n 2, pp. 3 et seq.

3.3 The International Perspective

As mentioned, economic expertise has gained an increasingly prominent role in recent years. In line with this trend, a growing number of expert opinions have been submitted to competition authorities and competent courts. In response to this development, guidance documents have been issued in a growing number of jurisdictions in order to assure the quality of the submissions.[41] To put the Bundeskartellamt's Best Practices into perspective, this section offers an international overview and contains a brief comparison with other guidance documents published by various competition authorities (sub-section 3.3.1). A few remarks then follow concerning jurisdictions where expert opinions are submitted despite the absence of a guidance document (sub-section 3.3.2).

3.3.1 A Comparison with Guidance Documents from Six Other Jurisdictions

Apart from Germany, competition authorities have issued guidance documents for expert opinions in several other jurisdictions.[42] Table 4 below lists relevant documents from six jurisdictions, three of them from Europe (the European Union, France, the United Kingdom) and another three from overseas (Australia, South Korea, USA).[43] Interestingly, with the exception of the Best Practices by the US Federal Trade Commission, all listed documents were issued or revised[44] around 2010, the year in which the Bundeskartellamt issued its Best Practices.

41 See also Christiansen and Locher, *supra* n 30, pp. 451 et seq.; Christiansen, *supra* n 3, pp. 16 et seq.; Ewald, *supra* n 3, pp. 40 et seq.; M. Walker, 'Background Note', in *OECD Competition Committee: Economic Evidence in Merger Analysis*, DAF/COMP(2011)23, 19–51, pp. 30 et seq.

42 The list reflects the authors' best knowledge based on a review of the relevant literature combined with a search of the websites of selected competition authorities. We do not claim completeness but we are fairly certain that we have tracked down most of the relevant documents as well as the most important ones. We would, however, be very thankful if further guidance documents were brought to our attention.

43 The abbreviations used in the following footnotes are explained in table 4.

44 The Australian Federal Court issued its first guidelines in 1998, which are revised regularly.

Table 4. Notices and comparable guidance documents for expert opinions in other jurisdictions

Jurisdiction	Title of document, source online, date of publication, abbreviation
Australia	Australian Competition and Consumer Commission, Formal merger review process guidelines 2008, available at http://www.accc.gov.au/content/index.phtml/itemId/776055, June 2008 (henceforth 'ACCC, Guidelines') Federal Court of Australia, Practice Note CM 7: Expert Witnesses in Proceedings in the Federal Court of Australia, available at http://www.fed court.gov.au/ case-management-services/ ADR/?a=16333, 01 August 2011 (henceforth 'FCA, Note')
European Union	Directorate General for Competition, Best Practices for the submission of economic evidence and data collection in cases concerning the application of Article 101 and 102 TFEU and in merger cases, available at http://ec.europa.eu/competition/ consultations/2010_best_practices/best_ practice_submissions.pdf, January 2010 (henceforth 'DG COMP, Best Practices')
France	Autorité de la Concurrence, Lignes directrices de l'Autorité de la concurrence relatives au contrôle des concentrations, available at http://www. autoritedelaconcurrence.fr/doc/ld_concentrations_dec09.pdf, paras 558 et seq., December 2009 (henceforth 'AdlC, Lignes directrices'),
South Korea	Korea Fair Trade Commission, Guidelines on the Submission of Economic Analysis Evidence, available at http://eng.ftc.go.kr/ files/static/ Legal_Authority/Guidelines on the Submission of Economic Analysis Evidence_mar 14 2012.pdf, July 2010 (henceforth 'KFTC, Guidelines')
United Kingdom	Competition Commission, Suggested best practice for submissions of technical economic analysis from parties to the CC, available at http://www.competition-commission.org.uk/rep_pub/corporate_ documents/ corporate_ policies/best_practice.pdf, February 2009 (henceforth 'CC, Suggested best practice') Civil Justice Council, Protocol for the Instruction of Experts to give Evidence in Civil Claims, http://www.justice.gov.uk/courts/ procedure-rules/civil/contents/form_section_images/practice_directions/pd35_pdf_eps/pd35_prot.pdf, June 2005 amended October 2009 (henceforth 'CJC, Protocol') Competition Commission and Office of Fair Trading, Good practice in the design and presentation of consumer survey evidence in merger inquiries, available at http://www.oft.gov.uk/shared_oft/ consultations/ merger-inquiries/Good-practice-guide.pdf, March 2011 (henceforth 'CC/OFT, Good practice')
United States	Federal Trade Commission, Best Practices for Data, and Economics and Financial Analyses in Antitrust Investigations, available at http://www.ftc.gov/be/bestpractices.shtm, 2002 (henceforth 'FTC, Best Practices')

Naturally, the content and scope of the documents vary somewhat between the jurisdictions due to differences in the substantive provisions, procedural frameworks and presumably also due to varying actual experiences with expert opinions. In the case of Australia and the United Kingdom, supplementary documents from the court system are also included in the table because they form an important part of the overall institutional framework.[45]

With respect to scope the most comprehensive document is the Best Practices of the EU Commission's DG Competition (DG COMP), which, among other things, contains some general remarks on economic models.[46] In contrast to the Bundeskartellamt's Best Practices, the documents by DG COMP and the US Federal Trade Commission also deal with requests by the respective authorities for quantitative data.[47] This is a separate but related issue because data requests typically form the basis for the quantitative analyses carried out by the authorities.[48] For example, DG COMP sets out the three following requirements for responses to a formal data request according to Article 18 of Regulation 1/2003 or Article 11 of the Merger Regulation: completeness, correctness and timely submission.[49] The documents by the French Autorité de la Concurrence and by the British Competition Commission and Office of Fair Trading also deal with one specific form of evidence often used in connection with economic submissions, namely customer survey evidence.[50] For example, data from such surveys can be used to estimate diversion ratios for the purpose of assessing merger effects.[51]

At the same time, all of the guidance documents display certain strong similarities in terms of substance. A common basic requirement is relevance – that is, relevance of the submitted analysis to the competition issue in question.[52] A closely related requirement is a clear statement of the questions that the expert was com-

---

45 See C. Veljanovski, 'Economists in Court: A Comparative Assessment of Procedures and Experience in Australia and England & Wales from an Economist's Perspective', SSRN Working Paper (2009), pp. 16 et seq.*supra* n 43. The underlying provisions of procedural law as for example in case of the UK Part 35 of the Civil Procedure Rules (CPR 35) and its associated Practice Direction (PD 35; available at http://www.justice.gov.uk/ courts/procedure-rules/civil/rules/pd_part35) have, however, not been included.

46 DG COMP, Best Practices, *supra* table 4, paras 9 et seq.

47 DG COMP, Best Practices, *supra* table 4, paras 46 et seq.; FTC, Best Practices, *supra* table 4, p. 1.

48 DG COMP, Best Practices, *supra* table 4, paras 48 and 51.

49 DG COMP, Best Practices, *supra* table 4, paras 60 et seq.

50 AdlC, Lignes directrices, *supra* table 4, paras 577 et seq.; CC, Suggested best practice, *supra* table 4, paras 25 et seq.; CC/OFT, Good practice, *supra* table 4,

51 K. Edwards, 'Estimating Diversion Ratios: Some Thoughts on Customer Survey Design', in P. Lowe and M. Marquis (eds.), *European Competition Law Annual 2010. Merger Control in European and Global Perspective* (Hart 2013), 31–42.

52 DG COMP, Best Practices, *supra* table 4, para 16; AdlC, Lignes directrices, *supra* table 4, para 568; KFTC, Guidelines, *supra* table 4, Article 4; CJC, Protocol, *supra* table 4, paras 4.4 and 6.1.

missioned to address and any specific hypotheses tested.[53] In some jurisdictions a non-technical summary of the analysis and main results or a summary of conclusions are also required.[54] Transparency, especially with regard to the specification of models used and assumptions made, is generally obligatory. The complete documentation of the analyses and replicability of the results by the authority are also common requirements.[55] More specifically, in the case of empirical analyses, the submission of the complete dataset – and, in some guidance documents, programme codes – is typically asked for.[56] By complete dataset, the guidance documents generally mean both the raw data and any alterations or modifications made by the experts, such as the removal of 'outliers' or the standardisation of certain variables. Another standard requirement concerns the robustness of the results.[57] This last point entails, in particular, the documentation of tests conducted as part of the submission. Typically, the guidance documents also express a preference for the use of established methods, and require the relevant literature to be cited.[58]

Taken together, all of the mentioned requirements fall under the principles of relevance and reliability. Both are of equal importance. Failure to conform to the first principle means that the expert opinion will be deemed unsuitable for influencing the outcome of a case, since it offers no relevant evidence. This consequence occurs irrespective of the technical quality or sophistication of the analysis in question. Failure to conform to the second principle will also lead an expert opinion to be discounted, but for a different reason. In this case the analysis may be relevant, but the results are viewed as unreliable, i.e. because they lack probative value. Consequently, a good expert opinion must conform to both principles. Only then can the expert opinions be successfully integrated into the decision-making process. A final common requirement relates to procedure. Most if not all guidance documents stress the need to inform the authority (or the court) about the

---

53 DG COMP, Best Practices, *supra* table 4, paras 17 et seq.; AdlC, Lignes directrices, *supra* table 4, para 559; ACCC, Guidelines, paras 3.40 and 3.41; FCA, Note. para 2.1.

54 AdlC, Lignes directrices, *supra* table 4, para 562; CC, Suggested best practice, *supra* table 4, para 8; CJC, Protocol, para 13.14.

55 DG COMP, Best Practices, *supra* table 4, para 32; AdlC, Lignes directrices, *supra* table 4, para 570; CC, Suggested best practice, *supra* table 4, para 8; KFTC, Guidelines, *supra* table 4, Articles 4 and 5; ACCC, Guidelines, *supra* table 4, para 3.42; FCA, Note, *supra* table 4, para 2.1.

56 DG COMP, Best Practices, *supra* table 4, para 32; AdlC, Lignes directrices, *supra* table 4, para 571; CC, Suggested best practice, *supra* table 4, paras 8 and 19 et seq.; FTC, Best Practices, *supra* table 4, p. 2; ACCC, Guidelines, *supra* table 4, para 3.41.

57 DG COMP, Best Practices, *supra* table 4, paras 37 et seq.; AdlC, Lignes directrices, *supra* table 4, paras 569 and 580; CC, Suggested best practice, *supra* table 4, paras 18 and 30; KFTC, Guidelines, *supra* table 4, Article 4; FTC, Best Practices, *supra* table 4, p. 2; ACCC, Guidelines, *supra* table 4, para 3.41.

58 DG COMP, Best Practices, *supra* table 4, paras 29 and 40; AdlC, Lignes directrices, *supra* table 4, para 562; CC, Suggested best practice, *supra* table 4, paras 14 and 32; CJC, Protocol, *supra* table 4, para 4.5; KFTC, Guidelines, *supra* table 4, Article 4.

involvement of economic experts at an early stage of the proceedings, emphasizing the time limits in merger control proceedings in particular.[59]

Another important similarity between the compared guidance documents lies in the fact that they all abstain from detailed prescriptions as to the specific theoretical models, empirical methods and kinds of data that should be used in individual cases. This is left to the discretion of the parties and their advisors. Likewise, the guidance documents do not define a range of issues in which the submission of expert opinions is necessary or even advisable. Effectively, all of the reviewed guidance documents focus on the process after a party has decided to make use of economic expertise, thus dealing with the presentation of the economic study and results to the authority or court.

3.3.2 A Quick Glance at Jurisdictions Without Guidance Documents

In many more jurisdictions than those reviewed above, no guidance documents have been issued so far.[60] This may be due to various reasons which can only be conjectured at here. The lack of guidance documents may indicate that quality problems with economic studies have not arisen thus far.[61] Second, the respective competition authorities and courts may dispose of other means of dealing with the issue: General rules for submitting opinions may make special provisions with regard to economic assessments dispensable. Alternatively, a reliance on existing guidance documents from other jurisdictions may have been sufficient to date.[62] In any event, an inquiry into whether and to what extent these reasons hold true is beyond the scope of this article. The point here is merely that the underlying challenge of integrating the opinions of economic experts into competition law enforcement is certainly relevant in more jurisdictions than the ones that have taken the formal step of issuing guidance documents for expert opinions. This point is corroborated by a quick glance at three other jurisdictions that differ in terms of the maturity of their competition law regimes, country size and geographic position.

---

59 DG COMP, Best Practices, *supra* table 4, para 2; KFTC, Guidelines, *supra* table 4, Article 6; AdlC, Lignes directrices, *supra* table 4, para 564; FTC, Best Practices, *supra* table 4, p. 2.

60 See for example the various country contributions in the OECD Roundtables on Managing Complex Mergers (DAF/COMP(2007)44, available at http://www.oecd.org/daf/competition/mergers/41651401.pdf) and on Economic Evidence in Merger Analysis (DAF/COMP(2011)23, available at http://www.oecd.org/daf/competition/ EconomicEvidenceInMergerAnalysis2011.pdf.

61 This in turn may have two reasons: either economic opinions have suffered from quality problems but these have not been detected or there have been no submissions of poor quality so far.

62 This may particularly be the case in the European Union where authorities from smaller Member States could look to the guidance offered by DG COMP as the arguably most important authority.

The first jurisdiction is Canada, where, according to some observers, 'the use of expert economists [...] is reasonably common in more complex merger cases'.[63] Goldman et al.[64] specifically refer to econometric analyses conducted by experts, mentioning the availability of data and time constraints as the most important limiting factors. In fact, beyond specific econometric work, the entire assessment of mergers is informed by economics and thus amenable to expert opinions.[65] An area particularly amenable to economic analysis is the efficiency defence incorporated in the Canadian Competition Act.[66] The Canadian contribution to the 2011 OECD Roundtable on Economic Evidence in Merger Control emphasized the 'considerable productive interaction between the parties' economists and the Bureau's internal and external economists'[67] in a recent – not further specified – case.

The second jurisdiction is New Zealand, where economic experts appear to be regularly involved in competition law proceedings, although no guidance documents have been issued by the Commerce Commission. To begin with, the Mergers and Acquisitions Guidelines issued in 2003 contain at least a brief reference to economic modeling, which by itself makes the perceived usefulness of such modelling clear.[68] The draft revised Guidelines issued for consultation in March 2013 make repeated references to 'economic evidence' and 'expert economic evidence the applicant wishes to provide' as relevant evidence in merger control proceedings.[69] Moreover, the Commerce Commission has conducted its own economic analyses in a number of cases.[70] The agency has reportedly also developed an

---

63 C. Goldman, R. Kwinter, N. Joneja and C. Leddy, 'A Canadian Perspective on the Evaluation of Evidence in Antitrust and Merger Cases in the Context of Recent Changes to Canada's Competition Law', in C.-D. Ehlermann and M. Marquis (eds.), *European Competition Law Annual 2009. The Evaluation of Evidence and its Judicial Review in Competition Cases* (Hart, 2011), 697–711, p. 702.

64 Goldman et al., *supra* n 62.

65 T. Ross, 'Merger Review in Canada and the Role of Economics', *UBC Sauder School of Business Working Paper* (2006).

66 See T. Ross and R. Winter, 'The Efficiency Defense in Merger Law: Economic Foundations and Recent Canadian Developments', 72 *Antitrust Law Journal* (2005), 471–504.

67 OECD Competition Committee: Economic Evidence in Merger Analysis, DAF/COMP(2011)23, available at http://www.oecd.org/daf/competition/EconomicEvidenceInMergerAnalysis2011.pdf, p. 99.

68 New Zealand Commerce Commission, Mergers and Acquisitions Guidelines (2003), available at http://www.comcom.govt.nz/assets/Imported-from-old-site/BusinessCompetition/MergersAcquisitions/ClearanceProcessGuidelines/ContentFiles/Documents/Mergers-and-AcquisitionsGuidelines-2003.pdf, p. 32.

69 New Zealand Commerce Commission, Draft Mergers and Acquisitions Guidelines for consultation, March 2013, available at http://www.comcom.govt.nz/assets/Business-Competition/Mergers-and-Acqusitions/Commerce-Commission-draft-Mergers-and-Acqusitions-Guidelines-for-consultation-08-March-2013.pdf, pp. 37, 38, 39.

70 See D. Law, M. Pickford and Q. Yang, 'Quantitative Methods in Competition Cases: A New Zealand Perspective', 17 *Competition and Consumer Law Journal* (2010), 252–275.

'approach to modeling' and, among other things, has implemented a 'quality control policy' for its own modeling work that also applies to external studies.[71] Furthermore, with regard to the abuse of dominance, economic analyses are commonly used to implement what is known as the counterfactual test under section 36 of the New Zealand Commerce Act of 1986.[72]

Finally, the People's Republic of China may be mentioned as an example of a relatively young competition law regime. Not until August 2008 did the Anti-Monopoly Law (AML) enter into force. Numerous pieces of secondary legislation have followed suit.[73] The prescriptions in the AML with regard to anti-competitive agreements and abuse of market power generally provide for a 'rule of reason' approach that leaves ample room for the application of economics.[74] Merger control is another important and quickly developing area of enforcement that is open to economic analysis.[75] The coming into force of the AML and related secondary legislation has led to an increase in public and private enforcement in lower and appellate courts.[76] Especially with respect to the latter China's Supreme People's Court issued a judicial interpretation (JI) in May 2012, in order to offer some guidance in resolving private disputes.[77] Article 12 of the JI states that parties may use specialists, including economic experts, and Article 13 states that the courts may also appoint economic experts on their own initiative.[78] Although case-law to date is limited, the framework outlined above makes it likely that economic experts will be employed regularly in the future.

---

71 See also New Zealand, 'Country Contribution', in *OCED Roundtable Managing Complex Mergers*, DAF/COMP(2007)44, 55–64 (available at http://www.oecd.org/daf/competition/mergers/41651401.pdf), 63–64.

72 C. Veljanovski, 'Market Power and Counterfactuals in New Zealand Competition Law', 9 *Journal of Competition Law and Economics* (2013), 171–201.

73 With regard to merger control, see the overviews by D. Wei, 'Antitrust in China: An Overview of Recent Implementation of Anti-Monopoly Law', 14 *European Business Law Review* (2013), 14, 119–140 and M. Furse, 'Merger Control in China: Four and a Half Years of Practice and Enforcement – A Critical Analysis', 36 *World Competition* (2013), 285–313.

74 See D. Lu and G. Tan, Economics and Private Antitrust Litigation in China, *USC CLEO Research Paper No. C12-13* (2012). One particular area especially amenable to economic input is the efficiency defense in merger control (see Wei, *supra* n 72, p. 126).

75 See the overview by Furse, *supra* n 72.

76 See Z. Li, 'New Developments in Civil Antitrust Litigation in China', *CPI Antitrust Chronicle*, January 2012, at https://www.competitionpolicyinternational.com/file/view/6622 and Wei, *supra* n 72.

77 Provisions on Several Issues Concerning the Application of the Law in Adjudication of Monopoly-Related Civil Disputes, issued on May 8, 2012, effective from 1 June 2012, available in Chinese at http://www.court.gov.cn/qwfb/sfjs/201205/t20120509_176785.htm.

78 Lu and Tan, *supra* n 73, p. 15.

4 A Special Look at the US: The Daubert Trilogy and Beyond

To provide a full picture of the different approaches used to promote the effective integration of economic analysis into competition law enforcement, a more detailed treatment of the developments in the U.S. seems to be useful for several reasons. In the U.S. in particular a distinct body of case-law exists regarding the admissibility of experts and their testimony in (all kinds of) court proceedings. This case law and the related debate among both academics and practitioners are of great interest in the context of this article, although they are not confined to antitrust law. Still, they have formed the basis for the specific debate occurring in antitrust circles until today.[79] The obvious difference compared to the agency guidance documents reviewed above lies in the identity of the decision-maker, which, in the U.S. context, is the court as opposed to the competition authority in the European context. Still, the basic issue is the integration of scientific expertise into decision-making. The most important reason why the debate in the U.S. focuses on court proceedings is that – in contrast to the administrative systems of public competition law enforcement prevailing in Germany and, in particular, at the European level – in the adversarial enforcement regime of the U.S., courts are involved to a greater extent in public competition law enforcement.[80] The federal antitrust agencies (the DoJ and FTC) have far more limited formal decision-making powers compared to their European counterparts.[81] Typically, the DoJ and, to a lesser extent, the FTC must bring formal complaints before courts, which can then order remedial relief. In addition, private enforcement, which naturally takes place before courts, has traditionally played a greater role in the U.S. than in Germany and certainly in the EU, at least outside the area of merger control.[82] This greater

---

79 A. Gavil, 'Defining Reliable Forensic Economics in the Post-Daubert/Kumho Tire Era: Case Studies from Antitrust', 57 *Washington & Lee Law Review* (2000), 831–878; A. Gavil, 'Competition Policy, Economics, and Economists: Are We Expecting Too Much?', in *Annual Proceedings of the Fordham Corporate Law Institute on International Antitrust Law & Policy*, (Juris Publishing 2006); H. Hovenkamp, 'Expert Testimony and the Predicament of Antitrust Fact Finding', in H. Hovenkamp, *The Antitrust Enterprise* (Harvard University Press 2005), 77–91; J. Langenfeld and C. Alexander, 'Daubert and Other Gatekeeping Challenges of Antitrust Experts', 25 *Antitrust* (2011), 21–28; G. Werden, 'The Admissibility of Expert Testimony', in ABA Section of Antitrust Law, *Issues in Competition Law and Policy* (ABA Publishing 2008); G. Wrobel and E. Meriwether, 'Economic Experts: The Challenges of Gatekeepers and Complexity', 25 *Antitrust* (2011), 8–12.

80 There has been no private enforcement before European courts to date since there is no supranational law with regard to damages.

81 See, e.g., M. Trebilcock and E. Iacobucci, 'Designing Competition Law Institutions', 25 *World Competition* (2002), 361–394, pp. 368 et seq.; D. Crane, *The institutional structure of antitrust enforcement* (Oxford University Press 2011), pp. 93 et seq.

82 See C. Jones, *Private Enforcement of Antitrust Law in the EU, UK and USA* (Oxford University Press 1999); Crane, *supra* n 80, pp. 49 et seq. For an analysis of recent

involvement of the judiciary implies that the courts deal with economic opinions more often in the U.S. and, accordingly, have an opportunity (and perhaps duty) to gather experience and devise strategies to deal with them adequately. In this latter regard the U.S. experience has important insights to offer.

With respect to the integration of scientific evidence into the different stages of law enforcement, the U.S. Supreme Court issued three landmark decisions in the 1990s, which are commonly referred to as the 'Daubert trilogy'[83]. In the constitutive Daubert decision issued in 1993, the Supreme Court assigned an obligatory 'gatekeeping' function to trial judges in order to screen out scientifically inferior expert opinions at an early procedural stage.[84] In interpreting the relevant piece of legislation, i.e. Rule 702 of the Federal Rules of Evidence, the Supreme Court laid out a threshold that expert testimony must satisfy in order to be admissible. The guiding principles are, again, relevance and reliability. As in the guidance documents reviewed above, the Supreme Court abstained from detailed prescriptions with respect to the substantive content of expert testimony. Instead, the Court outlined the focus of the inquiry in the following way:[85]

> The inquiry envisioned by Rule 702 is, we emphasize, a flexible one. Its overarching subject is the scientific validity - and thus the evidentiary relevance and reliability - of the principles that underlie a proposed submission. The focus, of course, must be solely on principles and methodology, not on the conclusions that they generate.

As regards the examination of reliability, a number of factors are mentioned that, together, have come to be known as the Daubert criteria.[86] These consist of

- the possibility of and extent to which the theory or technique can be tested,

---

case practice, see R. Lande and J. Davis, 'Benefits from Private Antitrust Enforcement: An Analysis of Forty Cases', 42 *University of San Francisco Law Review* (2008), 879–918.

83 Daubert v. Merrell Dow Pharmaceuticals, 509 U.S. 579 (1993); General Electric Co. v. Joiner, 522 U.S. 136 (1997); Kumho Tire Co. v. Carmichael, 526 U.S. 137 (1999). The usual shorthand references for the decisions are 'Daubert', 'Joiner' and 'Kumho'. As regards the subject matter of the underlying legal disputes the first two related to toxic tort suits while the third one concerned a case of product liability.

84 See M. Berger, 'The Supreme Court's Trilogy on the Admissibility of Expert Testimony', in *Reference Manual on Scientific Evidence*, Second Edition (2000), 9–38; B. Hawk and J. Keyte, 'Separating the Wheat from the Chaff: How the U.S. Courts Analyze Antitrust Evidence', in C.-D. Ehlermann and M. Marquis (eds.), *European Competition Law Annual 2009. The Evaluation of Evidence and its Judicial Review in Competition Cases* (Hart 2011), 713–749, esp. pp. 720 et seq. The procedural framework differs between merger cases according to Section 7 of the Clayton Act and other antitrust issues because in contrast to the other cases Section 7 challenges typically proceed on the preliminary injunction track which, among other things, does not provide for a final jury decision (Hawk and Keyte, *ibid.*, esp. pp. 741 et seq.).

85 Daubert v. Merrell Dow Pharmaceuticals, 509 U.S. 579 (1993), at p. 593.

86 Daubert v. Merrell Dow Pharmaceuticals, Inc., 509 U.S. 579 (1993), at pp. 593f.

- whether the theory or technique has been subjected to peer review and publication,
- the known or potential rate of error of a theory or technique, and finally
- the question of whether the theory or technique enjoys general acceptability in the relevant scientific community.

With regard to the second criterion (peer review and publication), the Supreme Court does not stipulate that only established theories and methods should be used. On the one hand, the Court makes clear that 'submission to the scrutiny of the scientific community is a component of 'good science' [...] because it increases the likelihood that substantive flaws in methodology will be detected'; but on the other hand, the Court also acknowledges that 'publication (which is but one element of peer review) is not a sine qua non of admissibility; it does not necessarily correlate with reliability [...] and, in some instances, well-grounded but innovative theories will not have been published.' Accordingly, the Court considers 'the fact of publication (or lack thereof) in a peer reviewed journal [...] [as] a relevant, though not dispositive, consideration in assessing the scientific validity of a particular technique or methodology on which an opinion is premised.'[87]

Moreover, the Court made clear in the Daubert decision that it did not hold this set of criteria to be definitive.[88] This implies that the courts must decide on the relevance and weighting of the factors to be considered in a particular case. In the Kumho decision, the last of the abovementioned trilogy, the Supreme Court in 1999 once again stressed the importance of the 'gatekeeping requirement' and described the basic rationale as follows: [89]

> The objective of that requirement is to ensure the reliability and relevancy of expert testimony. It is to make certain that an expert, whether basing testimony upon professional studies or personal experience, employs in the courtroom the same level of intellectual rigor that characterizes the practice of an expert in the relevant field.

Again, relevance and reliability are mentioned as guiding principles. According to *Gavil*[90] the key objective is to keep 'junk science' out of the courtroom and to at least limit the prevalence of so-called 'hired gun' experts who appear to be ready provide whatever expert testimony the client needs.

In another noteworthy passage of the Daubert decision, the Supreme Court dealt with the relationship between scientific research and the application of scientific knowledge in law enforcement, which is the precise domain of expert testimony. The relevant point here is the tension between, on the one hand, requiring the expert to adhere to scientific standards[91] in order to provide reliable evidence

---

87 Daubert v. Merrell Dow Pharmaceuticals, Inc., 509 U.S. 579 (1993), at p. 595.

88 Daubert v. Merrell Dow Pharmaceuticals, Inc., 509 U.S. 579 (1993), at p. 591.

89 Kumho Tire Co. v. Carmichael, 526 U.S. 137 (1999), at p. 152.

90 Gavil (2000), *supra* n 78, p. 857.

91 In fact, according to the Supreme Court the relevant Federal Rule of Evidence 702 requires 'a grounding in the methods and procedures of science'; Daubert v. Merrell Dow Pharmaceuticals, 509 U.S. 579 (1993), at p. 590.

and, on the other hand, acknowledging that scientific methods and findings cannot be transplanted directly into legal proceedings. The Court thus pointed to the fundamental differences between science and law enforcement in the following way:[92]

> Yet there are important differences between the quest for truth in the courtroom and the quest for truth in the laboratory. Scientific conclusions are subject to perpetual revision. Law, on the other hand, must resolve disputes finally and quickly. The scientific project is advanced by broad and wide-ranging consideration of a multitude of hypotheses, for those that are incorrect will eventually be shown to be so, and that in itself is an advance. Conjectures that are probably wrong are of little use, however, in the project of reaching a quick, final, and binding legal judgment – often of great consequence – about a particular set of events in the past.

In 2000 the relevant legislation, that is the Federal Rule of Evidence 702, was revised to take into account the aforementioned trilogy.[93] It now reads:

> If scientific, technical, or other specialized knowledge will assist the trier of fact to understand the evidence or to determine a fact in issue, a witness qualified as an expert by knowledge, skill, experience, training, or education, may testify thereto in the form of an opinion or otherwise, if (1) the testimony is based upon sufficient facts or data, (2) the testimony is the product of reliable principles and methods, and (3) the witness has applied the principles and methods reliably to the facts of the case.

The first condition is further strengthened by the subsequent Federal Rule of Evidence 705, which stipulates that the expert 'may in any event be required to disclose the underlying facts or data on cross-examination'. This in turn is closely related to Rule 26(a)(2) of the Federal Rules of Civil Procedure[94] on disclosure of expert testimony. This Rule does not prescribe the substantive content but stipulates wide-ranging disclosure obligations in abstract terms and basically mirrors a strict transparency requirement. In general, an expert witness must provide a written report which contains, among other things, a 'complete statement of all opinions the witness will express and the basis and reasons for them and the facts or data considered by the witness in forming them' (Rule 26(a)(2)(B)(i) and (ii)). Moreover, comprehensive information with regard to the expert and the conditions of his or her engagement is required.[95]

In conclusion, the Daubert trilogy as well as the legal framework in the U.S. address a number of fundamental issues with regard to the inclusion of scientific

---

92 Daubert v. Merrell Dow Pharmaceuticals, Inc., 509 U.S. 579 (1993), at p. 592.

93 See Werden, *supra* n 78. The current version of the Federal Rules of Evidence can be accessed at the website of the United States Courts at http://www.uscourts.gov/uscourts/RulesAndPolicies/rules/2010_Rules/Evidence.pdf.

94 Available at http://www.uscourts.gov/uscourts/RulesAndPolicies/rules/2010Rules/CivilProcedure.pdf.

95 These include a list of all publications authored by the witness within the preceding 10 years, a listing of any other cases in which the witness has testified as an expert within the preceding 4 years and the agreed compensation (Rule 26(a)(2)(B)(iv) to (vi)).

expertise in law enforcement and, indeed, do so in much the same manner as the guidance documents issued by the Bundeskartellamt and other competition authorities. Our analysis shows that the same core principles for ensuring the quality of expert submissions are used – that is, relevance and reliability.

U.S. Supreme Court decisions as well as the Federal Rules of Evidence apply to all kind of expert testimony in court proceedings. Their implications are further spelled out in the 'Reference Manual on Scientific Evidence' and the 'Manual for Complex Litigation' published by the Federal Judicial Center, the influential training and research institution of the U.S. federal courts.[96] Especially the latter Manual contains an entire section (30.2) devoted to the procedural handling by judges of voluminous datasets and expert economic testimony as forms of evidence. As regards the effects of these quality standards in the field of competition law enforcement, both Werden[97] and the Economic Evidence Task Force, a group of leading practitioners and academics set up by the Antitrust Section of the American Bar Association, in their report from August 2006 provide an overall positive assessment. For example, Werden[98] states: 'Daubert and its progeny are improving the quality and clarity of economic testimony in antitrust cases, and they are thereby increasing the sophistication of the discourse in antitrust litigation and the accuracy of judge and jury decisions.'[99] At the same time, some members of the Task Force have also pointed to the high costs associated with Daubert motions.[100] The group also recommends the further specification of the Daubert factors with regard to antitrust law.[101] Hovenkamp[102] is more critical and sees a tendency by judges to look at experts' testimonies in a 'superficial manner', (80) which is said to result in the erroneous admission of testimony that should (and could) have been excluded.

The most comprehensive empirical analysis of the relevant jurisprudence was done by Langenfeld and Alexander.[103] Their analysis confirms first of all the great relevance of what is known as the gatekeeping challenges, i.e. the motions by op-

96 Federal Judicial Center, Reference Manual on Scientific Evidence, Second Edition (2000), available at http://www.fjc.gov/public/pdf.nsf/lookup/sciman00.pdf/$file/sciman00.pdf; Manual for Complex Litigation, Fourth, 2004, available at http://www.fjc.gov/public/pdf.nsf/ lookup/mcl4.pdf/$file/mcl4.pdf.

97 See Werden, *supra* n 78.

98 See Werden, *supra* n 78, p. 817.

99 Similarly, the Economic Evidence Task Force wrote: 'Our review of the reported cases suggests that the judges who chose to write published opinions understood the economic issues and made sensible decisions. As a result, Daubert likely deters at least some types of unprofessional economic testimony, particularly by encouraging efforts to match the economic argument with the facts of the case'. Economic Evidence Task Force, *Final Report* (ABA Publishing 2006), p. 7.

100 Economic Evidence Task Force, *supra* n 99, 8.

101 Economic Evidence Task Force, *supra* n 99, 8.

102 Hovenkamp, *supra* n 78.

103 See Langenfeld and Alexander, *supra* n 78. By comparison, Appendix IV on Daubert Antitrust Decisions of the Final Report of Economic Evidence Task Force, *supra* n 99, lists 42 decisions from 1990 to 2005.

posing parties to exclude expert testimony in economics. Between 2000 and early 2011 they find a total of 113 antitrust economist challenges, of which 97 were based on Federal Rule of Evidence 702, which reflects the Daubert criteria.[104] Furthermore, according to their data, the plaintiff's experts were much more likely to be challenged than the defendents', and the expert testimony from plaintiffs had a 40% chance of being (partially or fully) excluded, compared to a 0% chance for defendants' experts.[105] According to Langenfeld and Alexander, this demonstrates that gatekeeping challenges have become a routine element of litigation strategies, especially for the defence. Defendants have a greater incentive to plea for the exclusion of economic evidence, as this may effectively undermine the plaintiffs' case, particularly given that the plaintiffs bear the burden of proof, and thus have to establish a breach of law, e. g. by putting forth a definition of the relevant market or the possession of market power by the defendant.

The empirical analysis by Langenfeld and Alexander and the critical points raised by the Economic Evidence Task Force and Hovenkamp show that certain challenges remain beyond the establishment of minimum quality standards, even though there seems to be a growing international consensus concerning the substance of such quality standards. Specifically, the effects of the standards on enforcement practice and their actual use should be monitored closely in order to detect undesirable side effects, which may result in particular from their strategic leveraging in legal disputes.

5 Conclusion

In recent years economic analysis has become increasingly relevant to competition law and policy in Germany, Europe as well as worldwide. As a result, issues surrounding how to effectively integrate the expertise of economists into competition law enforcement has gained prominence. This text argues that the most relevant issues and challenges in this context are best encapsulated under the term 'forensic economics in competition law enforcement'. Expert opinions constitute one specific input channel for forensic economics in competition law proceedings. However, in order to ensure that expert testimony supports sound decision making, minimum quality standards for the submission of expert assessments have been adopted in a number of jurisdictions.

A comparative analysis of the Best Practices issued by the Bundeskartellamt in October 2010 and similar guidance documents published by other competition authorities reveals a reliance on common core evaluation criteria. These are: relevance, reliability/robustness, replicability/transparency and accessibility/comprehensibility. Despite sometimes expressing a preference for established theories and methods, these guidance documents abstain from detailed prescriptions with respect to the substantive content or the methodology used in economic

104 See Langenfeld and Alexander, *supra* n 78, p. 23.

105 See Langenfeld and Alexander, *supra* n 78, p. 23 and Annex, Table 3.

assessments. Furthermore, a special look at the U.S. clearly indicates that court-based adversarial enforcement regimes apply almost identical principles for judging the admissibility of expert testimony. Accordingly, there is a growing international consensus concerning the quality standards that should be adopted to guide forensic economics in competition law enforcement.

Access to Evidence and Presumptions – Communicating Vessels in Procedural Law

Andreas Heinemann

1 General Context

In the discussion on the European Commission's White Paper on Damages Actions,[1] the proposals on the disclosure of evidence have attracted great attention and have met with approval by some observers and with rejection by others. The critics point to the risk of introducing a US-style litigation culture in Europe. What is less noticed in this discussion is the fact that some continental legal orders have found another way to fix the problem of evidence: special presumptions are used. In this contribution, the relationship between disclosure obligations and presumptions will be scrutinized. We will see that the success of presumptions is not necessarily due to their substantial persuasiveness but to their role of filling in the continental gaps in the field of disclosure. The advantages and disadvantages of both instruments and their economic rationale shall be discussed.

2 Burden of Proof

2.1 Burden of Production, Burden of Persuasion, Burden of Proof

The starting point is the difference between questions of law and questions of fact. Public authorities have to find their own interpretation of the law (*iura novit curia*). As regards facts, a distinction has to be made between the burden of production, the burden of persuasion and the burden of proof. The burden of production concerns the question of who has to bring forward evidence for a certain fact. In private law, under the adversary system, facts and evidence have to be introduced by the parties whereas under the inquisitorial system (in administrative and crimi-

1 European Commission, 'White Paper on Damages Actions for Breach of the EC Antitrust Rules', COM(2008) 165 final, 2 April 2008.

nal law) the public authority or the court has to investigate the facts, including those in favour of the accused party. This does not exclude duties of the parties to cooperate, which often are imposed in administrative procedure.

The burden of persuasion relates to the standard of proof, i.e. the degree of certainty an authority or court has to have with respect to the facts. Common law prefers objective criteria: In private law, preponderance of the evidence has to be found, in criminal law, the existence of the fact must be beyond a reasonable doubt. By contrast, continental systems rely on the inner conviction of judges (and civil servants). The court must not have serious doubts with respect to the existence of a certain fact. Absolute certainty is not required. The degree of certainty in administrative and criminal law has to be higher than in private law.[2] In all systems, the appreciation of evidence is based on free evaluation. Formal rules of evidence have become very rare.[3]

Finally, the burden of proof (in the narrow, material sense of the word) indicates the one to bear the consequences if a certain fact cannot be proven (situation of *non liquet*). In private law, according to a generally accepted rule, doubts go against the party claiming rights from the fact in question.[4] In administrative law, doubts go against the public authorities if the statute does not otherwise provide. In criminal law, the presumption of innocence has to be respected.[5] Cooperation duties of the parties are admissible if they do not violate the principle of *nemo tenetur se ipsum accusare.*

2.2 An Example: The Cartel Interdiction

These principles may be applied to the prohibition of restrictive agreements in art. 101 TFEU. From a private law perspective, the application of the general rules on the burden of proof would mean that the party that bases its rights on a violation of competition law has to prove the conditions of Art. 101 (1) TFEU, whereas

2 See rule 21.2 of the American Law Institute & Unidroit, *Principles of Transnational Civil Procedure* (available at www.unidroit.org/english/principles/civilprocedure/main.htm): 'Facts are considered proven when the court is reasonably convinced of their truth.' J. P. Westhoff, *Der Zugang zu Beweismitteln bei Schadensersatzklagen im Kartellrecht – Eine rechtsvergleichende Untersuchung* (Nomos 2010), p. 215 n. 1084 interprets this rule as a compromise between the subjective approach on the continent and the objective standard in common law.

3 For an in-depth analysis of the European Courts' approach including a comparative perspective on the law of the EU Member States, see E. Gippini-Fourier, 'The Elusive Standard of Proof in EU Competition Cases', 33 *World Competition* (2010), 187.

4 This principle seems so self-evident that many legal orders refrain from stating an express rule. For an exception see art. 8 of the Swiss Civil Code: 'Unless the law provides otherwise, the burden of proving the existence of an alleged fact shall rest on the person who derives rights from that fact.' See also rule 21.1 of the ALI & Unidroit Principles (*supra* note 2): 'Ordinarily, each party has the burden to prove all the material facts that are the basis of that party's case.'

5 See *infra* 5.2.

the other party has to prove the conditions for the efficiency defence in Art. 101 (3) TFEU.[6] Therefore, for the purpose of private law, the rule in Art. 2 Regulation 1/2003[7] has a purely declaratory character.

This is different in public law. Even if it is important to underline that rules on the burden of proof do not affect the duty of the authorities to investigate the facts,[8] they determine the outcome of the procedure in case of *non liquet*. The alleged infringer bears the risk that the investigation will not bring out sufficient facts for the efficiency defence. In the language of the *error cost approach*, the danger of false positives increases.[9] Moreover, in the field of criminal law, shifting the burden of proof onto the accused party collides with the presumption of innocence. For these reasons, there has been intense discussion on the question whether and, if so, to what extent the transfer of the burden of proof should apply in administrative and criminal law. Art. 2 Regulation 1/2003 apparently strives to apply the principle in public law, too. We will come back to this problem later.[10] At this

---

6 The Guidelines on Vertical Restraints (European Commission, OJ 2010, C 130/1, n. 47) go one step further: 'Where such a hard-core restriction is included in an agreement, that agreement is presumed to fall within Article 101(1).' This presumption is not very clear. Although the existence of a hard-core restriction may lead to the presumption of a restriction of competition, it is not relevant for the question if the parties are undertakings or if there is an effect on trade between Member States.

7 See also Recital 5 s. 2 and 3 of Regulation 1/2003: 'It should be for the party or the authority alleging an infringement of Article 81(1) and Article 82 of the Treaty to prove the existence thereof to the required legal standard. It should be for the undertaking or association of undertakings invoking the benefit of a defence against a finding of an infringement to demonstrate to the required legal standard that the conditions for applying such defence are satisfied.'

8 See Recital 5 s. 4 of Regulation 1/2003: 'This Regulation [does not affect the] obligations of competition authorities and courts of the Member States to ascertain the relevant facts of a case, provided that such [...] obligations are compatible with general principles of Community law.'

9 This concept, developed by Frank H. Easterbrook, 'The Limits of Antitrust', 63 *Texas Law Review* (1984), is that error costs of false positives (type 1 errors) and false negatives (type 2 errors) have to be weighed. If the costs of type 1 errors are higher than of type 2 errors, the conduct in question is to be allowed. The error cost approach is problematic particularly when the long-term effects on innovation are unclear, but possibly high. In these cases, the error cost approach will often advocate against the application of competition law although intervention may be particularly important in order to safeguard a competitive structure in the long run. See the critique of J. Drexl, 'Is There a 'More Economic Approach' to Intellectual Property and Competition Law?', in J. Drexl (ed.), *Research Handbook on Intellectual Property and Competition Law* (Edward Elgar Publishing 2008), p. 27, 40 *et seq.* See also J. Fingleton and A. Nikpay, 'Stimulating or Chilling Competition', 2008 (available at www.oft.gov.uk/news-and-updates/speeches/2008/0808), who warn against the tendency of the error cost approach to underestimate the chilling effect of under-intervention.

10 See *infra* 5.3.

point, it is sufficient to mention that EU law does not contain special rules on the standard of proof. According to Recital 5 of Regulation 1/2003, national rules on the standard of proof are not affected.

2.3 Specific Lack of Evidence in Private Competition Law?

According to a widespread, but not undisputed opinion, there are specific information asymmetries in private competition law.[11] They are due to the factual and economic complexity of competition law cases, e.g. the existence of secret practices and the difficulties in the context of market definition, the determination of a dominant position and the cost structure (relevant for the proof of predatory pricing or price abuse). While these points concern the competition law infringement, problems in providing evidence also arise when establishing the loss, the causation between infringement and loss and the requirement of fault if the national rule does not provide for strict liability. On the other hand, certain competitive parameters are quite visible, as for example restrictive terms in distribution agreements, boycott, refusal to deal and refusal to licence as well as the level of selling prices.[12] As regards the quantification of damages, most European countries provide for flexibility. If through no responsibility of the aggrieved party the precise calculation presents difficulties, then the courts often have the discretion to estimate the extent of losses incurred.[13]

In spite of these qualifications, then, the search for evidence in private competition law cases often poses difficulties. This conclusion does not imply that there are no other fields of law in which difficulties of comparable degree exist (as for example product or environmental liability). But the existence of other problematic issues does not affect the necessity to react to the problems in competition law. The question has to be answered if special rules for competition cases ought to be adopted or if a 'horizontal' approach (covering all fields of law showing comparable difficulties) ought to be preferred. In our view, problems in private competition law are so huge that reforms should start here if the adoption of general rules

---

11 For a definition, see European Commission, 'Commission Staff Working Paper – Annex to the Green Paper on Damages Actions for Breach of the EC Antitrust Rules', SEC(2005) 1732, 19.12.2005, para. 81: 'Information asymmetry exists when one party (usually the defendant) has in its control or has access to more evidence relating to a given claim than the (potential) claimant.'

12 A. Heinemann, 'Interferenzen zwischen öffentlichem Recht und Privatrecht in der Wettbewerbspolitik', in Epiney, Haag, & Heinemann (eds.), *Challenging Boundaries – Essays in Honor of Roland Bieber* (Nomos 2007), 681, at p. 695.

13 See Communication from the Commission on Quantifying Harm in Actions for Damages Based on Breaches of Article 101 or 102 of the Treaty on the Functioning of the European Union, OJ 2013 C 167/19, and the accompanying Practical Guide, Commission Staff Working Document SWD(2013) 205 of 11.6.2013, available at http://ec.europa.eu/competition/antitrust/actionsdamages/quantification_guide_en.pdf.

would delay the reform to some day in the indefinite future.[14] The example of intellectual property shows that specific problems in a certain legal field constitute a sufficient reason to adopt procedural rules going beyond the general standards.[15] The initiative of the European Commission to address the problem of scattered damages by introducing collective redress at least for the fields of competition and consumer protection law will serve as an indicator for the chances of success of a horizontal approach.[16]

3 Coping with Problems of Proof

3.1 Options

There are a number of ways of solving or at least alleviating the problem of proof. Here we find marked differences between common law and the continent.[17] In common law countries, comprehensive duties of discovery alleviate the burden of proof considerably.[18] In civil law countries, by contrast, the claimant has to prepare his case carefully. If he realizes that he will not be able to produce comprehensive evidence, it is not advisable for him to go to court. In order to solve the problems – particularly pressing in civil law countries – several options exist:

1. Transition to an inquisitorial system in private competition law
2. Active role of the competition authority in civil procedure
3. Use of administrative decisions in follow on actions
4. Right to information (in substantive law)

---

14 In this sense, see C. Kersting, 'Perspektiven der privaten Rechtsdurchsetzung im Kartellrecht', *Zeitschrift für Wettbewerbsrecht* 2008, 252, p. 270; J. P. Westhoff (*supra* n. 2), p. 181 *et seq.* For an opposing view, see J.-S. Ritter, 'Private Durchsetzung des Kartellrechts', *Wirtschaft und Wettbewerb* 2008, 762 (pp. 768–769).

15 Under Article 6 and 7 of the Enforcement Directive (Directive 2004/48/EC of the European Parliament and of the Council of 29 April 2004 on the enforcement of intellectual property rights, OJ 2004 L 195/16) EU Member States have to provide for special disclosure mechanisms following the principle of fact pleading.

16 See Commission Recommendation on Common Principles for Injunctive and Compensatory Collective Redress Mechanisms in the Member States Concerning Violations of Rights Granted under Union Law of 11.6.2013, OJ L 201/60.

17 D. Woods, A. Sinclair and D. Ashton, 'Private Enforcement of Community Competition Law: Modernisation and the Road Ahead', 2 *CPN* (2004), 31, p 34.

18 For this reason, it may be attractive to take legal action in British courts. See F. W. Bulst, 'The Provimi Decision of the High Court: Beginnings of Private Antitrust Litigation in Europe', *European Business Organization Law Review* 2003, 623; and *id.*, 'Internationale Zuständigkeit, anwendbares Recht und Schadensberechnung im Kartelldeliktsrecht', *Europäisches Wirtschafts- und Steuerrecht* 2004, 403, p.404.

5. Easing of the standard of proof: plausibility instead of full proof?
6. Presumptions
7. Access to evidence in possession of the other or a third party (procedural law)

Option (1) is the most radical one. The principle of administrative procedure would be applied to civil procedure as well (as it is already the case in many countries e.g. in certain areas of family law).[19] Option (2) would be similar. However, here it is not the court, but the competition authority that actively investigates the relevant facts in a civil procedure. Already today, competition authorities have the possibility of acting as *amicus curiae* in private competition cases. Art. 15 Regulation 1/2003 provides for a close cooperation of national courts with the European Commission, which applies to private enforcement, too.[20] Option (3) establishes an authoritative effect of administrative decisions for civil procedure: civil courts are bound by final decisions of the competition authority. Option (4) strives to solve the problems in substantive law: rights to information against infringers are to be strengthened. These rights may be enforced, or the failure to perform may entail negative conclusions against the disrespectful party. Option (5) would revolutionize the requirements for the standard of proof. The plaintiff would not be obliged any longer to adduce full proof, but it would be sufficient for him to render his claim plausible. Less far reaching is the plea for more presumptions (Option (6)) concerning selected elements of competition law violations. Finally, option (7) would strengthen the competence of the court to impose disclosure of evidence in possession of the other party or of third parties.

3.2 Discussion

In our view, reforms in the field of evidence are overdue. Evidentiary difficulties are particularly strong in the field of private competition law enforcement. As the result is an undue preference of the respondent, it is appropriate to modify the rules on evidence to the advantage of the plaintiff. If private enforcement is to be strengthened, there have to be improvements in this field. The goal is to re-establish an adequate balance between the interests of both sides.

---

19 See R. Zäch and R. A. Heizmann, 'Durchsetzung des Wettbewerbsrechts durch Private', in *Essays in Honor of Stanislaw Soltysinski* (Poznan 2005), 1059, p. 1066; R. Zäch, *Schweizerisches Kartellrecht* (Stämpfli, 2nd ed. 2005), para. 850.

20 See Commission Notice on the co-operation between the Commission and the courts of the EU Member States in the application of articles 81 and 82 EC, OJ 2004 C 101/54. As Art. 15 Regulation 1/2003 only establishes a minimum level, national law may confer wider powers on competition authorities of the Member States. See for example Art. 90 (2) of the German Act against Restraints of Competition (ARC), which gives the Federal Cartel Office the right 'to submit written statements to the court, to point out facts and evidence, to attend hearings, to present arguments there, and to address questions to parties, witnesses and experts.' Pointing out evidence does not confer a formal right to take certain evidence; rather, it allows the authority to play an active role.

3.2.1 Inquisitorial System

For this reason, no use should be made of option (1). The adoption of the inquisitorial system in private law would confer the same tasks to the courts that competition authorities have in administrative procedures. It is highly doubtful if courts – without the organizational substructure competition authorities have – would be able to cope with such a far-reaching task.

3.2.2 *Amicus curiae* Function of Competition Authorities

The *amicus curiae* function of competition authorities in private enforcement should be expanded. The European Commission's Report on the Functioning of Regulation 1/2003[21] has revealed that national courts tend to hesitate before asking questions to the European Commission. Therefore, competition authorities should be given the right to intervene in private procedures on their own initiative, since this is already the case in some countries. On the other hand, for the sake of the independence of competition authorities and with respect to their limited funding, this should not be understood in the sense that competition authorities would be obliged to make a full-fledged investigation. Rather, it is desirable that they can give input and indicate evidence which might be important to consider. Therefore, it is not about introducing an inquisitorial system through the backdoor of a competition authority's intervention. It is about strengthening the *amicus curiae* function of these authorities.

3.2.3 Binding Effect of Administrative Decisions

In some countries, courts are formally bound by (final) decisions of competition authorities. In the EU, Art. 16 Regulation 1/2003 provides for a binding effect of the European Commission's decisions for national courts. In the European Union, this principle could be extended to the decisions of national competition authorities in the EU Member States, as it is already the case in German law.[22] The argument in favour of a binding effect is the high authority of a decision that has been taken on the basis of a comprehensive investigation and that was open to judicial challenge. But this should not raise too many expectations: even in countries without a formal binding effect, administrative decisions will have a high level of persuasive authority.

---

21 European Commission, 'Communication from the Commission to the European Parliament and the Council – Report on the Functioning of Regulation 1/2003', COM(2009) 206 final, 29 April 2009.

22 See Art. 33 (4) ARC.

3.2.4 Right to Information

Already today, in many legal orders rights to information in substantive law exist.[23] They may be useful in certain contexts. But compared with the procedural duties of disclosure they appear laborious. It is more effective if the court orders disclosure of evidence directly. Therefore, procedural duties of disclosure will be looked at more closely later.

3.2.5 Easing of the Standard of Proof

Option (5) would transfer the pleading standard in the US (which is plausibility[24]) to standard of proof. It would be up to the defendant to rebut the plaintiff's allegations once they have reached the level of plausibility. A general presumption of a competition law violation in case of plausible allegations would be introduced. This does not seem adequate, however. The standard of proof determines the outcome of a civil suit. If it is too low, the risk of wrong judgments increases considerably. This does not seem compatible with fundamental principles of private law. It is with good reason that the European Commission rejected proposals going in this direction.[25]

3.2.6 Access to Evidence and Presumptions

Hence, the discussion on alleviations should focus on the rules governing access to evidence in civil procedure and on specific presumptions as a means to shift the burden of proof. Both concepts stand in close relationship to each other. Before analyzing the justification of presumptions, proposals on how to create better evidence access will be discussed.

---

23 With respect to German law, see the analysis by R. Wilhelmi, 'Zugang zu Beweismitteln und Auskunftsanspruch – Die Regelungen des deutschen Rechts und des Weißbuchs im Vergleich', in Möschel and Bien (eds.), *Kartellrechtsdurchsetzung durch private Schadenersatzklagen?* (Nomos 2010), 99, p. 104 *et seq.*

24 See US Supreme Court in the *Bell Atlantic Corp. v. Twombly* case, 550 U.S. 544 (2007). The Supreme Court underlined that for fulfilling the plausibility standard it is not sufficient that the claim – on the basis of the facts mentioned – is merely conceivable: 'Asking for plausible grounds does not impose a probability requirement at the pleading stage; it simply calls for enough fact to raise a reasonable expectation that discovery will reveal evidence of illegal agreement.'

25 European Commission, 'Commission Staff Working Paper accompanying the White Paper on Damages Actions for Breach of the EC Antitrust Rules', SEC(2008) 404, para. 91.

4 Access to Evidence

In public enforcement, access to evidence is not a major problem. Under the inquisitorial system, competition authorities have on hand a variety of instruments, e.g. the enforceable right to request for information, the power to take statements and the conduct of inspections in undertakings or other premises. Leniency programmes create incentives for infringers to reveal secret practices. Problems of access to evidence have recently been discussed as far as the access of accused parties is concerned. Inspired by the US model, the question is raised if cross-examining of witnesses should be introduced into administrative and court procedure.[26]

4.1 The Proposal of the European Commission

In the White Paper, based on the assumption of a structural information asymmetry, the European Commission has proposed a system of *fact pleading* as opposed to *notice pleading* known from US law.[27] A minimum level of disclosure is considered desirable that is linked to detailed conditions. The claimant has to present all facts and means of evidence reasonably available. They have to show plausible grounds for a harm caused by the defendant. The claimant must be unable to produce the requested evidence. Precise categories of evidence have to be specified.[28] If the requested evidence is relevant, necessary and proportionate, the court will order the defendant (or third parties) to submit this evidence. An exception applies in the case of corporate statements by leniency applicants.[29]

---

26 F. Castillo de la Torre, 'Evidence, Proof and Judicial Review in Cartel Cases', 32 *World Competition* (2009), 505, p. 534 *et seq.* with further references. For the subject of cross examination in the context of civil procedure, see R. Stürner, 'Duties of Disclosure and Burden of Proof in the Private Enforcement of European Competition Law', in J. Basedow (ed.), *Private Enforcement of EC Competition Law* (Kluwer Law International 2007), 163, at p. 180–181.

27 For the difference between fact pleading and notice pleading, see e.g. R. Stürner (*supra* note 26), p. 170–171.

28 The European Commission gives the following examples (Commission Staff Working Paper, *supra* note 25, para. 106): Documents about price discussions between cartelists for a clearly described product, period and territory to the extent that they may concern the claimant; disclosure – for a specified product, period and territory – of facts to enable the claimant to determine what the pricing structure on the market would have been in the absence of the cartel (including details of prices prior to the cartel and of price discussions during the life of the cartel).

29 European Commission, White Paper (*supra* note 1), p. 4–5.

4.2 Discussion

Continental systems oblige the claimant to produce all the evidence relevant for his claim. In specific situations, rights of information or procedural rules of disclosure exist but they are of limited scope. Although these alleviations have been subsequently extended,[30] they are not of great help in the field of secret anticompetitive behaviour. This contributes to the phenomenon of private underenforcement in the field of stand-alone actions.[31] By contrast, US-style notice pleading creates the danger of fishing expeditions, high procedural costs and the risk of blackmail settlements.[32] Therefore, a middle ground has to be found.[33]

A useful text identifying a way between extremes are the Principles of Transnational Civil Procedure adopted by the American Law Institute and Unidroit.[34] Rule 16 states the principle that each party should have access to all relevant, non-privileged and reasonably identified evidence in the possession or control of another party or, if necessary and on just terms, of a non-party. It is not a basis of objection to such disclosure that the evidence may be adverse to the party or person making the disclosure.' Even if the Principles appear as a compromise between different systems of disclosure, it has to be underlined that they start from the idea of fact pleading. Hence, they do not pave the way for fishing expeditions, but they invite states to leave behind rules that inadequately favour alleged infringers.[35] The English example demonstrates that balanced rules on disclosure may solve the difficulties of producing evidence without causing excessive litigation. The proposal of the European Commission in the White Paper is perfectly in line with these specifications. It may be added that an expansion of disclosure rules does not violate unwritten rules of procedural law. The often-quoted principle of *nemo ten-*

---

30 See R. Stürner, 'The Principles of Transnational Civil Procedure – An Introduction to Their Basic Conceptions', 69 *Rabels Zeitschrift für ausländisches und internationales Privatrecht* (2005), 201, p. 233 *et seq.*

31 In follow-on suits, problems of adducing evidence are mitigated by the information supplied by competition authority decisions, especially if they have a binding effect. See W.-H. Roth, 'Private Enforcement of European Competition Law – Recommendations Flowing From the German Experience', in J. Basedow (*supra* n. 26), 61, p. 77–78.

32 See P. Beschorner and K. Hüschelrath, 'Ökonomische Aspekte der privaten Durchsetzung des Kartellrechts', in Möschel and Bien (*supra* note 23), 9, p. 12. These risks are not removed, but only reduced by the fact that the US Supreme Court has tightened the requirement of plausibility, see *supra* note 24.

33 For a comparative perspective, see D. Gerber, 'Extraterritorial Discovery and the Conflict of Procedural Systems: Germany and the United States', 34 *American Journal of Comparative Law* (1986), 745.

34 *Supra* note 2.

35 See the assessment of R. Stürner (*supra* note 30), p. 237: 'In this way the Principles reach a reasonable solution appropriate to avoid the excesses of both traditional legal systems; namely, the tendency of the American procedure towards overbroad discovery on the one hand, and the danger of a too early termination of fact finding in the continental tradition on the other.'

etur edere contra se is not compatible with modern developments in private procedure.[36] With respect to EU law, the European Court of Justice has decided that *nemo tenetur* does not apply in civil proceedings, which cannot lead to the imposition of a penalty.[37]

In the area of competition law, specific reasons may be added. The more economic approach taken in European competition law and partial spilling over into the legal orders of the EU Member States has replaced the form-based by an effects-based analysis. Under the new approach, the importance of the factual basis has increased considerably.[38] The appreciation of all circumstances of the individual case has taken center stage and creates the tendency to push back general rules. This is not the place to discuss the pros and cons of this development.[39] For the purpose of private enforcement, this development means that access to evidence has become crucial. The important role of economics only makes sense in a system where access to the factual material is granted. Therefore, the increasing role of economics in competition law should go along with improved access to evidence. Fishing expeditions will not be possible if the necessary precautions are taken, and if access is placed under close judicial control.

5 Presumptions and Other Rules on the Burden of Proof

5.1 Concept

A presumption bases the existence of a certain fact or legal situation on the existence of other facts. Rebuttable presumptions are an instrument to shift the burden of proof. Thus, they modify the general rules in this area. For a rebuttal of the pre-

36 R. Stürner (*supra* note 30), p. 235 para. 163.

37 Case C-60/92 *Otto/Postbank* [1993] ECR, I-5683, para. 21.

38 See the interesting observation of D. Gerber, *Global Competition – Law, Markets, and Globalization* (Oxford University Press 2010), p. 137 according to which it is not only true that the economic approach requires broad access to facts, but that – conversely – the expansion of discovery rights in US law 'has played a major role in the ascendancy of economics-based analysis' and thus has promoted the change of substantive law in the direction of the economic approach.

39 For an analysis, see for example M. Hellwig, 'Effizienz oder Wettbewerbsfreiheit? Zur normativen Grundlegung der Wettbewerbspolitik', in Engel & Möschel (eds.), *Recht und spontane Ordnung – Festschrift für Ernst-Joachim Mestmäcker zum achtzigsten Geburtstag* (Nomos 2006), p. 231 *et seq.*; Schmidtchen, Albert & Voigt (eds.), *The More Economic Approach to European Competition Law* (Mohr Siebeck 2007); R. Zäch and A. Künzler, 'Freedom to Compete or Consumer Welfare: The Goal of Competition Law according to Constitutional Law', in Zäch, Heinemann and Kellerhals (eds.), *The Development of Competition Law – Global Perspectives* (Edward Elgar Publishing 2010), p. 61 *et seq.*

sumption, full proof of the contrary has to be provided. It is not sufficient to offer evidence giving reason for doubt.[40] This is different from *prima facie* or *res ipsa loquitur* evidence (*evidential presumptions*[41]), a sort of indirect evidence based on general experience, where rebuttal simply requires the creation of serious doubts.[42] Conclusive presumptions (*praesumptio iuris et de iure*) cannot be rebutted. They are in most cases disguised rules of law.[43]

5.2 Different Effects of Presumptions in Private, Administrative and Criminal Law

In private law, as we have seen, a presumption shifts the burden of production *and* the burden of proof onto the other party. Thus, presumptions have full effect in private law. The situation is different in public law (administrative and criminal). In an inquisitorial system, presumptions do not affect the mission of the authorities to investigate the facts. Therefore, presumptions do not in principle affect the burden of production on administrative authorities and the courts. However, presumptions may add a secondary burden of production onto the parties[44] in addition to general cooperation duties. In administrative law, presumptions determine the outcome if it is not possible to clear a matter up (*non liquet*).

---

40 In the German terminology the rebuttal requires a *Hauptbeweis*, not only a *Gegenbeweis*. See Art. 292 of the German Code on Civil Procedure; for Swiss law, see A. Staehelin, D. Staehelin and P. Grolimund, *Zivilprozessrecht* (Schulthess Verlag 2008), p. 258.

41 See the distinction between evidential, substantive and procedural presumptions by D. Bailey, 'Presumptions in EU Competition Law', 31 *European Competition Law Review* (2010), 362–369.

42 Normally, *prima facie* situations are identified by the courts. An example for a legal *prima facie* rule is Art. 20 (4) of the German ARC, which imposes on the other party the task of clarifying circumstances in his field of business if on the basis of specific facts and of general experience there seems to be exclusionary abuse. See R. Stürner (*supra* note 26), p. 185–186, who criticizes the combination of *prima facie* evidence and obligations to cooperate and who concludes that it 'is difficult enough to formulate helpful evidentiary rules, and it is more difficult to do so in special fields of law in accordance with the general law of evidence.' For a more favourable view of *prima facie* assumptions, see W.-H. Roth (*supra* note 31), p. 77–78.

43 On the historical development of presumptions, see Helmholz & Sellar (eds.), *The Law of Presumptions: Essay in Comparative Legal History* (Duncker & Humblot 2009).

44 See Joined Cases C-204/00 P, C-205/00 P, C-211/00 P, C-213/00 P, C-217/00 P and C-219/00 P *Aalborg Portland and Others/Commission* [2004] ECR I-123, para. 79: 'Although according to those principles the legal burden of proof is borne either by the Commission or by the undertaking or association concerned, the factual evidence on which a party relies may be of such a kind as to require the other party to provide an explanation or justification, failing which it is permissible to conclude that the burden of proof has been discharged.'

In criminal law, the legal prerequisites are different. First, it has to be underlined that, for the purpose of the European Convention on Human Rights, competition law has to be qualified as criminal law as far as fines of a certain amount are concerned.[45] Therefore, the presumption of innocence, laid down in Art. 6 (2) ECHR, applies.[46] This does not rule out the use of presumptions in criminal law; it only establishes restrictions. According to the European Court of Human Rights, the presumption of innocence 'requires States to confine them [*scil.* presumptions] within reasonable limits which take into account the importance of what is at stake and maintain the rights of the defence.'[47] As regards the importance at stake, it has to be underlined that the fundamental rights do not apply to all forms of criminal offences with the same intensity. According to the European Court of Human Rights, outside the hard core of criminal law, 'the criminal-head guarantees will not necessarily apply with their full stringency'.[48] The Court has explicitly mentioned competition law as an example of 'cases not strictly belonging to the traditional categories of the criminal law'.[49] Therefore, careful use of presumptions may be made in this area. As regards the rights of defence, it is essential that presumptions are rebuttable. Hence, conclusive presumptions are excluded in the field of criminal law. Likewise, it would be incompatible with the rights of defence if a rebuttal of the presumption were impossible for practical reasons (*probatio diabolica*). In order to strike an appropriate balance, presumptions should be interpreted as mere *prima facie* rules in the context of criminal law. Thus, not the proof of the contrary would be necessary, only the creation of serious doubt. In the case law of the European Court of Justice, this requirement is fulfilled by the rules on a secondary shift of the burden of proof.[50]

5.3 The Efficiency Defence

We have already seen that the burden of proving the conditions for the efficiency defence in Art. 101 (3) TFEU is on the party claiming the benefit of this defence.[51] In private law, this rule is immediately plausible. By contrast, the application of this rule in public law proceedings has been criticized.[52] In order to assess this crit-

---

45 See W. Wils, 'The Increased Level of EU Antitrust Fines, Judicial Review and the ECHR', 33 *World Competition* (2010), 5, p. 12 *et seq.*.

46 The same is true for the presumption of innocence in EU law. See ECJ, Case C-199/92 P *Hüls/Commission* [1999] ECR I-4287, para. 149–150; and Art. 48 (1) Charter of Fundamental Rights of the European Union.

47 ECtHR, case no. 10519/83 of 7 October 1988 – *Salabiaku v. France*, no. 28.

48 ECtHR, case no. 73053/01 of 23 November 2006 – *Jussila v. Finland*, no. 43.

49 *Ibid*; confirmed by ECtHR, case no. 43509/08 of 27 September 2011 – *Menarini Diagnostics v. Italy*.

50 *Supra* note 44.

51 *Supra* 2.1.

52 See for example J. Schütz in Hootz (ed.), *Gemeinschaftskommentar* (Heymann, 5th ed. 2004), Art. 2 Regulation 1/2003 n. 1 *et seq.* For Swiss law, see A. Raas, 'Verfehl-

icism, we have to inquire after the rationale of this rule. An explanation can be found in the legal basis of Art. 2 Regulation 1/2003, which is Art. 103 (2) lit. b TFEU. The rules for the application of Art. 101 (3) TFEU shall take 'into account the need to ensure effective supervision on the one hand, and to simplify administration to the greatest possible extent on the other'. It is certainly in the interest of effective supervision and of simplified administration to attribute the burden of proof for the efficiency defence onto the alleged infringer. At the same time, error costs caused by false positives are increased if the burden of proof in *non liquet* situations is placed on private parties. In our view, shifting the burden of proof onto private parties is nevertheless justified, as the facts suited for proving the four conditions in Art. 101 (3) TFEU are typically situated in the sphere of the parties to the agreement, making it much easier for them to find and to present these facts in an administrative procedure. According to case law, it is sufficient for the parties to deliver convincing arguments and evidence. If the Commission does not succeed in refuting these arguments and evidence, the enterprise has discharged the burden of proof.[53] This seems to be an efficient distribution of the burden of proof. The danger of false positives is reduced by the rules on the secondary burden of proof, and social costs will decrease because administrative costs are reduced considerably.[54]

In criminal law, however, different standards apply. There is an intense debate on the question whether, in competition law fining procedures, charging the undertakings with the burden of proof for the efficiency defence is compatible with the presumption of innocence.[55] As we have already seen, competition law has to

te Beweislastumkehr in Kartellrechtsverfahren – Im Zweifel für die Vertragsfreiheit', *sic!* 2007, 423.

53 *Supra* note 44 and Case T-168/01 *GlaxoSmithKline Services/Commission* [2006] ECR II-2969, para. 235–6; Joined Cases C-501/06 P, C-513/06 P, C-515/06 P and C-519/06 P *GlaxoSmithKline/Commission*, [2009] ECR I-9291, para. 81–88.

54 For an economic analysis of procedural law, see *infra* 6.

55 For favourable views of the full application of Art. 2 Regulation 1/2003, see Dalheimer in Grabitz & Hilf (eds.), *Das Recht der Europäischen Union, Kommentar* (C.H. Beck 2012), nach Art. 83, Art. 2 Regulation 1/2003 para. 12 *et seq.*; and Lampert, Niejahr, Kübler and Weidenbach, *EG-Kartellverordnung – Praxiskommentar* (Verlag Recht und Wirtschaft 2004), Art. 2 Regulation 1/2003 para. 82. For a critical view of this kind of allocation, see Bechtold, Brinker, Bosch and Hirsbrunner (eds.), *EG-Kartellrecht – Kommentar* (C.H. Beck, 2nd ed. 2009), Art. 2 Regulation 1/2003, para. 24; G. Dannecker and J. Biermann, in Immenga & Mestmäcker (eds.), *Wettbewerbsrecht Band 1, EU/Teil 2, Kommentar zum Europäischen Kartellrecht* (C.H. Beck, 5th ed. 2012), Vorbemerkungen zu Art. 23 ff. Regulation 1/2003 para. 66; and K. Schmidt in Immenga & Mestmäcker (eds.), *Wettbewerbsrecht Band 1, EU/Teil 2, Kommentar zum Europäischen Kartellrecht* (C.H. Beck, 5th ed. 2012), Art. 2 Regulation 1/2003 para. 39. The German delegation submitted a statement on Art. 2 Regulation 1/2003 that was entered into the Council minutes at the time that Regulation 1/2003 was adopted: 'Supplementary in particular to Recital 5 of the Regulation under consideration, the Government of the Federal Republic of Germany reiterates its view that Article 83 of the Treaty does not constitute a sufficient legal basis for intro-

be qualified as criminal law as far as fines of a certain amount are concerned.[56] But as pointed out above, the presumption of innocence does not categorically exclude presumptions or a distribution of the burden of proof that disfavours undertakings. It all depends on the 'reasonable limits', i.e. the importance of the offence and the maintenance of the rights of the defence.[57] In this respect, it has to be stressed that competition law fines are imposed for clear violations, mostly in the field of hard-core restrictions. It is very rare for undertakings to be fined in a situation where the scope of the efficiency defence is in dispute.[58] For the distribution of the burden of proof provided for in Art. 2 Regulation 1/2003, objective reasons exist. As we have already seen, it is hardly possible to prove the absence of the efficiency defence. The investigation has to be based on the arguments of the parties in question. Of course, as shown in the context of administrative law, it is up to the authority to rebut the factual evidence brought forward by an undertaking. Because of secondary rules of this type, there is no 'automatic reliance'[59] on the distribution of the burden of proof. The 'reasonable limits' underlined by the European Court on Human Rights are respected.

5.4 Per se Prohibition and Rule of Reason

Whereas presumptions refer to single facts or legal terms (e.g. dominance), the distinction between per se prohibition and rule of reason refers to a legal rule in its entirety. If a certain conduct is caught by a *per se* prohibition, the plaintiff has to prove the elements of the prohibition. If he succeeds, the defendant cannot object since the prohibition in its entirety works as an irrefutable presumption. The most famous example is the *per se* rule of US Antitrust Law in its classical conception. By contrast, a legal rule modelled according to the rule of reason, provides for a prohibition with exceptions. In the US version, pro- and anti-competitive effects have to be balanced. According to the European approach, prohibitions and exceptions are formulated in a more specific way, which might be called a structured rule of reason. The plaintiff has to prove the elements of the prohibition. The de-

ducing or amending provisions governing criminal law or criminal proceedings. This especially applies with regard to fundamental procedural guarantees in criminal proceedings such as the presumption of innocence of the accused. The Government of the Federal Republic of Germany points out that, in Germany, these procedural guarantees also apply to proceedings equivalent to criminal proceedings such as proceedings on administrative fines, and that they enjoy constitutional status. The Government of the Federal Republic of Germany thus expects that the Regulation under consideration, in particular Article 2, will neither amend nor impair Member States' criminal-law or criminal-proceedings provisions or legal principles applicable to criminal proceedings or proceedings equivalent to criminal proceedings.'

56 *Supra* 5.2.

57 *Supra* note 47.

58 K. Schmidt, *supra* note 55.

59 See ECtHR, case no. 13191/87 of 25 September 1992 – *Pham Hoang v. France*, no. 36.

fendant may rely on an exception; in this case he has to prove the prerequisites of this exception. For both types of rules, there may be presumptions with respect to certain elements, normally in favour of the plaintiff, but sometimes also in favour of the defendant (e.g. safe harbours).[60]

In US law, the clear distinction between *per se* prohibitions and rule of reason has been blurred by the *quick look* or *truncated* analysis under which hard-core restrictions may be open to justification.[61] This process goes along with the development of the *rule of reason* to a 'structured' rule creating (rebuttable) presumptions. In European law, there has never been a *per se* rule, as the defence in Art. 101 (3) TFEU applies to all restraints, be they hard-core or simple restrictions.[62] For a long while it has been said that the prerequisites of justification will virtually never be met if there is a hard-core restriction. But under the more economic approach, there is more space for justification even in the hard-core area.[63]

---

60 An interesting approach to presumptions is to be found in Swiss competition law. According to Art. 5 (3) and (4) of the Swiss Cartel Act (CartA), there are presumptions for an elimination of effective competition in case of certain hard-core restrictions. If there is an elimination of effective competition, the law does not admit the efficiency defence (which is available only if the agreement restricts but does not eliminate competition). Since these presumptions are refutable, the rules in question do not constitute per se prohibitions. See A. Künzler and R. A. Heizmann, 'Art. 5 Abs. 4 des schweizerischen Kartellgesetzes im Lichte der Leegin Entscheidung des U.S. Supreme Court', in Weber, Heinemann & Vogt (eds.), *Methodische und konzeptionelle Grundlagen des Schweizer Kartellrechts im europäischen Kontext* (Stämpfli 2009), p. 133 *et seq.*; R. Zäch and A. Künzler, 'Abschaffung der Vermutung von Art. 5 Abs. 4 des schweizerischen Kartellgesetzes – ein Schildbürgerstreich', in Oertle, Wolf, Breitenstein & Diem (eds.), *M&A: Recht und Wirtschaft in der Praxis – Liber amicorum für Rudolf Tschäni*,(Dike 2010), p. 465 *et seq.*

61 See L. A. Sullivan and W. S. Grimes, *The Law of Antitrust: An Integrated Handbook* (Westgroup 2000), p. 167–168.

62 See R. Whish, *Competition Law* (Oxford University Press, 6th ed. 2009), p. 150: 'In this sense EC law differs from US law, since there are no agreements that are "per se" illegal in the EC system.' For the same reason, the distinction in European competition law between restrictions by object and by effect cannot be put on the same level as the distinction between *per se* prohibitions and the rule of reason in US antitrust law. See Whish, *ibid.*, p. 118–119.

63 Compare the old Guidelines on Vertical Restraints (*European Commission*, OJ 2000, C 291/1, para. 46: 'Individual exemption of vertical agreements containing such hardcore restrictions is also unlikely.') with the new one (*European Commission*, Guidelines on Vertical Restraints, OJ 2010 C 130/1, para. 47: 'However, undertakings may demonstrate pro-competitive effects under Article 101(3) in an individual case.').

6 An Economic Analysis of Disclosure Obligations and Presumptions

6.1 Justification of Presumptions

When should the legislature or the courts provide for presumptions? A starting point may be found in the rationale of *per se* interdictions in US Antitrust Law. The US Supreme Court has held that 'per se rules of illegality are appropriate only when they relate to conduct that is manifestly anticompetitive.'[64] Certain categories of restraints 'always or almost always tend to restrict competition and decrease output',[65] and 'lack [...] any redeeming virtue'.[66] These requirements apply to the *per se* prohibition, i.e. an irrefutable presumption. Which conditions should apply to rebuttable presumptions? With respect to the rule of reason, the US Supreme Court has held in the *Leegin* case that 'courts can, for example, devise rules over time for offering proof, or even presumptions where justified, to make the rule of reason a fair and efficient way to prohibit anticompetitive restraints and to promote pro-competitive ones.'[67] So, the leading principle should be the search for a 'fair and efficient way'. This requires an economic analysis of presumptions and of procedural rules.

Procedural law is an instrument for applying substantive law. The use of the procedural system causes administrative costs (courts, lawyers, fact-finding) and errors in outcome, which distort incentives (error costs). From an economic perspective, the goal of procedural law is to minimize social costs, which are the sum of administrative and error costs.[68] There is a trade-off between administrative costs and error costs: the bigger the procedural efforts are, the less likely errors are to occur (and vice versa).[69]

---

64 *Sylvania*, 433 U.S. 36 (1977) at 49–50.

65 *Broadcast Music v. Columbia Broadcasting System*, 441 U.S. 1 (1979) at 19–20.

66 *Northern Pacific Railroad Co. v. United States*, 356 U.S. 1 (1958) at 5.

67 *Leegin Creative Leather Products, Inc. v. PSKS, Inc.*, 551 U.S. 877 (2007) at 898–899.

68 See R. Cooter and Th. Ulen, *Law and Economics et al.* (Prentice Hall, 6th ed. 2011), p. 384 *et seq.*; and R. Posner, *Economic Analysis of Law* (Wolters Kluwer, 7th ed. 2007), p. 593 *et seq.*

69 On a more general level, it could be asked what effect the arrangement of civil procedure has on total welfare or on consumer welfare. The interaction of public and private enforcement would have to be analyzed in this respect, including the impact of private enforcement on leniency programmes. This article starts from the idea that victims of competition law violations should be compensated so that the impact on public enforcement only allows a cautious interference with that goal. In the US, a link between compensation and leniency exists. See US Department of Justice, *Corporate Leniency Policy* (1993, www.usdoj.gov/atr/public/guidelines/0091.htm), A5 and B6: 'Where possible, the corporation makes restitution to injured parties.'

6.2 Economics of Disclosure Obligations

Disclosure obligations increase administrative costs for the parties because they have to screen the evidence in their possession as to their relevance for the procedure. In many cases, this requires that a large number of documents be produced. There may be disputes on the extent of the duty to submit documents. If business secrets are not protected sufficiently, disclosure may harm the business prospects of the party concerned. As for error costs, disclosure obligations will diminish them since the judgment is given on a broader factual basis. But error costs may also rise because of the risk of discovery blackmail.

Disclosure obligations will reduce social costs if a reduction of error costs outweighs an increase in administrative costs. The increase in administrative costs may be moderated by a careful limitation of disclosure obligations and by an adequate protection of business secrets. This would also reduce the risk of 'discovery blackmail'. It is imaginable to provide for discovery obligations of a different weight depending on whether a competition law violation (more protection of the defendant) or the extent of damages is concerned once such a violation has been established (less protection of the defendant, such as with follow-on suits). For a complete analysis, many other factors would have to be taken into consideration, e.g. the introduction of evidence known from administrative procedures into civil procedures, disclosure obligations of third parties or the possibility of disclosing only towards independent experts.

6.3 Economics of Presumptions

Presumptions aim to influence the trade-off between administrative costs and error costs.[70] They diminish administrative costs, but increase error costs. Irrefutable presumptions reduce administrative costs more than rebuttable presumptions by creating absolute legal certainty (e.g. *per se* prohibitions or *per se* legality). At the same time errors of presumption cannot be straightened out. The closer a presumption is to reality, the more likely savings in administrative costs will be higher than the increase in error costs. Hence, presumptions allow social costs to be reduced in situations where it is highly probable that the presumed fact has occurred or that the legal situation is given.

70 For an economic analysis of presumptions, see A. Bernardo, E. Talley and I. Welch, 'A Theory of Legal Presumptions', 16 *The Journal of Law, Economics, & Organization* (2000), 1. For the purpose of economic analysis, presumptions are qualified here as procedural law. This qualification is made notwithstanding the legal qualification of (some) presumptions as substantive law in many legal orders. For EU competition law, see Case C-8/08 *T-Mobile Netherlands* [2009] ECR I-4529, para. 44–53.

7 Examples

Three examples of presumptions shall be analysed as to their economic justification. In part, these presumptions are provided for by the law (or are being proposed to become law); others have been established by the courts.

7.1 Dominant Position

7.1.1 Market Shares

In several countries, a dominant position is presumed if a firm holds a certain market share. There are presumptions for single dominance and for dominance in oligopolies. If we look only at single dominance, according to German law, 'an undertaking is presumed to be dominant if it has a market share of at least 40 per cent', Art. 18 (4) ARC. In Austria, the presumption of dominance starts from a market share of 30 per cent according to Art. 4 (2) n. 1 of the Austrian Cartel Act.[71] In EU law, there is no written presumption of dominance but the European Court of Justice has resumed its practice in the AKZO case: 'With regard to market shares the Court has held that very large shares are in themselves, and save in exceptional circumstances, evidence of the existence of a dominant position … . That is the situation where there is a market share of 50% …'.[72]

These presumptions cannot simply be explained by historical remnants of an old-fashioned structuralist approach inspired by the out-dated model of perfect competition. To the contrary, market share presumptions also seem to be attractive for more recent competition laws. In Article 19 of the Chinese Antimonopoly Act of 2007, for example, dominance is presumed starting from a market share of 50 per cent. Apparently, presumptions of dominance based on market shares are attractive for states that have introduced competition law quite recently because it facilitates the application of the new law.[73] Does this mean that mature competition law nations may renounce on these presumptions since they are more appropriate for an early stage of advancement?[74] In order to answer this question, an economic analysis of presumptions of dominance has to be made.

---

71 See also R. A. Heizmann, 'Relative Marktmacht, überragende Marktstellung – Eine Analyse nach sechs Jahren Praxis', *recht* 2010, 172, p. 184 *et seq.*, who proposes that such presumptions be introduced into Swiss law. According to this proposal, the threshold for single dominance would be fixed at 40% (*ibid.*, at p. 187).

72 Case C-62/86 *AKZO/Commission* [1991] ECR I-3359, para. 60.

73 For the influence of German law on the Chinese Antimonopoly Act, see D. Gerber (*supra*, note 38), p. 228 para. 33, p. 233.

74 See OECD, *Judicial Enforcement of Competition Law* (Paris 1997), p. 13: 'There is a trend away from the use of such presumptions in some countries, however, as enforcement officials and the courts gain experience and sophistication in competition analysis.'

7.1.2 Assessment

Above we saw that presumptions can fulfil their economic function of reducing social costs only if it is highly probable that the presumed situation is true. So we have to ask if it is highly probable that a dominant position exists if the market share is 30%, 40% or 50%. The assumption of such a simplistic correlation has met with scepticism. The existence of dominance has to be based on many indicators of which market share is only one.[75] So whether the threshold is set at 30% or 50% is not the question. The concept of 'contestable markets' has shown that even a monopoly may be a competitive market if barriers to entry are low or non-existent.[76] If there are no barriers to entry and no sunk costs, the incumbent is under pressure from potential competitors who might access the market on short notice if he charges monopoly prices.

Accordingly, scepticism about the adequacy of market share-based presumptions is widespread and the importance of other factors for conferring independent power has been stressed.[77] The discussion in Germany about the legal status of these presumptions is revealing. Although the law expressly states that an undertaking is presumed to be dominant if it has a market share of at least forty per cent (Art. 18 (4) ARC), there is an ongoing debate whether this is a regular presumption, *prima facie* evidence or a way to impose a secondary burden of proof.[78] As an intermediary result, we may note that it is far from clear that the reduction of administrative costs due to the presumption of dominance will exceed the additional error costs.

---

75 See J. Vickers, 'Some Economics of Abuse of Dominance', University of Oxford, Department of Economics – Discussion Paper Series no. 376 (2007), www.economics.ox.ac.uk/Research/wp/pdf/paper376.pdf, 2007, p. 4: 'High shares alone never imply dominance.'

76 W. Baumol, J. Panzar and R. Willig, *Contestable Markets and the Theory of Industry Structure* (Harcourt Brace Jovanovich 1982).

77 See A. Fuchs and W. Möschel, in Immenga & Mestmäcker (eds.), *Wettbewerbsrecht Band 1, EU/Teil 2, Kommentar zum Europäischen Kartellrecht* (C.H. Beck, 5th ed. 2012), Art. 102 AEUV para. 73 *et seq.*

78 A recent study concludes that the significance of these presumptions for private enforcement is not conclusively resolved. See J. P. Westhoff (*supra* note 2), p. 90. For a position in favour of the full effect of presumption, see P. Pohlmann, 'Die Marktbeherrschungsvermutungen des GWB im Zivilprozess', 164 *Zeitschrift für das gesamte Handelsrecht und Wirtschaftsrecht* (2000), 589, p. 596 *et seq.*

7.2 Predatory Pricing

7.2.1 Sales Below Cost

Under which conditions should low selling prices be qualified as abusive? According to German law, exclusionary conduct exists if an undertaking with superior market power sells below cost (Art. 20 (3) ARC).[79] In the AKZO case, the European Court of Justice has held that prices below average variable costs must be regarded as abusive. The same is true for prices below average total costs, but above average variable costs if they are determined as part of a plan for eliminating a competitor.[80] In its Enforcement Priorities with respect to Art. 102 TFEU, the European Commission has adopted a modernized version of these rules. The central question is whether pricing is capable of foreclosing efficient competitors from the market.[81]

7.2.2 Assessment

The rules of the Court of Justice and the European Commission start from the idea that it is highly probable that sales below cost constitute an abuse pursuant to Art. 102 TFEU. This assumption has been criticized. According to *Martin Hellwig*, the assertions of the European Court of Justice in the *AKZO* case are wrong, at least in the general way as they have been made by the court. For example, it may make economic sense to sell below average variable costs in the case of introductory prices or of cross-subsidizing in multi-product firms.[82]

Even if we take into account that it is generally accepted that the dominant firm may invoke an objective justification (for which it has to provide the necessary evidence[83]), it is again not clear if savings in administrative costs are higher than the increase of error costs due to a (perhaps overly inclusive) rule.

---

79 For the *prima facie* rule in Art. 20 (4) ARC, see *supra* note 42.

80 Case C-62/86 *AKZO/Commission* [1991] ECR I-3359, para 71–72.

81 European Commission, *Guidance on the Commission's enforcement priorities in applying Article 82 of the EC Treaty to abusive exclusionary conduct by dominant undertakings*, OJ 2009, C 45/7, para. 63 *et seq*. The average variable costs are replaced by the average avoidable costs (AAC), the average total costs by the long-run average incremental costs (LRAIC).

82 M. Hellwig, *Wirtschaftspolitik als Rechtsanwendung – Zum Verhältnis von Jurisprudenz und Ökonomie in der Wettbewerbspolitik* (Forschungsgemeinschaft für Nationalökonomie an der Univ. St. Gallen, 2007), p. 6 *et seq.*

83 Enforcement Priorities (*supra* note 81), para. 31.

7.3 Passing on

7.3.1 Passive and Active Use

One of the most intricate questions in the context of private enforcement of competition law is the problem of 'passing on'. Can the respondent defend himself against a damage claim with the argument that the claimant has shifted the cartel overcharge onto the next market level?[84] In German law (Art. 33 (3) 2 ARC) the following rule is to be found: 'If a good or service is purchased at an excessive price, a damage shall not be excluded on account of the resale of the good or service.' This rule is not conceived as a presumption but as a rule on the calculation of damages, i.e. on the mitigation of damages by benefits received. This rule has an effect on the *onus probandi*, however: mitigation of damages has to be proven by the party pleading this argument, i.e. by the infringer. In other countries, this distribution of the burden of proof can be deduced from the general rules (if the passing on defence is recognized).

The European Commission has gone one step further by suggesting a presumption for the active use of the passing-on argument in the White Paper on damages actions: 'Indirect purchasers should be able to rely on the rebuttable presumption that the illegal overcharge was passed on to them in its entirety.'[85] But as perpetrators bear the burden of proof for the passive use of the passing on defence, a *non liquet* would burden them twice, first in damages claims from direct purchasers where they could not prove the passing-on defence, and second in damages claims of lower commercial levels, where they could not rebut the presumption for the active use of passing on.[86]

7.3.2 Assessment

Here again, we have to ask the question if it is highly probable that the overcharge has been passed on to the next market level. This depends on many circumstances, such as the degree of competition on downstream markets as well as on the price

84 See the study of F. W. Bulst, *Schadensersatzansprüche der Marktgegenseite im Kartellrecht* (Nomos 2006). For the context of Art. 102 TFEU, see M. O. Mackenrodt, 'Private Incentive, Optimal Deterrence and Damage Claims for Abuses of Dominant Positions', in Mackenrodt, Conde Gallego & Enchelmaier (eds.), *Abuse of Dominant Position: New Interpretation, New Enforcement Mechanisms?* (Springer 2008), p. 174 *et seqq*.

85 European Commission, White Paper (*supra* note 1), p. 8. But see now the balanced rule in Art. 13 of the Commission Proposal for a Directive of the European Parliament and of the Council on Certain Rules Governing Actions for Damages under National Law for Infringements of the Competition Law Provisions of the Member States and of the European Union, COM(2013) 404 final.

86 See the critique of J. Bornkamm, 'Cui malo? Wem schaden Kartelle?', *Gewerblicher Rechtsschutz und Urheberrecht* 2010, 501, p. 504–505.

elasticity of demand.[87] Error costs appear to be particularly high if presumptions do not only influence the outcome of a case between two parties, but also asymmetrically favour the claims of indirect purchasers, thus creating the risk of multiple liability.

8 Conclusions

The topic of presumptions touches the foundations of competition law. Whereas US antitrust law was based from the start on the prohibition principle, in Europe the abuse model initially prevailed. Under the abuse principle, the anticompetitive conduct is identified, but not prohibited. In abuse systems, competition law rules may be qualified as presumptions for the government to intervene.[88] With the transition to the prohibition principle, presumptions have received a more specific task. Within a competition law rule, they alleviate evidentiary burden with respect to single elements of that rule.

8.1 Insights

Presumptions deploy full effect in private law.[89] By shifting the burden of proof to the other party, presumptions ease difficulties of providing evidence. In administrative procedure, their consequences are tempered by the inquisitorial system. In the field of criminal law, the presumption of innocence applies, albeit with qualifications in the field of administrative offences. At least with respect to the three examples considered here, the economic rationale of presumptions seems to be rather weak.

8.2 The Link Between Presumptions and Disclosure Rules

Yet an overall assessment has to take into account the contribution of presumptions to private enforcement in general. Their function is to cure the problem of access to evidence virulent in continental legal systems (without comprehensive systems of disclosure). Their evaluation has to be made in this context. Presumptions and the rules on access to evidence are communicating vessels: presumptions may compensate difficulties in accessing evidence, and better access to evidence may render presumptions dispensable.

The preceding remarks suggest the following conjecture: The fact that presumptions have found their way into the law and into court practice, although the economic rationale of many of these presumptions is weak, proves their urgent

87 See F. W. Bulst (*supra* note 84), p. 281 *et seq.*

88 See D. Gerber (*supra* note 38), p. 49.

89 But also see the discussion on the status of the presumptions of dominance in German law, *supra* note 78.

need at least if the rules on access to evidence tend to be restrictive. Hence, in an evolutionary sense, these presumptions attest to the existence of a special information asymmetry in competition law. Apparently, the one-size-fits-all approach for evidence access is counterbalanced by the emergence of rules on the distribution of proof.

8.3 Preference for Improved Disclosure or for Presumptions?

This raises the question if preference should be given to better access to evidence or to presumptions. *Rolf Stürner* has clearly opted for the former option: 'When aiming at redressing asymmetries, shifting or lowering the burden of proof should be considered a worse solution compared with a well working system of procedural obligations to disclose and cooperate.'[90] This is even truer when the probability of the presumption's veracity is not very high.

On the other hand, presumptions have the advantage of focusing on specific aspects, whereas disclosure obligations are more general and regularly raise the problem of what is to be disclosed. There is the danger of 'underdisclosure' and 'overdisclosure': either too little is given so that the claimant is not able to discharge his burden of proof, or too much is given so that the other party has difficulties in finding what is relevant for his case. Presumptions avoid this problem: the party burdened by the presumption will have an interest to produce exactly the evidence pertinent for the question. Moreover, in most cases, presumptions focus on a certain aspect that very often may be better elucidated by the party burdened by the presumption.

In sum, disclosure obligations and presumptions have their pros and cons. The requirements of disclosure rules have to be high if an excessive litigation culture is to be avoided. This is why the proposals of the European Commission in the White Paper – restricting disclosure obligations to precise categories of evidence – seem promising. It is the task of the courts to submit disclosure obligations for a strict control of proportionality. Yet if the plaintiff cannot determine 'certain categories' of evidence he will not be able to discharge the burden of proof. Presumptions may fix this shortcoming: they are more targeted with respect to certain questions, and they create incentives to produce exactly the evidence needed for the assessment of certain questions. In this way some problems linked to disclosure obligations (plausibility or sufficient probability of an infringement, *nemo tenetur*, protection of business secrets) can also be avoided.

90 See R. Stürner in Basedow (*supra* note 26), p. 184.

8.4 Outlook

Therefore, in our view, a combination of carefully shaped disclosure rules and presumptions is the best option. Whereas presumptions are less important in public enforcement, they are essential for private law, especially if disclosure obligations are restrictive (or do not exist at all). The economic approach of competition law has amplified the need for an appropriate mix of disclosure and presumptions.[91] But an effects-based analysis is costly and will often require the production of economic expertise.[92] Administrative costs may be reduced if the burden of proof is shifted to the respondent. If presumptions are restricted to facts that the respondent is better placed to produce, the social costs will also be reduced. Hence, it is essential to look at the problem of evidence in a holistic way without isolating single elements. In particular, presumptions have to be assessed with the rules on evidence access in mind. Since these rules are constantly changing, assessments may vary over time.

---

91 See D. Gerber (*supra* note 38), p. 310–312 with respect to the consequences on the global level.

92 See R. A. Heizmann and R. Zäch, 'Expertisekosten als neue Hürden für Kartellklagen', in Leupold, Rüetschi, Stauber & Vetter (eds.), *Der Weg zum Recht – Festschrift für Alfred Bühler* (Schulthess 2008), p. 3 *et seq.*

Economic Evidence in Competition Litigation in Germany

Jochen Burrichter and Thomas B. Paul

1 Introduction

Economic evidence plays a crucial role in all areas of competition law, but nowhere is this more apparent than in private damage litigation. Since most damage lawsuits that go to trial are follow-on cases – meaning that the infringement as such is normally established beyond question under Article 16 Regulation (EC) No 1/2003[1] or Section 33(4) of the German Act Against Restraints of Competition (*Gesetz gegen Wettbewerbsbeschränkungen*, hereafter GWB) – the parties will typically focus their attention and energy on the most important issues remaining (arguably) open to discussion: causation and quantum. Both issues are intrinsically linked, and both require a proper analysis of a hypothetical but-for situation. In some cases, such analysis might be done using a simple before-and-after approach or a direct 'yardstick' comparison with other markets, but more often than not simple tools like these will not be sufficient. Different markets are seldom directly comparable, and prices and quantities are normally dependent on a number of different explanatory variables such as input costs, demand fluctuations, or market entries and exits by competitor firms. In order to control for these variables, more sophisticated techniques are required. Here is where economic evidence comes into play.

Building upon a study prepared by Oxera in 2009, the European Commission has recently published a very helpful practical guide which is referred to in an accompanying Commission Communication and directed at the courts of the Member States.[2] It is intended to provide an accessible explanation of the most popular

---

1 Council Regulation (EC) No 1/2003 of 16 December 2002 on the implementation of the rules on competition laid down in Articles 81 and 82 of the Treaty, O.J. 2003, L 1/1.

2 See *Communication from the Commission on quantifying harm in actions for damages based on breaches of Article 101 or 102 of the Treaty on the Functioning of the European Union*, O.J. 2013, C 167/19, and *Guidance to national courts: Quantification of harm caused by infringements of the EU antitrust rules* (11 June 2013), avail-

economic techniques and methods that can be used for proving causation and for calculating damages. In view of this, one can certainly expect to see a significant EU-wide trend toward standardization in the usage of economic evidence. However, the concrete role and responsibilities of economic experts and the significance of their testimony and reports in court proceedings will remain contingent on procedural rules in place in each respective forum. Moreover, the content of economic testimony needs to be adapted to applicable substantive laws and take into account the relevant distribution of the burden of proof. These factors effectively place an upper limit on the development of harmonized European standards and make it necessary to consider the procedural and substantive law environments in which the respective economic evidence is presented.

In the following article, we provide an overview of recent experience with economic evidence presented in German courts. Naturally, we will focus our attention on private enforcement – in the form of damage claims, to be exact – where economic evidence typically lies at the heart of any proceeding. However, a well-known peculiarity in the German law on administrative fines also allows us to draw some insights from public enforcement: Until the entry into force of the 7th GWB Reform Act in July 2005, administrative fines in Germany were determined on the basis of the illicit profits derived from the infringement, which meant that the calculation of cartel profits and but-for prices was intensely debated in public enforcement as well. As a consequence, there exists some illustrative case law, including a decision by the Higher Regional Court of Düsseldorf in the Cement cartel case, which may well be regarded as a blueprint for the treatment of complex econometric evidence in German courts.

2 Expert Evidence in German Civil Courts – Basic Features

One of the hallmark features of German procedural rules on evidence is the high regard that is traditionally afforded to expert testimony. According to a phrase coined by an early Federal Court of Justice judgment, experts are considered as neutral 'aides to the judge',[3] assisting the judge with their specific knowledge.[4]

able at http://ec.europa.eu/competition/antitrust/actionsdamages/quantification_guide_en.pdf.

3 Federal Court of Justice, Judgment of 30 January 1957, ref. V ZR 186/55, *Entscheidungssammlung des Bundesgerichtshofs in Zivilsachen (BGHZ)* 23, 207, at p. 213; Rosenberg, Schwab & Gottwald, *Zivilprozessrecht* (C.H. Beck, 17th ed. 2010), § 120 I.

4 This is a notion that is markedly different from the understanding in other jurisdictions, most notably the United States, where the hearing of expert evidence is more governed by the adversarial system of presenting information and where experts are usually nominated by the parties. Although it is possible for the court, under certain circumstances, to appoint an expert on its own motion under Rule 706 of the Federal

Obviously, this description relates primarily to the court-appointed expert, whose testimony is considered 'strict evidence' (*Strengbeweis*). Under the appurtenant German procedural rules on evidence, this latter quality refers to the ability to provide formal proof under Section 286 of the Civil Procedure Code (*Zivilprozessordnung*, hereafter ZPO) for a disputed statement of fact, and it is this ability which sets the court-appointed expert apart from their party-appointed colleagues. The latter's testimony – referred to as 'party expertise' or *Parteigutachten* – is usually only considered as 'qualified allegations' (*qualifizierter Parteivortrag*) and may raise the bar for the opposing party's counter-allegations in terms of detailedness and substantiation but does not normally possess any evidentiary value.[5]

Nonetheless, party-appointed experts are used regularly and often considered indispensable in cartel damage litigation. As we will see in more detail below, this is primarily due to the fact that the discussion about *quantum* lends itself to the use of party-appointed experts in (at least) two respects: First, it is often impossible for either party to prepare even the necessary pleadings without assistance and advice from economic counsel. Second, when it comes to quantum, the court enjoys a broad discretion in appreciating the facts (see Section 287 ZPO), which implies that strict evidence has less importance in this respect and that a well-drafted statement of 'party expertise' may be sufficient to support the court's estimate.

2.1 Court-Appointed Experts (*Gerichtssachverständige*)

In principle, German courts will resort to a court-appointed expert whenever the parties are in dispute over a statement of fact whose resolution requires expert knowledge that the judge does not possess. Normally, the appointment will also necessitate a motion from the party bearing the burden of proof, but this can be a blanket motion ('Proof: Expert Testimony'), and the court may even consider appointing an expert *ex officio* under Section 144(1) 1st sentence ZPO, although this latter discretionary power is used sparingly. It is primarily the court that is responsible for selecting a qualified expert, but the parties may be asked to submit suggestions for suitable candidates (Section 404(3) ZPO). In fact, due to their relative inexperience in dealing with economic evidence, most judges appreciate the opportunity to discuss their selection of an appropriate expert with the parties. Whether the courts would prefer to work with academic experts (as is the norm in cases involving medical malpractice) or with economic consulting firms is diffi-

Rules of Evidence (= 28 U.S.C. Appendix Rule 706), such court-appointed experts are rarely used in practice.

5 Federal Court of Justice, Judgment of 22 April 1997, ref. VI ZR 198/96, *Neue Juristische Wochenschrift* 1997, 3381, p. 3382; Huber, in Musielak (ed.), *Zivilprozessordnung* (Franz Vahlen, 10th ed. 2013), section 402 para. 5; Leipold, in Stein & Jonas (eds.), *Zivilprozessordnung* (Mohr Siebeck, 22nd ed. 2006), Introductory remarks to section 402 para. 74; Zimmermann, in Rauscher, Wax & Wenzel (eds.), *Münchener Kommentar zur Zivilprozessordnung* (C.H. Beck, 4th ed. 2012), section 402 para. 9.

cult to say based on experience to date. In any event, it seems clear that the issue of *remuneration* for the chosen expert plays a significant role in the selection process and may well become a standard point of dispute and tactical manoeuvring. Court-appointed experts are normally remunerated on an hourly basis according to the statutory rates set forth in the Act on Compensation for Witnesses and Experts (*Justizvergütungs- und Entschädigungsgesetz*, hereafter JVEG), which range from €50 to €95 (Section 9 JVEG), thus making it almost impossible to attract qualified experts who would be willing to invest much time and effort in the case. Although most typical candidates for economic expert testimony, such as university professors or economic consultants, are under a statutory obligation to prepare a report on that basis if they are called upon to do so by the court (Section 407(1) ZPO),[6] experience from other areas shows that courts are reluctant to 'force' experts into providing evidence at rates that are significantly below market standards.[7] This means that the court will need either the consent from all parties agreeing to the higher rates that a particular candidate requests – in which case the costs will be distributed according to the ordinary loser-pays rule (see Section 13(3) JVEG) – or the confirmation from at least one of the parties that it will bear the full balance of excess costs even if it wins the case (Section 13(5) JVEG).[8] Needless to say, this makes it difficult to have someone appointed as an expert when all parties are not in agreement.[9]

As for the introduction of expert evidence, the expert's written report would in theory suffice (cf. Section 411(3) ZPO). In practice, however, the party burdened by the results of the report can, and usually will, apply for an oral testimony, as this will provide the opportunity to direct questions at the expert and address po-

---

6 See Higher Regional Court of Munich, Decision of 23 January 2001, ref. 11 W 3216/00, *Neue Juristische Online-Zeitschrift* 2001, 1203, at p. 1206.

7 See, e.g., District Court of Kiel, Decision of 20 March 2008, ref. 11 O 110/07, *Der Sachverständige* 2009, 120, where the expert was simply released – although without compensation for work already done – after he had indicated that he would not be prepared to work on the basis of the statutory JVEG rates.

8 If at least one party agrees, a third option would be that the court renders a decision that substitutes the consent from the other parties, see section 13(2) JVEG. However, such decision 'shall' not be made when the stipulated rates exceed 1.5 times the normal rates, which means that the maximum hourly rate that can normally be attained this way would be €142.50. This is still significantly below market standards for economic evidence.

9 The Commercial Property Insurance cartel case (Higher Regional Court of Düsseldorf – Joined Cases VI-Kart 18 – 55/06 (OWi)) presents a rather drastic example of the difficulties that can arise in remuneration issues. Here, the Higher Regional Court obviously overstretched the statutory boundaries set forth in section 13 JVEG by misinterpreting the consent from one of the defendants as an assumption of the entire costs (under section 13(5) JVEG) for two economic experts that the court intended to appoint. This was subsequently overturned by the Federal Constitutional Court: Decision of 24 March 2010, ref. 2 BvR 1257, 1607/09, *Der Sachverständige* 2010, 319.

tential weaknesses in the report.[10] More importantly still, the fact that this interview is more often than not conducted by the judge implies that an oral hearing could provide welcome insights into the issues which the judge may consider critical. Moreover, according to the settled case law of the Federal Court of Justice,[11] any additional statements made by an expert in an oral hearing in response to questions and objections would automatically give the party burdened by the results the right to procure additional expert advice from its own party-appointed expert – and to submit another written brief in response thereto. This in turn may provide a welcome opportunity for the affected party to elaborate on its own economic arguments.

In view of the aforementioned high regard for court-appointed experts, it comes as no surprise that the evidentiary status of their written reports and oral testimony is equally highly regarded. Triers of fact sometimes tend to assume that disputes over questions requiring expert knowledge may be considered settled once the court-appointed expert has rendered his or her opinion. However, the Federal Court of Justice has always been watchful of such tendencies and has recently reaffirmed that the trier of fact cannot ignore conflicting expert reports submitted by either one of the parties but instead must provide a plausible and logical reason for its decision to follow the findings of the court-appointed expert.[12] If the court finds itself incapable of providing said plausible and logical explanation, it would need to consider commissioning a supplementary report from the court-appointed expert or arranging a direct confrontation between court-appointed and party-appointed experts. And if the latter does not suffice to resolve the conflict, the court would need to commission a completely new expert report under Section 412 ZPO.

As we will discuss in more detail further on under 7.3., the foregoing points present a considerable challenge for judges and their appraisal of economic evidence. By definition, economic models are based on simplifying assumptions, and the calculation of hypothetical but-for market results is a particularly thorny and controversial task due to the virtually limitless number of potential explanatory variables and the complex interactions between these variables. Moreover, there are no universally recognized standards in economics which will decide whether an economic model or a particular specification thereof is 'appropriate' or 'sufficient' to describe a given market and to deliver reliable estimates that account for

10 See section 402 in conjunction with section 397. See also Reichold, in Thomas & Putzo (eds.), *Zivilprozessordnung* (C.H. Beck, 34th ed. 2013), section 411 para. 5.

11 See Federal Court of Justice, Judgment of 13 February 2001, ref. VI ZR 272/99, *Neue Juristische Wochenschrift* 2001, 2796.

12 Federal Court of Justice, Decision of 12 January 2011, ref. IV ZR 190/08, *Neue Juristische Wochenschrift – Rechtsprechungsreport* 2011, 609; Decision of 18 May 2009, ref. IV ZR 57/08, *Neue Juristische Wochenschrift – Rechtsprechungsreport* 2009, 1192; Judgment of 24 September 2008, ref. IV ZR 250/06, *Neue Juristische Wochenschrift – Rechtsprechungsreport* 2009, 35; Judgment of 22 September 2004, ref. IV ZR 200/03, *Neue Juristische Wochenschrift – Rechtsprechungsreport* 2004, 1679.

the counterfactual.[13] For example, there is no universally accepted minimum 'threshold' for the 'coefficient of determination' R^2 that is often used to describe the goodness of fit[14] of an econometric model, not least because from an economic perspective such a threshold would be nonsensical.[15] Therefore it is difficult for the judge to distinguish between reasonable and serious criticism of a given model and what might be considered unmeritorious nit-picking or outright distraction. More importantly, all this means that it is ultimately up to the judge to decide on the basis of legal standards whether a particular model can be considered satisfactory. This decision, in turn, requires judges to undertake their own critical evaluation of the proposed model or technique.

2.2 Expert Counsel for the Parties (*Privatgutachter*)

As already mentioned, reports and analyses prepared by party-appointed experts have limited evidentiary value *per se*, given that under the applicable German procedural rules (Section 404 *et seq.* ZPO), only the testimony of a court-appointed expert will count as strict evidence. From a practical perspective, this means that the party bearing the burden of proof (typically the claimant) should not simply rely on a report prepared by its own economic counsel but needs to supplement this with an explicit motion to hear expert evidence from a court-appointed expert on all technical points that have been raised in the report. To foreign observers, this may seem excessive and redundant, but it is nonetheless necessary in order to avoid rejection of an argument on the basis of a lack of suitable evidence (*Beweisfälligkeit*).

---

13 The standards for 'statistically significant' results are a notable exception. Statistical significance refers to the fact that a particular result is unlikely to be the consequence of mere chance. Here, it is conventional practice to work with certain pre-defined levels, the most popular being the 90%, 95%, and 99% levels of confidence.

14 In its simplest form, the coefficient of determination R^2 can be described as measuring how good the econometric estimate fits the data in comparison to the simple average out of all observations. An R^2 value of 1 indicates a 'perfect fit', whereas a value of 0 indicates no fit at all.

15 To begin with, R^2 tends to be higher for time-series analyses (i.e., 'before-and-after comparisons') than for cross-sectional analyses (i.e., 'yardstick comparisons'), as any explanatory variable that increases over time automatically provides a good 'explanation' for any other variable that also increases over time, see Bauer, Fertig and Schmidt, *Empirische Wirtschaftsforschung* (Springer, 2009), 213. Needless to say, this does not imply that time-series analyses are 'better' than cross-sectional analyses in any meaningful sense. Also, R^2 cannot decrease, but may well increase, when additional explanatory variable are added to the model, even if they have absolutely nothing to do with the explained variable ('overfitting'). Besides, R^2 does not tell anything about other possible sources of errors such as, for example, an omitted-variable bias, which occurs when the econometric model 'compensates' for missing factors by over- or underestimating the factors that are accounted for.

As a corollary to this, experts retained by one of the parties will not normally be granted the opportunity to explain and defend their report in an oral hearing. In theory, the court could hear them out informally, but the legal basis for this is uncertain and it is not clear whether the court could conduct such an informal hearing if objections are raised by the other party.[16] In our experience, judges are reluctant to conduct such an informal interview, even if the party in question brings its experts to the hearing. However, as explained above, the case of conflicting reports from a court-appointed expert and a party-appointed expert is a notable exception to this rule. In this context, the Federal Court of Justice has explicitly stated that a direct confrontation in an oral hearing between the experts in disagreement is one possible method of resolving the conflict.

Because of these limitations, we can sometimes observe attempts by the parties to elevate their party-appointed expert to the status of an 'expert witness' under Section 414 ZPO.[17] Expert witnesses, as they are usually understood, have witnessed an event which is pertinent to the case and have been able to discern the relevant facts because of their particular knowledge or skills.[18] They are treated as regular witnesses and would therefore not only be afforded the opportunity to testify in an oral hearing but their testimony would also attain the status of strict evidence (i.e., a higher evidentiary value than ordinary reports from party-appointed experts). However, in a typical case where economic evidence is presented such attempts to elevate party-appointed experts will rarely succeed. According to settled case law in the German courts, the defining feature of an expert witness is his or her 'irreplaceability', which means that an expert witness cannot be replaced by someone else with similar skills and expertise.[19] This defining feature is normally absent when the focus lies on the construction and application of appropriate economic models rather than on a witness's first-hand experience with the inner workings of the industry.

As for the costs of economic counsel, it is important to distinguish between the claimant and the defendant. The claimant typically has two options from which to choose in how it will pursue reimbursement: On the one hand, it could treat the expenses as part of the damage caused by the infringement and try to recover these under substantive law (Section 249 BGB). In fact, so long as the defendant's lia-

16 Outside the formal hearing of evidence – where in principle only 'strict evidence' such as testimony from witnesses and court-appointed experts is admissible – only the parties themselves and their respective legal counsel have a procedural right to be heard by the court (see sections 128, 138 and 139 ZPO). An informal hearing of a party-appointed expert would therefore seem to undermine the procedural rules on evidence.

17 A motion to have the expert appointed by the court (i.e., as court-appointed expert under section 404 ZPO) is obviously bound to fail due to concerns of prejudice, see section 406(1) ZPO and Reichold, cited *supra* note 10, section 406 para. 2. 'Expert witnesses', on the other hand, are not subject to the same standards.

18 A prime example would be a surgeon who observes a surgery performed by colleagues in which something goes wrong (giving rise to the respective lawsuit).

19 See Reichold, cited *supra* note 10, Introductory remarks to section 373 para. 1.

bility as such can be established and the costs appear reasonable for the aim of asserting legal rights (which is *not* measured by the standards set by the JVEG), the claimant would normally be entitled to recover costs in full from the defendant. Since this claim is part of the substantive claim for damages, it must be included in the relief sought (*Klageantrag*) and be revised upwards under Section 264 No. 2 ZPO near the end of the proceedings in order to account for any additional costs that have accrued in the interim. The primary advantage of this method is that the claimant might still be able to seek partial reimbursement even if his action is otherwise dismissed for lack of verifiable damage.[20] On the other hand, the claimant could also rely on the procedural claim for cost reimbursement under Section 91(1) ZPO, which does not require a specification of the costs in the relief sought but is dependant on the relative success of the main claim. In other words: If the claimant partly wins and partly loses, the cost of economic counsel would be proportionally allocated according to the relative degree of success or, alternatively, declared as compensated. Although most claimants will normally leave the quantum to the estimation of the court – which significantly reduces the risk of said partial defeat[21] – this presents an important disadvantage in comparison with reimbursement under substantive law.

For the defendant, on the other hand, the procedural claim under Section 91(1) ZPO is typically the only means available for recovering the cost of economic counsel.

3 Role and Significance of Economic Evidence in Competition Litigation

Since most cartel damage cases are follow-on lawsuits, the range of procedural topics and factual disputes is determined to a large extent by the scope of the binding effect that the competition authority's decision may have. To appreciate the role and significance of economic evidence more fully one therefore needs to take account of the legal provisions pertaining to this binding effect, i.e., Article 16 of the Procedural Regulation and Section 33(4) GWB. As we will see below, the scope of the binding effect is still subject to certain legal controversies, but causa-

20 If the defendant's liability as such is undisputed, as is often the case in follow-on litigation, it does not seem far-fetched to argue that an economic expert report commissioned by the claimant for the purpose of ascertaining the amount of damage could still be considered reasonable for the purpose of asserting legal rights even if the amount of damage eventually turns out to be zero.

21 Under section 92(2) ZPO, the claimant will normally not be considered to have partly lost his case merely because the court's damage estimation deviates from the indications given in the statement of claims unless the claimant indicated a minimum amount – which most claimants do in order to ensure the admissibility of an appeal in case the court awards an unsatisfactory sum – and the sum awarded falls more than 20% short.

tion and quantum should normally be regarded as lying outside of the binding effect, which means that these two topics will lie at the heart of any economic evidence, albeit with certain alleviations for the claimant regarding the legal and evidential burden of proof. As for economic evidence brought to bear in stand-alone cases, in particular as a means of proving the existence of an infringement as such, we find reason for scepticism.

3.1 Scope of the Binding Effect of Decisions by Competition Authorities

In EU cases, Article 16 of the Procedural Regulation stipulates that national courts are barred from making a decision that runs counter to the decision adopted by the Commission. This binding effect certainly extends to the finding of an infringement as such (as set forth in the operative part of the Commission's decision), and it also seems clear that the content of the reasoning behind the decision can be used to interpret this finding and to give it a more concrete and identifiable shape. However, one may be led to wonder if the binding effect also covers the entire findings of fact and all economic and legal assessments that the Commission typically makes in the reasons of a particular decision. To make this concrete, consider the *Prokent/Tomra* case, where the Commission examined several types of rebates and exclusivity arrangements employed by the market-dominant supplier of reverse vending machines (Tomra) and, after having established that this conduct was *capable* of restricting competition (which was sufficient under *British Airways*[22] and *Michelin II*[23] to establish abuse under Article 102 TFEU), went on to consider the *actual* anti-competitive effects on five national markets, stating that Tomra did in fact achieve market foreclosure.[24] Against this background, one might expect that the findings on actual anti-competitive effects should be binding for any follow-on litigation, effectively making a damage lawsuit an almost assured 'home-run'. However, the appeal proceedings before the General Court make one pause to consider: In these proceedings, Tomra tried to put forward several reasons why the Commission's analysis of actual anti-competitive effects was flawed, but all of these reasons the Court rejected as irrelevant. In view of *British Airways* and *Michelin II*, the General Court went so far as to say that 'even if the Commission had made a manifest error of assessment, as the applicants allege, in holding that those agreements actually eliminated competition, the legality of the

---

22 CFI, Case T-219/99, *British Airways v. Commission* [2003] ECR II-5917, para. 293. Confirmed by ECJ, Case C-95/04 P, *British Airways v. Commission* [2007] ECR I-2331.

23 CFI, Case T-203/01, *Michelin v. Commission* [2003] ECR II-4071, para. 239.

24 Decision of 29 March 2006, Case COMP/E-1/38.113, *Prokent-Tomra*, paras. 331 *et seq.* In general, one may state that the 'more economic approach' has lead to a growing practice on the part of the European Commission and national competition authorities to garnish their decision with at least a lose assessment of the effects on customers, consumers, and competitors even where this is not strictly necessary.

contested decision would not be affected.'[25] In essence, it seems that findings which are not necessary to support the operative part of the decision cannot be contested before the General Court. It would therefore seem extremely questionable, especially in light of the requirement of effective judicial control,[26] to endow such findings with a binding effect under Article 16 of the Procedural Regulation, thereby making them effectively incontestable in either proceeding. Even the use of such findings in the 'free appraisal of the evidence' by the trier of fact under Section 286 ZPO ('freie tatrichterliche Beweiswürdigung'), to which German courts often resort when considering criminal convictions in the same matter[27] (since they are not procedurally binding for civil courts[28]), would be highly contentious.

Under German law, this issue is equally prevalent, as the German legislator in 2005 introduced a new legal provision concerning the binding effect of decisions by competition authorities and courts that was explicitly intended to go beyond Article 16 of the Procedural Regulation and facilitate private enforcement (Section 33(4) GWB). Many prominent authors[29] have therefore argued that Sec-

---

25 Case T-155/06, *Tomra Systems v. Commission* [2010] ECR-II 4361, para. 290. The appeals against this decisions were rejected by the ECJ, Case C-549/10 P, *Tomra Systems v. Commission* (not yet published).

26 The principle of effective judicial protection is recognized by the ECJ as a general principle of EU law stemming from the constitutional traditions common to the Member States, which has been enshrined in Articles 6 and 13 of the European Convention for the Protection of Human Rights and Fundamental Freedoms, see, e.g., ECJ, Case 222/84, *Johnston* [1986] ECR 1651, paras. 18 *et seq.*, and, recently, Case C-279/09, *DEB v. Germany* [2010] ECR I-13849, para. 29.

27 See Federal Court of Justice, Judgment of 16 March 2005, ref. IV ZR 140/04, *Neue Juristische Wochenschrift – Rechtsprechungsreport* 2005, 1024; Judgment of 27 September 1988, ref. XI ZR 8/88, *BGH-Rechtsprechung* ZPO § 286 Abs. 1 Strafurteil 1. See also Higher Regional Court of Düsseldorf, Judgment of 6 Mai 1993, ref. 5 U 160/92, para. 37: 'The decision [by the FCO] … along with its findings needs to be considered as evidence'.

28 See section 14(2) No. 1 of the Introductory Act to the Civil Procedure Code (Einführungsgesetz zur Zivilprozessordnung). See also Higher Regional Court of Saarbrücken, Judgment of 4 December 2002, ref. 1 U 501/02-121, *Neue Juristische Wochenschrift – Rechtsprechungsreport* 2003, 176; Stadler, in Musielak (ed.), *Zivilprozessordnung* (cited *supra* note 5), section 148 para. 6.

29 See, e.g., Bornkamm, in Langen & Bunte (eds.), *Kommentar zum Deutschen und Europäischen Kartellrecht, Vol. 1: Deutsches Kartellrecht* (Luchterhand, 11th ed. 2010), section 33 paras. 136, 144; Dreher, 'Der Zugang zu Entscheidungen mit Bindungswirkung für den kartellrechtlichen Schadensersatzprozess', *Zeitschrift für Wettbewerbsrecht* 2008, 325, at p. 328–330; Schütt, 'Individualrechtsschutz nach der 7. GWB-Novelle', *Wirtschaft und Wettbewerb* 2004, 1124; Bechtold, *Kartellgesetz: GWB – Kommentar* (C. H. Beck, 7th ed. 2012), section 33 para. 42; Jüngten, *Die prozessuale Durchsetzung privater Ansprüche im Kartellrecht* (Carl Heymanns, 2007), 138 *et seq.*; Meessen, *Der Anspruch auf Schadensersatz bei Verstößen gegen EU-Kartellrecht* (Mohr Siebeck, 2011), 133 *et seq.*

tion 33(4) GWB contains a 'Feststellungswirkung', which implies that more or less the entire content of the decision is binding for a follow-on lawsuit.[30] But once again, this is a highly contentious proposition, not only because legislative materials[31] used the term *Tatbestandswirkung* – which is normally used to denote a more narrow reading, endowing only the operative part of the decision with a binding effect[32] – but also because a broad reading raises similar concerns about effective judicial control.

We would therefore agree with a view endorsed by a substantial part of the legal literature according to which causation and quantum, among other things, should usually be considered as lying outside the scope of Article 16 of the Procedural Regulation and Section 33(4) GWB.[33] In fact, recent experience from court hearings in several on-going cases confirms that even in follow-on litigation German courts would normally expect claimants to provide reliable facts and evidence on both counts.

3.2 Proof of Causation

In economic studies, causation and quantum are often interrelated and not normally considered separately. In fact, to an economist, causation as such cannot be 'proven' but only inferred from the fact that a well-specified model taking into account all relevant explanatory factors shows a statistically significant relationship between the infringement and the variable under consideration (e.g., the price at which the claimant bought from the cartel members). Nevertheless, when preparing a report for use in a court proceeding in Germany, economists are well advised to keep causation and quantum separate because the evidentiary thresholds for establishing causation are arguably higher than for calculating the quantum. In cases involving an infringement of legal rights (such as property, health, or personal freedom), this is indeed settled case law: While causation in the form of a causal link between the defendant's behaviour and the violation of the claimant's legal right must be proven 'to the full conviction of the court' under Section 286 ZPO, the extent of the damage caused thereby can then be estimated under the more re-

30 See Federal Court of Justice, Judgment of 4 February 2004, ref. XII ZR 301/01, *Neue Zeitschrift für Verwaltungsrecht* 2004, 763.

31 Bundestag-Drucksache No. 15/3640 dated 14 August 2004, 54.

32 Such a more narrow reading of section 33(4) GWB is endorsed, *inter alia*, by: Rehbinder, in Loewenheim, Meesen & Riesenkampff (eds.), *Kartellrecht – Kommentar* (C. H. Beck, 2nd ed. 2009), section 33 GWB para. 54; Emmerich, in Immenga & Mestmäcker (eds.), *GWB – Kommentar* (C.H. Beck, 4th ed. 2007), section 33 GWB para. 78; Meyer, 'Die Bindung der Zivilgerichte an Entscheidungen im Kartellverwaltungsrechtsweg – der neue § 33 Absatz IV GWB auf dem Prüfstand', *Gewerblicher Rechtsschutz und Urheberrecht* 2006, 27, at p. 30.

33 See in particular the authors cited *supra* note 32. Interestingly, Bornkamm also supports a narrow reading of section 33(4) GWB in respect of causation and damage, despite arguing for a *Feststellungswirkung*. See *supra* note 29.

laxed standards set forth in Section 287(1) ZPO.[34] In cases of pure economic loss, on the other hand, the issue becomes somewhat more complicated, as the court's estimation under Section 287(1) ZPO seems to extend to the existence of damage as such, making it difficult to distinguish between causation and quantum.

The Federal Court of Justice has tried to resolve this dilemma by requiring full proof (under Section 286 ZPO) for the fact that the claimant was indeed adversely 'affected' by the defendant's behaviour, whereas the existence and the amount of damage would be subject to the court's estimate under Section 287(1) ZPO.[35] Unfortunately, the question as to how this is to be interpreted in the context of competition law is still up for debate.[36] Broadly read, one could argue that antitrust infringements are always capable of having harmful effects on other market participants, making this hurdle a mere formality. In our view, however, a sensible interpretation of the 'affectedness' criterion would require the claimant to prove that the defendant's behaviour did in fact result in anti-competitive effects (e.g., by raising the price above the competitive but-for level) and that the claimant was among those market participants that came into contact with these anti-competitive effects (e.g., that the claimant was a customer of a cartel member[37]). This interpretation would prevent the issue of causation from being entirely absorbed into the discussion about quantum (under Section 287 ZPO) and would not at the same time be unduly burdensome to claimants, especially in light of the fact that their burden of proof is often further alleviated by *prima facie* rules.

3.2.1 *Prima facie* Evidence of Causation in Hard-Core Cartel Cases

Although the Federal Court of Justice has not yet formally confirmed that civil claims for damages are allowed to rely on *prima facie* evidence for harm and/or damage, the Court has repeatedly invoked it in administrative cases where the Federal Cartel Office (*Bundeskartellamt*, hereafter FCO) was required to prove the

---

34 See, e.g., Federal Court of Justice, Judgment of 21 July 1998, ref. VI ZR 15/98, *Neue Juristische Wochenschrift* 1998, 3417, p. 3418.

35 Federal Court of Justice, Judgment of 15 June 1993, ref. XI ZR 111/92, *Neue Juristische Wochenschrift* 1993, 3073, at p. 3076.

36 This question was expressly left open by the Higher Regional Court of Berlin in the Ready-mix concrete cases, see Judgments of 1 October 2009, ref. 2 U 10/03 Kart, paras. 56 *et seq.* and ref. 2 U 17/03 Kart, paras. 69 *et seq.*

37 Whether or not 'umbrella effects', i.e., price increases from non-cartel members which slip under the 'umbrella' of the cartelized price, would also suffice to establish 'affectedness', is a difficult legal question and relates to issues of imputability/liability for autonomous third party acts ('Zurechenbarkeit von Drittverhalten') that lie outside the scope of this article. See Opinion of Advocate General Kokott delivered on 30 January 2014 in Case C‑ 557/12, *KONE AG and Others*. Under German law, the question would also depend on the proper interpretation of the 'protective scope' ('Schutzbereich') of Article 101 TFEU and section 1 GWB, i.e., the question of whether these provisions intend to protect customers and consumers also from the behaviour of third parties which use the cartel-induced price increase as an opportunity for their own price increases.

existence of a cartel overcharge. In the words of the Court: 'According to economic principles, cartels will typically involve a cartel overcharge. It is therefore highly likely...that a cartel is being formed and maintained because it leads to higher prices than could otherwise be obtained in the market.'[38] However, as the Federal Court of Justice recently held, this *prima facie* rule only applies to the market immediately affected by the cartel and not to downstream markets which may have been subject to pass-on effects. In other words: Indirect purchasers who are bringing claims for alleged damages from the pass-on of a cartel overcharge would be required to offer full proof of said pass-on effects.[39] Moreover, it is important to note that the *prima facie* rule is not tantamount to a full reversal of the burden of proof. As with all *prima facie* evidence, it would be sufficient for the opposing party (i.e., the defendant) to allege and prove the concrete possibility of an unusual course of events.[40] Indeed, in its recent Ready-mix Concrete decision, the Higher Regional Court of Berlin went so far as to state that the *prima facie* rule is inapplicable when the cartelized goods, on the basis of a simple before-and-after analysis, exhibit price movements which are incompatible with the assumption of an effective cartel.[41] In other words: To show the concrete possibility of an unusual course of events, it would seem to be sufficient for the defendant to demonstrate that prices did not increase after the start of the cartel and did not decrease after its break-up.

Needless to say, this inevitably leads to the question whether the claimant can restore the *prima facie* rule by presenting factors which might explain the absence of a 'typical' price development. For example, consider the price curve depicted in Figure 18. On the face of it, the sales price for the cartelized good (diagram on the left) does not show any noticeable cartel-induced increase – if anything, prices slightly decreased after the formation of the cartel. On the other hand, the cost of input X (say energy costs) exhibits a significant decrease that coincides with the duration of the infringement. One may therefore ask if it would suffice for the

38 Federal Court of Justice, Decision of 28 June 2005, ref. KRB 2/05, *Neue Juristische Wochenschrift* 2006, 163, p. 164 *et seq.*

39 Federal Court of Justice, Judgment of 28 June 2011, ref. KZR 75/10, *ORWI, Wirtschaft und Wettbewerb – Entscheidungssammlung* DE-R 3431, para. 45. In its judgment, the Federal Court of Justice explicitly confirmed that all indirect purchasers down to the level of ultimate consumers have a right to sue for their cartel-induced losses in German courts. However, in view of the economic complexities that determine if, and how much of, the cartel overcharge is passed on by direct customers, the Court also held that there is no presumption or *prima facie* evidence of pass-on, even in the retail industry. It is therefore upon the claimant to prove the occurrence and the extent of pass-on. In this context, the Court cited the price elasticity of demand, the extent of the cartel, and the degree of competition between direct purchasers as relevant factors for the assessment.

40 Federal Court of Justice, Judgment of 23 May 1952, ref. I ZR 163/51, *Neue Juristische Wochenschrift* 1952, 1137; Judgment of 18 December 1952, ref. VI ZR 54/52, *Neue Juristische Wochenschrift* 1953, 584; Judgment of 15 December 1970, ref. VI ZR 116/69, *Neue Juristische Wochenschrift* 1971, 431, at p. 432.

41 Judgment of 1 October 2009, ref. 2 U 17/03 Kart, para. 96.

claimant (and his economist) to point out the possibility that the cartel held the sales price constant and thereby prevented a significant pass-on of energy cost savings.

Fig. 18. Seemingly ineffective cartel

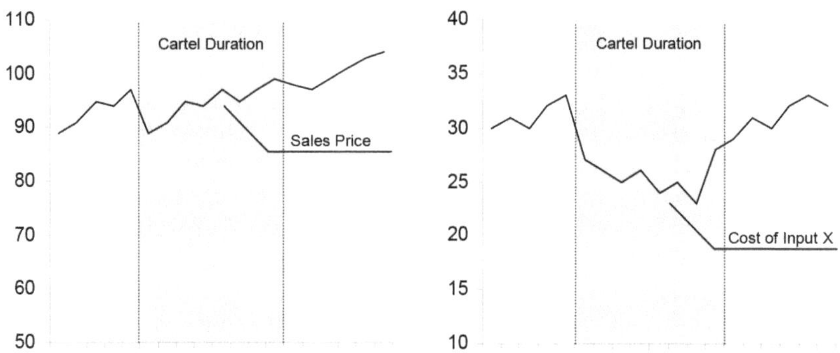

From an economic point of view, this is a difficult question: Although the available empirical evidence seems to indicate a relatively low percentage of unsuccessful cartels,[42] there is little reliable evidence which allows the deduction of the *conditional* probability that a cartel which did not result in an outright price increase was nevertheless successful in other ways. Moreover, from a legal point of view, *prima facie* evidence, once unsettled, cannot normally be 'revived'. As the Federal Court of Justice explained in an early judgment, if the defendant succeeds in proving the concrete possibility of an unusual course of events, it would then be up to the claimant to provide full proof under Section 286 ZPO.[43] In this context, the court may still take into account that unsuccessful cartels seem to be the exception, but the *prima facie* evidence would be gone.

3.2.2 Alleviations of the Standard of Proof in Other Cases

Whether or not the aforementioned *prima facie* rule extends beyond hard core infringements is still open for discussion. As of yet, there are no decisions by German courts regarding vertical restraints or abuses of market power. On the other hand, claimants will typically point to the fairly extensive body of case law under

42 See in particular Connor & Lande, 'Cartel Overcharges an Optimal Cartel Fines', in Wayne D. Collins (ed.), *Issues in Competition Law and Policy: Volume III* (Section of Antitrust Law of the American Bar Association 2008), chapter 88, 2203–2218; Connor, 'Price Fixing Overcharges: Revised 2nd Edition' (available at SSRN: http://ssrn.com/abstract=1610262, 2010), finding that in 8% of all cartel cases under review there was no overcharge). See also the external study of Oxera *et al.* prepared for the Commission 'Quantifying antitrust damages' (2009), p. 88 *et seq.*, which finds that in roughly 7% of all cases no overcharge could be detected.

43 Judgment of 23 May 1952, ref. I ZR 163/51, BGHZ 6, 169 *et seq.*

the Act Against Unfair Competition (*Gesetz gegen den unlauteren Wettbewerb*, hereafter UWG), where the Federal Court of Justice has invoked *prima facie* evidence of damage on the part of competitors in cases dealing with misleading advertisements,[44] infringements of IP rights,[45] and other instances of unfair competition directly aimed at obstructing competitors (*mitbewerberbezogene Verstöße*)[46]. However, it remains to be seen to what extent these principles can be carried over to antitrust infringements, outside of hard core cartel cases. An uncritical, across-the-board application of *prima facie* evidence would certainly not be warranted, especially in view of the fact that it is often sufficient for the competition authority to establish the mere possibility of foreclosure effects.[47] Against this background, claimants would in any case be well advised to offer a review of the existing economic literature on the typical effects of the market behaviour in question when submitting evidence from a party-appointed expert.

3.3 Quantum

When discussion comes around to the quantum, this typically marks the point where claimants are most reliant on expert evidence and where it is often inevitable to seek help from a party-appointed expert. Although Section 287(1) ZPO allows – in fact, obligates – the court to estimate the loss if the claimant is unable to prove an exact amount, it still requires a sufficiently firm factual basis upon which such an estimate can be founded. Moreover, the alleged damage must be 'preponderantly likely'.[48] According to an oft-cited phrase by the Federal Court of Justice, the judge would therefore be barred from estimating the damage when the resulting estimate would appear as if it had been 'pulled out of thin air' (*in der Luft hängen*).[49]

---

44 Federal Court of Justice, Judgment of 29 June 2000, ref. I ZR 29/99, *Filialleiterfehler, Gewerblicher Rechtsschutz und Urheberrecht* 2000, 907.

45 See, e.g., Federal Court of Justice, Judgment of 17 June 1992, ref. I ZR 107/90, *Tchibo/Rolex II, Gewerblicher Rechtsschutz und Urheberrecht* 1993, 55, p. 57; Judgment of 22 April 1993, ref. I ZR 52/91, *Kollektion 'Holiday', Gewerblicher Rechtsschutz und Urheberrecht* 1993, 757, p. 758; Judgment of 2 February 1995, ref. I ZR 16/93, *Objektive Schadensberechnung, Gewerblicher Rechtsschutz und Urheberrecht* 1995, 349, at 351.

46 For a recent account see Köhler, in Köhler & Bornkamm (eds.), *Gesetz gegen den unlauteren Wettbewerb – Kommentar* (C. H. Beck, 32nd ed. 2014), section 9 para. 1.35; Goldmann, in Harte-Bavemann & Henning-Bodewig (eds.), *Gesetz gegen den unlauteren Wettbewerb – Kommentar* (C.H. Beck, 3rd ed. 2013), section 9 para. 133.

47 See, e.g., the decisions in re *Michelin II* and *British Airways* on abusive rebates, cited *supra* notes 22 and 23.

48 Federal Court of Justice, Judgment of 21 July 2005, Case IX ZR 49/02, *Neue Juristische Wochenschrift* 2005, 3275, at 3277; Judgment of 18 March 2004, Case IX ZR 255/00, *Neue Juristische Wochenschrift* 2004, 1521.

49 See e.g. Judgment of 2 July 1992, Case IX ZR 256/91, *Neue Juristische Wochenschrift* 1992, 2694, at 2695.

Thus the cases in which these standards can be met without having recourse to external economic advice are rare and most often confined to price-fixing cases in which the competition authority's decision contains concrete information detailing the amount of agreed price increases. For example, the Higher Regional Court of Karlsruhe, in a recent decision arising out of the Carbonless Paper cartel, was able to estimate the damage without economic evidence by using simple information from the Commission's decision COMP/E-1/36.212 on the percentage increases agreed upon among the members of the cartel.[50] Similar calculation methods were employed by the District Court of Dortmund in the Vitamins case[51] and the Higher Regional Court of Berlin in the Ready-mix Concrete case.[52] Under such circumstances, it would then be incumbent upon the defendant to retain economic counsel and prepare analyses which demonstrate that the observed price increases – or at least a significant part thereof – were objectively justified and would have occurred even in the absence of the cartel.

In many cases, however, explicit information on the amounts of agreed price increases may not be available. Moreover, all of the decisions cited above dealt with relatively minor claims,[53] and it is unclear as to whether German courts would be equally willing to award multi-million EUR amounts without any concrete economic evidence.

As for the economic techniques that may be used to establish the quantum, the Commission's practical guide distinguishes broadly between comparator-based methods, simulation models, and cost-based methods, echoing the classification in the Oxera report, albeit using a slightly different and arguably more familiar terminology. Although this is not the place to discuss these techniques in great detail, their respective core ideas can be briefly summarized as follows:

- Comparator-based methods try to estimate the damage using statistical comparisons between affected and non-affected markets. They range from simple before-and-after studies and regional yardstick analyses to more complex econometric studies in which a number of explanatory factors are considered.

50 Judgment of 11 June 2010, Case 6 U 118/05 (Kart) (unpublished).

51 See Judgment of 1 April 2004, Case 13 O 55/02 Kart, *Wirtschaft und Wettbewerb – Entscheidungssammlung* DE-R 1352. The European Commission in its decision (Case COMP/E-1/37.512 – *Vitamins*) had found cartel-induced price increases in the range of 20–50% for the relevant vitamins. On this basis, the District Court considered the claim to be sufficiently established and awarded roughly €1.6 million ≈ 30% of the claimant's total turnover with the affected vitamins (excluding interest).

52 See Judgments of 1 October 2009, Case 2 U 10/03 Kart, paras. 62 *et seq.* and Case 2 U 17/03 Kart, paras. 75 *et seq.* Although the defendants had filed motions to have a court-appointed expert perform a regional yardstick analysis, the court considered the price development during the cartel period, in particular the consistent price differential of roughly €10–30/m³ as compared with the national average, to be sufficiently clear and meaningful to allow a reliable estimation of the damage.

53 Higher Regional Court of Karlsruhe: €100 thousand, Higher Regional Court of Berlin: €670 thousand, District Court of Dortmund: €1.6 million.

Econometric studies can be further subdivided according to the identification strategy pursued:[54] Time-series analyses, sometimes also called 'benchmark' analyses, are a more sophisticated version of the before-and-after approach, and they can be performed either by estimating the model solely on the basis of control period data and then 'forecasting' the explained variable (e.g., the but-for price in a price-fixing case) for the infringement period and comparing it with the observed data, or by using data from the entire period – infringement and non-infringement – and applying a so-called 'dummy variable' in the regression equation, which is set at 1 for the infringement period and at 0 for the control period and whose estimated coefficient then represents the average effect of the infringement on the explained variable.[55] Cross-sectional analyses, on the other hand, are a more sophisticated version of the yardstick approach, comparing data from the affected market with data from unaffected markets or market segments. Finally, difference-in-difference analyses (DID) are a combination of cross-sectional and time-series comparisons in which the difference between the affected market and unaffected markets during the infringement period is compared with the same difference during the non-infringement period(s). Provided that certain assumptions hold, the difference between these two differences then gives an estimate that approximates the effect of the infringement.[56]

- Simulations models attempt to estimate the damage on the basis of a theoretical prediction about market outcomes in the absence of the infringement. For this purpose, a theoretical model for competition is used, which is normally some variant of the basic *Cournot* and *Bertrand* models of oligopoly. These models are rooted in game theory and rely on the concept of *Nash* equilibrium for their prediction of market outcomes, which means that the outcome predicted can be interpreted as a state in which all market participants pursue strategies that are mutually optimal/profit-maximizing in the sense that, given the other partici-

---

54 See Bauer *et al.*, cited *supra* note 15, 156–166.

55 Both methods have advantages as well as drawbacks: The forecasting approach is often considered as a good 'disciplining' exercise, because it minimizes the dangers of 'overfitting'. Furthermore, it alleviates the problems that arise if the infringement had effects on other – seemingly independent – explanatory variables (such as input factor costs). On the other hand, the dummy variable approach allows the economist to use a broader database for choosing the appropriate model. This can be of considerable importance in rapidly-evolving markets. For a recent technical discussion of both approaches see McCrary and Rubinfeld, 'Measuring Benchmark Damages in Antitrust Litigation' (January 2011, available at http://www.econ.berkeley.edu/~jmccrary/mccrary_and_rubinfeld2011.pdf).

56 One of the most important sources of bias in DID estimates is a *disproportionate* development of the affected and the unaffected market, e.g. because the unaffected market is subject to different explanatory factors. Uncritical usage of DID estimates in cases of serially correlated outcomes may also be a serious problem. For a critical account of this latter problem see Bertrand, Duflo & Mullainathan, 'How Much Should We Trust Differences-in-Differences Estimates?', 119 *The Quarterly Journal of Economics* (2004), 249–275.

pants are also pursuing their respective *Nash* equilibrium strategy with respect to price (*Bertrand*) or quantity/capacity (*Cournot*), no player can achieve a better outcome than can be achieved by duly adhering to its *Nash* equilibrium strategy.
- Finally, cost-based methods use a bottom-up approach for calculating the hypothetical but-for price in hard core cartel cases. With this approach, the calculation starts with some measure of production costs per unit, to which is added a profit margin that would have been 'reasonable' in the non-infringement scenario. The resulting amount is then compared with the actual observed data.

Which method will be capable of delivering reliable results obviously depends on the particulars of each case and can only be assessed with the help of an economist. However, from a practical perspective, the following considerations should be taken into account:

- According to the *Paper Wholesale* decision of the Federal Court of Justice, comparator-based methods in the form of regional yardstick analyses which use comparable geographical markets that are demonstrably not under the influence of the same or similar infringements are typically preferable to cost-based models.[57] Although the decision is sometimes interpreted as paving the way for introducing econometric studies in German court proceedings, a careful reading shows that the Court primarily had simple comparisons with other regional markets in mind. In a similar fashion, the Court also held that for the purpose of estimating on-going cartel effects that could possibly last longer than the infringement itself, the trier of fact should analyze an 'appropriate period (e.g., one year)' post-infringement and take the difference between the price shortly before the end of the cartel and the lowest price in the post-cartel period as an indication of the magnitude of such lasting cartel effects.[58] Indeed, one should not underestimate the suggestive power of such simple ('naïve') evaluations, and both parties would be well advised to begin here, even if it becomes necessary to move on to more sophisticated econometric techniques at a later stage.[59]
- Before a complicated simulation model or econometric analysis is suggested, the party making the suggestion (usually the claimant) would be well advised to undertake a critical assessment of the method's limitations, in particular in view

57 Decision of 19 June 2007, Case KRB 12/07, *Neue Juristische Wochenschrift* 2007, 3792, at 3794. In the Cement cartel case, the Higher Regional Court of Düsseldorf reaffirmed that regional yardstick analyses cannot be used if there are indications of similar infringements on the comparator market, see Judgment of 26 June 2009, Joined Cases VI-2a Kart 2 – 6/08, para. 463 *et seq.*

58 Federal Court of Justice, Judgment of 28 June 2011, Case KZR 75/10, *ORWI*, *Wirtschaft und Wettbewerb – Entscheidungssammlung* DE-R 3431, para. 83 *et seq.*

59 Reviewing the experience with economic arguments in US courts, Connor finds that the lack of rigorous training in economics on the part of judges and juries '*will put a premium on simple analytical approaches and on the persuasive skills of testifying experts.*' See Connor, *Global Price Fixing* (Springer, 2nd ed. 2008), 92.

of existing data constraints. For example, if it is clear that the development of the market in question is determined to a significant extent by explanatory factors for which neither party can provide reliable data (and for which publicly available sources are missing), it may be futile and even counterproductive to advocate for the use of such techniques. Under such circumstances, better results may be achieved by starting from a more descriptive/qualitative analysis of the industry, which would begin with a review of the theoretical and empirical literature on the average effects of the infringement at issue and then move on to consider concrete indications about the magnitude of the infringement's effect in relation to those averages. Quantitative methods may then still be used as reinforcement.

- Due to their stringent assumptions, simulation models are likely to be met with scepticism on the part of the court and should perhaps not be used as the primary tool for estimating the amount of damage.[60] Their main drawback lies in the fact that they often yield predictions about market outcomes that are significantly off the mark when compared with actual market results, which means that they require extensive fine-tuning before they can provide reliable estimates. This, in turn, may be difficult for the court to understand and may even raise suspicions of possible manipulation. Moreover, simulation models also typically require extensive information about demand and supply curves, which may or may not be available. On the other hand, insights gained by the economic research community on the basis of simulation models can be applied rather well, not least because the scientific peer-review process can be expected to sift out results that are insufficiently robust or incompatible with indications derived from empirical research.
- In some markets, choosing an appropriate explained variable will also require some attention. If, for example, the cartel-affected market is characterized by significant price differentials across customers, an economic model that estimates the *average* but-for price for the entire market may be of little interest. Rather, in instances like these, it would be necessary to estimate the but-for price for each specific individual claimant.

Finally, it should also be taken into account that the preparation of a report by a party-appointed expert will require extensive cooperation between said expert and legal counsel, in particular when it comes to defining an appropriate counterfactual. This is not only an economic question, depending on which period and/or panel data can be regarded as sufficiently 'free' from infringement effects in order to serve as a comparator, but it is also a legal question concerning the distribution of the burden of proof. For example, in a price-fixing case, it would be misguided for the claimant's economist to try to assess the share of the cartel overcharge that the claimant was able to pass on to his customers, as passing-on is a defence that it is

60 In his review of forensic economics in the US, Connor did not find a single case where simulation models were used for damage quantification, see Connor, 'Forensic Economics: An Introduction With a Special Emphasis on Price-Fixing', 4 *Journal of Competition Law & Economics* (2008), 31–59.

up to the defendant to prove.[61] Conversely, an economist retained by the defendant would not normally have reason to try to estimate possible volume or umbrella effects when the claimant's calculation has been based solely on the alleged cartel overcharge for the quantity actually procured from the defendant. While seemingly straightforward, there are instances in which the construction of an appropriate counterfactual may not be so clear-cut: For instance, in cases where competitors sue on the basis of the alleged market foreclosure effects of a certain competitive behaviour (say a certain pricing practice), it will often be necessary to make some rudimentary assumptions about the hypothetical but-for behaviour in the non-infringement scenario, because otherwise it would be impossible to calculate an estimate. These assumptions, however, should then be fine-tuned so that the model accurately reflects the relative distribution of the burden of proof among the parties.

3.4 Economic Evidence as a Means of Detecting and Proving Collusion?

Moving beyond the familiar follow-on cases, one may also ask whether economic evidence might be used as a means of detecting and proving the infringement as such, thereby giving claimants the opportunity to pursue cartel damage claims

---

61 See Federal Court of Justice, Judgment of 28 June 2011, cited *supra* note 39. According to the Court, it is upon the defendant cartelists to prove that the claimant (i.e. the direct purchaser) was able to wholly or partially pass on the overcharge to his customers (para. 68 *et seq.*). Contrary to earlier case law established by several Higher Regional Courts, which had rejected the defence as altogether inadmissible, pass-on is now basically an evidentiary issue. There are, however, several signs in the Court's reasoning that seem to indicate that the defence will not often succeed in practice: *First*, the Court made it clear that the defence will not be accepted if and to the extent that the direct purchaser achieved pass-on by virtue of his 'own commercial efforts' or his 'pricing power that was not causally related to the cartel'. The precise content of these references remained rather vague. Of course, it makes perfect economic sense to control for other factors beside the cartel that could also explain or justify a price increase by the direct customers (e.g. improved product quality), but it seems that the Court wanted to go beyond that and also include notions of fairness in the assessment. If that is indeed the case, even a pitch-perfect econometric analysis of the amount of the pass-on would not be enough to establish the defence, as the trier of fact may still reject it for normative reasons. *Second*, the Court also held that the defendant must show that the clamaint's gains from passing on the cartel-induced price increase were not offset by reduced demand/lost sales (i.e. the foregone revenue which the direct purchaser could have generated at the lower – competitive – but-for-price). Economically, this is certainly well-founded, but it once again raises the bar for defendants, because the lost sales volume is notoriously hard to quantify (as it depends on two but-for figures: price *and* volume). It is certainly noteworthy in this context that Connor & Lande (cited *supra* note 42) did not find a case in U.S. antitrust litigation in which the lost volume effect had been quantified.

even in the absence of a binding decision.[62] Indeed, from a theoretical point of view, the same economic models that can be used in establishing causation and estimating the amount of damage might also be employed as proof of the existence of a cartel. For example, with time-series analyses one could attempt to establish the presence of a 'structural break',[63] which may be taken as an indication for the formation or break-up of a cartel. Somewhat easier to apply are 'variance screens' for collusion, which look for suspicious drops or spikes in the statistical *variance* of prices or margins, as these may also indicate the presence of a collusive understanding among competitors.[64] Another body of research focuses on decreases in the frequency of price changes, with a bias toward price increases (relative to the competitive situation), which are often observed in analyses of known cartels.[65]

Nonetheless, from a practical perspective, it would still be somewhat unrealistic to expect claimants to succeed on the basis of a mere economic model. Even from a purely economic perspective, using a model or 'screen' as proof of collusion seems to require a significant leap of faith. One of the main problems lies in the fact that legitimate oligopolistic interaction ('tacit collusion') and explicit cartel agreements are often practically indistinguishable on the basis of data alone. For example, theoretical and empirical research suggests that discipline among cartel participants is liable to break down if a 'maverick' competitor enters the industry and starts to undercut the cartelized price. The same, however, can also be said about tacit collusion, which is equally prone to collapse when market entries significantly change the market structure. In other words: The 'structural break' in the observed price data will be quite similar and therefore insufficient to overcome the burden of proof for collusion.

---

62 For a discussion see Friederiszick and Maier-Rigaud, 'Triggering inspections ex officio: moving beyond a passive EU cartel policy', 4 *Journal of Competition Law and Economics* (2008), 89–113; Haucap and Schultz, 'Forensische Kartellforschung', *Frankfurter Allgemeine Zeitung* 15 August 2011, 10.

63 In time-series analyses, the presence of a structural break means that two separate regressions on subintervals deliver a higher goodness of fit than the combined regression over the whole time period.

64 See, e.g., Abrantes-Metz, Taylor, Froeb, and Geweke, 'A Variance Screen for Collusion', 24 *International Journal of Industrial Organization* (2006), 467–486. See also Bolotova, Connor and Miller, 'The Impact of Collusion on Price Behaviour: Empirical Results from Two Recent Cases', 26 *International Journal of Industrial Organization* (2008), 1290–1307.

65 See, e.g., the analysis of 10 major EU-wide cartels by v. Blanckenburg, Geist and Kholodilin, 'The Influence of Collusion on Price Changes: New Evidence from Major Cartel Cases', 13 *German Economic Review* (2012), 245–256.

4 Content and Form of Presentation

For court-appointed experts, the most important guidance regarding content will obviously come from directives set by the court under Section 404a ZPO. This section in particular covers the facts that are to be taken as undisputed when the expert prepares his testimony (Section 404a(3) ZPO), e.g., whether or not causation should be regarded as established. As for the concrete questions posed to the expert, one can expect the courts to make generous use of the opportunities offered by Section 404a(2) ZPO, which allows the judge to engage in a discussion with the expert before settling on precise formulation.[66]

In addition to this, all experts – including those appointed by the parties – are well advised to use the standards for economic evidence published by the FCO[67] and by the European Commission[68] as a point of reference. For the most part, these standards are self-evident and simply concerned with ensuring a sufficient degree of transparency, which means that they would be equally valid in private damage lawsuits. For example, it seems natural to require that any assumptions made in the construction of an economic model should be carefully laid out and that all models should be subjected to robustness checks to assess their sensitivity to changes in the data, in the choice of the empirical method, and in the underlying assumptions. Similarly, a full description of the data compilation process should also be included in any empirical analysis; this description would need to explain how the data sample was selected and whether any 'data cleansing' (e.g., disregarding certain outliers) had been necessary.

Another requirement that can be found both in the standards published by the FCO and in those employed by the European Commission concerns the submission of all raw data that have been used in the expert opinion. Again, German procedural rules would demand that similar standards be observed in private litigation. According to the Federal Court of Justice case law, the rule of law (*Rechtsstaatsprinzip*) as enshrined in Article 20(3) of the German Constitution (*Grundgesetz*, hereafter GG) requires equal access for all parties to the entire factual basis upon which the court's judgment is founded. Therefore, a strong argument can be made that an economic expert report which contains data analyses cannot be used as evidence unless all parties were granted full access to the underlying database. While it is immediately apparent that this presents a major prob-

---

66 Such was the case in the Cement cartel proceedings before the Higher Regional Court of Düsseldorf, see *infra* 6.

67 Bundeskartellamt, 'Standards für ökonomische Gutachten' (dated 20 October 2010, available at http://www.bundeskartellamt.de/wDeutsch/download/pdf/Merkblaetter/Merkblaetter_deutsch/Bekanntmachung_Standards_final.pdf). More generally on the application of economic techniques and standards by the FCO, see Ewald, 'Ökonomie im Kartellrecht: Vom more economic approach zu sachgerechten Standards forensischer Ökonomie', *Zeitschrift für Wettbewerbsrecht* 2011, 15–47.

68 European Commission, 'Best practices for the submission of economic evidence and data collection in cases concerning the application of Articles 101 und 102 TFEU and in merger cases'.

lem in terms of protecting the confidentiality of sensitive data (see below under 7.2.), it seems equally clear that restricting access to the underlying raw data would significantly undermine the procedural rights of the opposing party.

5 Tactical Considerations

Naturally, the use and presentation of economic evidence is determined not only by legal standards (such as evidentiary thresholds and the distribution of the burden of proof) but also by a number of tactical considerations, some of which have already been addressed above. On the claimant's side, a critical assessment of the available data would normally be one of the first steps in the preparation of a lawsuit. Obviously, in cases of hard core cartel infringements, explicit information concerning the amount of agreed price increases is of considerable value. If such information is lacking, claimants are typically well advised to undertake an assessment as to whether the available data from their own books and from public sources is sufficient to support a convincing economic study, in particular a comparator-based analysis. If the data is insufficient, claimants need to assess their prospects for filling in the gaps with data and/or information from the defendant, which in turn depends on the available methods of discovery (see below under 7.1.).

Another important concern will be the timing of economic submissions. For example, it is often possible for an economist to produce at least a very rough damage estimate on the basis of the claimant's data and publicly available information. Nonetheless, it is not always in the claimant's best interest to make use of preliminary estimates at such an early stage. Although they may lend additional credibility to the claim, these estimates can also seriously undermine pending information and data requests, especially in the first stage of an action-by-stages.[69]

On the defendant's side, tactical considerations will typically revolve around the question of what kind of expert report is most appropriate to the particular procedural situation. For example, if the price development in a hard core cartel case shows a discernible increase after the formation of the cartel, defendants will normally need to engage an economist at an early stage in order to identify possible legitimate explanations for the observed price increases and to develop a consistent line of argument. If, on the other hand, no such development trend can be found in the data, the defendant will have considerably more freedom to confine him/herself to a purely defensive role. For this, it may be sufficient to procure an economic report that merely exposes the limitations and weaknesses in the arguments submitted by the claimant. Such a 'pure critique' will be less costly and may still have significant force, in particular when the claimant proposes to use simulation models or econometric analyses that are based on rather stringent economic assumptions.

69 For more on this method of gathering information see *infra* 7.1.

The limits of this purely defensive role are determined to a large extent by the concept of a 'secondary' burden of allegation (*sekundäre Darlegungslast*) which requires the defendant to counter the claimant's allegations by offering a specific account of the matter in question instead of flatly denying it. In general, the courts will hold the defendant to a secondary burden of allegation if the events in question are unknown and inaccessible to the claimant while the defendant could easily produce the relevant facts.[70]

6 Case Study: The Cement Cartel

So far, the experience with economic evidence in cartel damage cases mainly relates to on-going proceedings[71] which are still pending before the respective triers of fact and not yet advanced enough to provide much insight as case studies. However, given the fact that until the entry into force of the 7th GWB Reform Act on July 1, 2005, administrative fines had been calculated upon the basis of the 'illicit gains' (*Mehrerlös*), we are able to derive some insights from public enforcement as well. In fact, while earlier case law did not exhibit an extensive use of economic evidence, the Cement cartel decision by the Higher Regional Court of Düsseldorf which was recently upheld in all material aspects by the Federal Court of Justice[72] can certainly be taken as a prime example of complex econometric studies being used in a German court proceeding.[73]

In this case, the FCO, after having conducted initial dawn raids in July 2002, found the six largest producers of cement in Germany to be guilty of hard core cartel infringements between 1997 and 2001. In its decisions in March and April 2003, the FCO levied record fines totaling €660 million, which is tantamount to an overcharge estimate of roughly €10/ton of cement (~10-15% overcharge). All six

70 Federal Court of Justice, Judgment of 17 January 2008, Case III ZR 239/06, *Neue Juristische Wochenschrift* 2008, 982; Judgment of 12 June 2007, Case X ZR 87/06, *Neue Juristische Wochenschrift* 2007, 2549, at p. 2553.

71 The most prominent cases currently pending are perhaps the Cement case before the Higher Regional Court in Düsseldorf (which relates to the same allegations as the decision by the FCO and the Higher Regional Court of Düsseldorf); the Hydrogen Peroxide litigation before the District Court in Dortmund (now referred to the Court of Justice of the European Union); the TV Advertising cases before the District Court of Düsseldorf; and the Car Glass case before the District Court of Düsseldorf. Recently, the Rail Cartel case before the District Court of Frankfurt a.M. was added to this list.

72 Decision of 26 February 2013, ref. KRB 20/12, *Entscheidungssammlung des Bundesgerichtshofs in Strafsachen* (BGHSt) 58, 158.

73 For an economic account of the Cement case, see also Friederiszick and Röller, 'Quantification of harm in damages actions for antitrust infringements: Insights from German cartel cases', 6 *Journal of Competition Law & Economics* (2010), 595–618; Frank and Lademann, 'Economic Evidence in Private Damage Claims: What lessons can be learned from the German Cement Cartel case?', 1 *Journal of European Competition Law & Practice* (2010), 360–366.

cement producers filed appeals to the Higher Regional Court of Düsseldorf, which in June 2009 reduced the fine to roughly €330 million, despite finding that the infringements had already begun as of March 13, 1991, and extended throughout the entire German market.[74]

While the proceedings before the Higher Regional Court proved extremely time-consuming (mainly due to several requests from the court for additional investigations by the FCO), economic evidence was not actually taken before November 5, 2008, when the court rendered its first evidence order (*Beweisbeschluss*) in which it appointed Professor Röller as economic expert. After having delivered, on December 9, 2008, a preliminary opinion on the possible methods of calculating the illicit gains – to which the parties could respond with written comments – the expert was then summoned to an oral hearing on February 17, 2009, in which the advantages and drawbacks of the various methods were extensively discussed.[75] In this hearing, simple yardstick approaches were quickly discarded, not least due to the fact that the break-down of the cartel triggered an extensive 'price war' that arguably lasted until nearly the end of 2004 (see below Figure 19).

Fig. 19. Price index for cement in Germany

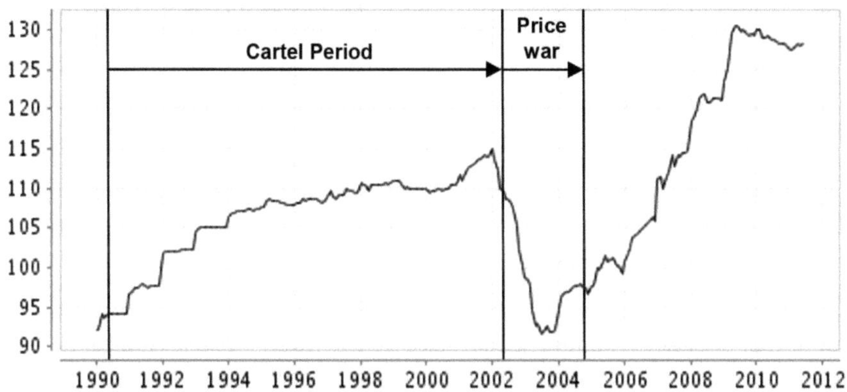

Source: Federal Statistical Office, 2005=100

Regional comparisons were also rejected due to concrete suspicion of cartel activities and spill-over effects in comparator markets, especially in the Benelux countries, France, Poland, and Austria, and because of significant differences in

74 Judgment of 26 June 2009, Joined Cases VI-2a Kart 2 – 6/08.

75 A similar procedure was also employed in the Commercial Property Insurance case cited *supra* note 9. In this case, the taking of evidence began in March 2009, and in April 2009, the two experts (Professors G. Götz and M. Morlok) gave their testimony on the appropriate methods. In May 2009, they were then instructed by the court to employ a time-series approach, before the proceedings were cut short by the withdrawal of the appeals by all parties except HDI-Gerling Industrie Versicherung AG (who was later acquitted on legal grounds).

market characteristics. By court decree dated February 27, 2009, the court eventually ordered the expert to employ a time-series approach using quantitative techniques to control for other price-driving factors.

In April 2009, the court gave additional guidance to the expert concerning the duration of the infringement period and the legal requirement that facts relating to prior infringements already fined by the FCO in 1989 could not be used in calculating the illicit gains (due to *non bis in idem*). On May 7, 2009, the expert then delivered a preliminary version of his testimony which employed a time-series approach in the form of a 'during and after' analysis with a dummy variable to account for the infringement (see above 3.3. on the characteristics of the dummy variable approach). Shortly after the expert delivered his testimony, all raw data and statistical programmes used were forwarded to the parties and their economic counsels for review. In the following month, the court then conducted three separate hearings with the expert, in which the parties posed questions and put forward several criticisms regarding, *inter alia*, the robustness of the model and the treatment of the alleged price war period shortly after the break-down of the cartel. While the FCO argued that the price war period should be regarded as a normal element of unrestricted competition and therefore be included in the comparator period, leading to higher overcharge estimates, the defendants took the position that the assumed 'phasing-out' period for the price war should actually be considered longer since this would improve the statistical properties of the model (as well as *lower* the overcharge estimate). After a final hearing on June 9, 2009, the expert, taking these comments into account, arrived at an overcharge estimate of approx. €5/ton, albeit with strong regional differences that stemmed mainly from different HHI concentrations. The FCO's argument that a price war should be considered as normal competition was rejected, but so was the defendants' argument in favour of a longer 'phasing-out' period. In its final judgment, the court followed the expert's testimony on both counts, although it made clear that the exclusion of the 'price war' from the comparator period was not based on legal but on factual considerations relating to the ordinary and economically reasonable behaviour of competing producers in industries with high fixed costs. Nonetheless, the court employed an additional 25% safety margin in favour of the defendants to account for the remaining uncertainties in the estimate.

In sum, the hearing of economic evidence on the illicit gains was relatively swift and efficient, taking only seven to eight months and requiring a total of five oral hearings. The judgment itself contains a rather extensive and knowledgeable appraisal of the results of Professor Röller's testimony, the techniques employed, and the price-driving factors considered. While some elements of the trial are obviously going to differ considering the procedural setting of administrative fine cases – which are governed by the Criminal Procedure Code and thus subject to a judge's much more active and inquisitory role – the overall approach would be quite similar in a private damage case.

7 Unresolved Problems

While experience with recent competition litigation, including the Cement case just discussed, has certainly shown that German courts are in fact willing to deal with complicated economic evidence, it seems clear that there are several key problems for which there are, as of yet, no satisfactory solutions. All of these problems have considerable practical importance and may well determine the future course of private enforcement in German courts.

7.1 Access to Relevant Data

One of the most pertinent issues concerns access to relevant information and data necessary to feed economic models. How significant an issue this is obviously depends on the particulars of the case: If a competitor sues on grounds of foreclosure effects that may have occurred due to vertical restraints or abusive pricing practices employed by the defendant, the claimant's economist will often ask for access to the defendant's transaction data, in order to draw a direct comparison. In hard core cartel cases, on the other hand, claimants may be able to use their own transaction data, although the defendant's database could also be of significant value, especially when the claimant generates limited turnover with the cartel-affected product, so that few data points are available for analysis. Needless to say, common law-style discovery is unknown in German civil proceedings, which means that claimants need to resort to other instruments. The available tools for gaining access to information are indeed plentiful, but it is far from clear how they will work in the context of economic evidence.

To begin with, most claimants will try to gain unrestricted access to the file of the European Commission or the FCO under the EU Transparency Regulation or Section 406e(1) of the German Criminal Procedure Code (*Strafprozessordnung*, hereafter StPO),[76] respectively. While the Commission has in the past denied any access to its file (though it has recently suffered some setbacks in taking this position before the General Court[77]), the FCO has always granted at least partial ac-

[76] In conjunction with section 46(1) of the German Act on Administrative Offences (*Ordnungswidrigkeitengesetz*).

[77] See Judgement of 15 December 2011, Case T-437/08, *CDC Hydrogen Peroxide v. Commission* (where the General Court quashed the Commission's decision to deny access to the full statement of contents of the Commission's case file in re COMP/F/38.620, *Hydrogen Peroxide and Perborate*) and Judgment of 22 May 2012, Case T-344/08, *EnBW v. Commission* (where the Court annulled the Commission's decision to deny access to the entire case file in re COMP/F/38.899, *Gas-insulated switchgear*). Upon the Commission's appeal, however, the CJEU annulled the General Court's decision in the EnBW case arguing, inter alia, that general considerations (i.e. the principle that any person is entitled to claim compensation for the loss caused to him by a breach of Article 81 EC) are not, as such, capable of prevailing over the reasons justifying the refusal to disclose the documents in the Commission's case file

cess to 'aggrieved parties', and the County Court of Bonn, which has jurisdiction over access requests in the event they are denied by the FCO, has shown a certain degree of claimant-friendliness in this regard.[78] On the other hand, even after the ECJ's judgment in *Pfleiderer,*[79] the German courts have not gone so far as to require the FCO to disclose leniency applications to potential claimants.[80] In any event, while the content of the file may be of considerable interest in other respects, it often will not contribute much that can be used in an economic study, as competition authorities are usually not concerned with data analysis nor with estimating the amount of harm caused by the infringement.

Indeed, current experience shows that, in order to obtain data for economic studies, claimants in German proceedings normally prefer the action-by-stages (*Stufenklage*) under Section 254 ZPO, which allows claimants to demand disclosure of data and/or information first, i.e., before the proceedings progress to the actual claim for damages.[81] The substantive basis for the claim for disclosure is firmly rooted in Federal Court of Justice case law,[82] and it is no longer controversial that a claimant can, in principle, expect to succeed with its claim for disclosure once it has established all preconditions for liability (other than the amount of damage) and has shown that it is, through no fault of its own, ignorant as to the precise extent of the claim. However, the information sought must be reasonable

and that it is highly unlikely that the action for damages will need to be based on all the evidence in the file relating to that proceeding (see CJEU, Judgment of 27 February 2014, Case C-365/12 P, at para. 105 et seq.).

78 See in particular Decision of 4 August 2009, Case 51 Gs 53/09, *Neue Zeitschrift für Gesellschaftsrecht* 2010, 60.

79 ECJ, Judgment of 14 June 2011, Case C-360/09, *Pfleiderer v. Bundeskartellamt* (not yet published). For a recent account of the interests involved, see Mäger, Zimmer and Milde, Konflikt zwischen öffentlicher und privater Kartellrechtsdurchsetzung, *Wirtschaft und Wettbewerb* 2009, 885 *et seq.*

80 See Higher Regional Court of Düsseldorf, Decision of 22 August 2012 – Case V-4 Kart 5 + 6/11 (OWi), *Kaffeeröster*, *Betriebs-Berater* 2012, 2459; County Court of Bonn, Decision of 18 January 2012, Case 51 Gs 53/09, *Neue Juristische Wochenschrift* 2012, 947. See, however, Higher Regional Court of Hamm, Decision of 26 November 2013, ref. 1 Vas 116/13, *Betriebs-Berater* 2014, 526, which denied any special protection for leniency documents contained in the files of a state prosecutor's office and ordered the handing-over of such documents to the civil court deciding over damage claims.

81 One of the main advantages of using the action-by-stages stems from the fact that the underlying substantive law claim is for *information*, not for documents (cf. Federal Supreme Court, Judgment of 17 May 2001, Case I ZR 291/98, *BGHZ* 148, 26 at 37), which means that the costs for gathering the requested data will typically fall upon the defendant, and obvious obstruction tactics such as overwhelming the claimant with truckloads of (mostly useless) files will not work.

82 See, e.g., Federal Court of Justice, Judgment of 6 February 2007, Case X ZR 117/04, *Neue Juristische Wochenschrift* 2007, 1806; Judgment of 28 October 1953, Case II ZR 149/52, *BGHZ* 10, 385, at p. 387.

in light of all the circumstances, which typically entails a weighing of interests[83] and it remains unclear from existing case law just how far claimants can go before a data request would be considered unreasonable. For example, there are currently several cases before German courts in which claimants are requesting the defendants disclose essentially all transaction data for all customers and for the whole duration of the infringement period including the years before and after, all of which information must be presented in an ordered Excel file ready for processing by the claimants' economists. These requests understandably led to extensive quarrelling as to their reasonableness and have not yet been resolved. This controversy also has a *constitutional law* dimension, as the claim for information has been developed by case law and therefore lacks a specific statutory basis. Thus, one may well question whether or not a judgment that obligates the defendant to hand over its complete books covering a several year period would still be within the boundaries set by the Federal Constitutional Court for the development of case law (*Richterrecht*).

In theory, claimants could also resort to other methods of gathering information, but there is as of yet little experience with deploying these tools in antitrust damage lawsuits. For example, under Section 142 ZPO – sometimes seen as a watered-down version of common law discovery rules[84] – the court can order claimant and defendant as well as third parties to produce documents in their possession. Since Section 142 ZPO requires only that reference had been made to the document in question, the court enjoys considerable discretionary powers, which claimants often urge the court to make use of. However, the Federal Court of Justice has recently emphasized that Section 142 ZPO should not be used for fishing expeditions,[85] and the courts have so far shown some reluctance in bringing their discretionary powers to bear. Moreover, it is unclear how Section 142 ZPO would work in case of a *data request*: To begin with, its wording refers specifically to 'documents', which means that the procedure cannot be used to request specific datasets unless they have already been compiled in one or more separate documents. Obviously, it is possible to interpret the defendant's books as 'documents' in this sense, and indeed the German Commercial Code (*Handelsgesetzbuch*, hereafter HGB) contains an explicit – albeit completely disregarded[86] – provision which gives the court discretionary powers to subpoena the books belonging to ei-

---

83 Federal Court of Justice, Judgment of 6 February 2007, cited *supra* note 82.

84 See Gruber and Kießling, 'Die Vorlagepflichten der §§ 142 ff ZPO nach der Reform 2002 – Elemente der 'discovery' im neuen deutschen Gerichtsverfahren? ', *Zeitschrift für Zivilprozeß* 116 (2003), 305–333 and Saenger, 'Grundfragen und aktuelle Probleme des Beweisrechts aus deutscher Sicht', *Zeitschrift für Zivilprozeß* 2008, 139–163.

85 Federal Court of Justice, Decision of 14 June 2007, Case VII ZR 230/06, *Neue Juristische Wochenschrift-Rechtsprechungsreport* 2007, 1393.

86 Besides a 19th century decision from the Reichsgericht (Decision of 14 November 1896, Case I 219/96, *Juristische Wochenschrift* 1896, 699), there is only one reported case in which section 258(1) HGB was employed (see *Sammlung des Bayrischen Obersten Landesgerichts in Zivilsachen* 1993, 156).

ther party (Section 258(1) HGB). However, according to prevailing opinion, the court cannot order the disclosure of books for the purpose of allowing the other party to perform a 'general analysis' of their content but only for the verification of specific allegations.[87] Moreover, both Section 142 ZPO and 258(1) HGB require the court to weigh the interests in a manner similar to that governing the substantive claim for information in an action-by-stages.[88] Finally, it should also be noted that there is no way of directly enforcing a disclosure order – be it under Section 142 ZPO or Section 258(1) HGB – if it is directed at one of the parties. Rather, an unjustified refusal to produce the documents would enable the court to take as uncontested the other party's assertions concerning the content of the documents (Section 427 ZPO).[89] This, however, does no good in cases in which the claimant requests large datasets and is completely ignorant of their content.

In addition to issuing disclosure orders directed at the parties, the court could also request the disclosure of files or information from public authorities, most notably the FCO or the European Commission, under Section 273(2) No. 2 ZPO. In German cases, however, experience shows that courts are often disinclined to make use of these powers because, on the one hand, claimants can typically gain access to the FCO's file for themselves (under Section 406e(1) StPO), and, on the other, to the extent they cannot gain access (because the FCO asserts confidentiality), it seems that a request from the court itself would not receive a substantially different treatment. The FCO's reticence here is due largely to the fact that the transmission of files would be considered 'administrative assistance' (*Amtshilfe*)[90]

---

87 See Reichsgericht, Decision of 14 November 1896 (cited *supra* note 86): 'The disclosure of books of account shall only occur for the purpose of clarifying specific disputes and shall be limited to the parts that are necessary for this. A general analysis [German: *Eine allgemeine Durchmusterung*] of the books of account by the other party is not permitted by the law.' See also Graf, in Kropff & Semler (eds.), *Münchener Kommentar zum Aktiengesetz* (C.H. Beck, 2nd ed. 2003), section 258 HGB para. 4; Winkeljohann and Philipps, in Ellrott *et al.* (eds.), *Beck'scher Bilanz-Kommentar* (C. H. Beck, 8th ed. 2012), section 258 HGB para. 2, with further ref.

88 For section 142 HGB see: Wagner, 'Urkundenedition durch Prozessparteien - Auskunftspflicht und Weigerungsrechte', *Juristenzeitung* 2007, 706 *et seq.*, and Becker, 'Die Pflicht zur Urkundenvorlage nach § 142 Abs. 1 ZPO und das Weigerungsrecht der Parteien', *Monatsschrift für Deutsches Recht* 2008, 1309 *et seq.* For section 258 HGB see: Wiedmann, in Ebenroth *et al.* (eds.), *Handelsgesetzbuch*, section 258 para. 5.

89 For section 142 ZPO see: Federal Court of Justice, Judgment of 26 June 2007, Case XI ZR 277/05, *Neue Juristische Wochenschrift* 2007, 2989, at 2992. For section 258 HGB see: Wiedmann, in Ebenroth & Boujong *et al.* (eds.), *Handelsgesetzbuch* (C. H. Beck, 2nd ed. 2008), section 258 para. 11; Graf, cited *supra* note 87, section 258 HGB para. 4; Hüffer, in Canaris *et al.* (eds.), *Großkommentar zum HGB* (De Gruyter, 4th ed. 1988), section 258 para. 23.

90 Reichold, cited *supra* note 10, section 432 para. 7; Schreiber, in Rauscher, Wax & Wenzel (eds.), *Münchener Kommentar zur Zivilprozessordnung* (C.H. Beck, 4th ed. 2012), section 432 note 9; Greger, in Zöller *et al.* (eds.), *Zivilprozessordnung: ZPO – Kommentar* (O. Schmidt, 28th ed. 2010), section 273 para. 8.

and would thus be governed by Section 5 of the Federal Act on Administrative Procedure (*Verwaltungsverfahrensgesetz*, hereafter VwVfG), which allows that a request be denied if and to the extent it would run counter to confidentiality considerations or would jeopardize the accomplishment of the FCO's tasks (see Section 5(2) 2nd sentence and (3) No. 3 VwVfG). These are by and large the same standards that are also relevant for direct access requests under Section 406e StPO.

Similarly, in European cases, recent decisions by the General Court regarding access requests under the EU Transparency Regulation suggest that claimants can now gain access to the Commission's files directly.[91] This right of direct access may further disincline German courts to resort to Section 273(2) No. 2 ZPO and request that Commission files be handed over. Moreover, a request from a national court does not seem to have any better prospect of success, given that the Commission Notice on the cooperation between the Commission and the courts clearly stipulates that the Commission will not transmit to the national courts (a) any confidential information and business secrets unless the court offers to guarantee their protection (which it usually cannot do for reasons we will discuss in a minute, below under 7.2.) and (b) any information voluntarily submitted by a leniency applicant without the consent of that applicant.[92] In light of this, one can expect court requests made under Section 273(2) No. 2 ZPO will remain the exception.[93]

There may also be other means available for gaining access to certain documents (see Sections 422, 423, and 432 ZPO), but they have thus far been of no practical significance.

7.2 Confidentiality of Data

As indicated above, another unresolved issue concerns the confidentiality of the raw data used in economic analyses. For key reasons that are grounded in constitutional law (cf. Article 20(3) GG), it would seem that neither party can avail itself of economic evidence without disclosing the underlying data to the court and to all other parties, including recipients of third party notices that have decided to join the proceedings. Indeed, in the Cement case, all parties received the entire raw dataset used by the court-appointed expert so that they were able to validate the expert analyses and to carry out their own data investigations. This disclosure of data poses a problem in (at least) two regards: On the one hand, the loss of confidentiality will make it harder for a court to grant a request for disclosure in the first place (be it through an action-by-stages or any of the other methods described above under 7.1.), given that any potential negative consequences must be taken into account as the interests are weighed. If, for example, the claimant requests ac-

91 See the decisions cited *supra* note 77.

92 European Commission, Commission Notice on the cooperation between the Commission and the courts of the EU Member States in the application of Articles 81 and 82 EC, O.J. 2004, C 101/1, paras. 25 and 26.

93 See, however, Higher Regional Court of Hamm, cited *supra* note 80.

cess to the defendant's transaction data for use in an economic study and the granting of this access would make the data available to competitors – as will often be the case since these competitors are often themselves defendants in the same proceedings or have joined the proceedings upon a third party notice – the interests of the defendant will typically carry significantly more weight.

On the other hand, loss of confidentiality is also a concern that may have substantial influence on what the parties themselves are prepared to submit as evidence. If a claimant sues competitors on account of alleged foreclosure effects and is contemplating the submission of an econometric study as proof, the fact that all underlying data would need to be disclosed may well act as a deterrent, particularly if the time span between the infringement and the lawsuit is short, so that relatively new or recent data would have to be used. Similarly, a defendant may find himself unwilling to put forward economic studies out of concern that the harm caused by a loss of confidentiality could possibly exceed any expected gain from mustering an adequate defence.

Unfortunately, the existing procedural tools for protecting confidentiality do little to mitigate the situation: Excluding the public and conducting the proceedings partly *in camera* under Section 172 No. 2 GVG makes no strategic sense when the real concern is not whether confidentiality is lost before a courtroom audience (who will not gain any useful insights into confidential data on the basis of a mere oral hearing anyway), but that it is lost before other parties to the case, who necessarily cannot be excluded from the trial. In cases involving unfair competition, the courts have occasionally allowed defendants to disclose confidential data to an auditor, who then examines the data and reports only the results to the court and to the claimant (*Wirtschaftsprüfervorbehalt*).[94] However, even this method does not provide a workable solution, as it only covers simple and straightforward examinations (e.g., an inspection of the financial accounts to ascertain certain turnover figures) and is therefore evidently misplaced in cartel damage lawsuits where complex economic analyses need to be performed. Using data in an anonymized form may sometimes help, but more often than not it is equally pointless, as the claimant will normally need to combine data from several defendants (and from other sources, including his own books). Moreover, the parties will often be able to undo most of the anonymization quite easily by cross-referencing the anonymized data with their own database. In sum, it would therefore seem that there is currently no suitable way that would allow a party to build an economic argument on confidential data without jeopardizing the confidentiality vis-à-vis the other parties to the proceedings.

---

94 See Federal Court of Justice, Judgment of 2 April 1957, Case I ZR 58/56, *Rechnungslegung, Gewerblicher Rechtsschutz und Urheberrecht* 1957, 336; Judgment of 13 February 1976, Case I ZR 1/75, *Fernschreibverzeichnisse, Gewerblicher Rechtsschutz und Urheberrecht* 1978, 52, p. 53; Judgment of 7 December 1979, ref. I ZR 157/77, *Monumenta Germaniae Historica, Gewerblicher Rechtsschutz und Urheberrecht* 1980, 227, p. 232; Decision of 13 February 1981, ref. I ZR 111/78, *Wirtschaftsprüfervorbehalt, Gewerblicher Rechtsschutz und Urheberrecht* 1981, 535.

7.3 Resolution of Conflicting Expert Reports

Finally, the resolution of conflicts and contradictions in expert testimony – be it between court- and party-appointed experts or between several party-appointed experts – will also pose a significant challenge to the courts. As described above, courts cannot expect to find the resolution in economics itself, as there are no intrinsic economic 'thresholds' to identify models that deliver sufficiently reliable results. 'Robustness' is often cited as a desirable quality in an economic model, but this is a somewhat elusive concept and not easily applied in many real-world cases. Moreover, most sophisticated economic techniques for estimating damage have serious drawbacks that are both highly technical and difficult to understand for non-economists. To give but three examples: In a time-series regression analysis that uses a dummy variable to account for the infringement, it is normally possible to use an in-sample model selection mechanism which produces a damage estimate of *zero*, because it adds a number of explanatory variables that actually have little relevance for the explained variable, thereby leading to what is usually termed 'overfitting'.[95] Overfitting is particularly 'easy' to do with explanatory variables whose development exhibits a shape similar to that of the explained variable (i.e., in a price-fixing case: explanatory variables that have developed in parallel to the observed market price during and after the infringement). Another drawback to the dummy variable approach stems from the possible influence that the infringement may have had on other apparently independent explanatory variables. For example, a cartel may have succeeded not only in raising the sales price but also in lowering the purchase price for certain input factors (by exercising buyer power). In such a setting, a dummy variable approach may significantly underestimate the impact of the infringement.[96] On the other hand, if the model disregards important explanatory variables and therefore suffers an 'omitted-variable bias', it may well yield results that overstate the actual damage because the model wrongly attributes the effects of the 'hidden' variables to the infringement (while at the same time indicating deceptively high goodness of fit and statistically significant coefficients). It is therefore almost always possible to explore different variations of an econometric model until arriving at one variation that is is beneficial to one side or the other.

To a certain extent, remaining uncertainties might be resolved by employing safety margins, as the Higher Regional Court of Düsseldorf did in the Cement case – albeit not in the examples mentioned previously in which the problem concerns *underestimating* the damage. Moreover, it should be noted that the Cement case was still relatively 'simple' in that it dealt with an almost perfectly homogenous product and an industry with little dynamic development and little structural change. There was therefore no fundamental dispute about the overall suitability of the econometric model and the explanatory variable under consideration; in-

---

95 See, e.g., White, Marshall and Kennedy, 'The Measurement of Economic Damages in Antitrust Civil Litigation', 6 *ABA Antritrust Section – Economic Committee Newsletter* (2006), 17, at p. 21; McCrary and Rubinfeld, cited *supra* note 55.

96 See White, Marshall and Kennedy, cited *supra* note 95, 18.

stead there was a rather limited disagreement over determining the parameters of the control period (particularly, to what extent the alleged 'price war' period that began once the cartel broke up should be included in or excluded from the control period). In future cases, one can expect to see more elementary battles over the choice of economic models, and disputes of this nature can easily result in a stalemate which only the judge will be able to settle, according to legal standards. This resolution of stalemate, however, will require the judge to confront and understand the disputed technical issues and their potential impact on the reliability of the results.

In light of this, the recent initiative by the European Commission to provide a practical guide on economic techniques for damage calculation is certainly worth endorsing. However, given the relatively low degree of specialization among German civil courts, where cartel damage claims are regionally concentrated[97] though still typically tried by judges who preside over a variety of other matters, it remains to be seen to what extent this initiative will actually reach those to whom it is addressed. It is not inconceivable that future claimants, when choosing the appropriate forum, will include in their considerations the economic proficiency of the court.

8 Concluding Remarks

While private enforcement of competition law has always been a central pillar in the German competition law tradition, high stakes cartel damage claims are a rather recent phenomenon, and so is the use of economic evidence that inevitably accompanies almost every major damage lawsuit. Although expert testimony is traditionally considered the domain of court-appointed experts, the special features of damage litigation (e.g., the difficulties both parties experience in gathering the necessary pleadings and the more relaxed evidentiary thresholds that govern the court's damage estimation) provide strong incentives to retain party-appointed economic counsel. A number of on-going cases before German courts confirm this.

The German courts' initial experience with economic evidence, especially their comparatively swift and knowledgeable hearing of economic expert testimony in the Cement cartel case before the Higher Regional Court of Düsseldorf, may be considered rather encouraging but should not drive us to premature conclusions. In fact, there are several significant stumbling blocks concerning, inter alia, access to the data necessary to perform economic analyses, the protection of confidentiality

[97] Most German States have passed State ordinances that concentrate cartel matters with one or several District Courts, see, e.g., the respective ordinance for North Rhine-Westphalia: *Verordnung über die Bildung gemeinsamer Kartellgerichte und über die gerichtliche Zuständigkeit in bürgerlichen Rechtsstreitigkeiten nach dem Energiewirtschaftsgesetz,* dated 30 August 2011, Gesetz- und Verordnungsblatt für das Land Nordrhein-Westphalen (Official Journal of North Rhine-Westphalia), 469.

of the raw data used in such analyses, and, perhaps most importantly, the significant technical pitfalls that lay concealed in almost any economic method of damage quantification and may give rise to prolonged battles over what can be considered a reliable estimate. In this context, it is worth noting that, according to some estimates,[98] well over 90% of all treble-damage cases filed in the U.S. are eventually resolved through settlements, often even before the discovery process is initiated, thus sparing the courts the trouble of having to hack their way through the thicket of conflicting economic expert testimony. Obviously, this high share of early settlements is possible because of the unique features of the US litigation system, in particular its considerable claimant-friendliness[99] and the sometimes prohibitively high costs associated with the discovery process.[100] Given that the German system does not share these features, litigants here can typically afford a higher 'perseverance', implying that to expect a similar share of early settlements in German courts would be deeply misguided. Consequently, German courts face a considerable challenge and the European Commission's initiative to provide non-binding guidance on the relevant economic techniques is all the more praiseworthy.

98 See Connor, cited *supra* note 60, 31 *et seq.*

99 For example, the U.S. Supreme Court in a landmark decision in 1981 held that there is no basis, either in the federal antitrust laws or in federal common law, for allowing federal courts to create a right of contribution among antitrust defendants, *Texas Industries, Inc. v. Radcliff Materials, Inc.*, 451 U.S. 630 (1981). This has generated significant incentives for defendants to settle early.

100 The discovery process is regularly estimated to cost up to $10 million, see O'Donoghue, 'Europe's Long March Towards Antitrust Damages Actions', 2 *CPI Antritrust Chronicle* (2011), 4.

Private Damage Claims – Recent Developments in the Passing-on Defence

Mario Siragusa

1 Introduction: POD and Effective Private Enforcement

In recent years the European Commission has focused its concern on bolstering new developments within European legal systems aimed at facilitating actions for damages caused by infringements of antitrust laws. Debates and initiatives surrounding the matter are clearly animated by an objective to provide better and more efficient enforcement of competition law while at the same time allowing customers access to redress for their losses. Specifically, the Commission states that the absence of an effective legal framework for antitrust damages actions (i) causes victims of antitrust infringement to forego a considerable amount of compensation, and (ii) also hampers full enforcement of antitrust rules, thus having a negative bearing on vigorous competition in an open internal market.

In an effort to avoid these effects, a number of initiatives have been taken whose intended purpose was to identify those obstacles barring the path to a more efficient system of processing damages claims in the EU and to propose several options by which such obstacles might be overcome. Let us recall the 2005 Green Paper, followed by the 2008 White Paper and, in March 2009, the proposed, then retired EU Directive, as well as the publication of a comprehensive study of the methods used to calculate damages which were expressly aimed at establishing a guidance tool for national courts in assessing antitrust damages.[1]

More recently, with the Almunia Commission, the effort continues, albeit with a more nuanced approach. As we will see, public consultation on the issue of collective redress has only now begun in earnest. What we see happening at present will likely prove to be only the first steps in the new approach that Commissioner Almunia has taken since beginning his work at the Commission. In short, this new path focuses on collective redress as a general means to support private enforcement of EU law – not limited to competition law – and aims at a deeper involvement with the European Parliament.

1 See Oxera, *Quantifying antitrust damages* (December 2009).

In this general framework, the 'passing-on defence' ('POD') represents a key issue insofar as it allows defendants, while being held responsible for an infringement, to rebut the claims of direct purchasers; at the same time, passing-on can also represent a legitimate circumstance for arguing for an indirect purchaser's standing in antitrust damages actions. Scholars refer to these two guises of the POD, stressing both its *offensive* use – i.e., as an argument enabling indirect purchasers to claim damages – as well as its *defensive* use – i.e., as an argument allowing defendants to limit the amount of the damages that can be claimed.

The sensitivity of POD in orienting the direction and force of antitrust policy is obvious. Consider the US system where a focus on deterrence has led federal courts to ban both the use of POD as a defensive argument and the possibility for indirect purchasers to claim damages. Under these conditions, direct purchasers may recover an overcharge in full, even if they have already passed it on in its entirety to their customers. Admittedly, even in the US, the issue is still up for debate and national courts are broadening their scope of definition for indirect purchasers' standing.[2]

In the following, I will begin by providing a description of the Commission's approach to POD, with particular attention paid to the consequences the Commission's choices with regard to POD are likely to have on private enforcement actions. I shall then move on to discuss national experience of the issue, namely the Italian experience, detailing some interesting judgments which help in clarifying the scope and the actual impact of the POD. This is followed by a brief look into some interesting recent developments in France, Germany, and the United Kingdom. I will then briefly outline what problems passing-on estimation is likely to bring up in national courts, and finally I will conclude with a discussion of recent initiatives on collective redress and their potential impact on the POD issue.

2 POD and Indirect Purchaser Standing: Definition and Main Issues

As is well known, the POD is strictly based on simple market dynamics: in multistage distribution chains, firms having to pay supra-competitive prices resulting from an antitrust infringement may be able to pass overcharges downstream to indirect purchasers. These indirect purchasers may be producers deploying the cartelized component in their manufacturing process, distributors, or end-consumers. The phenomenon typically occurs in a price-fixing setting, which is how it will be discussed here, although passing-on of overcharges can also occur in the context

2 *Hanover Shoe v. United Shoe Machinery*, 392 US 481 (1968) and *Illinois Brick v. Illinois*, 431 US 720 (1977). A number of states allow, however, for indirect purchasers to sue under state law. In *California v. ARC America*, 490 US 93 (1989), the US Supreme Court held that such state laws are not preempted by Section 4 of the Clayton Act. See also US Antitrust Modernization Commission, *Report and Recommendations* (April 2007), Chapter II.B 'Indirect Purchaser Litigation'.

of an (especially exploitative) abuse of dominant market position and, to a lesser extent, in a situation where vertical restraints are in place (given that the producer's interest is usually aligned with the consumer's, whose mutual interest is in compressing the distributor's margin).

Therefore, when considering the passing-on phenomenon, one ought to ask whether or not the passing-on of anti-competitive charges bears any relevance when it comes to adjudicating antitrust claims and, if so, to what extent the burden of proof for said passing-on needs to be attributed, and to whom.

Unfortunately, there is no simple solution to this problem. The approaches proposed in legal scholarship and followed in national litigation systems tend to vary, ranging between two extreme positions, each inspired by a particular philosophy of enforcement.

On the one hand we have what is known as the 'zero option', which consists in fully recognizing both the POD as well as indirect standing. This approach is strictly compensatory in nature, insofar as it remedies possible multi-liability of the defendants and ensures that direct purchasers do not receive compensation greater than the harm actually incurred. This approach is common among most European member states.

On the other hand we have the opposite approach, which denies both POD and indirect standing. This scenario relies heavily on direct customers as the leading force in private antitrust enforcement, given their close ties with infringers and their greater knowledge of market dynamics. At the same time, denying POD strongly incentivizes direct customers to claim damages and may lead to substantial over-deterrence and excess of litigation (the literature here refers to direct purchasers as the '*most efficient enforcers*' or '*better detectors*'[3]).

As I mentioned earlier, the latter approach was the one originally adopted in the US. In *Hanover Shoe v. United Shoe Machinery Corp* (1968), the Court rejected the POD argument raised by the defendant on the grounds of '*insurmountable*' practical difficulties in proving the event of passing-on and its amount[4]. Moreover, reference was made to the actual dispersion of indirect purchasers and to their consequent weakness in claiming antitrust damages. Later, in *Illinois Brick Co. v. Illinois* (1977), the court denied the indirect purchaser the right to claim for damages that had allegedly been passed on to it.[5]

---

3 CEPS, *Making Antitrust Damages Action More Effective in the EU, Report for the European Commission* (Brussels 2007), at para. 470.

4 Particularly, the Supreme Court observed that it is too difficult to establish the passing-on to consumers, as it would require convincing proof of '*virtually unascertainable figures*' and it would render already complex antitrust damages actions completely unmanageable. Parlak, 'Passing-on Defence and Indirect Purchaser Standing: should the Passing-on Defence Be Rejected Now the Indirect Purchaser Has Standing after Manfredi and the White Paper of the European Commission', 33 *World Competition* (2010), at p. 34.

5 The court pointed out two major factors that would run counter the hypothetic assumption of passing-on of price overcharge: (i) direct purchasers often sell in an imperfectly competitive market; and (ii) they often compete with other sellers not af-

This approach was, however, subject to criticism. First, state court decisions began to legitimize indirect purchasers' suits, and a number of states passed what is referred to as the *Illinois Brick* repealer laws or applied consumer protection statutes in order to permit consumer standing. Secondly, at the federal level, the Antitrust Modernization Commission has recommended that 'direct and indirect purchaser damages claims [be made to fall] more in line with their actually lost profits from the cartel'[6].[7]

With regard to the European system, in 2005 the Commission's conclusion was that 'there is no passing-on defense in Community law: rather, there is an unjust enrichment defense which requires: (1) proof of passing on [...] and (2) proof of no reduction in sales or other reduction to income'.[8,9]

This principle essentially relies on the law established by the *Comateb* case, according to which the ECJ accepted that, faced with a restitutionary claim, POD was compatible with the European legal system.[10]

From the point of view of consumers' standing, both the *Courage* and *Manfredi* judgments are more clear-cut: 'Any individual can claim compensation for the

---

fected by the overcharge. See Parlak, *ibid.*, at p. 33, for further description of the US experience.

6 T. Van Dijk and F. Verboven, 'Cartel damages and the passing-on defense' (2007, available at http://www.cresse.info/uploadfiles/Paper%20Verboven%20-%20Dijk.pdf), at 4.

7 Particularly, the Commission recommended adopting '*major statutory changes to overrule Illinois Brick to allow indirect purchasers to sue for damages in federal court*' and to limit the POD '*to those cases where only direct purchasers sue in federal court*'. See CEPS (2007), *supra* note 3, para. 673.

8 *Green Paper* (2005), para. 48

9 The need to avoid unjust enrichment is recognized by European case law, according to which: '*Community law does not prevent national courts from taking steps to ensure that the protection of the rights guaranteed by Community law does not entail the unjust enrichment of those who enjoy them (see, in particular, Case 238/78 Ireks-Arkady v. Council and Commission [1979] ECR 2955, paragraph 14, Case 68/79 Just [1980] ECR 501, paragraph 26, and Joined Cases C-441/98 and C-442/98 Michaïlidis [2000] ECR I-7145, paragraph 31)*' (Case C-453/99, *Courage c. Crehan*, para. 30)' (Joined cases C-295 and 298/04, *Manfredi* [2006] ECR I-6619, para. 94).

10 Joined cases C-192/95 to C-218/95 *Société Comateb* [1997] ECR I-165, para. 21-22: '*There is, however, an exception to that principle. As the Court stated in Just, Denkavit and San Giorgio, cited above, the protection of the rights so guaranteed by the Community legal order does not require repayment of taxes, charges and duties levied in breach of Community law where it is established that the person required to pay such charges has actually passed them on to other persons (see, in particular, San Giorgio, paragraph 13). In such circumstances, the burden of the charge levied but not due has been borne not by the trader, but by the purchaser to whom the cost has been passed on. Therefore, to repay the trader the amount of the charge already received from the purchaser would be tantamount to paying him twice over, which may be described as unjust enrichment, whilst in no way remedying the consequences for the purchaser of the illegality of the charge.*'

harm suffered where there is a causal relationship between that harm and an infringement of Article [101] or [102 TFEU]. This principle also applies to indirect purchasers'.[11]

With a view to supporting damages actions and to adopting a common pan-European approach toward POD, in its 2005 Green Paper the Commission discussed a number of options,[12] each of which involved different benefits in terms of effective enforcement in addition to potential drawbacks. The most relevant problems posed by the main options regarding POD were that:

- prohibiting the POD would be contrary to the principle of strict compensation, according to which claimants must receive compensation for damages actually incurred and this ultimately would result in claimants being over-compensated (above all direct purchasers), thus increasing the associated risk of abusive 'US-style' litigation;
- denying indirect purchasers' standing would lead to unjust enrichment of the authors of the antitrust infringement, diminishing any possible deterrent effect;
- allowing the POD would consequently introduce complex issues involving allocation of damages among the various actors who had any part in the passing-on; and
- allowing indirect purchaser standing would then require that effective means be established in order to coordinate and prosecute several damages actions against a single infringer.

3 The European Commission's Proposals

After having assessed the different scenarios associated with the proposed options, in the 2008 White Paper the Commission eventually suggested that defendants be allowed to rely on POD in order to limit or block claims for compensation by a purchaser, whether direct or indirect, who is not an end consumer. The latter are indeed able to claim damages, according to *Courage* and *Manfredi* case law. Therefore, the principle of full compensation should be followed.

Consequently, once POD and indirect-purchaser standing are recognized, equilibrium must be found between the need to encourage private actions without at the same time allowing over-compensation or unjust enrichment by either the claimant or the defendant, and this equilibrium ultimately rests on where the burden of proof is located. Therefore, proper allocation of the burden of proving the passing-on becomes crucial, and might very well involve presumptions or alleviation.

---

11 Joined cases C-295 and 298/04 *Manfredi* [2006] ECR I-6619, para. 61.

12 Namely: (i) to allow both POD and indirect-purchaser standing; (ii) to deny both POD and indirect-purchasers standing; (iii) to deny POD, while allowing indirect-purchaser standing; and (iv) to deny POD, while allowing indirect purchasers to sue only direct purchasers.

According to the Commission, the burden of proving that overcharges have been passed on necessarily lies with the defendant who is alleging the argument as a defense. Furthermore, the standard of proof must be equivalent to the standard required of the claimant for proving the damages suffered.[13]

As for indirect purchasers and end consumers suing for damages, the Commission proposes that their standing be grounded on a rebuttable presumption that the illegal overcharge was passed-on in its entirety to their level in the market stream.[14] Thus, an indirect purchaser has to prove only the infringement and the overcharge. The rationale for this presumption can be found in the Commission's desire to ease the burden in favour of claimants, given its political objective of encouraging private enforcement actions.

Indeed, proving the passing-on, both its existence and its amount, is an equally difficult task for both parties. However, were a defendant to fail the burden of proof, the negative potential consequences of this failure (i.e., risk of multiple liability for defendants and over-compensation for claimants) are considered less likely to actually happen than the negative consequences associated with a claimant's inability to meet the burden of proof (i.e., under-deterrence and unjust enrichment of the infringer). In fact, the the defendant may risk incurring charges of multiple liability for the same infringement in the unlikely event that (i) several purchasers sue for the same over-charge, (ii) the defendant cannot successfully demonstrate the passing-on, and (iii) the court does not take into account damages already paid on an equitable basis. Furthermore, easing the claimant's burden of proof is considered far more politically acceptable.[15]

By contrast, no presumptions lie with direct purchasers. Indeed, direct purchasers are closer to the violation and are generally better placed to prove both infringement and the amount of an overcharge than are purchasers further down the distribution chain.

Moreover, it should be noted that the Commission calls on national courts to adopt every possible means to avoid under- or over-compensation of the harm incurred, by taking recourse in any mechanism that national law may provide. The Commission also mentions, among the possible means for defendants to rebut the passing-on presumption, the existence of an award or any other prior judgment which has already ordered him or her to compensate a direct purchaser.[16]

Thus, it is apparent that the approach taken by the Commission is inspired by the principle of full compensation, adjusted with a view to obtaining corrective justice by means of a rebuttable presumption of passing-on in favour of indirect purchasers and end consumers.

This approach has been further developed and was confirmed in the 2009 Draft Directive on rules governing actions for damages prepared by the EU Commission shortly before the end of its mandate. Concerning POD, Article 11 states, 'Member states shall ensure that the defendant in an action for damages can invoke as a

13 *White Paper*, p. 8; *Staff Working Paper*, para. 214.

14 *Staff Working Paper*, para. 220.

15 *Staff Working Paper*, para. 217–218.

16 *Staff Working Paper*, para. 219.

defense against a claim for damages the fact that the claimant passed on the whole or part of the overcharge imposed upon him.' At par. 2, it then introduces a rebuttable presumption of passing-on in favour of the claimant.

Stakeholders fiercely objected to the rebuttable presumption in favour of indirect purchasers and/or end consumers. According to the majority of NCA's and lawyers' associations, this presumption would be hard to rebut and would systematically lead to multiple liability for defendants.[17]

However, while the content of the Draft Directive was largely based on the White Paper, it also fails to address some major points connected to the POD, such as methods for allocating and calculating damages. Moreover, the Draft Directive was heavily criticized, especially with reference to its undue interference with internal procedural systems and the risk it poses of inconsistencies with other EU initiatives in the field of collective redress (such as those in the area of consumer law and environmental law).[18]

Therefore, as we will see further on, Almunia's new stance with respect to collective redress actually aims at representing a general and cohesive framework within which private enforcement of antitrust law may be debated and further defined in the future.

4 Italian Case Law on Antitrust Damage Claims: What Can We Draw from National Experience?

Moving on to national experience, it should be noted that the passing-on defense is not recognized as such by Italian legislation or case law. Therefore, the issue shall be construed in accordance with general civil liability principles, which provide that a claimant may only seek compensation for those damages it actually suffered, provided that it did not collude in causing them.

In looking at the few antitrust cases that address this issue, we find that courts actually did apply general principles, concluding that claimants have no standing with respect to damages they passed along to their customers. This reasoning appears to have been endorsed in a number of Italian cases.

In *Indaba v. Juventus*,[19] a travel agency entered into a contract with the Juventus Football Club, undertaking to sell tickets to the 1997 Champions League

---

17 See the specific criticism reported in Prosperetti, *Il danno antitrust* (Il Mulino 2009), p. 201.

18 To this regard, *see* European Parliament's Resolution adopted in March 2009, which insisted on the need to involve European institution through 'the co-decision procedure' in any legislative initiative in the area of collective redress. The Commission, however, chose to ignore the Parliament's wishes. In any case, it appears that, due to these oppositions, Barroso may have personally intervened to pull the directive.

19 Court of Appeal of Turin, judgment of 6 July 2000, *Indaba vs. Juventus* (è '*privo di legittimazione attiva sostanziale il soggetto che abbia concorso a traslare il danno a*

final match in Munich only if bundled with travel packages that included services not normally needed by football supporters. The venture proved unsuccessful, and the travel agency sued Juventus for antitrust damages. The court found that the agreement unduly restricted competition and that Juventus had abused its dominant position in the relevant market for the sale of those tickets by imposing excessive prices and illegally tying the sale of the tickets to the entire travel package. However, no damages were awarded to the plaintiff. In fact, according to the court, the plaintiff had actually stipulated in the restrictive agreement its intention to 'pass on the damage' to its customers and it therefore was not entitled to any damages, since it had intentionally contributed to causing the harm. It is unclear whether the passing-on defense was actually raised by the defendant or considered by the court on its own motion.

In that case, it seems that national judges applied the rule provided for by Art. 1227 of the Civil Code, which acknowledges the relevance of the injured party's causal contribution to the occurrence of the damage. As a consequence, the injured party must behave with due diligence in order to lessen the harmful effects of the unlawful conduct and may only claim damages to the extent that said damages are not a consequence of its own misconduct.

In a second case, *Unimare v. Geasar*,[20] the judge, while concluding that there was no violation of antitrust law, nevertheless added that in any event the claimant would not have been entitled to recover any damages since it had already passed on its additional costs to its customers.

Unimare, a former provider of handling services at the Olbia airport in Sardinia, claimed that Geasar, the current management body of Olbia Airport, had abused its dominant position by (i) increasing its fees excessively and without justification, and (ii) stealing Unimare's main client, the US Naval Service Order (NSO), by presenting itself as the only entity qualified to supply ground-handling services at the airport.

The court maintained that no abuse took place though it went on to state that in any event it is not possible to claim damages caused by an abuse of dominant position when the damages have been completely passed on to the customers. In the case at issue, the fees imposed by Geasar were passed on from Unimare to the NSO, as explicitly stated in the contract between the parties that provided for the reimbursement of expenses. More specifically, the court found that (i) the U.S. Naval Service Order had actually reimbursed any fees paid by Unimare, pursuant to a specific contractual duty, and (ii) the tariff increase had not caused the U.S. Naval Service Order to switch to another supplier, because the new fees equally applied to all operators. Therefore, since Unimare had entirely passed on the tariff increase to its client, it could claim no damages.

More generally, Italian courts have often dealt with the issue of passing-on in the context of tax or subsidy refund cases, because under Italian law the public administration is not required to refund illegally levied taxes if it is able to prove

---

terzi, e così ai consumatori finali [...] [o]*nde a costoro spetterebbe il risarcimento del danno per l'esborso non voluto*').

20 Court of Appeal of Cagliari, judgment of 23 January 1999, *Unimare vs. Geasar*.

that the claimant has passed on the charge to its customers.[21] In these cases, the courts have maintained that (i) refund to the claimant of an illegally levied tax, a charge which the claimant has already passed on to its customers, does not necessarily imply unjust enrichment; (ii) the claimant may obtain damages for any harm caused by the undue or discriminatory application of the tax (e.g., the shortage of goods imported from other countries); and (iii) the claimant may also obtain damages for any reduction in its sales that was caused by the passing-on (i.e., by an increase in prices aimed at compensating an increase in costs caused by the illegally applied tax).[22] With regard to indirect purchasers' standing, this is generally recognized in national case law. In *Indaba v. Juventus* (cited above), the Court of Appeals of Turin maintained that the actual victims of Juventus's abuse were its football supporters (who had been forced to spend more than they would have otherwise), rather than the travel agency. The court thus stated in an *obiter* that, because of the passing-on, those indirect customers 'would be the ones entitled to claim damages for the overcharges they did not want' (our translation from Italian). Indirect purchasers are also entitled to sue the antitrust infringer for damages (App. Roma, 31 marzo 2008).

5 Recent Developments in France, Germany, and the United Kingdom

In concluding my remarks on national case-law, it seems useful to mention the approach recently taken by French and German courts with respect to the POD issue. Certainly the difference of opinion is striking between the two national judges and the references they make to the above mentioned main conceptions of antitrust private enforcement, as being divided between deterrence and compensation.

First: In France, a recent judgment of the French Commercial Supreme Court recognized the POD in an antitrust damages claim, following on the *Synthetic ly-*

---

21 According to the Court of Cassation in a tax refund case, '*in our legal system, and particularly in the tax sector, there is no general principle which would rule out the recipient's duty to return undue payments when the payer has already obtained elsewhere the restitution of the unduly paid sum*' (judgment of 24 May 2005, no. 10939). By the same token, absent special circumstances, any indemnifications collected owing to an own insurance policy do not reduce the damages that the injured party is entitled to claim from the defendant (see, e.g., Court of Cassation, judgments of 12 May 2003, no. 7269, and 15 April 1993, no. 4475).

22 See, for all instances, Court of Cassation, judgment of 24 May 2005, No. 10939, cited above. With respect to a previous law, pursuant to which claimants could obtain a refund only if they proved that the illegally levied taxes had not been passed on to their customers, the Constitutional Court stated that '*the inversion of the burden of proof*', aimed at requiring from the claimant '*the (negative) proof of the absence of passing on*' was so manifestly unreasonable as to violate the Italian Constitution (Constitutional Court, judgment of 9 July 2002, no. 332).

sine cartel decision.[23] Doux Aliments, a poultry farmer group and indirect purchaser of lysine, has sued the production company that was fined by the European Commission (Ajinomoto) before French courts. In 2009, the Paris Court of Appeal awarded damages amounting to €380,000, rebutting the POD by stating that it was irrelevant to decide whether the claimant could have passed the overcharge on to its clients.[24] On appeal brought by the cartel participant, the French Supreme Court overturned the prior judgment, stating that 'awarding damages without assessing whether Doux Aliments had fully or partly passed on to its clients the overcharge resulting from AE's infringement could have resulted in an unjust enrichment'.[25]

This approach has been further confirmed by the Paris Court of Appeal. In a judgment issued in February 2011, the Court dismissed the direct purchasers' claims, noting that claimants did not demonstrate they 'were faced with a supply price increase without having the possibility to pass it on to their clients, this assertion being insufficiently evidenced by concrete demonstrative elements'.[26]

It should be noted that the judgment of the French Supreme Court confirms the one already adopted in a prior follow-on action regarding the *Vitamins* case.[27] In that case, given that the cartel had an actual effect on prices paid by end consumers, as ascertained by the European Commisison, the claimant (an indirect purchaser) had to demonstrate that it 'not only did not increase its sale price to consumers as was claimed, but that moreover it would have been impossible for it to have done so'.[28]

It follows that direct and indirect purchasers (other than end consumers) who claim damages occurred as a result of an anti-competitive overcharge have to demonstrate that they did not pass the higher costs on to the next level, especially where final prices actually increased as a result of the cartel. One may infer a sort of reinforced presumption of passing-on in favour of end consumers, whereby direct and indirect purchasers have to demonstrate the impossibility of passing the damage on in order to claim the damages from the producer. Indeed, this approach seems to place a further burden on claimants and, potentially, could eventually discourage private actions, given that direct and indirect purchasers are more confident in suing infringers before national courts. At the same time, POD would become an important instrument for defendants.

---

23 Chambre commercial de la Cour de cassation, judgment of 15 July 2010.

24 '*La circonstance que les société DOUX auraient été en mesure de répercuter ce surcoût sur les hausses de prix du produit est sans incidence sur l'étendue du droit des appelantes à réparation*' (Paris Court of Appeals, judgment of 10 Juin 2009).

25 See Parmentier H.-Descote M., *The French Commercial Supreme Court validates the passing-on defence in a follow-on action based on the lysine cartel*, 15 June 2010, e-Competitions Bulletin June 2010.

26 Paris Court of Appeals, judgment of 16 February 2011 (our translation).

27 Tribunal de Commerce Nanterre, 11 May 2006.

28 Original: '*non seulement n'a pas augmenté ses prix de ventes aux consommateurs comme elle le soutient mais surtout qu'elle était dans l'impossibilité de procéder à une telle augmentation*'.

Second: In Germany, literature argues that POD can be based on a 'consistent application of the 'adjustment of benefits principle' (*compensatio lucri cum damno*), according to which the defendant must establish that the purchaser of its goods or services managed to reduce its loss by passing on the excessive prices to its own customers.[29]

In this regard, it should be noted that in a judgment related to the *Vitamins* cartel, the Karlsruhe Higher Regional Court refused to award compensation to direct customers, based on the POD argued by defendants.[30] Specifically, the Court based its ruling on the necessity to assess damages by taking into account the overall economic effect in its entirety, which includes an examination as to whether the customers in question were in turn able to pass on their cost increase to their own customers.

More recently – and following an amendment to the German Act against Restraints of Competition that entered into force in 2005[31] – the same Court has taken a different stance on POD.[32] In a follow-on suit concerning the *Carbonless Paper* cartel, the Karlsruhe Higher Court awarded €100,000 in damages to an indirect purchaser, a printing firm which purchased paper from the subsidiary of a cartel participant. The relevance of this ruling lies in that it lays out two main principles: (i) indirect purchasers do not have the right to claim damages, given that they are not directly affected by the infringement (an exception applies if the potential cartel victim has purchased products from a wholly-owned subsidiary of a cartelist)[33]; and (ii) the defendant is not entitled to advance POD in order to reduce the damage claim.

Importantly, the Court held that, although in principle defendants could prove the passing-on of the damage, allowing the passing-on defense in cartel damages cases would impede an efficient enforcement of EU law (citing Manfredi) as it

---

29 Böge and Ost, 'Up and Running, or is it? Private Enforcement – the Situation in Germany and Policy Perspectives', 19 *European Competition Law Review* (2006), 200.

30 Judgment of the Higher Regional Court of Karlsruhe, 28 January 2004, *Vitaminpreise, Neue Juristische Wochenschrift* 2004, 2243. See Thomas L., *Several German courts of first instance decide on damages claims brought by the customers of the vitamins cartel (Vitaminpreise)*, in e-Competitions Bulletin, 2004, noting that this approach was not followed in a similar cartel damages suit by the Regional Court of Dortmund, which eventually awarded compensation (only German text available at: http://ec.europa.eu/competition/antitrust/national_courts/court_2004_023_de.pdf).

31 According to A§33, '*If a good or service is purchased at an excessive price, a damage shall not be excluded on account of the resale of the good or service*'.

32 Judgment of the Higher Regional Court of Karlsruhe, 11 June 2010

33 With respect to the ECJ precedents *Courage* and *Manfredi*, the Court noted that both cases did not concern damages claims of indirect purchasers. For this reason the Court held that both precedents could not be consulted on the question of the standing of indirect purchasers. Moreover, the Court held that the legal materials of the new Section 33 of the ARC would show that the legislator intended to limit the standing to direct purchasers in order to avoid multiple liability of the defendant.

would lead to a decrease of the level of deterrence.[34] The standing of potential cartel victims is therefore limited to direct purchasers based on the argument that this group is in the best position to prove damages. In this context, the court explicitly rejected the view taken by another court of appeals in October 2009[35] that stated that direct and indirect purchasers are entitled to cartel damages as joint and several creditors. Following these conflicting decisions, the Federal Court of Justice overturned the Karlsruhe Court of Appeal's judgment and held that indirect customers also have standing to bring damages actions, provided that damages were passed-on by the direct customers to the indirect customers. However, indirect customers bear the burden of proof for such a passing-on of damages, and to this regard it is not sufficient to show a price increase on the downstream market. Instead, it has to be analyzed whether the market conditions make it likely that damages were passed on.[36]

Third: In the United Kingdom, POD was successfully leveraged by a defendant in order to block the admissibility of a representative action brought by a direct purchaser on behalf of 'other direct or indirect purchasers of air freight services the prices for which were so inflated'.[37] With reference to the second requirement stipulated for introducing representative actions by claimants (i.e., that the relief sought must be 'equally beneficial for all members of the class'), the Chancellor observed that there was 'an inevitable conflict between the claims of different members of the class' insofar as damages suffered by a member of the class 'will depend on where in the chain of distribution he came and who if anyone in that chain had absorbed or passed on the alleged inflated price' (*id.*, § 36). Significantly, the court rejected the possibility of introducing in the English court the US *Hanover Shoe* rule denying a defendant the possibility of relying on POD.

The judgment was later upheld by the UK Court of Appeal, which in principle seems to confirm the admissibility of Passing-on Defence for defendants by stating that 'members of the represented class do not have the same interest in recovering damages for breach of competition law if a defence is available in answer to the claims of some of them, but not to the claims of others: for example, if BA could successfully run a particular defence against those who had passed on the inflated price, but not against others. If there is liability to some customers and not to others, they have different interests, not the same interest, in the action'.[38]

---

34 Decision of the Karlsruhe Court of Appeal (OLG Karlsruhe) of May 12, 2010, 6 U 118/05 (Kart) (08)

35 Judgment of the Berlin Court of Appeal, October 1, 2009, ref. 2 U 17/03Kart.

36 Judgment of the Federal Court of Justice (BGH), June 28, 2011 (case no. KZR 75/10).

37 High Court of England and Wales, 8 April 2009, *Emerald Supplies v. British Airways Plc* [2009] EWHC 741 (Ch). This was a follow-on action concerning the *Air Freight Services* cartel. The claimant was a direct purchaser of freight services from British Airways and sought damages for infringement of EC competition law rules and regulations.

38 UK Court of Appeal, *Emerald Supplies Limited v. British Airways* [2010] EWCA Civ. 1284.par. 64.

6 Practical Issues in Estimating Passing-on

POD and indirect-purchaser standing make it necessary to estimate passing-on within the context of damages allocation and quantification. That can indeed be a rather complex issue, eventually requiring the judge to apply equitable methods or presumptions in order to assess the *quantum* that has been passed-on.

Toward this end, economic literature has tried to establish workable models for calculating passing-on.[39] These models rely primarily on a 'decomposition' of the claimant's lost profits into three effects:

- Direct Cost Effect: the price overcharge (the cartel input price minus the but-for input price), multiplied by the total inputs purchased from the cartel;
- Pass-on Effect: the increase in revenue that follows if the claimant passes part of the input price increase on to its customers in the form of a higher output price; and
- Output Effect: representing the lost profits associated with any sales lost as a consequence of the higher input price set by the passing-on claimant.

While the direct cost effect is always negative and represents a loss borne by the direct purchaser, the pass-on is always positive, thus counteracting at least in part the direct damages suffered as a consequence of the initial price overcharge. In this assessment, the output effect deriving from the passing-on would eventually determine the overall effect of the anti-competitive practice on the claimant: in fact, the output effect could override the pass-on effect, thus leaving the claimant with damages to be redressed <u>or</u> to be compensated for by the pass-on, ultimately to the claimant's advantage.

Therefore, the magnitude of these effects depends largely on the market circumstances of each case, and in particular on:

1. The degree of competition in the downstream market:

- In a market characterized by perfect competition, a marginal cost increase affecting all firms in the market can be expected to be passed on *in full*. At the same time, the output effect is non-existent, since lost sales do not reduce the original margin.
- On the contrary, in an imperfect competition structure, the pass-on can be very significant (i.e., a monopolist is expected to pass on 50% of a marginal cost increase to its customers) and the resulting output effect even moreso: in the extreme case of a cartelized downstream market, the output effect may even fully offset the pass-on;[40]

---

39 See Parlak, see *supra* note 4, p. 37; Van Dijk and Verboven, *supra* note 6, p. 5.

40 J.-P. Van der Veer and A. Lofaro, 'Estimating Pass-On', *The CPI Antitrust Journal*, May 2010, p. 3; Van Dijk and Verboven, see *supra* note 6, p. 8.

2. The number of firms affected by the cost increase:

- If some but not all downstream competitors have incurred higher input costs, their ability to pass on these higher costs will necessarily be somewhat constrained given that other competitors will have been able to leave their prices unchanged.
- Moreover, the output effect can be exacerbated by an increased likelihood that passing-on firms will lose market shares to rival firms unaffected by higher input costs.

Other factors that may be relevant to the assessment of pass-on effects include:

- Demand Elasticity: if the demand is inelastic (because of price-insensitive customers), firms tend to pass on a larger part of the price overcharge given that few customers will stop purchasing as a direct result of an increase in price. Conversely, if demand is very elastic (because of price-sensitive customers), firms tend to pass on a smaller part of the price overcharge.
- Buyer Power: passing-on phenomena are more likely when downstream customers cannot oppose a material countervailing buyer power.
- Margins: undertakings with high margins can potentially pass on less of the overcharge, since they may absorb it by lowering their mark-ups in order to sustain demand.
- Competition Constraints: constraints imposed by competition among other players may induce a firm not to pass on its cost increases in order to avoid any loss of sales.

Access to empirical data, in principle, makes it possible to estimate the actual pass-on rates relevant to any given case. However, access to such data (i.e., the precise data on a defendant's actual prices and costs) is not always guaranteed under national procedural laws. Alternatively, complex econometric models can be construed by both the claimant and the defendant in order to determine the 'but-for' scenario at the downstream market level and ultimately define the overcharge that is actually being passed-on.[41]

7 Concluding Remarks: Recent Initiatives on Collective Redress and Action for Damages

As we mentioned in the introductory remarks, after the White Paper and the 2009 Draft Directive, the Commission's initiatives in the field of competition enforcement have been suspended, at least temporarily, and a new consultation on collective redress has been launched, which aims at defining a new general framework for collective enforcement.

[41] *See* Oxera, *supra* note 1, at p. 116 and followings.

Collective redress has been at the heart of EU initiatives on private enforcement of competition law since the Green and White Papers were issued. It was quite evident to the Commission that victims rarely bring actions individually when they have suffered low-value damages, and that therefore, in cases where the damages caused by an infringement are fragmented and diffuse, almost no compensation is granted to the victims. Thus, absurdly, the more diffuse the damage is (i.e., the greater the number of victims involved) the less likely it is that any action for damages will be filed, with the consequence that an infringer may retain an illegitimate profit from the violation, even after a fine is imposed by a competition authority. Three basic factors influence this outcome: the disadvantageous risk/benefit ratio for a single complainant in filing such an action; the difficulties in identifying and demonstrating the violation, the damages suffered, and their causal link; and the fact that the cost of civil litigation is often higher than whatever compensation may be awarded.

Therefore, in order to improve both access to justice as well as the efficiency of civil litigation, and to ensure that victims do receive proper compensation, it is crucial that a mechanism of collective redress be established. The Commission is well aware of this need, and in the White Paper it has proposed two separate procedural instruments laid out in the Draft Directive: (i) opt-in collective actions[42] and (ii) representative actions.[43]

The mechanisms are considered to be complementary. Opt-in mechanisms correspond more closely with European legal culture; however, in comparison with opt-out mechanisms, they are more complicated since they require the identification of the claimants as well as the identification and demonstration of the damage suffered by each plaintiff. Opt-out actions, by granting the advantage of a wider representation of the victims, are by contrast more efficient and offer greater deterrence and corrective-justice effects, albeit they are also more likely to lead to excessive litigation.

---

42 The opt-in collective action combines in one single procedure the claims by all victims of the infringement who have expressed their intention to file an action and that are all equally party of the procedure. This type of action has the advantage of making litigation more attractive (including low-damage victims) by improving the risk/benefit ratio and allowing the claimants to share evidence in the same proceeding. This kind of collective action is closer to the legal traditions of the Member State than the opt-out action that is more linked to the US legal culture.

43 Representative actions, by contrast, allow a 'qualified entity', representing interests of a category or of a defined group of subjects, to bring an action for damages on behalf of the individuals or companies represented who are not in this case party to the proceeding. The interests represented must be sufficiently precise as to clearly individuate the subjects represented and allegedly harmed. The Draft Directive and the White Paper suggested the establishment of two different kinds of qualified entities: (1) entities, representing legitimate and defined interests and having determined requirements set by law, which are designated in advance by each Member State; (2) entities which are certified on an ad hoc basis by each Member State regarding a particular antitrust infringement.

The scope of the new initiative is wider by far than the one discussed in the 2008 White Paper. Indeed, in light of stakeholders' worries about possible 'inconsistencies between the different Commission initiatives on collective redress'[44], its scope of application virtually covers private enforcement of 'any EU legislation creating substantive rights'.[45] At the same time, the scope of the intervention seems to be a bit narrower, given that its main focus is on mechanisms and procedures intended to grant effective access to justice by identifying 'common legal principles on collective redress' (para. 12). Furthermore, the subsidiarity principle requires that 'any action at EU level should address the specific cross-border dimension of collective redress', thereby limiting possible direct interference in national procedure (*id.*, para. 14).

In any case, collective redress mechanisms are tightly linked to the enforcement scenarios that POD would introduce in private antitrust litigation. In fact, allowing defendants to claim POD necessitates that effective mechanisms for indirect purchasers and consumers be in place in order to avoid any potential unjust enrichment by infringers that would ultimately result in under-compensation and under-deterrence. Therefore, the new initiative on collective redress aims to encompass not only the interests of consumers, but of 'EU citizens and business' (*id.*, para. 7).

Conversely, even without a rebuttable presumption concerning passing-on in the interests of indirect purchasers, a workable mechanism of collective redress may offer claimants more effective means to allege and demonstrate the fact of passing-on and consequently their own standing. Ultimately, they are meant to represent a means to balance and counteract the procedural strength of defendants in antitrust claims, thereby guaranteeing a fair and effective judicial process. Indeed, 'collective redress is a matter of fundamental rights'.[46]

Following the consultation, the Commission is now undertaking the 'definition of a general legal framework for collective redress' and, subsequently, 'this framework will be used to launch specific legislative initiatives in the different policy domains'.[47]

44 Reding, Almunia and Dalli, 'Renfrocer la coherence de l'approche en matiere de recours collectif: prochaines etapes' (Brussels, 5 October 2010), para. 11.

45 EU Commission, *Towards a Coherent European Apporach to Collective Redress* (Brussels, 4 February 2011), para. 7.

46 The Charter of Fundamental Rights of the EU establishes the right to effective remedy for everyone whose rights and freedoms are violated (Art. 47(1); see also Art. 19(1) of the EU Treaty, incorporating the principle of effective judicial protection).

47 Almunia, 'Common standards for group claims across the EU', Speech/10/554 (Valladolid, 15 October 2010). In the wake of stakeholders' responses and the position of the European Parliament, the Commission confirmed the intention to pursue an horizontal approach on this matter. This would allow to define common rules for all policy fields in which scattered harm frequently occurs and where consumers and SMEs struggle in their claims for compensation. After the consultation, the Commission adopted the Communication 'Towards a European Framework for Collective Redress' (COM(2013) 401 final), and a Commission Recommendation on common principles for injunctive and compensatory collective redress mechanisms in the Member States concerning violations of rights granted under Union Law (C(2013) 3539 final).

More recently, in June 2013, the Commission finalized a new proposal for a directive on certain rules governing actions for damages for infringements of competition law. [48] The Proposal is intended to pursue two "inextricably linked" goals, namely: i) ensuring the effectiveness of Articles 101 and 102 TFEU; and ii) creating a more uniform level playing field for undertaking and citizens. The latter objective requires amending national provisions governing damage actions and, based upon Article 114 TFEU, the Proposal seeks to introduce uniform provision on certain procedural issues, such as disclosure of evidence and the treatment of leniency documentation. [49]

The new initiative deals specifically with POD and indirect consumer standing. To this regard, the Proposal confirms the strict compensation approach laid down in the 2009 Draft Directive (*see* above par. 3). Indeed, it explicitly recognises the possibility for the infringing undertaking to invoke the passing-on as a defence (as well as the burden of prooving it, which rests on the defendant). At the same time, the proposal denies such a defence 'in situations where the overcharge was passed on to natural or legal persons at the next level of the supply chain for whom it is legally impossible to claim compensation'. [50] The latter provision aims at avoiding unjustified enrichment by the infringer, where the party actually hit by the anticompetitive conduct is indeed prevented from claiming compensation (for example, by reason of national rules governing access to the court or other procedural or substantive requirements). It remains however unclear under which circumstances such legal impossibility can be invoked, and how to avoid that direct customers are finally over-compensated for damages thay did not suffer. [51]

Article 13 then defines standing of indirect or end-consumers. It lays down the general principle that indirect consumers claiming damages from an anticompetitive conduct shall proove the passing-on of the overcharge. Futhermore, in order to ease such a burden, it provides for a presumpion in favor of indirect customers which contracted with a direct customer and purchased the goods or services subject of the infringement. Acknowledging the complexity of such evalutation, especially where the exact existence and scope of the passing-on is essential in order to

48 Proposal for a Directive of the European Parliament and of the Council on certain rules governing actions for damages under national law for infringements of the competition law provisions of the Member States and of the European Union (2013/0185 COD), Strasbourg, 11.6.2013 (the 'Proposal').

49 To this regard the Proposal recalls two institutonal initiatives, namely the resolution of the Heads of the European Competition Authorities on the 'Protection of leniency material in the context of civil damages actions', and the European Parliament resolutions of 2 February 2012 on 'Towards a Coherent European Approach to Collective Redress' which emphasised that public enforcement in the competition field is essential, and called on the Commission to ensure that private enforcement does not compromise the effectiveness of either the leniency programmes or settlement procedures.

50 See Commission's Proposal, p. 17 and Article 12.

51 See Reindl A., The European Commission's Package on Private Enforcement in Competition Cases, CPI (August 2013-1), which notes that Art. 12 'is a defensible solution, though, but only if one accepts a deterrence maximizing rationale. 17 It has nothing to do with compensation'.

allow standing or award damages in favor of indirect customer or end-consumers, the Proposal recommends Member States to grant national courts 'powers to estimate which share of the overcharge was passed on'. [52] Eventually, [53] Article 15 deals with coordinating possible actions brought by claimants from other levels in the supply chain. The Commission is fully aware of possible inconsistencies that may occur in parallel actions against the same infringer by customers or consumers variously positioned in the supply chain, and calls national judges to take 'due account' of such actions and of the judgments deriving therefrom.

The much awaited Proposal is surely to be welcomed and, overall, its provisions seem to encourage private litigation. It remains to be seen how the proposed solutions on certain technical and specific issues could work in national experience, as well as their practical consequences. In any event, it is desirable that within the legislative debate following the Proposal, the provisions contained therein shall be further defined and specified.

---

52 To make it easier for national courts to quantify harm, the Commission has also published non-binding guidance on this topic in its Communication on quantifying harm in actions for damages based on breaches of Article 101 or 102 TFEU (C(2013) 3440).

53 Article 14 confirms that loss of profits are inherent in damages' claim by the injuerd party. Indeed, as noted supra, where a loss is passed on, the price increase by the direct purchaser is likely to lead to a reduction in the volume sold. Therefore, the loss of profit, as well as the actual loss that was not passed on (in the case of partial passing-on) remains antitrust harm for which the injured party can claim compensation (Proposal, p. 17).

Competition Law Enforcement in England and Wales

Sebastian Peyer[1]

1 Introduction

Competition law enforcement in England and Wales underwent significant changes in the 21st century with the entry into force of the Competition Act 1998 in 2000 and the Enterprise Act 2002 in 2004. [2] The Competition Act and the Enterprise Act have altered both the substantive provisions applicable within the UK as well as the institutional framework for the enforcement of UK and European competition law.[3] The reform aligned UK with European law, created enforceable national prohibitions, and modified enforcement institutions. The domestic system of competition law now parallels the Community rules on competition. Chapter I of the Competition Act (Chapter I Prohibition) prohibits agreements which have as their object or effect the prevention, restriction, or distortion of competition within the United Kingdom.[4] The Chapter II Prohibition bans the abuse of a dominant position by a firm if this abuse affects trade within the UK. Like the Chapter I Prohibition, the restrictions on unilateral conduct are modelled after Community law. The only difference between Community rules and national law is that a breach of national law is defined as having an effect on trade within the UK.[5]

---

1 The author gratefully acknowledges the support of the ESRC Centre for Competition Policy of the University of East Anglia. I would like to thank Ali Massadeh for his helpful comments. The article was written in 2011 and last updated in March 2013.

2 Although reference is made to UK, this article will only deal with the public and private enforcement in England and Wales.

3 The reform repealed, for instance, the Restrictive Trade Practices Acts 1976 and 1977, the Resale Prices Act 1976 and the provisions on anti-competitive practices in the Competition Act 1980.

4 Section 2 Competition Act 1998.

5 For the scope of this requirement see *Aberdeen Journals v. Office of Fair Trading* [2005] CAT 4 and *P&S Amusements v. Valley House Leisure* [2006] EWHC 1510 (Ch). With an analysis Ben Rayment, 'The Consistency Principle: Section 60 of the Competition Act 1998' in Barry J Rodger (ed), *Ten Years of UK Competition Law Reform* (Dundee University Press, 2010), 81.

While the substantive provisions do not differ greatly from EU competition law – Community law is also used to interpret the national norms[6] – the institutional and procedural framework has some features which set it apart from most continental European enforcement systems. The Office of Fair Trading (OFT) is the primary enforcement agency empowered to enforce consumer and competition law. The Enterprise Act created a special body, the Competition Appeal Tribunal (CAT), which reviews public enforcement decisions and adjudicates monetary private follow-on claims. Private enforcement benefited from enforceable substantive national provisions introduced by the Competition Act as well as from advantageous rules for bringing follow-on actions implemented with the Enterprise Act. Although the new enforcement framework has had less than a decade to fine-tune and settle, the OFT and the Competition Commission (CC), both of which are responsible for market investigations and Phase II merger investigations, will be abolished and their functions transferred to the Competition and Markets Authority (CMA).[7]

The extensive changes at the beginning of the millennium and the proposed new reform compel to take a closer look at how public and private antitrust enforcement have developed through the present. While it is unrealistic to expect the new Competition Act to have an instant, far-reaching impact within its first years in force, now, after a decade of its existence, some traits characteristic of the enforcement system are emerging. This article surveys the current state of competition law enforcement in England & Wales. It examines the features of the new enforcement framework created by the Competition Act and the Enterprise Act as well as the key decisions that are likely to shape the future of competition law enforcement. This chapter focuses on the progress that has been made in England and Wales since the Competition Act 1998 came into force in 2000, largely excluding developments prior to its implementation. The first part of the text analyses the public enforcement of competition law while the second part deals with private enforcement of UK competition law. The third section offers concluding remarks.

---

6 See also section 60 Competition Act 1998.

7 See Department of Business, Innovation and Skills (BIS) 'A Competition Regime for Growth: A Consultation on Options for Reform. Impact Assessment' (March 2011); Stephen Wilks, 'Institutional Reform and the Enforcement of Competition Policy in the UK', 7 *European Competition Journal* (2011), 1–23. James Aitken and Alison Jones, 'Reforming a World Class Competition Regime: The Government's Proposal for the Creation of a Single Competition and Markets Authority' forthcoming in *Competition Law Journal* (2011).

2 Public Enforcement

This section considers the role of the OFT and the Competition Appeal Tribunal. It briefly describes the enforcement institutions, investigates the relationship between national and EU law enforcement, and summarizes the history of criminal and civil sanctions.

2.1 The Institutions

The Office of Fair Trading is the central competition enforcement agency in England and Wales. It was established with the Enterprise Act and replaced the Director of Fair Trading.[8] The Director's functions were allocated to the OFT because it was no longer considered appropriate to vest an individual with the considerable powers of market oversight.[9] The OFT's mission is to 'make markets work well for consumers' and to ensure that markets are competitive, innovative, and efficient.[10] In its most recent annual plan the OFT described its tasks as the enforcement of competition and consumer laws, analysis of markets, merger control, and advocacy.[11] It shares the task of enforcing Chapter I and II Prohibitions as well as EU competition law with various sector regulators whose powers are concurrent in regulated markets.[12] Certain tasks under the Enterprise Act, such as merger review and market monitoring, are institutionally divided between the OFT and the Competition Commission.[13] The OFT has the power to initiate proceedings (Phase I), and the Competition Commission has the power to decide the cases that are referred to it (Phase II).[14]

---

8 The Fair Trading Act 1973 introduced the Director of Fair Trading.

9 For the changes of the institutional structure with the coming into force of the Enterprise Act 2002 see Cosmo Graham, 'The Enterprise Act 2002 and Competition Law', 67 *The Modern Law Review* (2004), 273–288; Richard Whish, *Competition Law* (Oxford University Press, 6th ed. 2009), 64. See also Whish for the internal structure of the OFT.

10 OFT, *Annual Plan 2011–12*, OFT 1294 (2011).

11 Other areas of activity are licensing and supervisory work in the consumer credit and estate agency markets, including anti-money laundering supervision, education and consumer advice through Consumer Direct.

12 The following regulators can also enforce the provisions of the Competition Act: Office of Communications (OFCOM), the Gas and Electricity Markets Authority (OFGEM), the Northern Ireland Authority for Energy Regulation (OFREG NI), the Director General of Water Services (OFWAT), the Office of Rail Regulation (ORR) and the Civil Aviation Authority (CAA). See also the OFT's guidance on the 'Concurrent Application to Regulated Industries' OFT 405 (December 2004).

13 Market investigations and mergers will not be discussed in this article.

14 Sector regulators and the Secretary of State also have the right to refer investigations to the Competition Commission.

The Competition Appeal Tribunal (CAT) is an important part of the institutional framework for both public and private enforcement.[15] It functions as a review body for public enforcement decisions and as a forum for private follow-on damages actions.[16] The Competition Appeal Tribunal reviews CC, OFT, and regulatory decisions that have been made under the Competition Act. The CAT is an independent judicial body comprised of specialists which hears competition law and regulatory cases. With respect to public competition law enforcement, the CAT is the appeal instance for complaints against decisions made by the OFT and sector regulators.[17] CAT decisions can also be appealed based on points of law and with respect to the amount of sanctions; appeals are made to the Court of Appeal, conditional to the CAT's permission. If penalties are imposed on parties for the failure to comply with OFT notices, they are reviewed by the CAT. Appeals against OFT decisions are appeals on the merits of the case. Consequently, the CAT has the power to replace the OFT's assessment with its own findings, and it has done so in the past.[18] The Tribunal is a specialized court in which it is not necessary that ordinary members be lawyers. Thus, the case-hearing panels can be composed according to the demands of case; for example, the panel will consist of economists when the case at hand deals with technical regulatory issues. The number of public and private cases brought before the CAT has grown steadily over the years.[19]

2.2 Compliance with EU Law

The Competition Act introduced a 'consistency principle' in the application of national competition law.[20] Section 60 states that questions arising under the Competition Act are dealt with in a manner which is consistent with the treatment of corresponding questions arising in Community law, with respect to any relevant differences between the provisions concerned. The courts, the CAT, and the OFT must take into account relevant statements of the European Commission and the European Courts. Especially in the early days of the Competition Act, some cases dealt with disputes over the interpretation of the 'consistency principle', although it is said that the importance of Section 60 is overstated given that the substantial UK competition law provisions resemble Community rules.[21] Section 60 has been

15 Before the coming into force of the Enterprise Act, the CAT used to be known as the Competition Commission Appeal Tribunals.

16 For the CAT's functions in private antitrust proceedings see the next section on private enforcement.

17 If the CAT does not have jurisdiction, the OFT's behaviour may be subject to scrutiny before the Administrative Court.

18 *ME Burgess, JJ Burgess and SJ Burgess v. Office of Fair Trading* [2005] CAT 25.

19 David Bailey, 'The Early Case Law of the Competition Appeal Tribunal', in Barry J Rodger (ed), *Ten Years of UK Competition Law Reform* (Dundee University Press, 2010), 27, 32.

20 David Bailey, 'The Impact of Pernod v. OFT on Section 60 and the Enforcement of UK Competition Law', 3 *Competition Law Journal* (2004), 153.

21 Rayment (*supra* note 5).

applied to the 'effect on trade within the UK' test[22] and to the procedural question of third party rights in investigations.[23] With respect to the latter, this has helped to clarify the law which previously had not governed this issue. However, the prediction that this provision would lead to a significant amount of litigation did not come to pass.[24] The main issues concerning competition law enforcement do not stem from the interpretation of Community law but rather from the open-ended nature of competition law rules and their application to the facts of the case.[25]

Despite the inclusion of Section 60 in the Competition Act, the English courts do not show unconditional deference to the European Commission's findings in competition law cases. The House of Lords took a distinct stance in the private proceedings of *Inntrepreneur v. Crehan* – the case that prompted the ECJ to rule on the availability of damages in private antitrust proceedings.[26] The first-instance High Court disregarded evidence about the UK beer market that came from the Commission's *Whitebread* decision as it was not binding in the Crehan case.[27] The Court of Appeal determined that not taking the findings of the European Commission into account in a similar case could lead to a conflicting decision contrary to Article 16 of the Modernisation Regulation and the *Delimits* and *Masterfoods* standards.[28] The House of Lords overturned the Court of Appeal: as long as the legal and the factual context of the actual case is not completely identical with a Commission's decision, courts do not run the risk of adopting conflicting decisions should they arrive at different conclusions, even if the same market is concerned.[29]

2.3 Investigating Anticompetitive Conduct

The OFT opens an investigation into potentially anti-competitive conduct if there are 'reasonable grounds for suspecting' that EU or UK competition law has been violated pursuant to Section 25 of the Competition Act. The OFT is given discretion whether or not to conduct an investigation. Investigations into anti-competitive conduct can be based on written and reasoned third party complaints. The OFT offers pre-complaint discussions for third parties contemplating a complaint in order to help individuals decide whether or not it is worthwhile to commit

22 *Aberdeen Journal v. Office of Fair Trading* [2003] CAT 11, *P&S Amusements Ltd v. Valley House Leisure Ltd* [2006] EWHC 1510 (Ch).

23 *Pernod Ricard v. Office of Fair Trading* [2004] CAT 10.

24 Peter R Willis, 'Procedural Nuggets from the 'Klondike Clause': The Application of s. 60 of the Competition Act 1998 to the Procedures of the OFT', 20 *European Competition Law Review* (1999), 314–323.

25 Rayment (*supra* note 5).

26 *Crehan v. Inntrepreneur Pub* [2006] UKHL 38.

27 *Whitbread* (Case IV/35.079/F3) Commission Decision 99/230/EC [1999] OJ L88/26.

28 See Case C-234/89, *Delimitis v. Henninger Bräu AG* [1991] ECR I-935 and Case C-344/98, *Masterfoods Ltd v. HB Ice Cream Ltd* [2000] ECR I-11369.

29 *Crehan v. Inntrepreneur Pub* [2003] EWHC 1510 (Ch), *Crehan v. Inntrepreneur Pub* [2004] EWCA Civ 637.

their time and resources to filing a reasoned complaint. If an investigation is opened, the OFT can make use of its formal powers to obtain information. It can ask the firms under investigation to comply with an information request pursuant to Section 26 of the Competition Act, but it can also address customers, competitors, complainants, and others.

To supply misleading information or to refuse to comply with a request without a lawful excuse is a criminal offence.[30] Once a formal investigation has been opened, the OFT has the power to enter and search business and domestic premises ('dawn raid') and to seize documents, barring privileged communication. A business suspected of having violated a competition law cannot be forced to provide answers that would in turn violate their privilege against self-incrimination. However, it is difficult to establish when certain information is protected under this privilege or when such information must be disclosed in order to prove the breach of law.

The OFT can issue interim measures during its investigations.[31] In criminal cartel investigations, the OFT may seek evidence using covered or directed surveillance as well as gather information through informants.[32] If information requests and searches produce sufficient evidence of anti-competitive conduct, the OFT issues a statement of objection addressed to the firms concerned. The companies under scrutiny have the right to reply to the statement and, depending on their reply, may be subject to enforcement actions, including fines and directives. If a firm is found to have violated UK or EU competition law, it has the right to appeal the case on the merits to the Competition Appeal Tribunal.[33]

The OFT can also accept undertakings from the firms concerned in order to speed up proceedings. In cases where there is no evidence of anti-competitive behaviour, the competition authority may hand down a decision that there are no grounds for action. Investigations can also be closed on grounds of administrative priorities. As of March 21, 2011, the OFT began a one-year trial period in which a Procedural Adjudicator was assigned in order to quickly resolve procedural issues between the parties and the OFT's case team. The main aim was to implement a cost-effective and speedy mechanism meant to assist with disputes related to deadlines for responses, disclosure and submission of documents and the confidentiality thereof, and any other argument that might arise in the course of an investiga-

30 See sections 42 to 44 Competition Act.

31 Section 35 Competition Act.

32 Section 26 Regulation of Investigatory Powers Act 2000.

33 The OFT had issued a non-infringement decision for an alleged refusal to supply in *Harwood Park Crematorium* (Case CP/0055/02) OFT Decision CA98/06/2004 of 29 June 2004. The CAT set aside the OFT's decision finding that Harwood Park Crematorium abused its dominant position. *ME Burgess, JJ Burgess and SJ Burgess v. Office of Fair Trading* [2005] CAT 25. This also led to a private follow-on case in the CAT. *Burgess v. W Austin & Sons (Stevenage) Ltd* (Case 1088/5/7/07) which was settled.

tion.[34] If the OFT finds evidence of anti-competitive conduct it can, depending of the type of violation, commence criminal proceedings against individuals who engaged in cartel activities, apply for a director's disqualification order in court which would ban the individual from acting as director of a company,[35] or impose financial penalties and directives on firms.

2.4 The Cartel Offence and Company Director's Disqualification Orders

The Cartel Offence was introduced with the Enterprise Act 2002 and sanctions individuals who dishonestly engage in cartel agreements.[36] Section 188 of the Enterprise Act 2002 punishes an individual with unlimited fines and up to five years imprisonment if he or she dishonestly agrees with others to make or implement or to cause to be made or implemented a number of enumerated, strictly defined cartel arrangements such as price-fixing, limiting supply or production, sharing markets, or bid-rigging. The Cartel Offence applies to all individuals who violate the cartel prohibition, although the OFT grants immunity from criminal sanctions to individuals who come forward with information about cartels.[37] Individual immunity is granted in the form of 'no-action letters'. The individual has to admit that he or she participated in the cartel, provide the OFT with further information about the incriminating activity, and cannot have coerced others into the cartel.

Much criticism has been issued against the dishonesty requirement ('dishonestly agrees')[38] and it is likely to be removed from the new Cartel Offence in the reformed UK competition law enforcement system, according to the Enterprise and Regulatory Reform Bill 2012-2013. The cartel offence in its current form restricts criminal enforcement because dishonesty, as interpreted by the courts, is difficult to prove.[39] Juries, which are used in criminal trials, may struggle to find price fixing dishonest, especially against the background of a weak perception of criminality of cartels in the UK.[40] Only three businessmen have been sentenced for their

---

34 OFT, 'OFT announces Procedural Adjudicator trial as it publishes new competition act procedure guidance', Press release 27/11 of 02 March 2011.

35 Section 1 of the Company Director's Disqualification Act 1986.

36 For details see Jon Lawrence and Jane Moffat, 'A Dangerous New World – Practical Implications of the Enterprise Act 2002', 25 *European Competition Law Review* (2004), 1–4; Jeremy Lever and John Pike, 'Cartel Agreements, Criminal Conspiracy and the Statutory 'Cartel Offence': Part 1', 26 *European Competition Law Review* (2005), 90–97.

37 OFT, 'The cartel offence – Guidance on the issue of no-action letters for individuals' OFT 513 (2003).

38 Dishonesty is tested according to *R v. Ghosh* [1982] QB 1053, 75 Cr. AppR. 154 CA, 2 All ER 689, CA.

39 See for an overview Andreas Stephan, 'How Dishonesty Killed the Cartel Offence', *Criminal Law Review* (2011), 446–455.

40 Christopher Harding and Julian Joshua, *Regulating Cartels in Europe: A Study of Legal Control of Corporate Delinquency* (Oxford University Press, 1st ed. 2003), 51; Stephan (*supra* note 40).

participation in the *Marine Hoses Cartel*.[41] Although the OFT has brought one successful criminal case, the two other proceedings related to the cartel offence have shown flaws both in the design of the provision and in the OFT's case selection. The problematic dishonesty standard was discussed in the House of Lords' *Norris* decision, and the criminal proceedings launched against British Airways executives demonstrated the difficulties of building a criminal case.[42] In *Norris*, a US court indicted Ian Norris who, as the former CEO of Morgan Crucible, had allegedly been involved in the *Graphite* cartel.[43] The United States requested that Norris be extradited on the grounds that even prior to the enactment of the Enterprise Act Norris had satisfied the conditions of the common law offence of a conspiracy to defraud. Like the Cartel Offence, the common law offence is based on dishonesty. Ruling on the dishonesty standard, the House of Lords found that price fixing as such does not constitute dishonesty. The dishonesty standard is not satisfied by simply disguising the illicit conduct; rather, it requires aggregating circumstances.[44] This interpretation was criticized for having created a high bar for effective criminal prosecution.[45]

The latest criminal proceeding against BA executives collapsed spectacularly and has cast considerable doubts over the future of an unaltered Cartel Offence in the UK. Virgin Atlantic blew the whistle on an exchange of emails and telephone conversations with British Airways which allegedly lead to an increase in fuel surcharges. The OFT initiated criminal proceedings against four employees of BA, relying on the evidence it had obtained from Virgin Atlantic. After the trial had started Virgin produced new emails which had not previously been made available to the OFT or BA. Consequently, the OFT was forced to withdraw its case.[46] The OFT's unimpressive track record reveals the comparative difficulties of building a criminal trial versus carrying out administrative proceedings, the problems of the dishonesty test, and, finally, the OFT's inexperience in acting as a criminal prosecutor.[47] In the criminal cases that have so far been brought, the Cartel Offence has not lived up to the high expectations it excited when the Enterprise Act was first enacted.

---

41 *R v. Whittle, Brammar & Allison* (Marine Hose) [2008] EWCA Crim 2560. The defendants were arrested in the United States and a conviction (under UK law) was secured through a plea bargaining with the Department of Justice.

42 *Norris v. United States* [2008] UKHL 16; [2008] 1 A.C. 920.

43 *Electrical and mechanical carbon and graphite products* (Graphite Cartel) (Case C.38.359) Commission Decision 2004/420/EC [2004] OJ L125/45.

44 Ian Norris was finally extradited to the US and sentenced to 18 months in jail for conspiracy to obstruct justice. Ironically, his former employer Morgan Crucible received leniency from the European Commission for its participation in the Graphite Cartel.

45 Peter Whelan, 'Resisting the Long Arm of Criminal Antitrust Laws: Norris v. The United States', 72 *The Modern Law Review* (2009), 272–283; Angus MacCulloch, 'The Cartel Offence: Is Honesty the Best Policy?' in Barry J Rodger (ed.), *Ten Years of UK Competition Law Reform* (Dundee University Press 2010), 283.

46 OFT, 'OFT withdraws criminal proceedings against current and former BA executives', Press release 47/10 of 10 May 2010.

47 Stephan (*supra* note 40), p. 453.

The OFT has indicated that it will make more use of personal sanctions against executives, issuing new guidance on the disqualification of directors.[48] The OFT and sector regulators can request a court-imposed director's disqualification order (Section 9A of the Company Directors Disqualification Act 1986).[49] If an application for a director's disqualification order is successful, the individual concerned is banned from acting as director of a company; acting as receiver of a company's property; or in any way, whether directly or indirectly, being concerned or taking part in the promotion, formation, or management of a company.[50] The court will issue such an order if an undertaking of which that person is a director commits a breach of competition law and the court decides that person's conduct in his or her capacity as director makes him or her unfit to be concerned in the management of a company.

The maximum period of disqualification is 15 years. During the disqualification period it is a criminal offence to be the director of a company or to act in related duties. Individuals who act against the disqualification order are personally held liable for the debts of the company. The OFT can accept a competition disqualification undertaking instead of a court order. The OFT does not normally apply for a director's disqualification order against the director of a company that had sought leniency unless the director fails to cooperate under the terms stipulated in the leniency application.[51] Two of the three defendants in the Marine Hose criminal investigation were disqualified from executing director's duties for seven years, and the third defendant was prohibited from holding a director's position for five years. However, the orders were obtained under Section 2 of the Company Director's Disqualification Act 1986, which allows for a director to be disqualified for committing a criminal act. The OFT has not yet sought a director disqualification under Section 9(A).

2.5 The OFT's Fining Practice

The OFT may impose financial penalties on undertakings which have intentionally or negligently violated Article 101 or 102 TFEU or the Chapter I or Chapter II Prohibitions according to Section 36 of the Competition Act. The maximum penalty is set to ten per cent of the undertaking's worldwide annual turnover.[52] Minor

---

48 OFT, 'OFT sets out revised approach to director disqualifications', Press release 68/10 of 29 June 2010. See for more details on director's disqualification orders: Andreas Stephan, 'Disqualification Orders for Directors Involved in Cartels', 2(6) *Journal of European Competition Law & Practice* (2011), 537–550.

49 The Competition Disqualification Order was introduced with section 204 Enterprise Act.

50 Section 1 of the Company Director's Disqualification Act 1986.

51 OFT, 'Director disqualification orders in competition cases – an OFT guidance document', OFT 510 (2010).

52 OFT, 'OFT's Guidance as to the Appropriate Amount of a Penalty', OFT 423 (September 2012).

violations of Chapter I and Chapter II Prohibitions may be granted immunity from fines unless the breach in question is a price fixing agreement. The final penalty is calculated according to the turnover, and the OFT will take aggravating and mitigating factors into account. For example, it is considered to be aggravating if the company concerned was the leader of the infringing firms, undertook coercive measures, or continuously violated the law. The fine may be reduced if the illegality of the practice in question was genuinely uncertain, if the undertaking has installed a compliance programme, and if it has co-operated with the OFT. The OFT runs its own leniency programme for cartel violations, granting total immunity from fines to the first firm coming forward with information.[53] If the OFT has already started an investigation or possesses sufficient evidence to prove the illicit activity, the undertaking may not benefit from full immunity but fines may still be reduced by 100 per cent.

As of September 2011 the OFT has adopted 25 infringement decisions in relation to Chapter I and Chapter II.[54] After leniency and reductions through appeals are deducted, firms have paid more than £600 million in fines by November 2009.[55] The recent decisions have indicated two trends in enforcement: monetary sanctions imposed on firms have seemed to increase (although they are often lowered on appeal) while, at the same time, the OFT is also seeking early dispute resolutions with the firms involved ('settlements'). As for the trend toward higher fines, the £121.5 million imposed on British Airways for its collusion with Virgin Atlantic over fuel surcharges was the highest fine in a competition case at that time.[56] Yet, the £225 million penalty imposed in 2011 on the defendants in the *Tobacco* case for unlawful practices almost doubled the previous record sum for a single case, but the CAT quashed the OFT's decision in December 2011.[57] Of all the decisions the OFT has adopted so far only five investigations were concluded with a finding of a Chapter II violation.[58] As for the effect of its interventions, the OFT has conducted an *ex-post* assessment of its first infringement findings under

---

53 OFT, 'Leniency and no-action – OFT's guidance note on the handling of applications', OFT 803 (December 2008).

54 Wish counted 22 formal infringement decisions until the end of 2010. See Whish (*supra* note 10); Richard Whish, 'The Role of the OFT in UK Competition Law', in Barry J Rodger (ed.), *Ten Years of UK Competition Law Reform* (Dundee University Press, 2010), 1.

55 Whish (*supra* note 55), p. 12.

56 OFT, 'British Airways to pay record 121.5 million penalty in price fixing investigation' Press release 11/07 of 01 August 2007.

57 *Tobacco* (Case CE/2596-03) OFT Decision CA98/01/2010 of 16 April 2010; [2011] CAT 41.

58 *Napp Pharmaceutical Holdings Ltd and Subsidiaries* Decision of the Director General of Fair Trading CA98/2/2001 of 30 March 2001; *Aberdeen Journals I* Director General of Fair Trading CA98/5/2001 of 16 July 2001; *Abderdeen Journals II* (Case CE/1217/02) Director General of Fair Trading CA98/14/2002 of the 29 September 2002; *Cardiff Bus* (Case Case CE/5281/04) OFT Decision CA98/01/2008 of 18 November 2008; *Genzyme*, Director General of Fair Trading CA98/3/03 of 27 March 2003; *Reckitt Benckiser* (Case CE/8931/08) OFT Decision of 13 April 2011.

the Competition Act in *Napp*, including an academic review of this *ex-post* analysis.[59] The report states that the OFT's decision in *Napp* had a clear impact and enhanced competition for morphine products.

More recently the OFT, despite imposing record fines on companies, has relied on the cooperation of some or all firms under investigation in order to resolve cases.[60] The penalty guidelines encourage firms to cooperate, as cooperation may be rewarded with a reduced fine. The obvious advantage for the OFT is that the proceedings can be swiftly concluded and resources thereby saved. In spite of the discounts the fines are still significant, as for instance in the *Tobacco* case, where the OFT ordered twelve undertakings to pay an aggregated £225 million notwithstanding the leniency and cooperation discounts that were given to ten of the firms. Two tobacco manufacturers and ten retailers had allegedly manipulated the retail prices for tobacco products in the UK, linking retail prices for their tobacco products with the retail prices of competing products. Collusive agreements in the construction industry prompted the OFT to fine a number of companies in two separate proceedings.[61] Many of the firms involved in these cases cooperated with the OFT. In the *Bid-rigging* investigation, which involved 103 companies and a total penalty of £129 million, 33 undertakings received reduced fines under the leniency programme and 41 undertakings were given discounts of up to 35 per cent under settlement arrangements.[62] Overall, 25 companies appealed the fines to the CAT, of which six appellants also challenged the OFT's finding of an infringement. The CAT reduced the fines significantly – for some complainants by more than 90 per cent – and rejected the OFT's practice of applying a minimum deterrence threshold as being overly mechanistic.[63] The Tribunal criticized how the fines had been calculated, particularly the 'relevant turnover' chosen by the OFT and the starting point of five per cent as being excessive in light of the infringement. The OFT announced that it would rethink its fining policy and did not appeal the CAT's decision.[64] The OFT's investigation into anti-competitive practices in markets for dairy products was also aided by cooperation and resulted in fine

59 OFT, 'OFT evaluation of Napp case finds increased competition in morphine market', Press release No 63/11 (6 June 2011).

60 The first case terminated with an 'early resolution' decision was *Independent Schools*, OFT Decision CA98/05/2006 of 20 November 2006. See also OFT, 'Independent schools agree settlement' OFT Press release 88/06 (19 May 2006).

61 *Construction Recruitment Forum* (Case CE/7510-06) OFT Decision CA98/01/2009 of 29 September 2009; *Bid rigging in the construction industry in England* (Case: CE/4327-04) OFT Decision of 21 September 2010. In *Construction Recruitment Forum* the OFT found that eight companies had fixed prices for the supply of candidates to the construction industry. Two firms received leniency. Six firms received fines which were reduced on appeal. *CDI AndersElite Ltd and others v. Office of Fair Trading* [2011] CAT 8.

62 12 parties were given small reductions in fines after admitting to the violation.

63 *Kier Group plc and others v. Office of Fair Trading* [2011] CAT 3

64 OFT, 'OFT decides not to appeal recent Competition Appeal Tribunal judgments', Press release 61/11 (27 May 2011).

reductions.[65] However, despite cooperation with the OFT, the investigation turned out to be rather lengthy. Almost eight years after it had commenced scrutiny the OFT finally concluded its case, imposing £50 million on four supermarkets and five dairy processors. According to the OFT, the firms involved coordinated price increases for cheese and milk. One company, which had brought the collusive behaviour to the OFT's attention, benefited from complete immunity under the OFT's leniency programme. A number of firms received cooperation discounts once they admitted the breaches and facilitated the investigation. The OFT emphasized that the reductions were awarded in order to acknowledge the fact that the firms' concessions helped conserve OFT resources.[66] Nevertheless, in light of the eight years it took to conclude the investigation, irrespective of any appeals, one may doubt the cooperation strategy is effective in saving resources. It is also problematic that part of the investigation was dropped due to insufficient evidence, even after some firms had already admitted to this specific breach in 2007. The case against Morrison was completely withdrawn and Tesco received a no-contest penalty discount – a discretionary fine reduction – although it denied any wrongdoing. The only case in 2011 so far, *Reckitt Benckiser*, has been closed on the basis of an early resolution agreement in which Reckitt Benckiser admitted to violations of EU and UK competition law and agreed to pay a fine of £10.2 million.[67]

The OFT seems to focus on the pursuit of anti-competitive agreements, with the exception of its occasional scrutiny into dominant firms. It is sometimes criticized for its selection of cases and for the few infringement decisions it makes.[68] In light of its recent impact assessment, the OFT's work may well have an effect on markets. One must give the OFT credit for quickly establishing enforcement mechanisms, even if a bit more fine-tuning is needed in the way it calculates fines and brings criminal cases. The upsets and defeats the OFT has suffered are, to a certain extent, attending ills on the road to credible and predictable enforcement.

3 Private Enforcement

The development of private antitrust enforcement has also benefited from the overhaul of UK competition law. It is currently subject to further reform proposals that would introduce opt-out class actions for UK-domiciled claimants and extend the jurisdiction of the CAT. This section outlines the framework for private actions, scrutinizes the remedies available, and gives an account of key private cases.

---

65 *Dairy products retail pricing* (Case CE/3094-03) OFT Decision of 10 August 2011.

66 OFT, 'OFT fines certain supermarkets and processors almost £50 million in dairy decision', Press release 89/11 (08 August 2011).

67 *Reckitt Benckiser* (Case CE/8931/08) OFT Decision of 12 April 2011.

68 Whish (*supra* note 55), p. 14.

3.1 Legal Framework for Private Actions

The Competition Act introduced enforceable national prohibitions. As in all other EU member states, the modernisation of EU competition and the direct effect introduced with Article 101(3) TFEU have made private actions a more attractive option. The Competition Act and the Enterprise Act do not provide explicitly for private remedies for a breach of competition law, but the House of Lords already established in 1983 that a breach of competition law may give rise to a claim for damages.[69] The Enterprise Act introduced Sections 47A, 47B, and 58A in the Competition Act, and created the Competition Appeal Tribunal, giving it jurisdiction over damages and other monetary follow-on claims. Section 47A allows monetary follow-on claims to be brought before the CAT if the appeal process against decisions of the European Commission, the UK competition authorities, or the courts has been exhausted or if the time limit for doing so has elapsed. Section 47B introduced an opt-in representative action which can be brought by a designated body on behalf of consumers. According to Sections 58 and 58A of the Competition Act, the courts are also bound by the infringement findings of the OFT once the appeal period has elapsed.

Section 47A allows claimants to choose the forum for follow-on proceedings: it creates a new route to the CAT while also retaining that to the High Court.[70] Although the CAT is a specialized court which deals exclusively with competition law issues, there are several limitations which have spawned satellite litigation and diminished the attractiveness of the Tribunal for follow-on claims. Section 47A limits follow-on actions to the findings of the competition authority. A damages claim brought before the Tribunal cannot be extended to related infringements (and the loss originating from them) if they were not part of the competition authority's decision.[71] The CAT's jurisdiction is restricted to issues of causation and harm.[72] For a follow-on action brought before the High Court, no such limitation applies.

The time limit for bringing a follow-on action differs between the High Court and the CAT. In the High Court the limitation period is six years according to Sec-

---

69 *Garden Cottage Foods Ltd v. Milk Marketing Board* [1984] A.C. 130 (HL).

70 See section 47A(10) Competition Act. Follow-on claims which were decided in the High Court: *Devenish Nutrition Ltd v. Sanofi-Aventis SA* [2007] EWHC 2394 (Ch) and [2008] EWCA Civ 1086 (CA); *English, Welsh and Scottish Railway Ltd v. E.ON UK plc* [2007] EWHC 599 (Comm) and *National Grid Electricity Submission plc v. ABB Ltd* [2009] EWHC 1326. *Devenish* was brought in the aftermath of the Commissions' Vitamin decision. *Vitamins* (Case COMP/E-1/37.512) Commission Decision 2003/3/EC [2003] OJ L6/1. There are more follow-on actions pending.

71 *Enron Coal Services Limited (in liquidation) v. English Welsh & Scottish Railway Limited* [2009] CAT 36, [2011] EWCA Civ 2.

72 The existence of an infringement decision (and the finding of a competitive disadvantage) does not necessarily prove causation even if the competition authority finds that the defendant had engaged in anticompetitive conduct to the detriment of the plaintiff. *Enron Coal Services Limited (in liquidation) v. English Welsh & Scottish Railway Limited* [2009] CAT 36; [2011] EWCA Civ 2.

tion 2 of the Limitation Act 1980, while follow-on actions to the CAT must be brought within two years pursuant to Section 47A of the Competition Act.[73] The shorter CAT time limit begins to run when a final public decision has been adopted and the time period for appeals has elapsed, although the CAT can exercise discretion with respect to an action brought before or after the two-year period. It had been ambiguous as to when the time limit for CAT actions actually begins to run. The Court of Appeal ultimately clarified the issue.[74] If a company appeals the fine but not the infringement decision, the time limit for bringing an action begins running at that time, whereas if appeal is made against the infringement decision itself, the limitation period is barred from running and no action can be brought in the CAT. The limitation period in the High Court begins when the damage has accrued or, if the breach of law is concealed, when the victim discovers or should have discovered the infringement had he or she acted with reasonable diligence.[75] This may give victims of anti-competitive conduct, especially cartel victims, a more generous time frame to launch an action against the offender. It may be because of the limitations placed on private cases in the CAT that the High Court became a more attractive forum for claimants.[76]

If victims seek other than monetary relief or if there is no prior decision by a competition authority, the claim must be filed in the High Court because the CAT cannot adjudicate on stand-alone cases or injunction requests. All competition actions must be commenced in the Chancery Division (High Court) unless the case was commenced in the Commercial Court according to the Competition Law Practice Direction.[77] If the claim contains an element of competition litigation and has been commenced in another court, it will be transferred to the High Court. The concentration of cases in the High Court allows High Court judges to obtain the experience and expertise needed for complex competition law cases. Courts can also draw on the expertise of the OFT or sector regulators, as these entities are able to intervene in private proceedings. The competition authorities may submit

---

73 According to section 36 Limitation Act 1980 time limits do not apply to equitable remedies such as injunctions.

74 *BCL Old Co Ltd v. BASF SE* [2009] EWCA Civ 434 and the Tribunal's previous ruling [2008] CAT 24. See also *BCL Old Co Ltd v. Aventis SA* [2005] CAT 1; *Emerson Electric Co and others v. Morgan Crucible* (*Emerson I*) [2007] CAT 28, *Emerson II* [2007] CAT 30, *Emerson III* [2008] CAT 8. The confusion about limitation periods prompted a challenge before the UK Supreme Court in *BCL Old Co Ltd v. BASF SE* 2012, [2012] UKSC 45 *Deutsche Bahn AG v. Morgan Crucible Co Plc* [2012] EWCA Civ 1055.

75 Section 32 Limitation Act 1980.

76 The number of follow-on cases filed in the High Court in 2010 and 2011 exceed those that were filed in the CAT.

77 Civil Procedure Rules 1998 (SI 1998/3132), Practice Direction – Competition Law – Claims relating to the application of Articles 81 and 82 of the EC Treaty and Chapters I and II of Part I of the Competition Act 1998.

written observations or apply for permission to give an oral presentation in private proceedings.[78] The OFT intervened only once in the *Crehan* case.[79]

As for the jurisdiction of English courts in transnational competition cases, the High Court's decision in *Provimi Ltd v. Aventis* is said to have opened the floodgates to international damages actions being brought by non-UK claimants.[80] An English subsidiary of the defendant implemented the vitamin cartel in England.[81] The claimant, a German purchasing company, sued for losses it suffered from purchases that had taken place in Germany. It was allowed to bring its claims against the English company even though the English subsidiary, being part of a cartelist, had not made any sales to the claimant. It was believed that this decision would make London an attractive forum for Europe-wide losses claims because parties that had purchased from several of a cartelist's subsidiaries throughout Europe could now bring a single action for damages before the High Court provided that one subsidiary were domiciled in England. However, more recently, the High Court has narrowed its interpretation of jurisdiction, stating that there must be some direct connection to England and Wales in order for a claim to be brought before the High Court.[82]

Of particular issue with respect to bringing private actions in England are the costs of doing so.[83] Costs are considered to be the major obstacles for antitrust claimants.[84] Normally the losing party pays the winner's costs, including fees, charges, disbursements, expenses, and reimbursements in accordance with Civil Procedure Rule 43.2 (1)(a). The general rule is that the unsuccessful party will pay the costs of the successful party, also known as the indemnity principle or the 'costs will follow the event' standard.[85] Despite the prospect of a complete cost re-

78 This right is based on Article 15(3) Regulation (EC) No 1/2003 for Articles 101, 102 TFEU proceedings. The OFT can also submit statements in accordance with the Competition Law Practice Direction.

79 *Crehan v. Inntrepreneur Pub* [2006] UKHL 38. The Office of Rail Regulation has intervened in *English, Welsh & Scottish Railway Ltd v. E.ON UK plc* [2007] EWHC 599 (Comm).

80 Brian Kennelly, 'Antitrust Forum-Shopping in England: Is Provimi Ltd v. Aventis Correct?', 2 *CPI Antitrust Journal* (2010), 1–7.

81 *Provimi Ltd v. Aventis Animal Nutrition SA* [2003] EWHC 961 (Comm). See also Friedrich Wenzel Bulst, 'The *Provimi* Decision of the High Court: Beginnings of Private Antitrust Litigation in Europe', 4(4) *European Business Organization Law Review* (2003), 623–650. See also Articles 3 and 5 Council Regulation (EC) No 44/2001 of 22 December 2000 on jurisdiction and the recognition and enforcement of judgments in civil and commercial matters [2001] OJ L012/01.

82 *SanDisk Corporation v. Koninklijke Philips Electronics NV* [2007] EWHC 33 2 (Ch).

83 John Peysner, 'Costs and Financing in Private Third Party Competition Damages Actions', 3 *Competition Law Review* (2006), 97–115; Alan J Riley and John Peysner, 'Damages in EC Antitrust: Who Pays the Piper?', 31 *European Law Review* (2006), 748–761.

84 Peysner (*supra* note 84), p. 98; Office of Fair Trading, *Private Actions in Competition Law: Effective Redress for Consumer and Business – Discussion Paper*, 26.

85 Civil Procedure Rules 44.3 (2)(a).

covery for successful plaintiffs, the costs of running a case are high. To overcome this problem, English law provides for conditional fee agreements, which are not to be confused with damages based agreement ('no win, no fee').[86] In a conditional fee agreement, a solicitor normally charges an hourly rate with a hike of up to 100 per cent of this rate if he or she is successful.[87] Conditional fee agreements are supposed to reduce the burden of legal aid and facilitate access to justice. In a standard conditional fee agreement, the legal representative recovers his fee from the opponent in addition to the reward if the claim is won. The problem of litigation cost does not only occur in the context of competition law litigation but is recognized to be a general problem before the English courts.[88]

One factor contributing to litigation expenses is the disclosure procedure for documents held in the other party's possession. In addition to evidence which can be gained through settlements, disclosure is a favourable way for claimants to solve the problem of asymmetrically distributed information. According to Civil Procedure Rule 31, parties must disclose documents on which their case relies as well as documents which are adverse to their own case or which support or adversely affect another party's case. However, it may still be difficult to gather enough evidence to actually move on to the disclosure stage in trial. Disclosure before the Competition Appeal Tribunal is subject to directives of the Tribunal under CAT Rule 19(2)(K). In the *National Grid* litigation, the High Court ordered two defendants in a damages claim to disclose documents which originated from other defendants in the same proceedings.[89] These documents had come into the possession of the disclosing parties in the course of the European Commission's investigation of the Gas Insulated Switchgear Cartel.[90] The plaintiffs were likely to face difficulties in obtaining the documents from the other defendants and applied successfully for a disclosure order. However, the disclosure order does not apply to documents subject to a leniency application. Leniency documents in the possession of third parties and competition authorities remain a contentious issue, since the CJEU dodged a clear ruling in *Pfleiderer*.[91] The High Court weighed the interests of leniency applicants and claimants, applying the Pfleiderer test, in a second decision in *National Grid*, ordering the defendant to disclose certain paragraphs of the confidential version of the Commission's decision in *Gas Insulated Switchgear*.[92]

86 Third party professional litigation funding may be available. Public funding is barred in disputes arising from the carrying on of a business according to the Access to Justice Act 1998 Schedule 2. This will affect most private antitrust disputes.

87 Section 58 of the Courts and Legal Service Act 1999.

88 Rupert Jackson, *Review of Civil Litigation Costs, Final Report* (2009).

89 *National Grid Electricity Transmission Plc v. ABB Ltd* [2011] EWHC 1717 (Ch).

90 Gas Insulated Switchgear Case COMP/39.966.

91 Case C-360/09, *Pfleiderer AG v. Bundeskartellamt* [2011] ECR I-0000.

92 *National Grid Electricity Transmission Plc v. ABB Ltd* [2012] EWHC 869 (Ch).

3.2 Remedies

Damages claims are the most frequently discussed remedy in England and Wales.[93] The right to damages for the breach of EC competition rules under UK law was first recognized in *Garden Cottage Foods Ltd v. Milk Marketing Board* – a case that dates back to the days before the Competition Act.[94] In *Garden Cottage Foods*, the plaintiff sought interim relief which was denied on the grounds that damages were available and appropriate to remedy his injury. Despite the fact that damages were generally available, it was arguable as to whether damages actions were founded on the breach of a statutory provision or whether they constitute a new type of tort.[95] The courts finally adopted the breach of a statutory provision.[96] More recently, in *Crehan v. Inntrepreneur Pub Co*, the courts further clarified that a plaintiff is entitled to claim damages for the breach of a statutory duty even if he or she was also part of the anti-competitive agreement.[97] Damages payments normally include costs and pre-judgement interests.

English law also provides for exemplary damages which are meant to deter and punish the offender. However, in *Devenish* the High Court rejected a follow-on claim for exemplary damages and restitutionary damages, as this would have contradicted the compensation principle underlying damages actions. The main objective of damages actions is that of restoration rather than punishment.[98] The principle of *ne bis in idem* prevents a second 'fine' once the Commission has already punished the undertaking. The claimants in *Devenish* also requested restitutionary damages and an account of profits. Restitutionary damages are calculated on the basis of the defendant's gain from the violation. The High Court and, on appeal, the Court of Appeal held that restitutionary damages are not available in antitrust litigation. An account of profits allows the claimant to access the defendant's books and forces the defendant to surrender any unlawfully obtained profits. Lewison J. stressed that an account of profits and restitutionary damages are only

93 OFT, *Private Actions in Competition Law: effective redress for consumers and business*, OFT 916 (November 2007).

94 *Garden Cottage Foods Ltd v. Milk Marketing Board* [1984] A.C. 130 (HL).

95 See Clifford A. Jones, *Private Enforcement of Antitrust Law in the EU, UK and USA* (Oxford University Press 1999), 113; Mark Hoskins, 'Garden Cottage Revisited: The Availability of Damages in the National Courts for Breaches of the EEC Competition Law Rules', 13(6) *European Competition Law Review* (1992), 260; Nicholas Green, 'The Treaty of Rome, National Courts, and English Common Law – The Enforcement of European Competition Law After Milk Marketing Board', 48 *Rabels Zeitschrift für ausländisches und internationales Privatrecht* (1984), 509–551.

96 *Society of Lloyd's v. Clementson* [1995] *Common Market Law Review* 693 (CA); *Askin v. Borchard* [2000] UK CLR 495; *MTV Europe v. BMG Records (UK) Ltd* [1997] *European Law Reports* 100 (CA); *Crehan v. Inntrepreneur Pub Co* [2004] EWCA Civ 637 at para. 156.

97 *Crehan v. Inntrepreneur Pub* [2006] UKHL 38.

98 *Devenish Nutrition Limited v. Sanofi-Aventis SA* [2007] EWHC 2394; [2008] EWCA Civ 1086. See also Jennifer Skilbeck, 'Cartel Damages: The Court of Appeal Rejects a Gain-based Remedy', 30(3) *European Competition Law Review* (2009), 105–106.

awarded in extraordinary circumstances. Since the claimants can ask for compensatory damages, there is no exceptional case justifying an account of profits. The Competition Appeal Tribunal, however, awarded exemplary damages in its contentious *Cardiff Bus* follow-on decision.[99] The OFT had found the defending Cardiff Bus company guilty of engaging in predatory pricing, foreclosing the market to entrant 2 Travel. Cardiff Bus escaped a fine under Section 40 of CA98, which provides limited immunity from financial penalties for conduct of minor significance. While there was evidence that Cardiff Bus had attempted to shut out its competitor, little evidence was offered to prove harm to consumers. The competing bus service was also badly managed, thus raising the question as to why the CAT almost trebled the award – there is no mandatory trebling of antitrust damages in the UK – ultimately bestowing £60,000 on the claimant. Since the defendant had been found guilty by the OFT but not been fined, the CAT did not feel constrained by the *Devenish* considerations.

In a private case related to the abovementioned *Dairy Products* investigation, the British supermarket Safeway Stores (acquired by Morrisons) brought damages actions against former employees who it believed to be responsible for Safeway's anti-competitive conduct. Safeway sought to recover the fines that had been imposed on it but the action was blocked by the Court of Appeal.[100] The Court of Appeal held that the claimant cannot recover damages based on the consequences of its own illegal action (*ex turpi causa* doctrine). Although the decision weakens the deterrent effect on individuals, it has nevertheless clarified firms' liability for antitrust fines.

In a number of private antitrust cases, plaintiffs sought permanent or interim injunctions in order to stop current violations of the law or to prevent further harm.[101] In competition law litigation, claimants have mostly sought interim injunctions.[102] The CAT may also impose interim measures for which it has the power to make a final decision.[103] An interim injunction will be granted if the court is satisfied that a serious question will be tried, damages are not an adequate remedy for the party, and the balance of convenience lies with the claimant.[104] The first prerequisite is satisfied if the claim is not frivolous or vexatious. The second hurdle bars the plaintiff from interim relief if damages are regarded as an adequate remedy. This was the case in *Garden Cottage Foods Ltd v. Milk Marketing Board* where the claim for injunctive relief was rejected.[105] Thirdly, interim relief will on-

---

99 *2 Travel Group Plc (In Liquidation) v. Cardiff City Transport Services Ltd* [2012] CAT 19.

100 *Safeway Stores Ltd v. Twigger* [2010] EWHC 11 (Comm), [2010] EWCA Civ 1472.

101 Sebastian Peyer, 'Injunctive Relief and Private Antitrust Enforcement', *CCP Working Paper* No. 11–7 (2011).

102 Barry J. Rodger, 'Competition Law Litigation in the UK Courts', 27(5) *European Competition Law Review* (2006), 241–248.

103 CAT Rule 61(1)c. See the interim damages award in *Healthcare at Home v. Genzyme Ltd* [2006] CAT 29.

104 *American Cyanamid Co. v. Ethicon Ltd.* [1975] A.C. 396.

105 *Garden Cottage Foods Ltd v. Milk Marketing Board* [1984] A.C. 130 (HL).

ly be granted if there is a doubt as to the adequacy of damages, i.e. if the loss is irreparable, damages would have been unjust, or the predicted outcome might favour the plaintiff.[106] If the injunction would alter the status quo, courts are less likely to decide in favour of the applicant. Apart from the fact that plaintiffs have considerable difficulties in convincing courts to grant interim remedies and to bring complex economic evidence into interim hearings,[107] the damages hurdle seems to hamper claimants. Except for cases in which a business is in danger of being forced out of the market, competition law infringements are regarded as remediable with damages. Some plaintiffs have successfully asked for interim relief in competition law cases, and there are signs that the courts have begun to relax the requirements for interim injunctive relief. [108] As for permanent injunctions, the claimants in the recent *Purple Parking* case successfully fought an application for an injunction restraining Heathrow Airport from abusing its dominant position in the provision of parking space for meet and greet parking services.[109] This case is remarkable insofar as it represents both a stand-alone action as well as a rare permanent injunction.

Nullity is the only remedy mentioned in Article 101 TFEU and Section 2(4) of the Competition Act. In one case, the plaintiffs have used nullity like a sword and successfully asked the court to declare void certain provisions of a contract.[110] In *Hendry v. World Professional Billiards & Snooker Association LTD*, the claimants contended, among other things, that a rule requiring the prior written permission from the defendant to participate in billiard and snooker tournaments organized by other associations than the defendant is void.[111] The claimant also asked for damages but could not prove that they had incurred losses and lost their claim to that effect.

---

106 Mark Brealey and Mark Hoskins, *Remedies in EC Law* (2nd ed., Sweet & Maxwell 1998); Tim Ward and Kassie Smith, *Competition Litigation in the UK* (Sweet & Maxwell 2005), 169; *Healthcare at Home Ltd v. Genzyme Ltd* [2007] EWHC 565.

107 Barry J. Rodger and Angus MacCulloch, 'Wielding the Blunt Sword: Interim Relief for Breaches of EC Competition Law before the UK Courts', 17(7) *European Competition Law Review* (1996), 397.

108 *Cutsforth v. Mansfield Inns Ltd* [1986] *Common Market Law Review* 1; *Holleran v. Daniel Thwaites* [1989] C.M.L.R. 917. For a more relaxed approach see *Network Multimedia Television Ltd v. Jobserve Ltd* [2001] EWCA 2021; Adidas-Salomon AG v. Draper [2006] EWHC 1318 (Ch); Software Cellular Network v. T-Mobile (UK) Ltd [2007] EWHC 1790 (Ch).

109 *Purple Parking Ltd v. Heathrow Airport Ltd* [2011] EWHC 987 (Ch).

110 For cases in which the initial defendant invoked the voidness of an agreement see Barry J Rodger, 'Competition Law Litigation in the UK Courts: A Study of all Cases 2005–2008, Part I', 2 *Global Competition Litigation Review* (2009), 93–114 and *Passmore v. Morland Plc* [1999] All ER (D) 93, CA.

111 *Hendry v. World Professional Billiards & Snooker Association Ltd* [2002] U.K.C.L.R. 5.

3.3 Collective Actions

Group claims can be brought by a designated body on behalf of two or more consumers pursuant to Section 47B of the Competition Act. The representative model according to Section 47B is an opt-in rather than an opt-out action. It is argued that the broad definition of consumers in Section 47B(6), read in conjunction with subsections (2) and (7), allows indirect purchasers to bring claims, although this has yet to be put to test.[112] In order to bring a representative action, the claiming organisation must be granted the status of a specified body which has thus far only been granted to the consumer association *Which?*.[113] This consumer organisation has made use of its powers as such in its proceedings against *JJB Sports*, a retailer that had participated in the price fixing of replica football shirts.[114] For the legal proceedings consumers had to give their consent, and *Which?* managed to identify 130 individuals who had bought and held proof of purchase of the replica shirts in question. *Which?* and *JJB Sports* settled the case before the CAT, paying £20 to those consumers who were parties to the action and between £5 and £10 to other affected consumers upon presentation of the said shirt. Overall, *Which?* won probably less than £20,000 in the proceedings against JJB Sports, while the costs of the legal action were likely to be in the region of several hundred thousand.

Another attempt to bring a group action based on civil procedure rules has failed in *Emerald Supplies Ltd v. British Airways Plc*.[115] The claimants imported cut flowers and sought damages from BA which had allegedly participated in price fixing for air freight charges. In the absence of an explicit regulation of class actions in England and Wales, the claimants asked for collective damages under Civil Procedure Rule (CPR) 19.6. This rule states that representative actions can be brought if the individuals involved have the same interest and that the findings of the court are binding on all parties represented in the claim. The High Court as well as the Court of Appeal refused to accept that victims on different levels of the supply chain share the same interest, especially if BA invokes the passing-on defence against direct purchasers at a later stage of the proceedings. The courts continue to apply a very narrow test to CPR 19.6 which, for this reason, has not been widely used before the English courts. If Emerald had succeeded with its representative action, it would have effectively introduced an uncertified class action.

---

112 Barry J Rodger, 'UK Competition Law and Private Litigation', in Barry J Rodger (ed.), *Ten Years of UK Competition Law Reform* (Dundee University Press 2010), 53, p. 58.

113 Specified Body (Consumer Claims) Order 2005, SI 2005/2365.

114 *Price-fixing of replica football kit* (Case CP/0871/01) OFT Decision CA98/06/2003 of 1 August 2003; upheld on appeal to the CAT *JJB Sports PLC v. Office of Fair Trading* [2005] CAT 22 and Court of Appeal [2006] EWCA Civ 1318.

115 *Emerald Supplies Ltd v. British Airways PLC* [2009] EWHC 741 (Ch), [2010] EWCA Civ 1284.

3.4 Impact of Private Cases

The overall number of private actions is relatively low when compared with litigation levels in Germany or the United States.[116] Rodger counted 113 private competition cases up through 2008.[117] With the exception of the *Independent School Fees* case[118] all procedures were brought by legal persons.[119] Private plaintiffs became more active after the UK competition law was reformed, but there has not been an exponential increase in the number of litigated cases in recent years as had been expected.[120] If pre-trial settlements are taken into account, the number of disputes based on competition law is certainly higher, as Rodger has shown in his study of out-of-court settlements.[121] Those settlements play a particularly important role against the background of high litigation costs. The fact that cases are normally settled before a final judgement is handed down may also explain why, despite the number of claims brought over the years, there has only been one damages award to date. In *Healthcare at Home Ltd v. Genzyme Ltd*, the claimant also came very close to being granted a damages award when the CAT awarded interim damages of £2 million and the parties subsequently agreed on a settlement.[122]

It appears that there is a trend toward sword cases and more CAT follow-on proceedings.[123] Most follow-on proceedings are brought in the aftermath of cartel investigations, whereas stand-alone claims are often based on Chapter II or Article 102 TFEU violations. According to Rodger, the most significant case in relation to the Chapter I Prohibition is *Bookmakers' Afternoon Greyhound Services Ltd v. Amalgamated Racing Ltd*.[124] In this case the High Court handed down two judge-

---

116 Sebastian Peyer, 'Private Antitrust Litigation in Germany from 2005 to 2007: Empirical Evidence' 8(2) Journal of Competition Law and Economics, 331–359.

117 Rodger counted 86 cases prior to 2005 and 27 cases between 2005 and 2008. Barry J Rodger, 'Competition Law Litigation in the UK Courts, A Study of All Cases to 2004: Part 3', 27 *European Competition Law Review* (2006), 341–350; Barry J Rodger, 'Competition Law Litigation in the UK Courts, A Study of All Cases to 2004: Part 2', 27 *European Competition Law Review* (2006), 279–292; Barry J Rodger, 'Competition Law Litigation in the UK Courts, A Study of All Cases to 2004: Part 1', 27 *European Competition Law Review* (2006), 241–248; Barry J Rodger, 'Competition Law Litigation in the UK Courts: A Study of all Cases 2005–2008, Part I', 2 *Global Competition Litigation Review* (2009), 93–114; Barry J Rodger, 'Competition Law Litigation in the UK Courts: A Study of all Cases 2005–2008, Part II', 2 *Global Competition Litigation Review* (2009), 136–147.

118 *Wilson v. Lancing College Ltd* (Case 1008/5/7/07). The case was settled.

119 Rodger (*supra* note 108).

120 Aidan Robertson, 'UK Competition Litigation: From Cinderella to Goldilocks?', 9 *Competition Law Journal* (2010), 275–294.

121 Barry J Rodger, 'Private Enforcement of Competition Law, the Hidden Story: Competition Litigation Settlements in the United Kingdom, 2000–2005', 29 *European Competition Law Review* (2008), 96–116.

122 [2006] CAT 29.

123 Rodger (*supra* note 113).

124 Rodger (*supra* note 108).

ments on the merits in a dispute over exclusive licensing for horse race data, images, and sound.[125] Many stand-alone claims have dealt with the abuse of dominance and, more specifically, with a refusal to deliver, refusal to deal, or with the essential facility doctrine in the broadest sense.[126]

Considering the fact that the active enforcement of competition law provisions (sword cases) is relatively new, the courts and the CAT have had the chance to clarify a number of issues like, for instance, the binding effect of public decisions in follow-on proceedings, the rules for choosing England as the jurisdiction for damages actions, or the limitation period before the CAT. Thus, the impact of private enforcement must also be measured in terms of clarification and development of the law. The *Crehan* litigation, which originated in the UK courts, has not only helped to clarify the binding effect of Commission decisions for UK courts but has also established the Community right to damages for the violation of Articles 101 or 102 TFEU. Some issues still remain unresolved, like, for example, the passing-on defence or the standing of indirect purchasers. The passing-on problem was raised in *BCL Old Co Ltd v. Aventis S.A.* but the CAT refused to address it in a security for cost proceeding.[127]

4 Conclusion

In the recent shake-up of UK agencies, the government announced the merger of the OFT and the Competition Commission. While this concentration of expertise is likely to bolster the central role of the future Competition and Market Authority, the actual design of this agency has not been revealed.[128] Whether or not the institutional redesign will bring about swift improvements in the track record of the competition watchdog is doubtful. The OFT may have been unfortunate with some of the cases it selected for enforcement actions, and some cases it brought may not have sent the strong signals to the markets that are required from a public enforcer. However, a relatively new agency needs time to establish precedents and procedure and to learn from judicial defeats. Although scepticism as to the future of the Cartel Offence is justified on the grounds of the unfavourable dishonesty requirement and the difficult nature of criminal proceedings, the OFT is currently

---

125 [2008] EWHC 1978 (Ch) and [2008] EWHC 2688 (Ch).

126 *Getmapping v. Ordnance Survey* [2002] EWHC 1089 (Pat); *Suretrack Rail Services Ltd v. Infraco JNP Ltd* [2002] EWHC 1316 (Ch); *Land Rover Group Ltd v. UPF (UK) Ltd (in administrative receivership)* [2002] EWHC 3183; *Software Cellular Network v. T-Mobile (UK) Ltd* [2007] EWHC 1790 (Ch); *Purple Parking Ltd v. Heathrow Airport Ltd* [2011] EWHC 987 (Ch).

127 [2005] CAT 2.

128 Although the merger control and market investigation regime is most likely to be affected, the currently discussed change from an administrative to a prosecutorial system will have a major influence on how the future agency will enforce competition law.

pursuing a number of criminal investigations. Reacting to criticism of its fining practice in the recent bid-rigging case, the OFT has changed its fining guidance.

In private enforcement of competition law there are similar signs that the enforcement environment is beginning to settle. Nevertheless, more final court decisions are still needed in order to clarify some outstanding issues like, for example, indirect purchaser standing. One of the major challenges of private litigation in the UK is the cost of bringing a case. Private parties have to make considerable investments to successfully argue an action. This does not make it worthwhile for consumers or small firms to pursue their rights in the courts. Given the institutional constraints, it may be advantageous to introduce a small track procedure which would allow injunction claims or small-value damages claims to proceed at reasonable costs. The CAT could be given jurisdiction over stand-alone actions and draw on the expertise it has gained in follow-on proceedings. To improve the effectiveness of private enforcement, the OFT has suggested a reform of representative actions which, as the *JJB Sports* case has shown, are too difficult and costly to bring on an opt-in basis.[129] The UK Government is currently rethinking the framework for private actions and has released its proposals for reform.[130] It suggests introducing opt-out class actions, extending the CAT's jurisdiction to stand-alone cases, and a fast track procedure intended primarily for injunctions in the CAT.

Public and private enforcement of competition law has adapted quickly to the new environment created after the entry into force of the Competition Act and the Enterprise Act even though it may not have satisfied expectations with regard to the number of proceedings. Nevertheless, some key cases have had bearing on the enforcement of competition law and have clarified the law to the benefit of future actions. The fine-tuning process is on-going and will continue subject to input from EU institutions. The enforcement mode that has emerged may be characterized as cautious rather than overzealous. As enforcement institutions gain experience and expertise, it is only a matter of time before we will see more criminal convictions, OFT decisions which are upheld on appeal, and a greater number of final decisions in private damages litigation.

---

129 OFT, *Private Actions in Competition Law: effective redress for consumers and business*, OFT 916 (November 2007).

130 Department for Business, Innovation & Skills, *Private actions in competition law: a consultation on options for reform* (January 2013), https://www.gov.uk/government/consultations/private-actions-in-competition-law-a-consultation-on-options-for-reform.

Editors and Contributors

Thomas Ackermann holds the Chair of Civil Law and European and International Business Law at LMU. He was born in 1966, and arrived at LMU in October 2009. He studied law at the Universities of Bonn and Cambridge, obtaining his doctorate in Bonn in 1997 with a dissertation on the rule of reason in European antitrust law. In 2004, he completed his habilitation at the University of Bonn with a work on the protection of the reliance interest. In the same year, he was appointed to the Chair of German, European and International Civil and Business Law at the University of Erlangen-Nürnberg. His research interests cover the legal constitution of markets with a particular focus on contract law and competition law. One special focus of his work concerns the European dimension of these subjects. Thomas Ackermann is a member of the editorial board of *Common Market Law Review*, the leading international peer-review journal for European union law, and of *Neue Zeitschrift für Kartellrecht*. In addition, he is a member of the Munich Risk and Insurance Center, on faculty at the International Max Planck School for Competition and Innovation and head of the programme Munich University Summer Training in German and European Law.

Wolfgang Bosch passed the German bar exam in 1987 and received his doctorate in law from the University of Constance in 1989 with a dissertation titled *Rechtshängigkeit und Rechtskraft im Schiedsverfahren*. After serving as teaching assistant at University of Bern he joined Gleiss Lutz in 1990 and has been a partner at the firm since 1994. His Frankfurt-based practice concentrates on competition and transactional work. He has represented clients in major merger control and antitrust law infringement cases. Publications include *EG-Kartellrecht* (co-author) and *GWB* (co-author).

Jochen Burrichter has been a partner in the Düsseldorf office of Hengeler Mueller since 1977 and has been actively involved in developing the firm's Brussels office. Burrichter received his legal education at the Universities of Freiburg and Münster. A specialist in European and German competition law, he has been responsible for a large number of merger notifications to the European Commission and the German Federal Cartel Office, has acted in various cartel cases and has represented clients before the General Court and Court of Justice of the European Communities as well as at courts in Germany. Mr. Burrichter has served many years on the board – and is now an honorary member – of Studienvereinigung Kartellrecht e. V. (The Association of German Antitrust Lawyers). He is a co-founder of the European Competition Lawyers Forum and a former chairman of Committee C (antitrust affairs) in the Business Law Section at the International Bar Association. Burrichter is a co-author of the commentary *EU Competition Law* (eds. Immenga & Mestmäcker). He has lectured on competition law at various international competition conferences and has published several articles on European and German competition law.

Arndt Christiansen is an economist at the Bundeskartellamt, Germany's federal competition authority, in its Unit G3 – Economic Issues in Competition Policy. His work covers all areas of competition law enforcement with a particular focus on merger control and economic analyses in anti-cartel proceedings. He joined the Bundeskartellamt in 2008 and previously worked in the unit in charge of the application of competition law in the energy sector (8th Decision Division). He holds a PhD in economics from Philipps-University of Marburg. His PhD thesis, on EU merger control, was published in 2010 under the title *Der More Economic Approach in der EU-Fusionskontrolle: Darstellung, konzeptionelle Grundlagen und kritische Analyse* by Peter Lang. He has also published articles in leading German and international journals in the field of competition law and economics on topics such as the analysis of coordinated and unilateral effects in EU merger control, competence allocation in EU competition policy, the optimal differentiation of competition rules and minimum quality standards for expert economic opinions. He also regularly contributes book reviews in the fields of competition law and general economics to professional journals as well as to newspapers.

Gerhard Dannecker is Professor of Criminal Law and Law of Criminal Procedures and Director of the Institute for German, European and International Criminal Law and Law of Criminal Procedures in Heidelberg, Germany. Before joining Heidelberg University, he held the Chair for Criminal Law, Law of Criminal Procedures and Information Law in Bayreuth, Germany. He received his legal education in Freiburg and Göttingen, and he served as a research fellow at the Institute of Criminology and Criminal Business Law in Freiburg. He is a member of the presidium of the Association of European Criminal Law and of the editorial board of the *Neue Zeitschrift für Wirtschafts-, Steuer- und Unternehmensstrafrecht*. He has published widely on issues of criminal business law and criminal tax law on national, European and international levels, medical law, European criminal law and comparative law.

Christian Ewald is Chief Economist of the Bundeskartellamt. Core elements of his current work include the provision of economic advice and assistance to the decision bodies of the Bundeskartellamt in single cases and the assessment of policy issues on the role of economic analysis in competition law enforcement. From mid-2005 until mid-2007 he served as a National Expert in the Directorate-General for Competition in Brussels. He joined the Bundeskartellamt in 1994. He studied economics and law and holds a university degree in economics. He publishes regularly in leading German and international journals on issues in competition law and economics and he is also a visiting lecturer for competition economics and policy at the University of Düsseldorf (Düsseldorf Institute for Competition Economics, DICE).

Andreas Heinemann is Professor of Commercial, Economic and European Law at the University of Zurich and permanent visiting professor at the University of Lausanne. After studies in economics and law he was awarded the Diplôme International d'Administration Publique (DIAP) from the Ecole Nationale d'Administration (ENA), then in Paris. He passed his bar exam in Berlin and completed his PhD and habilitation at the University of Munich's faculty of law. His research focuses on Swiss, European and International Economic Law with a special emphasis on competition and intellectual property law. He is a member of the board of the Europa Institute at the University of Zurich and of the Scientific Advisory Board of the Munich Intellectual Property Law Center (MIPLC). He has been a member of the Swiss Competition Commission since 2011, and its vice president since 2012.

Kai Hüschelrath is head of the research unit "Competition and Regulation" at the Centre for European Economic Research (ZEW) and coordinator of the Mannheim Centre for Competition and Innovation (MaCCI). Since October 2013, he has also been Professor of Economics, Competition Policy, at the University of Mannheim. Kai Hüschelrath studied economics and management at the University of Würzburg. From 2001 to 2004 he was a research and teaching assistant of Jürgen Weigand at the Chair for Microeconomics and Industrial Organization at WHU Otto Beisheim School of Management in Vallendar. During that time, he spent several months as visiting scholar at the University of California at Berkeley and the University of British Columbia in Vancouver. After working as an economist in the London office of Frontier Economics for almost two years, he joined ZEW's Research Department "Industrial Economics and International Management" in October 2006, there he worked as researcher and later senior researcher until December 2011. From April 2009 until September 2013 he was also Assistant Professor of Industrial Organization and Competitive Strategy at WHU.

Ursula Kern is a doctoral candidate in the field of comparative criminal law and received her legal education in Heidelberg, Germany and Leeds, UK. For her dissertation she is studying the criminal liability of board members and of officers in supervising bodies when companies prepare and publish false financial statements, comparing German and British regulations and the effects of changes to European law. Her research project was accepted for the State Postgraduate Scholarship Programme of Baden-Württemberg (LGFG) and she has worked as a research assistant for Gerhard Dannecker at the Institute of German, European and International Criminal Law and Criminal Procedure in Heidelberg. She has published several papers in the area of accounting fraud and has conducted research at St. Catharine's College in Cambridge and at the University of Leeds. Since October 2012 she has been a law clerk at the Heidelberg district court.

Thorsten Mäger was admitted to the bar in 1996 and has been a partner with Hengeler Mueller since 2001. He graduated from Berlin Law School in 1993. Mäger specializes in all areas of European and German competition law. He provides general competition counselling to German and foreign companies and represents clients before the German and European competition authorities and courts. Mäger has also represented a company in the landmark Pfleiderer case before the European Court of Justice concerning access to leniency statements sought by a potential plaintiff in a damage claim. He advises clients in several complex follow-on damage claim proceedings before German courts. Mäger has also been involved in numerous high-profile merger control proceedings. He is editor and co-author of a German handbook on EC competition law (*Europäisches Kartellrecht*, 2nd edition, 2011), co-author of a 2012 handbook on international competition litigation and co-editor of the *Neue Zeitschrift für Kartellrecht*.

Gunnar Niels leads Oxera's work in competition policy and litigation, with 18 years of experience in the field covering mergers, agreements, abuse of dominance, damages and state aid. He has advised companies such as Nokia, easyJet, Mars, Belgacom and MasterCard, as well as government bodies and the European Commission. Gunnar has provided expert testimony before courts in a range of jurisdictions, including the UK, the Netherlands, Spain, South Africa and New Zealand. Gunnar is currently a non-governmental adviser (NGA) to the International Competition Network (ICN) Working Group on Unilateral Conduct. He is on the boards of the *Competition Law Journal* and *Oxford Competition Law*, has been guest editor for the *Antitrust Bulletin*, and has published in many leading journals, including *European Journal of Political Economy*, *Review of Network Economics* and *Journal of Competition Law and Economics*. Before joining Oxera, in 1999, Gunnar was deputy head of the Economics Directorate at Mexico's Federal Competition Commission. He is listed in *The International Who's Who of Competition Lawyers & Economists 2013* and was among the five nominees for Global Competition Review's 2011 Economist of the Year award.

Robin Noble specialises in quantifying damages. He led the Oxera team that worked together with the Directorate-General for Competition to develop a handbook to aid quantification of antitrust damages. He has a wide range of experience in damages matters, working on cases in the UK, the USA, the Netherlands, Germany and South Africa. He has been active on more than 30 of these cases in recent years, including cartel damages, exclusionary cases and breaches of contract. Notable examples include working with Nokia in its claim against the LCD cartel, and acting for RWE Dea in defending a claim for damages related to its involvement in the paraffin waxes cartel. Robin has testifying and cross-examination experience, and has been formally appointed as expert in several cases. Robin also specialises in competition economics. Recent work in the field has included providing advice on mergers to the European Commission, to the UK Office of Fair Trading, and to the South African Competition Tribunal in sectors such as retailing, wholesaling, water, forestry and mineral extraction. He is listed in *The International Who's Who of Competition Lawyers & Economists 2013*, and acts as reviewer on publications such as the *European Journal of Law and Economics*.

Thomas B. Paul is a senior associate at Hengeler Mueller in Düsseldorf, where he specializes in corporate and competition law and dispute resolution. A particular focus of his work lies on advising and representing clients in cartel damage lawsuits before German and European courts. In addition to being admitted to the bar, Paul holds master's degrees in economics and business administration, having graduated from the Universities of Bonn and Hagen in Germany, and Oxford in the UK. He is the author of a number of articles in German law journals and has published a book on the economic approach in European competition law. He is a co-author of Wolters Kuwer's 2012 *Handbook on International Competition Litigation* (eds. Blanke & Nazzini). During his *Referendariat*, he clerked for the litigation department of the Bundeskartellamt. Prior to work at Hengeler Mueller, he was a research fellow at the Institute for Commercial Law of the University of Bonn.

Sebastian Peyer is a Lecturer in Law at the University of Leicester. He received his legal education at the University of Potsdam (Germany), the University of Kazan (Russia) and the University of East Anglia (UK). He holds a degree in law (2004) from the University of Potsdam, and an LLM (2008) and PhD (2011) from the University of East Anglia (UK). Peyer researches and teaches in the area of competition law, European Union law, tort law as well as law and economics. He has worked extensively on public and private antitrust enforcement. He advised the UK government on private enforcement remedies in the Consumer Rights Bill. Before joining the University of Leicester, he worked as a postdoctoral research fellow at the ESRC Centre for Competition Policy. During that time, he spent several months as a visiting scholar at Georgetown University, D.C.

Ulrich Schwalbe studied economics and political science at the Free University of Berlin. After completing his studies, he held a teaching and research position at the university's Chair for Economic Theory (led by Elmar Wolfstetter). After receiving his PhD from the Free University of Berlin, he served as associate professor at the institute of economic theory at the University of Mannheim (under Volker Böhm) from 1990 through 1996. In 1996, he completed his habilitation with a work titled *The Core of Economies with Asymmetric Information.* He served as an acting professor at the universities of Mannheim, Bonn and Essen before accepting a position as a senior lecturer from the University of Canterbury, New Zealand. Since 1999 he has held the Chair for Microeconomics and Industrial Organization at the University of Hohenheim, Stuttgart. His major research interests comprise microeconomics with a special focus on general equilibrium theory, game theory, industrial organization, and competition theory and policy. He is also a research professor at the German Institute for Economic Research (DIW), a member of the scientific advisory board of the FIW, of the editorial board of the *Neue Zeitschrift für Kartellrecht* and a member of the expert group of the Federal Ministry of Economics and Technology on the 8th Amendment to the German Act against Restraints of Competition.

Heike Schweitzer is Professor of Private Law, European Economic Law and Competition Law in Mannheim, Germany. Before joining Mannheim University, she held the chair for European Competition Law at the European University Institute in Florence, Italy. She received her legal education in Freiburg, Germany, and at the Yale Law School, and she served as a research fellow at the Max-Planck-Institute for Comparative and International Private Law and at Columbia Law School. She has published widely on issues of competition law, including state aid and public procurement law, as well as on issues of regulation (telecommunications, media, health). She is director of the Mannheim Centre for Competition and Innovation (MaCCI), member of the academic board of the ASCOLA (Academic Society of Competition Law) and of the Florence School of Regulation (Communications & Media Area) and a member of the editorial board of the NZKart (Neue Zeitschrift für Kartellrecht).

Mario Siragusa, a Rome-based partner at Cleary Gottlieb Steen & Hamilton LLP, focuses on corporate and commercial matters in EU and Italian competition law and on cases involving complex commercial litigation. He lectures regularly at conferences throughout the United States and Europe and has published numerous articles in US and European legal journals. He is a professor at the College of Europe in Bruges and lectures at the Catholic University in Milan. He graduated with honours from the Law School of Rome University in 1970 and received a Diploma of High European Studies from the College of Europe in Belgium in 1971. He received an LL.M. degree from Harvard in 1972. Siragusa is a member of the Commission on Law and Practices Relating to Competition of the International Chamber of Commerce, located in Paris. He is also a member of the Rome Bar.

List of Figures

List of Tables

MIX
Papier aus verantwortungsvollen Quellen
Paper from responsible sources
FSC® C105338

FSC
www.fsc.org

If you have any concerns about our products,
you can contact us on
ProductSafety@springernature.com

In case Publisher is established outside the EU,
the EU authorized representative is:
Springer Nature Customer Service Center GmbH
Europaplatz 3, 69115 Heidelberg, Germany

Printed by Libri Plureos GmbH
in Hamburg, Germany